RETIREMENT MIGRATION IN AMERICA

CHARLES F. LONGINO JR., Ph.D

Edited by R. Alan Fox

VACATION

PUBLICATIONS

HOUSTON

RETIREMENT MIGRATION IN AMERICA

Edited by: R. Alan Fox

Art Direction and Cover Design: Fred W. Salzmann

Assistant Editor: Jill Boxrud

Editorial Assistants: Beth Ballew, Dawn Helm, Paula E. Rylander

Published by Vacation Publications, Inc.
1502 Augusta Drive, Suite 415
Houston, TX 77057

Library of Congress Catalog Card Number: 94-62150
ISBN 0-9644216-1-5

Printed in the United States of America

For Jeanne Biggar
educator, scientist, priest and friend

ACKNOWLEDGMENTS

The National Institute on Aging (NIA) provided the funds through a series of research grants over the past 18 years for the studies whose findings this book summarizes and reports. These research projects analyzed the 1960, 1970, 1980 and 1990 Census public use microdata samples on many topics related to retirement migration. The NIA project officer was Richard Suzman. The work literally could not have been done without their support.

The original research team in 1976 included Cynthia Flynn and Bob Wiseman from the University of Kansas and Jeanne Biggar from the University of Virginia. At that time I was also at the University of Kansas while a post-doctoral fellow in the Midwest Council for Social Research in Aging. The four of us, and our research assistants, worked very hard on the first three of these four NIA-funded projects and the work in this book reports the creative insights and research findings of all of us. There was strength in the diversity of the research team. Cynthia Flynn and Jeanne Biggar identify themselves as social demographers; Bob Wiseman is a social geographer; and I am primarily a social gerontologist. Over the first decade, we learned to work closely at a distance, long before e-mail, as I moved to the University of Miami, Bob moved to Washington, DC, then back to the University of Kansas, Cynthia to Seattle, and Jeanne to Arlington, VA, and back to Charlottesville. Many changes have occurred in nearly 20 years. Cynthia Flynn is now a nurse midwife with a recent degree from Yale. Jeanne Biggar is an Episcopalian priest with a parish in the Virginia mountains. Bob Wiseman, still a geographer, has turned to other intellectual pursuits. And, like Melville's surviving protagonist, Ishmael, I alone remain to tell the tale. However, the spirits of the original research team are present in this volume and their contribution is gratefully acknowledged.

Those fellow travelers who have also struggled in the little vineyard of retirement migration during the past two decades, whether for the whole day or the last hour of it, should be thanked. Most of the scholars listed below have collaborated with me on one or more writing projects, and have contributed, directly or indirectly, many of the ideas in this book. They are Steve Golant, Bill Serow, Eugene Litwak, Vic Marshall, Larry Mullins, Dick Tucker, Lee Cuba, Bill Crown, Diane Cowper, Ken Smith, Frank Biafora, Juli Bradsher, David Jackson, Rick Zimmerman, Mark Fagan, Bill Haas, Mark Smith, Dale Yeatts, Ralph McNeal, Hiram Friedsam, Andrei Rogers, Al Speare, Graham Rowles, John Watkins, Nina Glasgow, Merril Silverstein, Eleanor Stoller, Kevin McHugh, Tim Hogan, Gordon Bennett, Tony Warnes, Francoise Cribier, Herbert Northcott, Phil

ACKNOWLEDGMENTS

Perricone, Ian Taplin, Everett and Anne Lee, George Myers, Calvin Beale, Gladys Bowles and Doug Wolfe. These are the ones with whom I have corresponded over the years. I have listened to their presentations before learned societies and read their papers before publication. In addition, there are others, not named here, whose writings I have read and learned from along the way, many of whose works are cited in the text. Their contributions are also acknowledged.

Over the years, Cheryl Russell and Brad Edmundson, editors-in-chief of *American Demographics*, have both sought to include articles from our research projects about retirement migration in that magazine. These articles have acquainted a broad audience outside of academia with our research. For these opportunities, I am grateful.

Alan Fox, who wrote the foreword, was also a strong influence on this volume. He advised, nurtured, edited, supervised, encouraged and edited some more. He would not leave well enough alone, and the quality of the outcome owes much to his tireless effort. He was especially concerned that all of the numbers be right. The entire process, from our first discussion to the first printing, spanned two years. There is no way to express my gratitude for his vision, faith, intelligence and energy. Jill Boxrud managed much of the day-to-day editing operation, checking the facts and proofing the numbers. She also put the two appendices together.

Carol Corum, the office manager and calming influence of the Reynolda Gerontology Program at Wake Forest, and Will Corum, our research assistant, prepared and proofread most of the tables that appear in this book. Angela Worley, a programmer in the Department of Public Health Sciences at the Bowman Gray School of Medicine, went far beyond the call of duty in producing the 1990 tables from the census microdata files. She put up with unrealistic schedules, an impatient writer and an unwieldy data set, while juggling several other major responsibilities at work and at home. The great goodwill and competence of these three close associates is a cause for rejoicing. John Gregg, David Kammann and Andrea Badillo did their share of proofreading, copying and mailing, and Bret Marchant was a good library sleuth.

As the book unfolded, Loyce Longino provided nightly long-distance encouragement from Miami where she struggled with her doctoral dissertation project. It seems trivial to say "thank you" to a soulmate when one's gratitude is more profound than words can express. It was she who abided the downside of the entire 20-year process that resulted in this volume.

RETIREMENT MIGRATION IN AMERICA

TABLE OF CONTENTS

FOREWORD

There is a new, clean, growth industry in America today.

Still in its infancy, this industry already generates billions of dollars a year in sales of everything from real estate to financial services, health care, utilities and entertainment. Once believed to be cornered by three states, it has jumped the borders and spread throughout the Sun Belt and beyond. It is responsible for a massive redistribution of wealth and income and poised on the brink of a 30-year-long explosion in size that will create new towns, stem and reverse the population declines in many rural counties and communities and add to the economic woes of major metropolitan areas that are losing their best citizens.

The industry is retirement migration, and if you're involved or thinking of getting involved in attracting retirees to your state or community, *Retirement Migration in America* is the place to start.

The pages that follow will reveal the size and economic impact of the retirement migration industry, highlight the industry's major sending and receiving areas and provide developers, counties, county groups, states and regions a solid understanding of where they stand and what's ahead in the increasingly competitive battle for affluent retiree migrants.

This book is the result of more than two years of planning, programming, writing and editing. But the information presented covers three decades — four in some cases — in order to provide a historical perspective from which to view the current picture.

The core of this book is data extracted and analyzed from the 1990 Census tapes. These data are only a snapshot of a social phenomenon that is growing and changing continuously. New retirement towns are being created, established towns are growing and some of the earliest retirement meccas are losing their luster.

My first contact with the author of this book was three years ago, as my company prepared to launch *Where to Retire* magazine.

As we sought to gather facts about the size and nature of retirement migration, our research frequently led us to the same source, Chuck Longino, a social gerontologist at Wake Forest University who had authored or co-authored much of the work ever done on the subject.

Chuck's data helped to convince us that there were enough people moving in retirement to support a magazine on the subject.

Collaborating with Chuck on *Retirement Migration in America* has been a great pleasure and an education for me.

The new, clean, growth industry in America today is retirement migration. The best news is, there's still time to get in on the ground floor.

R. Alan Fox
Publisher, *Where to Retire* magazine

INTRODUCTION
A BRIEF RESEARCH CHRONOLOGY

Readers often enjoy the insights and new understandings that come from social research without knowing anything about the processes that generated the new knowledge. Those operations are backstage, out of view. As a result, it seems that knowledge flows from an artesian fountain, immediately, abundantly and effortlessly. Such slight of hand shortchanges the reader and the researchers.

This work looks back 20 years to the earliest sustained efforts to make sense of retirement migration in America. In 1975, the author and his colleagues first applied to the National Institute on Aging (NIA) for funding to study retirement migration using 1970 Census microdata. At that time, attention to the topic was practically nonexistent outside this tiny circle of interdisciplinary scholars. Jeanne Biggar and Cynthia Flynn worked primarily in the field of demography, Bob Wiseman in geography and the author in gerontology.

Migration research in demography was dominated at that time by economic considerations. Migration was seen as an "equilibrating mechanism" in a complex geo-economic system. As local economies expanded, migration distributed the labor force geographically so that the needed workers came to fill the new jobs. The earliest attempts to explore the subject of retirement migration, therefore, were disappointing. Most older migrants are not in the labor force. The migration models, as usually constructed, did not work very well.[1]

One of the major contributions of retirement migration is that it encouraged demography to expand its range of macrolevel explanations of mobility to explicitly include location-specific amenities, even in its study of youthful migration.[2] Nowadays, it is not unusual to find macro models including climatic, geographic and amenity factors in addition to economic variables.[3] There are, of course, economic factors that influence retirement migration, such as a lower cost of living and lower taxes. These are not the same factors, however, that motivate migration in the young adult population.[4]

In 1980, a special issue of the gerontology journal *Research on Aging* was devoted entirely to the subject of retirement migration. This publication showcased the major findings from the first NIA-funded project. Appearing in this collection were the state-to-state migration stream patterns produced by the project.[5] Jeanne Biggar's collection of studies on Sun Belt retirement migration began with data from the first project,[6] as did the author's work on migration to one's state of birth.[7] Retirement amenity migration was first discussed in the context of this study.[8]

Also in 1980, the National Institute on Aging funded a second migration project, proposed by the same team of researchers, which compared their findings from the 1970 Census with those from a decade earlier, 1960. This study produced the first decade comparisons and demonstrated the

stability of retirement migration over time.[9]

In 1982, the NIA funded a third migration project, now comparing retirement migration patterns over three periods, 1955-1960, 1965-1970 and 1975-1980. This study demonstrated the existence of counterstreams for the first time, suggesting indirectly that some who move soon after retirement may later return to their state of origin.[10] These findings shocked some observers who had assumed that persons move only once during retirement. The discovery of counterstreams gave rise to the life course model of migration. This model acknowledges that the post-retirement years are an extended period of time and that migration can be triggered by disparate issues at different times during retirement.[11] The third project also produced the first studies of ethnic retirement migration, for Hispanics[12] and African Americans.[13] Also, this study demonstrated the size of interstate income transfers resulting from retirement migration.[14] These disparate reports and papers have littered the intellectual landscape of retirement migration over a 20-year period.

This volume collects and integrates the research findings on all of these topics and brings trends up to date. The recent release of the 1990 Census microdata files, and the NIA's funding of a fourth research project make this update possible. A comprehensive overview of retirement migration in America is the goal.

Migration is now a standard part of any discussion of the demography of aging.[15] Geographers are also taking an interest in retiree migration. Finally, there is a growing interest in retirement migration in mainstream demography which had initially considered the topic unrelated.

The casual reader may not care where the numbers in the tables come from in this book. The readers who intend to use any of these numbers in their own work, however, will care very much. It is not possible to check the numbers in census reports and difficult to study census definitions of concepts and geography. For these reasons, the following section will summarize the appropriate information for the readers who need or want to know.

Census Microdata: Where the Numbers Come From

As the U.S. economy grew after World War II, the Census Bureau received an increasing number of requests for custom tabulations to answer the specific questions of business and government planners. The Bureau did not have the manpower to respond to most of these requests. In 1960, the Bureau responded by providing a sample of census records for public use. By using this sample, those with questions could answer them by producing their own custom tabulations. The Census Bureau's microdata program was born. Such samples have continued to be produced after each census since 1960.

Microdata is a strange word. It evokes the intriguing image of microfilm, secret codes and spies. Actually, the term is much more mundane in its derivation. Census data is usually reported for a number of geographic units: for the nation, states, counties, neighborhoods or census tracts, and even for city blocks. The smallest possible unit for reporting census data, however, is the individual person. The individual, therefore, is the "micro" unit of data. A microdata sample is drawn from individual census records. Items are removed that could identify the person, such as his or her name, address, Social Security number, etc. It is the demographic do-it-yourselfer's dream. With a microdata file, one can create any information that can be derived from the samples, for any subpopulation that can be defined by the samples, from Norwegian bachelor farmers in rural Minnesota to octogenarian physicians in Manhattan. The only big problem encountered by microdata users is the danger of overgeneralizing to a population from a small sample.

Estimating from samples — The Census Bureau always refers to the microdata program as producing "small samples" of individual records. The first samples were 1-in-100 and 1-in-1000. In 1980 a 1-in-20 sample was added. In that decade, however, the geographical codes of only half of the individual records were entered — as a cost-saving measure. Therefore, microdata migration analyses from that census were based on an actual sample of 1-in-40. In 1990, for the first time, the full 5 percent sample was available for studying migration.

It is very important to note that all of the "facts" derived from census microdata about migration, or anything else, are only estimates. Samples are commonly used for making estimations. Market research, political polls and social science surveys all estimate population parameters from samples. Polls usually make these estimates within certain confidence intervals, often stated as "give or take" a small percent. That error, called "sampling variation" by researchers, is larger when samples are smaller.

Therefore, estimates of a very small subpopulation from census microdata will be less certain than estimates of a large population. For example, estimates of the number of older migrants in the United States from the 5 percent sample would be very close to the total census count, off by less than 1 percent. Estimates of the number of migrants in the stream from South Dakota to Ocean County, NJ, however, would contain much greater sampling variation because the sample would be so small. All of the numbers in the many tables of this book are only estimates derived from a sample. The reader should keep this principle in mind: Small numbers reported are less trustworthy estimates than the larger numbers.

Because smaller samples produce less reliable estimates than larger samples, the likelihood of missing the estimation mark is greater in the estimates from the 1960 and 1970 (1-in-100), than the 1980 (1-in-40) and 1990 (1-in-20) samples. The best estimates are from the 1990 Census. For this reason, there are more tables from the 1990 Census than from earlier decades. In addition, the 1990 sample was weighted, while earlier samples were not.

Having thought about samples, estimations and sampling error, it is important also to have a clear understanding of the primary census concepts used in this book. How is migration actually measured by the census?

The census measure of mobility — The census contains only one item measuring residential mobility, and it appeared for the first time in the 1940 Census. The question asked Americans if they lived in the same house five years before the census date, excluding children born during the interim. If the respondent did not, the census item further asks in which city or town, county and state, or country, they did live at middecade. In this way, detailed information was provided about who has moved where in the second half of each decade. Because persons who moved in the first half of the decade would not be counted, and persons moving twice or more in the second half of the decade would be counted only once, the five-year question was considered as a mobility "average" for the decade.

There was so much mobility in the late 1940s, following World War II, that the five-year question was expected to greatly underestimate mobility in the decade. The question was changed in the 1950 Census to ask whether a person had moved in the past year. The question may have generated a better measure for immediate purposes. However, it made decade changes impossible to analyze between the 1940 and 1950 censuses, and between the 1950 and 1960 censuses. The five-year migration question was reinstated in 1960 and has remained the same since then. Decade trends in the study of older migrants is not possible before 1960.

In 1960, the first census microdata files included geographical codes on only the current place of residence. This file was obviously not constructed with migration in mind. In 1970, 1980 and 1990 the place of origin was also included on the sample records. Migration stream data (from place to place) do not exist for any period before 1970.

Geographical mobility is an umbrella concept that includes migrants and local movers. *Local movers* make moves within their counties. *Migrants*, as defined by demographers, are persons who move across significant political boundaries. There are two kinds of migrants, however. *Internal migrants* cross county or state lines (sometimes many of them), and *international migrants* move between nations. Retirement migration, as covered here, includes only those persons who moved across state lines. Although an occasional nod is given to persons of retirement age who move from abroad, the focus here is on long-distance internal migrants.

Unfortunately, there are important migration issues that census data cannot address. Only the residences at the time of the census and five years earlier are recorded. One cannot tell from census data whether a person is returning to a place where he or she has lived earlier. Only one's state of birth is recorded. Further, using census data, one cannot tell how frequently a person has moved. Nor can one tell whether people in counterstreams (those that move in the opposite direction to the major streams) are actually returning after an earlier retirement move. Census studies of migration, therefore, do a lot with a little.

Census microdata geography — Census microdata geography is a world unto itself, and needs some explaining. The District of Columbia is considered a state. Counties are not identified individually in the microdata samples. The geographical unit below the state level is an artificial one called a PUMA, the acronym standing for Public Use Microdata Area. These units are parts of counties, whole counties or collections of counties, identified by state planners in each state as the most useful for state planning purposes. The only limitation placed on the PUMA by the Census Bureau is that the geographical units must have more than 100,000 people in them. There may be several PUMAs in the largest cities, and very sparsely populated counties are bundled together into units that have more than 100,000 residents. In this study, when a densely populated metropolitan county is split into several PUMAs, those PUMAs were combined so that the county could be identified as a whole. However, nothing can be done about the sparsely populated combined counties. In the present analysis, PUMAs are seldom referred to directly; they are called "counties or county groups."

In a few cases we've identified independent cities rather than counties. These cities are not in any county; they exist as separate entities. For example, while the city of Baltimore is surrounded by Baltimore County, it is independent of that county. The state of Virginia has several independent cities. St. Louis, MO, and Carson City, NV, are also independent cities.

Unfortunately, making comparisons of PUMAs between 1970, 1980 and 1990 is not possible because they are redefined in each decade by state planners. Their boundaries do not stay the same over time. Therefore, the analysis of migration to counties or county groupings in this study is limited to the 1990 Census microdata.

Even with all of these limitations, the census microdata sample gives us the best vantage from which to glimpse the changing patterns of retirement migration in the United States. Furthermore, it is really quite remarkable how much more we know after examining these microdata files than was known before.

CHAPTER ONE
AN OVERVIEW OF RETIREMENT MIGRATION

Introduction

Retirement migration is one aspect of a broader cultural happening that is very old. Members of the social and economic elite have always traveled. Most countries boasting a history of monarchy have seasonal palaces that have become tourist attractions. Wintering in Southern Europe was considered a health-giving activity by the physicians of the wealthy in Northern and Western Europe. Travel to spas was popular among the rich and famous for centuries before Franklin Roosevelt made lengthy visits to Hot Springs, GA.

Retirement migration seems to have always been toward the coast and toward milder climates. When the United States was fighting for its independence from England, the town of Bath was a thriving community of wealthy seasonal residents and retirees. The Riviera beckoned Parisians to the southern coast of France. What was once an activity of the leisure class in Europe has found a much broader audience in our time.

Vacationing, seasonal migration and retirement resettlement to a more healthful climate offering leisurely lifestyles could become a widespread phenomenon in America only after the development of a substantial middle class and transportation technology that made land travel to distant places possible and affordable. Thus these activities have become common only in this century. Although the individual community histories of retirement settlement may extend back to the 1920s and 1930s in some places, retirement migration became more than a novelty only after World War II.

Most interstate migrants originate in large cities and move to smaller cities, and to places with different climates. In 1920, the U.S. Census reported for the first time that more than half of the U.S. population lived in communities of more than 2,500 persons. This year was the demographic tip point between a rural and an urban America. Today, more than half of our citizens live in cities of over 1 million residents. Urbanism is a recent phenomenon, and retirement migration has increased as a result.

Three related fields of study — demography, geography and gerontology — today feature research specialties in retirement migration. In addition, economic development researchers became interested in the topic when studies revealed the characteristics of migrants. Furthermore, a steady flow of useful knowledge about trends and places has attracted public interest, reflected in business and the media. People thinking about making such a move provide an audience. This text is written for individuals with business and lay interests as well as for scholars. The viewpoint taken in this book is one that respects scholarship and scientific research but is accessible to people who have no special training in demography, geography or gerontology. Demographers can describe the patterns of retirement migration and discuss the social characteristics of migrants, but the actual social psychological processes that lead to making and enjoying such a move cannot be firmly grasped from census data. Why retirees move, therefore, has been a topic of intense speculation by marketing strategists. Finally, first-rate theoretical understanding of this issue is emerging from its discussion.

Why Most Retirees Do Not Move

Dr. Robert Butler, former head of the National Institute on Aging, has been quoted as saying, "The best place to retire is the neighborhood where you spent your life."[1] For most people who are retiring, this statement is probably sound advice. The retiree's house is a comfortable, secure and familiar setting in which friends visit and to which children return for holidays. Ties to the community, the neighborhood, tavern, clubs and church are secure and socially rewarding. Opportunities to indulge recreational interest and to be useful are within driving distance and plentiful enough to match the lifestyle the retiree desires in retirement. And the climate in which the retiree has lived for years poses no serious health problems. Under these circumstances, why would anyone think of moving? In any recent five-year period, people of retirement age are only about half as likely to make long-distance moves as is the U.S. population as a whole. So most people tend to stay put when they retire.

Lifestyles and place ties — Like boats to a mooring, people are tied to their environments by investments in their property, by the many community contexts in which they find meaning, by friends and family whose proximity they value, by the experiences of the past and by lifestyles that weave these strands together into patterns of satisfying activity. Any lifestyle requires a unique combination of environmental resources, and a retirement lifestyle is no exception to this rule. It is the combination of place ties, person ties and resources that is the key to understanding what is behind a retirement move.

A minority of retired people seek to change their lifestyles in such a way that a change of territory is required, and some find that they must relocate in order to re-establish their desired lifestyles because the environments around them have changed. In the paragraphs that follow, the relationship between retirement and geographic mobility will be examined, with particular emphasis placed on the kinds of people most likely to move. For the researcher, these movers are a population or subject pool; for the businessperson, they are a market.

The retirees who are most likely to relocate are those who have the fewest moorings; those whose desired retirement lifestyles are not compatible with their present community, neighborhood and housing environments; and those with the economic, health and psychic resources to move.[2] Let us look at these one at a time.

Work itself is a major community mooring; it ties us, within commuting distance, to the place of our employment. If a retiree has no other strong ties to the community, then retirement alone might be enough to motivate a move. If some local friends move when they retire, they model the process and their leaving may loosen ties further. As children leave for college or jobs, community ties are also loosened. It is not unusual to hear a retiree explain a move by saying that he or she had "no reason to remain," followed by a litany of loosened or lost moorings.[3]

The weakening of ties to a place may make moving easier, but it is seldom the only factor behind a move. For some, the image of a retirement lifestyle calls for a different environment. Images of retirement are frequently drawn from leisure or vacationing experiences, and most popular retirement locations are in or near places that attract tourists and vacationers.[4]

There may be a dark side to the idealization of retirement lifestyles and environments.[5] They may be formed partly as opposite projections of negative experiences. An example of this process is the yearning to retire in a setting that has a climate with none of the bad aspects of one's own. If it is too cold, then the ideal place would be warm. Perhaps this accounts for part of the Sun Belt retirement patterns for people who have endured many bitter winters, and for the fact that native Floridians tend to seek out cool summer places, such as western North Carolina, as retirement sites. Place planning guided by such fantasies is problematical because it never broadly considers the person's basic needs, only the frustrated ones.

Sometimes the successful retirement moves of an earlier generation, especially moves by parents and their siblings and friends, provide powerful models for members of the next generation. The family history of retirement mobility, however, is unexamined in the research literature.

On the other hand, compulsive workers or others who neither enjoyed nor pursued leisure during their early adulthood and middle years may have no compelling images of retirement lifestyles when they retire. They may repudiate retirement as an appropriate life goal, and, in retirement, they may be helpless to piece together a tolerable lifestyle of any kind. Retirement-lifestyle-based marketing appeals to these people will fall on stony ground, indeed.

Person ties — Lifestyle-motivated moves tend to be place-centered. When migration researchers focus on particular popular retirement destinations, they tend to see amenity-seeking migrants there. Although they are more difficult to study, there are also person-centered motivations for moving that are equally important. Investigators normally infer that a retired person moving to Florida or Arizona is motivated primarily by the destination, when he or she may very well be moving to be near a child or friend already there. The climate change, in this case, is only a bonus. Patricia Gober and Leo Zonn, professors of geography at Arizona State University, surveyed the residents of nearby Sun City, AZ, a decade ago and found that more than 40 percent of all households had at least one relative in the destination region.[6] Marketers should consider other "relationships" as

well, including friendships, that effect migration. Also, person-motivated moves do not necessarily imply a need for assistance. Older relatives and friends often nurture and care for others, and sometimes the provision of such care requires a move.

Resources — If person ties and place ties often go undifferentiated when motives are assessed or inferred, it is equally true that place ties and resources are often confused. Retirees vary considerably in their possession of the resources needed to relocate — particularly their economic, health and psychic resources. Butler's observation that most retired persons are better off in the location where they have lived before retirement does not necessarily mean that persons who do not move prefer to stay where they are living. Some retirees simply do not possess the resources necessary to make a desired move.

On the whole, long-distance movers are better off economically than those who do not move and those who move short distances, perhaps because of the economic resources needed to make such a move.

Health resources cut two ways.[7] Good health can facilitate an early retirement move. When asked, retirees often justify their move by saying that they want to do this 'while they have good health and can enjoy their new lifestyle.' On the other hand, the author and his colleagues found in a study of mobility and health that a decline in functional health when one is older can trigger a move to another living environment.[8] This process is accelerated when combined with widowhood.[9]

Psychic resources are those that provide the inner strength and freedom to take the risks involved in moving. Retirees who have experienced relocation frequently during working years understand residential and community transition and the prospects generate fewer doubts and fears. Strong community moorings carry an emotional cost, however. They reduce one's ability to mount the effort it takes to move even if income and health resources are abundant. Rootedness, in this case, may be a psychic cost or handicap.

Lee Cuba, who studied retired migrants to Cape Cod, has argued that 'selves' as well as 'bodies' can be relatively mobile. Moving oneself physically to another community does not necessarily mean that one also moves emotionally.[10] There are some migrants who never put down roots but remain emotionally moored to their former communities. Perhaps the more mobile self is the one more likely to make lifestyle-based moves to exotic places.[11]

In conclusion, it is a combination of place ties (moorings), lifestyle attractions, person ties and resources that impact the decision of whether and where to move. There was a time when process theorists thought the decision to move was separate from the decision of where to move.[12] Now, the prevailing view claims that, for most retirees, these decisions are really inseparable.[13]

Search space — When a retired couple is considering a move and begins looking for housing, geographers define the acceptable territory in which the couple will search for a new residence as "search space."

The search space of the couple is defined by their previously acquired knowledge. This knowledge, of course, is

Table 1— Migration During Five-Year Periods Ending in 1960, 1970, 1980 and 1990

	1960 #	1960 %	1970 #	1970 %	1980 #	1980 %	1990 #	1990 %	% Change in Volume 1960-70	% Change in Volume 1970-80	% Change in Volume 1980-90
Total U.S. Population	179,323,000		203,302,000		226,546,000		248,710,000		13.4	11.4	9.8
Age 60+ Population	22,820,000		27,538,000		35,637,000		41,858,000		20.7	29.4	17.5
Interstate Migrants:											
Age 5+	14,141,000	9.2	16,081,000	9.3	20,358,000	9.9	21,585,000	9.4	13.7	26.6	13.0
Age 60+	931,000	4.1	1,079,000 [1]	3.9	1,622,000 [2]	4.6	1,901,000	4.5	15.9	50.0	17.2

Source: U.S. Census. [1]This figure was derived by extrapolating from a 1 in 100 sample. The actual census count was 1,094,014. [2]This figure was derived by extrapolating from a 1 in 40 sample. The actual census count was 1,654,000.

informed by earlier visits, discussions with migrants and travelers, and by reading. Rarely does one move to a place that was previously unknown to the person making the move, unless the move was forced. The primary reason that people choose new locations where they have vacationed and visited is because they have gained the necessary knowledge base to make a choice.

In addition to knowledge, there are motivational factors that assist in the decision-making process. These ordinarily fall into three categories: lifestyle, relational and cost of living factors. Retirees usually have an image of how they want to live in retirement, and they seek those features of the environment that would facilitate that lifestyle. There is sometimes a strong recreational component, such as golfing, boating or shopping. The presence of well-stocked libraries, entertainment establishments and restaurants may also be important. For some, the kind and quality of churches or temples and opportunities to participate in organized volunteer work or part-time employment may also be factors. The search space, therefore, may be narrow or wide depending upon the priorities of lifestyle elements. Relational issues primarily revolve around access to family members. Being too far away (or too near) must be balanced against the lifestyle issues. Finally, retirees frequently seek a new hometown with a cost of living advantage. For retirees who leave large cities, most smaller cities will carry this advantage.

Because the search space is conditioned by knowledge requirements and motivational factors, the size of the targeted area will vary from retiree to retiree. Thus, for example three couples may live in the same apartment building and move at about the same time. One couple might settle in a neighborhood in a Sun Belt state occupied by several of their friends and relatives who had moved before they did. Another may move to a neighborhood two hours further away with a different mix of lifestyle factors. And the third couple might choose a different destination state altogether, perhaps not so far away from the original residence, because of the lower cost of living. Migration flows, therefore, are less like laser beams than garden hoses because of varying amounts of search space.

What Migrants Want

Older migrants, like people in general, come in many types. The research literature tends to classify them into two major categories: dependency migrants and amenity migrants. Dependency migrants are typically forced to move due to deterioration of health or financial resources or the death of a spouse. Amenity migrants are looking for settings that will afford a new and better lifestyle. Communities located on or near lakes, beaches and mountains, and those in temperate climates, have an advantage in attracting this type of migrant, who tends to be recently retired, and therefore younger, usually married, and economically better-off than many other retirees. Interstate migration streams to the Sun Belt are laden with amenity migrants.

What are amenity migrants searching for in a retirement location? A survey of subscribers to *Where to Retire* magazine found the following to be the most important considerations for its readers:

1) low crime rate
2) good hospitals nearby
3) low overall cost of living
4) mild climate
5) low overall taxes
6) low housing cost
7) friendly neighbors
8) major city nearby
9) no state income tax
10) active social/cultural environment

People age 50 and older were asked by the Gallup Organization, "If you could live in any place, where would you choose?" Sixty percent idealized small towns and rural areas as better places to make ends meet and to get in touch with more important values. Tom Graff and Robert Wiseman argued that older migrants see the quality of life as better outside of large cities, but they still want to live near a city for the amenities that cities offer. Many of the tables in this volume tell the same story.[14]

Is Migration Increasing or Decreasing?

How many older people move across state lines before each census, and how does their migration rate compare with that of Americans in general? Is retirement migration increasing or decreasing?

These questions are answered in Table 1. The growth from 1960 to 1990 of the U.S. population in general, and for that part of it age 60+, is shown in the top two lines of the table.

In each decade the number of Americans, and older Americans, has increased. The decade change, shown on the right side of the table, indicates that the size of the older population is growing considerably faster than the population as a whole. Between 1980 and 1990, for example, the U.S. population increased nearly 10 percent while the older population grew nearly 18 percent.

The same general pattern is evident when the number of interstate migrants is compared in each decade. Migrants increased in the U.S. population over age 5 in each decade after 1960, from 14.1 million in 1960 to nearly 22 million in 1990. The increase was due to growth in the general population. The percent who had moved in the five-year period before each census grew very little, remaining between 9 percent and 10 percent.

The same pattern is seen among older Americans. The number of interstate migrants grew in each decade, from 931,000 during the five years prior to 1960 to nearly 2 million in the five years prior to 1990. Again, the proportion of the entire age group who moved to another state before each census remained relatively constant, between 3.9 percent and 4.6 percent, over the four census decades.

Will retirement migration continue to increase in the future? Having a stable trend that reaches back over four censuses encourages one to expect the same in the future. Much speculation has centered on the retirement of the large baby-boom generation, a process that will begin in another decade. The economic middle class in this 18-year age cohort is smaller than in earlier generations. The economic distribution is more polarized, with higher proportions of households in the upper and lower income categories. To the extent that higher income is associated with interstate migration, this polarization should suggest an increase in the rate of retirement migration among baby boomers. The retirement behavior of this generation, however, could be different from those of earlier generations. Adjusted projections should be made cautiously.

The Thrust of the Book

In Chapter 2, the gross national patterns of interstate migration are described. Trends are determined over the four-census period from 1960 to 1990. Resulting changes in state rankings are discussed. Chapter 3 goes one step further and focuses upon state-to-state stream migration. All of the state-to-state streams containing more than 2,000 retirees are charted and described. Also, in this chapter there is a description and discussion of counterstreams. Many older migrants in counterstreams may be returning from earlier destinations to their origin states. Chapter 4 is devoted to the first systematic census exploration of the most popular and least popular retirement counties in the United States. These data were drawn entirely from the 1990 Census files. This analysis explores those counties from which interstate migrants tend to move in large numbers, as well as those into which they migrate. And in Chapter 5, the major interstate county-to-county streams are described. Never before in the research literature on interstate retirement migration have the underlying principals of county-to-county migration been described and discussed. At this juncture, the case is made for three distinct patterns of out-migration, a New York City pattern, a Los Angeles pattern and a Chicago pattern.

The next three chapters concern special types of retirement migration. Chapter 6 explores returning to one's state of birth. Older migrants are no more prone to return to their home state than are American migrants generally. Nonetheless, it is an important variant, particularly popular among African-American and Hispanic-American retirees. A second special type of retirement migration, snowbirding, is illustrated in Chapter 7. Seasonal migration of retirees is not apparent in census data, which concerns itself only with "permanent" moves. This chapter, therefore, summarizes what is known about this special type of retirement migration from sample surveys in Florida, Texas and Arizona. Chapter 8 considers a final special type of retirement migration, moves of a shorter distance to regional destinations. Data for this chapter were drawn primarily from fieldwork conducted on Cape Cod and in the Missouri Ozarks among retirees who had moved to each destination predominately from the same and neighboring states.

Chapter 9 considers retirement migration as an economic development strategy. This chapter describes the amount of income that is transferred between states as a result of retirement migration, and the income distribution of migrants to the most popular retirement counties.

• • • • • • • • • •

In Chapter 2 we will consider state retirement migration patterns over four census decades.

CHAPTER TWO

STATE RETIREMENT MIGRATION PATTERNS

Introduction

Geographic strategic planning should always begin with the gross national patterns and then move progressively toward the local setting. In this chapter we will examine the flows of migrants in and out of states over four census migration periods: 1955-1960; 1965-1970; 1975-1980; and 1985-1990. In doing so, we will develop first impressions of the major sending and receiving states and their relative attractiveness.

Researchers have reported on the migration patterns of the older population since at least the early 1950s, and interest in the subject has been enduring. Early research, however, was tentative and sparse. The census did not contain a question about residential location until 1940, but its coverage of migration issues has improved substantially since that time. The census question on mobility asks where a person lived five years before the census — except in 1950 when the high levels of mobility following the war prompted its change to where a person lived one year ago. This one-time deviation in wording the key mobility question has made it impossible to trace decade trends earlier than 1960 using the census measure of mobility.

Even the kind of data used in the tables of this report has improved. In 1960 the state of origin was not included on the individual records of migrants, only their destination state. Therefore, only since 1970 have we been able to estimate both the state of origin and destination for each person who made long-distance moves. As a result, we have data from four census decades (1960-1990) on the states to which older migrants moved, and data from only three census decades (1970-1990) on the states from which migrants came.

Sun Belt Migration

After decades of labor force movement out of the rural Southern and Southwestern states to Northern industrial ones, the 1970 Census showed a major reversal. In a bulletin published by the authoritative Population Reference Bureau, the Sun Belt region was called the U.S. population "frontier of the 1970s," because it had become the most rapidly growing segment of the nation.[1] Between 1965 and 1970, nearly a quarter of interstate migrants of all ages moved into just three large states—California, Texas and Florida.

Retirees discovered the Sun Belt, however, decades before the general population began knocking on its door. The earliest study of migration patterns of the elderly examined interregional moves between 1935 and 1940. Hiram Friedsam reported that the Pacific Coast and South Atlantic regions were the most frequent destinations of older interregional migrants, and that migrants to the South Atlantic came mostly from east of the Mississippi.[2] These find-

ings have been remarkably stable over the intervening decades.

Professor Jeanne Biggar from the University of Virginia studied the migration of persons age 60 and older to the Sun Belt region during the 1965-1970 period. She defined the region as including all of the border states from Virginia southward to Florida and westward to California, adding two interior states, Arkansas and Missouri, because they straddle the Ozarks area.[3] She found that more than half (58 percent) of elderly interstate migrants moved to these 14 states. When she examined the exchange between the Sun Belt and the non-Sun Belt, she found that the exchange went both ways. The non-Sun Belt sent the majority of migrants to the Sun Belt, but there was a smaller flow of migrants back. In addition, in a study of the 1980 Census, Biggar found that the 1970 pattern had continued over the next decade; the same 14 states were capturing 59 percent of migrants age 60 and older between 1975 and 1980.

When the proportion of migrants entering these same states between 1985 and 1990 was calculated, again it captured 59 percent of the total. To summarize, nearly 60 percent of older migrants entered a Sun Belt state in each of the three decades.

A regional analysis such as this one is a sound place to begin examining retirement migration patterns because it affords such a good opportunity to consider the problems inherent in generalizing from census data. The broader the geographical area one considers as the recipient of migration, the greater the variation it will cloak. Some Sun Belt states receive floods of older migrants, and some receive hardly a trickle. It is true, as a generalization, that the Sun Belt is a large, stable receiving area for retirees who make interstate moves. The region is so broad, however, that a planner who wants to locate services for retirees in a place where many of them move would hardly be helped by such information. A belt is not needed; what is needed is a spot. The Sun Belt pattern is only useful in providing a context. Being aware of the Sun Belt pattern leads to the expectation that climate has something to do with the attractiveness of retirement destinations for many older migrants. This important insight is the first wisdom in understanding a prominent type of retirement migration, that associated with lifestyle enhancement, and often simply referred to as "amenity migration." The warmer the climate, the more golf days there are in a year.

A regional analysis misses the factors other than climate, however, that are consequential pulls for migrants. Such a complex phenomenon as retirement migration is motivated by many factors, climate among them, although climate by itself is insufficient or else the Sun Belt would be evenly spread with older migrants. It is not. As we shall soon see, Louisiana, the Sportsman's Paradise, is not more attractive to

Table 1 — Ten States Receiving Most In-Migrants Age 60+ in Five-Year Periods Ending in 1960, 1970, 1980 and 1990

Rank	1960 State	#	%	1970 State	#	%	1980 State	#	%	1990 State	#	%
1	FL	208,072	22.3	FL	263,200	24.4	FL	437,040	26.3	FL	451,709	23.8
2	CA	126,883	13.6	CA	107,000	9.9	CA	144,880	8.7	CA	131,514	6.9
3	NJ	36,019	3.9	AZ	47,600	4.4	AZ	94,600	5.7	AZ	98,756	5.2
4	NY	33,794	3.6	NJ	46,000	4.3	TX	78,480	4.7	TX	78,117	4.1
5	IL	30,355	3.3	TX	39,800	3.7	NJ	49,400	3.0	NC	64,530	3.4
6	AZ	29,571	3.2	NY	32,800	3.0	PA	39,520	2.4	PA	57,538	3.0
7	OH	27,759	3.0	OH	32,300	3.0	NC	39,400	2.4	NJ	49,176	2.6
8	TX	26,770	2.9	IL	28,800	2.7	WA	35,760	2.2	WA	47,484	2.5
9	PA	25,738	2.8	PA	28,600	2.7	IL	35,720	2.1	VA	46,554	2.4
10	MI	20,308	2.2	MO	25,300	2.3	NY	34,920	2.1	GA	44,475	2.3
Total Interstate Migrants	931,012			1,079,200 [1]			1,622,120 [2]			1,901,105		
% of Total in Top 10 States	60.7			60.4			59.5			56.3		

Source: U.S. Census. [1]This figure was derived by extrapolating from a 1 in 100 sample. The actual census count was 1,094,014. [2]This figure was derived by extrapolating from a 1 in 40 sample. The actual census count was 1,654,000.

older migrants than Minnesota, Wisconsin or New Hampshire.

Major Receiving and Sending States

When individual states are considered, rather than a multistate region, the picture that emerges is more interesting and far more useful. Interstate migration may be only half as common in the older population (4.5 percent) as in the general American population (9.4 percent) over a five-year period, but retirement migration is much more channelized for the former.[4] Retirees move in greater proportions to fewer states than migrants of all ages, thus metaphorically they dig deeper channels. Evidence of this migration pattern can be seen in Table 1. From 1985-1990, 56 percent of older migrants moved to only 10 states, 43 percent to only five. Retirement migration is not of much consequence in most states, but in some it is a major industry.

It's convenient to think of the in-migrant market as a pie, with cities and states vying for a slice. Which state's slice is the largest? From 1985-1990, Florida received nearly a quarter (23.8 percent) of all older interstate migrants. Less than a third that many migrants moved to California (6.9 percent). Arizona and Texas ranked third and fourth, receiving 5.2 percent and 4.1 percent respectively. So the market is dominated by Florida. Others among the top 10 receiving states were North Carolina (fifth), Pennsylvania (sixth), New Jersey (seventh), Washington (eighth), Virginia (ninth) and Georgia (10th).

When comparing the rankings of states over the four census decades, there are some interesting trends. The underlying master trend is one of a gradual dechannelization of retirement migration. That is, a gradual decrease in the market share of migrants received by the major destination states, a gentle spreading out of the flows. This process is very gradual, but as it happens, it is important to note the states that are sliding, inch by inch, losing their magnetism for migrants; those that are essentially stable over time; and those that are moving up in the rankings. Dechannelization is good news for all of those states interested in attracting retirees that are not already on the top of the list of destinations.

Now for some evidence. First, the master trend is evident in the fact that the leading four states all lost market share during the past decade, although they held their same ranking position relative to one another in 1990 as in 1980. The losses were small, but the pattern is clear and persistent. Florida, which has dominated retirement migration since at least 1960, increased its number of older migrants but lost more than 2 percent share between 1980 and 1990. Arizona, likewise, lost share but gained numbers. California lost both share and numbers. Texas lost share but held its numbers constant.

Most of these declines are not felt on the ground. Planners seeking out migrant concentrations would not notice the changes at all because there were more than a quarter million more interstate migrants age 60+ from 1985-1990 vs. 1975-1980. The pie chart representing the entire retirement migration market is considerably larger today, so the number of migrants to Florida increased by nearly 15,000 even though its share of all migrants was 2.5 percent smaller in 1990 than a decade earlier.

Within the broader context of slight declines in market share received by the major receiving states, there are some states that could be called "sliders." These are states that have experienced a decline in popularity over several decades. Chief among the sliders is California. It has been ranked second since 1960, but its share of migrants has declined in every decade since that time, from 13.6 percent to 6.9 percent, cutting its share nearly in half.

The other sliders are all Northern states. In 1960, the top 10 destination states included New Jersey (third), New York (fourth), Illinois (fifth), Ohio (seventh), Pennsylvania (ninth) and Michigan (10th). By 1990, most of these Northeastern and Midwestern states had dropped completely off the list, with only two exceptions, Pennsylvania (sixth) and New Jersey (seventh). Of these two, New Jersey is also a slider, having dropped in the rankings every decade since 1960. Though its slice of the pie is smaller, from 1985-1990 New Jersey continued to attract almost as many migrants as it did from 1975-1980.

Florida, Arizona, Texas, Pennsylvania and Washington may be considered the stable destination states. They have held onto their rankings over the past two or three censuses. Arizona had made an enormous leap between 1960 and 1970 from sixth to third place and had held onto third place and bettered its share in 1980. If Arizona had made the same proportional gain (1.3 percent) in the latest decade, it would have passed California to occupy the second place among retirement destination states in 1990.[5] Instead, it lost share, along with the other top destination states caught in the macrotrend of dechannelization.

Among the other stable destinations, Pennsylvania is particularly worthy of note. It has held sixth place in the rankings for the past two decades, and is the only Northern state to be a stable destination of retirees. In addition, its proportion of migrants increased in the 1990 Census. The state of Washington jumped onto the list in 1980 and maintained its eighth rank in 1990, also improving its share.

The other states listed among the top 10 destinations are located in the Atlantic Coast region between New York and Florida. They are the islands in the major migration stream between the Empire and the Sunshine states. North Carolina is the star. It ranked 27th in 1960, 17th in 1970, seventh in 1980 and jumped ahead of both New Jersey and Pennsylvania to land in fifth place, behind Texas, in 1990. Virginia (ninth) and Georgia (10th), replaced Illinois and New York, respectively, since 1980.

The consolidation of the Sun Belt as a retirement region can be seen in these rankings. In 1960, there were six Northern states and four Sun Belt states among the top 10 receiving states. In the latest census, there were two Northeastern states and seven Sun Belt states ranked among the top 10. With the exception of Pennsylvania and New Jersey, all of the remaining states on the 1990 list are located on the border of the United States from Virginia southward to Florida and west to California, with Washington, also a border state, thrown in. The Sun Belt as a regional destination of retirees is a belt after all, but it is on the sunny rim of the nation, not in the nation's sunny interior.

One of the defining characteristics of retirement migration is that migrants coming from all over the nation concentrate their destinations in a few states, forming highly channelized flows into these states. More than half arrive in just 10 states. Is the same picture also true of origin states? Are there a handful of states that contribute very high proportions of older migrants to the destination states? The answer to this question is "yes." Elderly migration is channelized both at destination and at origin. When the top 10 sending states are compiled for 1990, they collectively contribute 58 percent of all the migrants.

As seen in Table 2, New York has held the top position in this chart for three census decades, since 1970. In 1990, for the first time, the share of out-migrants that the Empire State contributed to the pool fell by almost three points. It is difficult to escape the comparison between New York's sending and Florida's receiving performance. Florida, also for the first time, dropped two-and-a-half points in this decade.

The dominant pattern found in Table 2 could be summarized in the quip "the major sending states are the states with the most to lose," that is, these are the states with the largest populations over age 60. Three of the top four receiving states, California, Texas and Florida, are also found on the list. It is difficult to argue, therefore, that only cold winters

Table 2 — Ten States Sending Most Out-Migrants Age 60+ in Five-Year Periods Ending in 1970, 1980 and 1990

Rank	1970 State	#	%	1980 State	#	%	1990 State	#	%
1	NY	154,300	14.3	NY	242,960	14.6	NY	222,781	11.7
2	IL	86,600	8.0	CA	141,440	8.5	CA	187,240	9.8
3	CA	74,400	6.9	IL	120,160	7.2	FL	128,561	6.8
4	(Tie) OH	53,400	4.9	FL	92,280	5.6	IL	107,136	5.6
5	(Tie) PA	53,400	4.9	NJ	86,880	5.2	NJ	106,556	5.6
6	MI	52,400	4.9	OH	85,760	5.2	PA	78,903	4.2
7	NJ	50,100	4.6	PA	81,280	4.9	MI	74,661	3.9
8	FL	46,000	4.3	MI	72,040	4.3	OH	74,271	3.9
9	TX	30,300	2.8	MA	47,000	2.8	TX	69,856	3.7
10	IN	29,200	2.7	IN	39,440	2.4	MA	56,737	3.0
Total Interstate Migrants		1,079,200			1,662,120			1,901,105	
% of Total in Top 10 States			58.4			60.7			58.2

Source: U.S. Census.

motivate out-migration. Arizona, the third leading destination state, is missing from the list of major origin states, following this logic, primarily because its older population is not large enough to make such a substantial contribution.

Several states appear decade after decade among the top 10 origin states. Even in this picture of stability, however, one cannot rightly assert that there has been no movement in rankings over the three decades. The most interesting trend in the data is the rise of California to challenge New York as the leading origin of older interstate migrants. California went from a distance of 7.4 percentage points behind New York in 1970 to 6.1 in 1980. In 1990, it moved to within two points of becoming the major contributor of older migrants. California is the second leading destination state; it is also the second leading origin state.

California is not the only major destination state which increased its contribution to the pool of out-migrants between 1980 and 1990. Florida has risen steadily through the ranks as well. In 1970, Florida ranked eighth among the origin states, moving up to fourth place in 1980 and to third place in 1990 when it contributed nearly 7 percent to the national pool of out-migrants.

The two states which made consistently downward moves in the rankings each decade were Illinois and Ohio.

Rising and Declining Popularity

What can be made of these temporal patterns of state inflows and outflows of older migrants? First, it is difficult not to be impressed by the stability inherent in these patterns. The proportion of older persons who make long-distance moves, the proportion who move to Sun Belt states, and indeed the share received or sent by the leading destination and origin states, are not volatile, rising and falling decade by decade. Minor changes occur within a framework of considerable stability, and this predictability provides the basis for strategic planning.

The changes that do occur, however, point to some long-term trends and processes that should be considered at this point. Humans and human populations are not boundless; they are finite and relatively easy to track over time and space. Discerning the long-term patterns in those tracks is one of the most interesting speculative aspects of social science.

There are generational changes that will certainly facilitate and motivate retirement moves in the future. A generation of "free agents," accustomed to making independent decisions about their lives with less loyalty to company and place than earlier generations, may be even more mobile in retirement.[6] On the other hand, they may be more inclined to move down the information highway and the flight path without moving their home base. Keeping up with scattered friends through e-mail and videophones may dull the desire to join them residentially. Certainly the dual professional households that have made up the economic elite of the baby boom's upper middle class will be in a financial position to move in retirement if they wish to do so.

The migration patterns that are evident in this chapter help very little in understanding the motivations of future movers. But they do hint at a long-term macroprocess that

should be kept in mind when considering retirement migration. Quality of life, or at least the perception thereof, is at the heart of this process.

When we pull from the bookstore shelf one of those reference volumes that offers advice about places to retire, we are only examining the most recent packaging of an old concept: quality of life. A geographical definition of quality of life incorporates the concept of individual well-being but focuses more on places than individuals. Quality of life, like a coin, has two sides — goals and appraisals.[7] The goal side is subjective and attempts to specify what a good place "ought to be." The appraisal side assesses the actual environment, usually with a variety of measures. It is the subjective nature of the ideal that creates the problem in rating places. The "ideal" environment differs from one rater to another, so the reliability of ratings is not high.

Some of the subjective goals of older migrants can be discerned from the population data we have already observed. We know, for example, that climatic conditions favor Sun Belt locations. We know also that there is a movement out of the most populous, presumably the most crowded, states. Moving to a place with less congestion and fewer of the problems that big cities tend to have must be attractive to many retirees. The fact that people tend to move to the rim states, most of which are on water, must imply that there is more than climate that is attractive about the physical environment. Water and mountains, and scenic beauty in general, are traditional pulls.

So long as there is a perceived quality of life difference in the environments at origin and destination, the better quality of life will attract new residents who are retired. Retirees who moved into and have lived in a Sun Belt community for 10 or 15 years will often complain that the quality of life has declined since they arrived, and they often blame the decline on the retirees who followed them, and those who keep coming. The reason that they keep coming is that even in its decline, as viewed by migrant old-timers, there is still a quality of life advantage as compared with where the new migrants originated. The quality of life of the environment of origin may also have declined over the past 15 years, holding the relative advantage of the destination about constant.

When the difference narrows, however, it begins to choke off in-migration and generate pressure for retirement out-migration from the destination. People who retire in Sun Belt cities sometimes subsequently move to less crowded places with greater scenic beauty, too, and feel that they have traded up on their quality of life.

This is the long-term pattern seen in California. Once a powerful magnet to retirees, California may be better known in the future as an origin than as a destination. In recent years, residents have faced water shortages, earthquakes, rising crime and riots, skyrocketing housing costs (recently moderating but still much higher than national averages), and a tarnished national reputation created and reinforced by the news media. An increasing rate of out-migration is not surprising in this context.

The same principle appears to be at work in certain regions of Florida. Dade County certainly has its share of

Table 3 — Volume and Impact* of In-migrants Age 60+ in All States

	1975-1980					1985-1990				
	In-migration			Impact*		In-migration			Impact*	
State	#	%	Rank	%	Rank	#	%	Rank	%	Rank
Alabama	18,520	1.1	27	3.0	36	25,336	1.3	24	3.6	30 (Tie)
Alaska	1,520	0.1	51	7.8	8	2,395	0.1	51	6.8	8 (Tie)
Arizona	94,600	5.7	3	21.6	2	98,756	5.2	3	15.6	2
Arkansas	33,760	2.0	12	7.9	6 (Tie)	29,848	1.6	23	6.5	12 (Tie)
California	144,880	8.7	2	4.2	24 (Tie)	131,514	6.9	2	3.1	37 (Tie)
Colorado	27,160	1.6	18	7.6	9	30,672	1.6	22	6.8	8 (Tie)
Connecticut	18,320	1.1	28	3.5	31	17,351	0.9	32	2.9	40
Delaware	6,680	0.4	42	7.5	10	8,026	0.4	43	7.3	7
D.C.	3,560	0.2	48	3.4	32 (Tie)	4,821	0.3	47	4.7	21
Florida	437,040	26.3	1	19.2	3	451,709	23.8	1	14.8	3
Georgia	33,360	2.0	14	4.5	20 (Tie)	44,475	2.3	10	5.0	20
Hawaii	5,640	0.3	43	5.0	16	8,053	0.4	42	4.6	22
Idaho	9,120	0.5	37	6.8	11	10,832	0.6	39	6.8	8 (Tie)
Illinois	35,720	2.1	9	2.0	47 (Tie)	36,897	1.9	15	1.9	50
Indiana	23,120	1.4	22	2.8	38	31,405	1.7	21	3.3	35 (Tie)
Iowa	11,320	0.7	36	2.2	43 (Tie)	11,669	0.6	38	2.1	48 (Tie)
Kansas	14,880	0.9	32	3.6	30	16,492	0.9	33	3.7	28 (Tie)
Kentucky	17,880	1.1	29	3.1	35	21,770	1.1	20	3.5	32 (Tie)
Louisiana	12,120	0.7	35	2.1	45 (Tie)	14,004	0.7	35	2.2	46 (Tie)
Maine	8,880	0.5	38	4.6	18 (Tie)	11,929	0.6	37	5.5	17
Maryland	24,600	1.5	20	4.2	24 (Tie)	32,428	1.7	19	4.5	23
Massachusetts	21,920	1.3	24	2.2	43 (Tie)	23,796	1.3	25	2.2	46 (Tie)
Michigan	24,920	1.5	19	1.9	49	31,885	1.7	20	2.1	48 (Tie)
Minnesota	13,800	0.8	33	2.1	45 (Tie)	19,370	1.0	30	2.7	41 (Tie)
Mississippi	16,120	1.0	31	4.0	27 (Tie)	17,637	0.9	31	4.1	27
Missouri	30,400	1.8	16	3.4	32 (Tie)	35,251	1.9	17	3.7	28 (Tie)
Montana	5,360	0.3	44	4.4	22 (Tie)	6,140	0.3	44	4.4	24 (Tie)
Nebraska	7,960	0.5	41	2.9	37	9,852	0.5	41	3.4	34
Nevada	24,160	1.5	21	23.9	1	43,131	2.3	13	23.8	1
New Hampshire	12,480	0.8	34	8.6	5	15,058	0.8	34	8.9	4 (Tie)
New Jersey	49,400	3.0	5	4.0	27 (Tie)	49,176	2.6	7	3.5	32 (Tie)
New Mexico	17,160	1.0	30	10.5	4	19,872	1.0	29	8.9	4 (Tie)
New York	34,920	2.1	10	1.3	51	42,802	2.3	14	1.3	51
North Carolina	39,400	2.4	7	4.5	20 (Tie)	64,530	3.4	5	5.9	16
North Dakota	2,560	0.2	50	2.4	41 (Tie)	3,140	0.2	50	2.7	41 (Tie)
Ohio	32,680	2.0	15	2.0	47 (Tie)	44,459	2.3	11	2.3	45
Oklahoma	22,600	1.4	23	4.4	22 (Tie)	23,572	1.2	26	4.2	26
Oregon	33,600	2.0	13	7.9	6 (Tie)	43,996	2.3	12	8.6	6
Pennsylvania	39,520	2.4	6	1.8	50	57,538	3.0	6	2.4	44
Rhode Island	4,360	0.3	46	2.4	41 (Tie)	5,842	0.3	46	3.0	39
South Carolina	20,560	1.2	25	4.9	17	34,251	1.8	18	6.3	14
South Dakota	4,000	0.2	47	3.3	34	4,141	0.2	49	3.1	37 (Tie)
Tennessee	29,040	1.7	17	4.0	27 (Tie)	36,306	1.9	16	4.4	24 (Tie)
Texas	78,480	4.7	4	4.1	26	78,117	4.1	4	3.3	35 (Tie)
Utah	8,520	0.5	40	5.5	14	10,751	0.6	40	5.3	18
Vermont	4,600	0.3	45	5.9	12	5,916	0.3	45	6.7	11
Virginia	34,160	2.1	11	4.6	18 (Tie)	46,554	2.4	9	5.1	19
Washington	35,760	2.2	8	5.8	13	47,484	2.5	8	6.2	15
West Virginia	8,600	0.5	39	2.6	39	12,919	0.7	36	3.6	30 (Tie)
Wisconsin	19,640	1.2	26	2.5	40	23,030	1.2	27	2.7	41 (Tie)
Wyoming	2,760	0.2	49	5.1	15	4,207	0.2	48	6.5	12 (Tie)

*Impact is calculated by dividing the number of older in-migrants by the total number of older residents.

Figure 1 — Positive or Negative Net Migration by State, Migrants Age 60+, 1985-1990

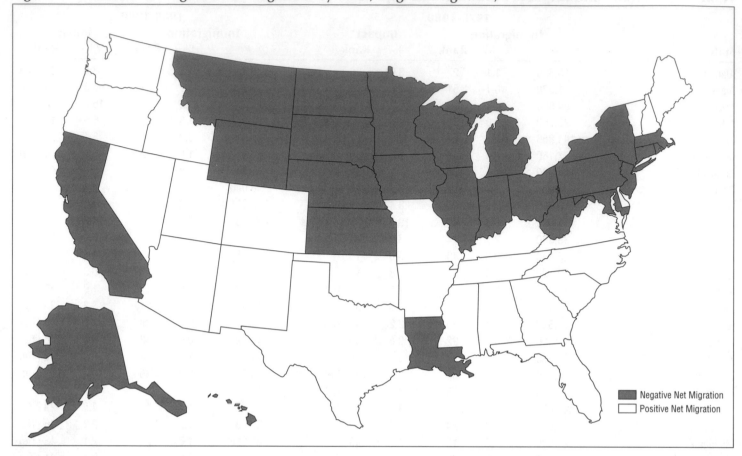

Negative Net Migration
Positive Net Migration

crowding, crime and natural disasters, not to mention its negative image in the news media. An exodus of retirees from Dade County, as the quality of life has declined in Greater Miami over the past two decades, has been evident.

The take-home lesson of this discussion is that the strategic planner should not forget to consider the long-term as well as the short-term prospects for the quality of life when considering retirement migration. For a future generation that values personal space, convenience and quality more highly than earlier generations did, unplanned and uncontrolled retirement development may carry within itself the seeds of its own destruction by hastening the decline in the quality of life as it is understood by retirees.

In-migration and Impact

There is another quality of life issue that affects continued migration flows. The attractiveness to recent retirees of a destination is certainly enhanced or depressed by the environment. It also is affected by the shape of the settlement population itself. When a retirement community or neighborhood, in which the median age is 72, ages in place, without the benefit of people moving in, the median age of the population increases year by year until after only a few years the people in the community or neighborhood seem much older. In Florida, these areas are sometimes unkindly referred to as "God's waiting room." You get the picture.

Retirees tend to move soon after retirement when they are relatively young. In their search for a place to reside, a median age of 12-15 years older than they are will be considered a negative neighborhood attribute. What keeps communities from aging as their original members age is the continuous stream of youthful retirees who enter the community, rejuvenating and enriching the environs and keeping it attractive as a retirement destination.

The impact of recent retirees moving into a community filled with earlier retirees is ordinarily a positive one, like the freshness, energy and school spirit brought to a college student body every year by the freshman class. In a very crude way, it is possible to examine impact using census data. Impact could be measured by the proportion of a state's 60+ population that is composed of recent migrants, assuming that their greater presence increases their impact. A qualification should be added. If the new migrants are culturally very different from those who came before, the old-timers could perceive a reduction in quality of life. Some stories of Californians who retire to Oregon and New Yorkers who retire to Georgia seem to carry this message.

In Table 3 the measures of in-migration and impact may be compared in 1980 and 1990. First, it is clear that older migrants into a state rarely form a very large percentage of all older people.

Second, the states where recent migrants make up more than 10 percent of the older population tend to be the major destination states of Florida and Arizona, and Southwestern states with strong migration potential, such as New Mexico (in 1980) and especially Nevada (in 1990). Nevada ranked number one in the impact of its retiree migrants in both 1980 and 1990. Indeed, Nevada may be "the next Arizona" in the

Table 4 — States Ranked by the Net Number of Migrants Age 60+, 1985-1990

Rank	State	# of In-migrants	# of Out-migrants	Net # of Migrants
1	Florida	451,709	128,561	323,148
2	Arizona	98,756	38,280	60,476
3	North Carolina	64,530	26,436	38,094
4	Nevada	43,131	16,193	26,938
5	Oregon	43,996	22,777	21,219
6	South Carolina	34,251	16,015	18,236
7	Washington	47,484	29,345	18,139
8	Georgia	44,475	28,475	16,000
9	Arkansas	29,848	18,454	11,394
10	Tennessee	36,306	26,133	10,173
11	Texas	78,117	69,856	8,261
12	Alabama	25,336	19,571	5,765
13	New Mexico	19,872	14,698	5,174
14	Mississippi	17,637	13,153	4,484
15	Virginia	46,554	42,695	3,859
16	Utah	10,751	8,148	2,603
17	Oklahoma	23,572	21,074	2,498
18	New Hampshire	15,058	12,785	2,273
19	Colorado	30,672	28,815	1,857
20	Delaware	8,026	6,345	1,681
21	Maine	11,929	10,534	1,395
22	Kentucky	21,770	20,444	1,326
23	Missouri	35,251	34,514	737
24	Idaho	10,832	10,205	627
25	Vermont	5,916	5,447	469
26	West Virginia	12,919	12,936	-17
27	Hawaii	8,053	8,335	-282
28	Nebraska	9,852	10,794	-942
29	Montana	6,140	7,226	-1,086
30	South Dakota	4,141	5,244	-1,103
31	North Dakota	3,140	4,320	-1,180
32	Wyoming	4,207	6,491	-2,284
33	Alaska	2,395	5,837	-3,442
34	Rhode Island	5,842	9,289	-3,447
35	Minnesota	19,370	23,958	-4,588
36	D.C.	4,821	10,288	-5,467
37	Indiana	31,405	38,426	-7,021
38	Kansas	16,492	23,644	-7,152
39	Louisiana	14,004	21,437	-7,433
40	Wisconsin	23,030	31,175	-8,145
41	Maryland	32,428	41,333	-8,905
42	Iowa	11,669	20,962	-9,293
43	Pennsylvania	57,538	78,903	-21,365
44	Connecticut	17,351	42,172	-24,821
45	Ohio	44,459	74,271	-29,812
46	Massachusetts	23,796	56,737	-32,941
47	Michigan	31,885	74,661	-42,776
48	California	131,514	187,240	-55,726
49	New Jersey	49,176	106,556	-57,380
50	Illinois	36,897	107,136	-70,239
51	New York	42,802	222,781	-179,979

region because of its steep climb in in-migration over the decade, from 21st to 13th place in the ranking.

State Winners and Losers: Net Gains and Losses

In the various reports of retirement migration over the years, the focus has been maintained steadfastly on the in-migrants, essentially ignoring the out-migrants. The reason for this focus is simple. It is the in-migrants that form the market for housing and other major initial purchases in the states to which they go. Out-migrants, especially those who are making their first move after retirement, will become part of the market in other states.

Before the Census Bureau provided microdata samples of individual census records for researchers to use, the only way to approximate migration was to take the difference in size of the retirement age category across two decades and adjust for everyone who had aged into the category or died in the previous decade. What was left was attributed to migration, and called "net" migration. If a person did not get into the older population by aging into it, and did not leave the older population by death, how else could one get there or leave but through migration? The correct answer is that the attribution category also contains miscalculations, mis-estimates, illegal immigrants who do or do not get counted and other "static" or "noise" in the statistical system.

By using the sample of individual census records, however, it is possible to subtract actual out-migrants from actual in-migrants and, thereby, to produce a picture that makes a much cleaner estimate of net migration, where the net migrants are persons. It is also an estimate because it is based on a sample, and it only estimates a five-year migration period because the mobility question asks whether a person had moved in the past five years.

The major destination and origin states have already been discussed. An analysis of net migration, using sample data, essentially merges the receiving and sending states into one list. If people vote with their feet, then the list represents the winners and the losers in that vote. Subtracting out-migrants from in-migrants may provide a better measure of relative popularity than the measures considered to this point. Popularity gradually changes over time as quality of life issues are perceived to change. A state may have a strong positive net migration of retirees and then gradually begin losing more than it is receiving. The trend, if not checked, would lead to a shift from positive to negative net migration, from winner to loser in exchanges with other states.

Figure 1 graphically depicts all states according to positive or negative net migration. Table 4 arranges the states from positive to negative net migration with the strongest winner on top and the strongest loser on the bottom. The net winners, those with a residual surplus of more than 10,000 migrants in 1990 are Florida, Arizona, North Carolina, Nevada, Oregon, South Carolina, Washington, Georgia, Arkansas and Tennessee. Conspicuously missing from the list are California, Texas, Pennsylvania, New Jersey and Virginia, states that received in-migration flows sufficient to rank them among the top 10. States that appear in the top 10 of Table 4, which were not listed earlier among the major

Table 5 — States Ranked by the Number and Proportion of Migrants Age 60+ Received from Abroad

Rank	State (1975-1980)	#	%	Rank	State (1985-1990)	#	%
1	California	53,600	29.9	1	California	77,638	32.9
2	New York	27,640	15.4	2	New York	32,692	13.9
3	Florida	23,640	13.2	3	Florida	30,746	13.0
4	Illinois	8,480	4.7	4	Texas	13,372	5.7
5	New Jersey	7,800	4.3	5	Illinois	10,293	4.4
6	Texas	7,680	4.3	6	New Jersey	10,013	4.2
7	Massachusetts	5,240	2.9	7	Massachusetts	6,835	2.9
8	Washington	3,600	2.0	8	Virginia	4,275	1.8
9	Hawaii	3,400	1.9	9	Maryland	4,266	1.8
10	Ohio	3,320	1.8	10	Pennsylvania	4,052	1.7
11	Pennsylvania	3,200	1.8	11	Washington	3,777	1.6
12	Connecticut	3,120	1.7	12	Arizona	3,556	1.5
13	Michigan	2,920	1.6	13	Hawaii	3,453	1.5
14	Virginia	2,840	1.6	14	Michigan	2,992	1.3
15	Maryland	2,640	1.5	15	Connecticut	2,329	1.0
16	Arizona	1,960	1.1	16	Ohio	1,955	0.8
17	Oregon	1,480	0.8	17	Georgia	1,867	0.8
18	Wisconsin	1,360	0.8	18	North Carolina	1,557	0.7
19	Minnesota	1,280	0.7	19	Oregon	1,535	0.7
20	Colorado	1,160	0.6	20	Colorado	1,533	0.7
21	Louisiana	1,040	0.6	21	Minnesota	1,488	0.6
22	Rhode Island	880	0.5	22	Wisconsin	1,308	0.6
(Tie) 23	Georgia	840	0.5	23	Nevada	1,249	0.5
(Tie) 23	Missouri	840	0.5	24	Missouri	1,053	0.5
(Tie) 23	North Carolina	840	0.5	25	Oklahoma	1,026	0.4
(Tie) 26	Alabama	640	0.4	26	Tennessee	999	0.4
(Tie) 26	South Carolina	640	0.4	27	Indiana	886	0.4
(Tie) 28	Kansas	600	0.3	28	Rhode Island	860	0.4
(Tie) 28	Oklahoma	600	0.3	29	South Carolina	771	0.3
(Tie) 28	Tennessee	600	0.3	30	D.C.	697	0.3
(Tie) 31	Indiana	560	0.3	31	New Mexico	660	0.3
(Tie) 31	Utah	560	0.3	32	Louisiana	648	0.3
33	Nevada	520	0.3	33	Kansas	644	0.3
34	D.C.	480	0.3	34	Arkansas	581	0.3
(Tie) 35	Arkansas	320	0.2	35	Iowa	531	0.2
(Tie) 35	Maine	320	0.2	36	Mississippi	465	0.2
(Tie) 35	Mississippi	320	0.2	37	New Hampshire	410	0.2
(Tie) 35	Vermont	320	0.2	38	Kentucky	402	0.2
(Tie) 35	West Virginia	320	0.2	39	Maine	399	0.2
(Tie) 40	Idaho	280	0.2	40	Alabama	371	0.2
(Tie) 40	Iowa	280	0.2	41	Utah	369	0.2
(Tie) 40	New Mexico	280	0.2	42	Alaska	257	0.1
43	Alaska	200	0.1	43	Idaho	252	0.1
(Tie) 44	Delaware	160	0.1	44	West Virginia	245	0.1
(Tie) 44	Kentucky	160	0.1	45	Montana	175	0.1
(Tie) 44	New Hampshire	160	0.1	46	Delaware	125	0.1
47	Montana	120	0.1	47	South Dakota	96	–
(Tie) 48	Nebraska	80	0.1	48	Nebraska	95	–
(Tie) 48	South Dakota	80	0.1	49	Wyoming	78	–
(Tie) 48	Wyoming	80	0.1	50	North Dakota	65	–
51	North Dakota	40	–	51	Vermont	37	–
Total		**179,520**	**100.5***			**235,978**	**100.4***

*rounding error

destination states, are Nevada, Oregon, South Carolina, Arkansas and Tennessee. The picture produced by net retirement migration, therefore, reinforces the Sun Belt regional pattern explored earlier.

None of the states that lost more than 10,000 migrants over those they received are Sun Belt states, with the notable exception of California. They are New York, Illinois, New Jersey, California, Michigan, Massachusetts, Ohio, Connecticut and Pennsylvania. Except for California, they would be characterized as Northern industrial states.

When the winners and losers are directly compared, the climatic difference stands out more clearly. The prominence of a Sun Belt state, California, among the major losers, however, calls for comment.

Climate obviously does not explain all. States that tend to send retirees to the Sun Belt are those with large metropolitan populations. Economic opportunities are greater in cities than elsewhere. Cities are places where resources can be accumulated more easily to support such a move in retirement. City workers confront higher levels of pollution, crime, traffic and noise than those who live and work in smaller cities and small towns. In addition to climate, therefore, there are quality of life issues, derived from city living, driving retirement migration. Ordinarily these are considered "push factors." If perceived quality of life has declined in metropolitan California, one would expect these greater push factors to motivate more out-migration from California to places in other states where quality of life is perceived to be higher.

Migrants from Abroad

Not all older long-distance migrants are from another state in the United States. From 1985-1990, nearly a quarter million migrants age 60+ moved to the United States. Compared to the nearly two million interstate migrants, their numbers are not great, but they are important in certain markets.

Where do they settle? As seen in Table 5, from 1975-1980 and from 1985-1990 migrants from abroad focused on relatively few states, primarily those with major ports of entry. The states that received more than 10,000 migrants who lived abroad in 1985 and who were 60 or older in 1990, were California, New York, Florida, Texas, Illinois and New Jersey. The overall volume of in-migration of the elderly has increased 31 percent from 179,520 in 1975-1980 to 235,978 in 1985-1990. Because of the smaller total volume, there were only three states that received more than

10,000 older migrants from abroad in 1975-1980: California, New York and Florida.

California suffered a net loss of nearly 56,000 older migrants to other states in 1985-1990, but it may have more than replaced them with nearly 78,000 migrants from abroad in the same age category. It is impossible to know how many Californians over 60 moved abroad during this period. They were not available to participate in the census. If Florida leads the way in attracting interstate migrants, California is in a similar position in attracting migrants from abroad. Almost one-third (32.9 percent) of these international migrants in 1985-1990 chose California as their destination. Even New York does not seriously compete, attracting less than half the proportion (13.9 percent). Florida nearly matches New York at 13 percent, and Texas, Illinois and New Jersey trail with 4-6 percent each.

Studies of Hispanic older migrants find that they tend to move to the destination state nearest to their country of origin.[8] For example, Cubans and Puerto Ricans tend to move to Florida. Mexicans tend to move to Texas and California, both states bordering Mexico. Other Hispanics, largely Central Americans, one would assume, are more evenly distributed between California, Florida and New York. Those who move the longest distance may be more dispersed in their destinations than those who have less territory to traverse. Because of these stream patterns, migration from abroad forms strong cultural enclaves. These enclaves later are attractive to Hispanics who make interstate moves in retirement. Among these, Cubans tend to move to Miami from Northern industrial states, and Mexicans to Texas and California, contributing their numbers to supporting the Sun Belt migration phenomenon. Generalizing to other racial and cultural populations from what is known about Hispanics, one would assume that Asian migrants would settle primarily in California and that Europeans would still tend to settle in New York and New Jersey, with some going also to Illinois. Although they are largely overlooked by students of interstate migration, migrants from abroad add diversity to older migrant populations.

• • • • • • • • • • •

Speculation about relations between sending and receiving states will be taken up in the next chapter, where the concept of stream migration is explored. It is only by connecting the origin with the destination that one can talk about streams, and it is the migration stream that holds the key to marketing to retirees before they become migrants.

CHAPTER THREE
STATE-TO-STATE STREAMS

Introduction

For an individual or family, residential mobility from one place to another would be called a "move." When many households move, a stream is formed that may grow or shrink over time. The defining characteristic of all migration streams is that each has an identified origin and destination.

The first students of migration were primarily interested in labor force movement.[1] Migration streams of workers formed between places where industry and commerce were developed and labor recruitment areas, and movement in those streams was overwhelmingly to places of greater perceived economic opportunity. Family ties between workers who moved earlier and those who came later helped to keep the stream viable. Sometimes these streams lasted for decades. Just as certain preparatory high schools are "feeders" for particular private universities, so also particular geographic origins provide large numbers of workers for the growing economies of certain cities.

When retirement migration streams were first discovered, how and why these streams developed was not understood at all by migration researchers who universally used labor force migration as their model. Retirement migration seemed like an oxymoron.[2] Over the past 20 years, however, a great deal has been discovered about how retirement migration streams get started and keep going. They seldom start and stop abruptly, and once started they provide a fresh supply of migrants in increasing or decreasing numbers for many years.

Streams and Stream Dynamics

What pulls people into migration streams to begin with? One significant force is tourism. There is a link between tourism counties and retirement counties in the United States, with many small towns in scenic tourist areas gradually turning into retirement communities.[3] Two specific studies look hard at this issue, one conducted in Cape Cod and another in the Ozarks.

Professor Lee Cuba of Wellesley College interviewed retired migrants in a community on Cape Cod and asked them how their tie to the community was first established. More than 90 percent of them had some previous vacation experience with their new hometown. Almost half had visited the Cape on a regular basis for an extended period of time; nearly one-quarter had been seasonal residents before they moved.[4]

There are three ways that tourism helps to cement the tie between origin and destination for older migrants. First, visiting a particular area repeatedly for a long time can come to be like a love affair; it predisposes one to greater commitments. In a similar way, visiting predisposes some toward moving "permanently." Cuba recorded many cases of migrants who had vacationed on Cape Cod since their childhood. Two-thirds of those surveyed said they did not consider any other retirement destination.

Second, tourism affects migrant expectations about community life. If they enjoyed living temporarily in an area and found the lifestyle satisfying during visits, they expect to find their life similarly pleasant in that community during retirement.

Third, repeat tourists often establish friendship networks that promote migration. Just as they do in labor force migration streams, friends and family members encourage migration by providing information about economic or social conditions where they are. Cuba found that more than 85 percent of those surveyed knew someone living on the Cape at the time they moved. This is the social glue that attaches visitors to the destination and transforms them from visitors into new residents. As this process is repeated hundreds of times a year in a vacationing area, the migration stream grows.

Streams tend to perpetuate themselves. How do they do it? In a study of several Ozark retirement communities conducted by the author, this question was considered.[5] The project concluded that there are three interdependent processes at work: self-selection, selective recruitment and network recruitment.

Self-selection occurs when an individual or household identifies problems with their current town and perceives advantages of a potential new location. Some communities were chosen by older retirees concerned about the cost of housing and the need for health care and special services. These persons tended to move within their county to their new residence. Persons who moved to the Ozarks area in and near Branson, MO, tended to be primarily concerned with the natural environment and social needs. They were younger, better educated, more often married and tended to move from greater distances than the migrants who moved to planned communities near metropolitan areas. There was a matching of the resources and opportunities in the destination environments with the needs of the individual. Retirees, therefore, made rational choices in their moves. Self-selection is essentially a matching process.

The second process involves the selective recruitment efforts of the community itself. In the Ozarks, land developers acquire and use large mailing lists of people nearing retirement age. These mailings proclaim the pleasures of picturesque mountain life and offer an invitation to visit. Retirement communities therefore selectively search with varying degrees of success for new residents, just as people self-selectively search for destinations that will meet their perceived needs. In the Ozarks, more than one-fifth of the retired migrants said that developers and realtors first approached them. Selective recruitment, then, cannot be ignored when considering the migration decision process.

The third process is called network recruitment. New

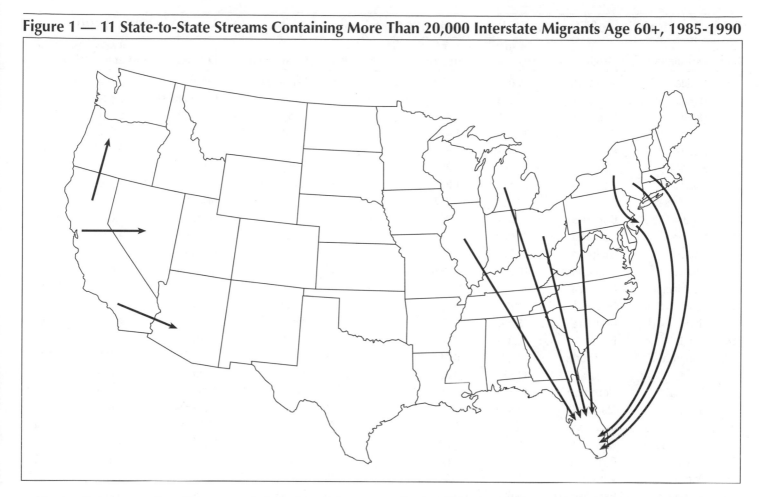

residents of a community often act as informal recruiters whose efforts facilitate self-selection on the part of their friends and family members considering a move. When retirees move into an area, a visiting pattern is frequently established, linking the new residents with other retired or soon-to-be retired friends and family members. This is especially the case in resort areas. In the Ozarks study, retired migrants were asked if they had known someone in the community before they themselves moved. Similar to Cuba's findings about the retirees who move to Cape Cod, more than half had known someone before they moved, and this proportion held regardless of the distance of the move. On average, they had known seven other people.

Network recruitment, like selective recruitment, is part of a filtering process that results in a general similarity of migrant backgrounds in each community. Selective recruitment may prime the pump, but network recruitment keeps the flow going.

Major State-to-State Streams

In Chapter 2 it was determined that retirement migration is very stable over time and highly channelized. Nearly 2 million persons of retirement age move across state lines every five years, but the majority of them are moving to fewer than 10 states. The ability to examine streams moves us much further down the road of understanding retirement migration. Mapping the streams allows us to see migration as a geographical system.

State-to-state retirement streams for three decades are displayed in Appendix A. Focusing on the 1990 results, there are 2,187 state-to-state streams large enough to register in the census microdata sample. The total network connects every state to nearly all the others, although most of these connections could best be described as trickles rather than streams. Only 202 of these streams, about 10 percent, carry more than 2,000 older migrants between pairs of states. Ranked in size, these larger streams are listed in Table 1. The largest seven streams are all to one state, Florida. These seven streams collectively contain 15 percent of all migrants. Each of the largest 11 streams consists of more than 20,000 migrants. Each contains more than 1 percent of the total national migration. These 11, together, account for nearly one-fifth of all older migrants.

Most of these first-tier streams can be placed into two categories: streams into Florida and streams out of California (Figure 1). There is one other large stream, from New York to New Jersey. The New Jersey shore has been a favorite vacationing spot for New York City residents since the 1920s. The only streams to non-contiguous states among these first-tier streams are to Florida. They are all from east of the Mississippi River. All others are to contiguous states.

The next 12 streams (ranked 12-23) vary in size from 10,134 to 18,952. Each contains between 10,000 and 20,000 migrants. This second tier of streams accounts for 8.1 percent of the total national migration, and the 23 largest streams together contain 27.9 percent of all migrants age 60 and older who changed states between 1985 and 1990.

The 12 second-tier streams are combined with the 11

Table 1 — Ranking of State-to-State Streams of More Than 2,000 Migrants Age 60+, 1985-1990

Rank	Destination	Origin	# of Migrants	% of all Migrants	Rank	Destination	Origin	# of Migrants	% of all Migrants
1	Florida	New York	104,019	5.472	52	Oklahoma	Texas	5,562	0.293
2	Florida	New Jersey	41,315	2.173	53	Florida	New Hampshire	5,504	0.290
3	Florida	Michigan	32,058	1.686	54	Arizona	Colorado	5,461	0.287
4	Florida	Ohio	27,986	1.472	55	Florida	Alabama	5,217	0.274
5	Florida	Pennsylvania	27,567	1.450	56	California	Nevada	5,199	0.273
6	Florida	Illinois	25,893	1.362	57	Illinois	Florida	5,148	0.271
7	Florida	Massachusetts	25,450	1.339	58	Arizona	New York	5,116	0.269
8	New Jersey	New York	23,903	1.257	59	Virginia	Maryland	5,109	0.269
9	Arizona	California	23,331	1.227	60	Texas	Florida	5,070	0.267
10	Oregon	California	23,069	1.213	61	Missouri	Illinois	4,943	0.260
11	Nevada	California	21,389	1.125	62	Texas	Louisiana	4,874	0.256
12	Florida	Connecticut	18,952	0.997	63	Arizona	Michigan	4,857	0.255
13	Washington	California	16,689	0.878	64	South Carolina	New York	4,794	0.252
14	Pennsylvania	New Jersey	14,820	0.780	65	Arkansas	Texas	4,783	0.252
15	Florida	California	13,407	0.705	66	Indiana	Florida	4,773	0.251
16	Florida	Indiana	13,327	0.701	67	Alabama	Florida	4,729	0.249
17	California	New York	11,695	0.615	68	Florida	Maine	4,726	0.249
18	Florida	Virginia	11,582	0.609	69	Florida	Kentucky	4,704	0.247
19	Georgia	Florida	11,533	0.607	70	Massachusetts	New York	4,680	0.246
20	Florida	Maryland	11,432	0.601	71	Missouri	California	4,675	0.246
21	Pennsylvania	New York	10,404	0.547	72	California	Michigan	4,639	0.244
22	North Carolina	New York	10,356	0.545	73	California	New Jersey	4,611	0.243
23	Texas	California	10,134	0.533	74	Tennessee	Florida	4,572	0.240
24	Florida	Wisconsin	9,763	0.514	75	Colorado	California	4,524	0.238
25	New Jersey	Pennsylvania	9,663	0.508	76	Florida	Missouri	4,507	0.237
26	California	Texas	9,597	0.505	77	Missouri	Kansas	4,490	0.236
27	Florida	Georgia	9,210	0.484	78	Oklahoma	California	4,451	0.234
28	California	Illinois	9,136	0.481	79	California	Pennsylvania	4,378	0.230
29	California	Arizona	9,134	0.480	80	Texas	Illinois	4,341	0.228
30	New York	Florida	9,063	0.477	81	Florida	Rhode Island	4,278	0.225
31	North Carolina	Florida	8,841	0.465	82	Florida	Tennessee	4,257	0.224
32	Ohio	Florida	8,707	0.458	83	Maryland	New York	4,185	0.220
33	Wisconsin	Illinois	8,568	0.451	84	New Jersey	Florida	4,173	0.220
34	Arizona	Illinois	8,460	0.445	85	Maryland	D.C.	4,160	0.219
35	California	Florida	7,731	0.407	86	Virginia	New Jersey	4,116	0.217
36	New York	New Jersey	7,716	0.406	87	California	Ohio	4,039	0.212
37	New Hampshire	Massachusetts	7,058	0.371	88	Pennsylvania	Maryland	3,945	0.208
38	Virginia	New York	6,972	0.367	89	Virginia	Florida	3,897	0.205
39	Washington	Oregon	6,870	0.361	90	Mississippi	Louisiana	3,891	0.205
40	Pennsylvania	Florida	6,831	0.359	91	Arkansas	California	3,879	0.204
41	Florida	Texas	6,787	0.357	92	Florida	Minnesota	3,836	0.202
42	Michigan	Florida	6,712	0.353	93	Kentucky	Ohio	3,810	0.200
43	California	Washington	6,460	0.340	94	Maryland	Virginia	3,802	0.200
44	Florida	North Carolina	6,385	0.336	95	New Mexico	Texas	3,768	0.198
45	California	Oregon	6,151	0.324	96	South Carolina	North Carolina	3,747	0.197
46	North Carolina	Virginia	6,102	0.321	97	Arizona	Washington	3,732	0.196
47	Texas	Oklahoma	5,965	0.314	98	Kansas	Missouri	3,711	0.195
48	North Carolina	New Jersey	5,871	0.309	99	New Mexico	California	3,708	0.195
49	Oregon	Washington	5,762	0.303	100	Arizona	Minnesota	3,704	0.195
50	Connecticut	New York	5,689	0.299	101	Utah	California	3,674	0.193
51	Indiana	Illinois	5,574	0.293	102	Michigan	Illinois	3,665	0.193

Rank	Destination	Origin	# of Migrants	% of all Migrants		Rank	Destination	Origin	# of Migrants	% of all Migrants
103	Texas	New York	3,642	0.192		154	Texas	Arkansas	2,599	0.137
104	Maryland	Pennsylvania	3,621	0.190		155	California	Minnesota	2,598	0.137
105	New York	Pennsylvania	3,570	0.188		156	California	Missouri	2,578	0.136
106	Maine	Massachusetts	3,557	0.187		157	Kentucky	Indiana	2,538	0.134
107	California	Colorado	3,555	0.187		158	North Carolina	Ohio	2,505	0.132
108	Texas	New Mexico	3,537	0.186		159	Maryland	New Jersey	2,494	0.131
109	Louisiana	Texas	3,525	0.185		160	California	Massachusetts	2,490	0.131
110	Maryland	Florida	3,470	0.183		161	Nevada	Illinois	2,465	0.130
111	Hawaii	California	3,459	0.182		162	Colorado	Texas	2,448	0.129
112	Florida	West Virginia	3,441	0.181		163	Massachusetts	Connecticut	2,447	0.129
113	Ohio	Michigan	3,433	0.181		164	Florida	Iowa	2,435	0.128
(Tie) 114	Georgia	Alabama	3,396	0.179		165	Indiana	California	2,433	0.128
(Tie) 114	Georgia	New York	3,396	0.179		166	Arizona	New Jersey	2,414	0.127
116	Arkansas	Illinois	3,380	0.178		167	Michigan	Ohio	2,394	0.126
117	Arizona	Ohio	3,375	0.178		168	Ohio	West Virginia	2,390	0.126
118	Indiana	Ohio	3,283	0.173		169	Texas	Michigan	2,343	0.123
119	Illinois	Missouri	3,282	0.173		170	Ohio	Indiana	2,341	0.123
120	New York	California	3,280	0.173		171	Tennessee	Illinois	2,337	0.123
121	Indiana	Kentucky	3,272	0.172		172	Missouri	Texas	2,335	0.123
122	Illinois	California	3,255	0.171		173	California	Wisconsin	2,330	0.123
123	Arizona	Texas	3,244	0.171		174	Michigan	Indiana	2,303	0.121
124	Ohio	California	3,241	0.170		175	Connecticut	Massachusetts	2,296	0.121
125	Massachusetts	Florida	3,232	0.170		176	Ohio	New York	2,263	0.119
126	North Carolina	South Carolina	3,204	0.169		177	Arizona	Iowa	2,257	0.119
127	Ohio	Pennsylvania	3,161	0.166		178	Kentucky	Florida	2,253	0.119
128	Minnesota	Kansas	3,154	0.166		179	Texas	Colorado	2,240	0.118
129	California	Hawaii	3,092	0.163		180	Georgia	Tennessee	2,210	0.116
130	Florida	South Carolina	3,090	0.163		181	South Carolina	Georgia	2,202	0.116
131	Texas	Missouri	3,085	0.162		182	North Carolina	Illinois	2,199	0.116
132	Illinois	Wisconsin	3,066	0.161		183	California	Virginia	2,173	0.114
133	South Carolina	New Jersey	3,021	0.159		(Tie) 184	Illinois	Indiana	2,172	0.114
134	North Carolina	Pennsylvania	3,003	0.158		(Tie) 184	North Carolina	Georgia	2,172	0.114
135	Pennsylvania	California	2,998	0.158		186	Arkansas	Missouri	2,164	0.114
136	Alabama	Georgia	2,958	0.156		187	Texas	Ohio	2,145	0.113
137	Ohio	Kentucky	2,944	0.155		188	North Carolina	Michigan	2,127	0.112
138	Wisconsin	Minnesota	2,914	0.153		189	Virginia	California	2,121	0.112
139	South Carolina	Florida	2,910	0.153		190	Florida	Louisiana	2,089	0.110
140	Virginia	North Carolina	2,901	0.153		191	Tennessee	Kentucky	2,082	0.110
141	Virginia	Pennsylvania	2,853	0.150		192	Nevada	Arizona	2,076	0.109
142	North Carolina	Maryland	2,844	0.150		193	Delaware	Maryland	2,074	0.109
143	Tennessee	Michigan	2,817	0.148		194	Indiana	Michigan	2,066	0.109
144	Arizona	Wisconsin	2,763	0.145		195	Tennessee	Ohio	2,058	0.108
145	California	Oklahoma	2,746	0.144		196	Colorado	Arizona	2,031	0.107
146	Michigan	California	2,721	0.143		197	Texas	Kansas	2,028	0.107
147	Mississippi	Tennessee	2,715	0.143		198	Texas	Arizona	2,025	0.107
148	Arizona	Florida	2,714	0.143		199	Florida	Arizona	2,021	0.106
149	Arizona	Pennsylvania	2,686	0.141		200	Georgia	Illinois	2,014	0.106
150	Idaho	California	2,680	0.141		(Tie) 201	Arizona	New Mexico	2,009	0.106
151	New York	Connecticut	2,672	0.141		(Tie) 201	Massachusetts	New Jersey	2,009	0.106
152	West Virginia	Ohio	2,638	0.139						
153	Pennsylvania	Ohio	2,607	0.137						

Figure 2 — 23 State-to-State Streams Containing More Than 10,000 Interstate Migrants Age 60+, 1985-1990

first-tier streams in Figure 2. The initial impression is altered little. The dominant pattern remains to Florida and out of California. Florida receives five additional streams, four from east of the Mississippi, and California originates three additional streams, now to non-contiguous states: Washington, Texas and Florida. The out-migration from California, Florida notwithstanding, is essentially a Southwest and Pacific Coast pattern.

There are some streams on the map that do not fit the overall pattern. Pennsylvania receives streams from New York and New Jersey. New York sends streams to North Carolina and California. The only stream out of Florida, to the contiguous state of Georgia, completes the picture.

In Table 1, there are 87 state-to-state streams of at least 4,000 migrants. How many states have become more than just regional retirement centers, as measured by significant migration streams from non-contiguous states?

There are only five states that receive three or more streams from non-contiguous states: Florida, California, Arizona, Texas and North Carolina.

Florida and California received large numbers of streams from non-contiguous states, 21 to Florida and nine to California. The leading streams to Florida are pictured in Figure 3 and those to California are seen in Figure 4. There is a similarity between the recruitment fields of these two states, with each drawing heavily from the Northeast and Great Lakes regions.

Streams to North Carolina, Texas and Arizona, the three smaller national destination states, are seen in Figure 5. Each

state attracts significant streams from three non-contiguous states. North Carolina receives streams from New York, New Jersey and Florida. The North Carolina mountains have attracted vacationers from all three states for many decades, and the state stands in the middle of the country's largest migration streams: New York to Florida and New Jersey to Florida. One wonders to what extent North Carolina siphons off some of the migrants who might otherwise have gone to Florida. Texas receives relatively large streams from Florida, California and Illinois. Arizona receives streams from the non-contiguous states of Illinois, New York and Michigan.

Counterstreams

If there are two streams between two states, going in opposite directions, which is the stream, and which is the counterstream? The answer to that question is easy. The stream is the larger and the counterstream is the smaller one.

One of the earliest "laws" of migration was that a stream, if persistent, will eventually produce a counterstream.[6] The reasons are obvious. Not everyone who moves from one place to another is going to like their new location and a few of them will return. Because migration studies were focused on labor force movement for so long, the principle was usually expressed in economic terms: Not everyone will find a job and some will return to their origin. It was thought that those with the least to offer employers would have the hardest time finding a job and would be the most likely, therefore, to return. Counterstream migration was conse-

Figure 3 — Streams of 4,000 or More Migrants Age 60+ from Non-contiguous States into Florida, 1985-1990

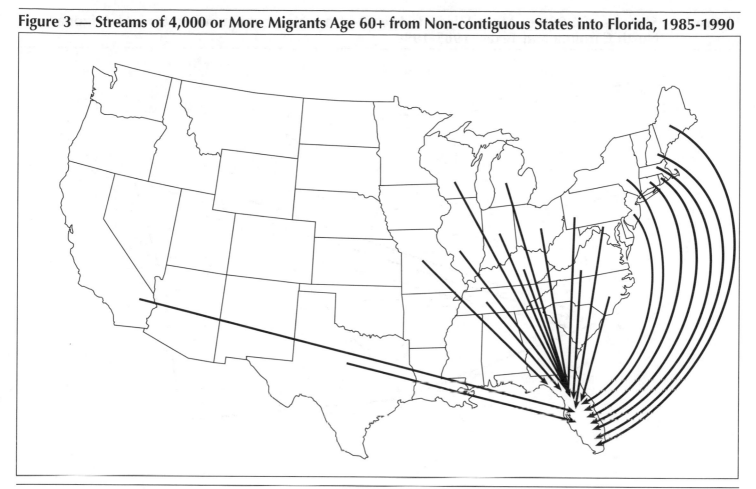

Figure 4 — Streams of 4,000 or More Migrants Age 60+ from Non-contiguous States into California, 1985-1990

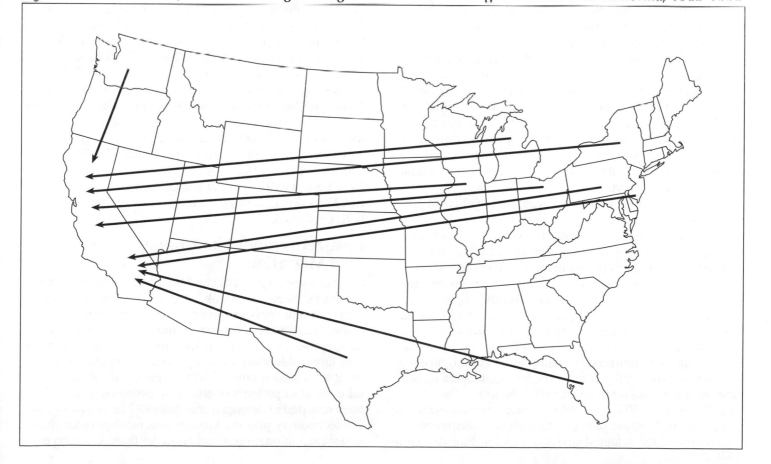

Figure 5 — Streams of 4,000 or More Migrants Age 60+ from Non-contiguous States into Arizona, North Carolina and Texas, 1985-1990

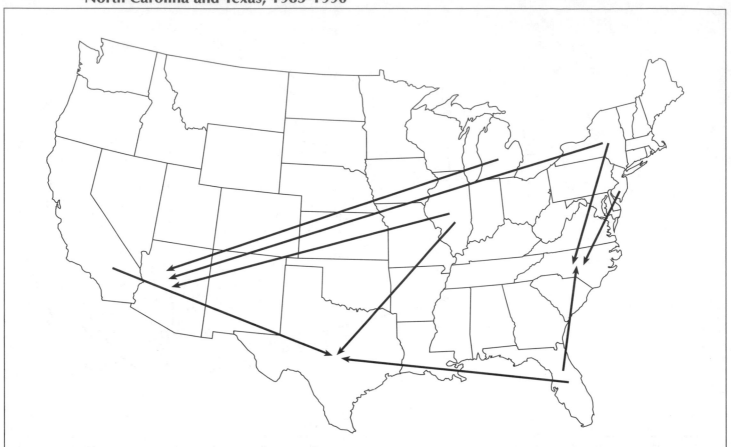

quently said to be "negatively selective," that is, to select migrants with less education and fewer job skills on average than those found in the streams.

When the state-to-state streams of older migrants were first studied, the researchers were not at all surprised to find counterstreams. They are a natural part of the migration landscape. They were, however, very surprised to find that they, just as labor force counterstreams, were negatively selective. That is, migrants in the counterstreams were somewhat older, on average, and more often widowed and living dependently with relatives or others at origin than migrants in the stream.[7]

Thus, elderly return migration is part of a cyclical migration process after retirement. Migrants making long-distance moves to popular destinations tend to do so soon after retirement, at the peak of their retirement income, while still married, living independently in their own home and interested in enhancing their lifestyle. After several years, and brushes with widowhood and disability, the opportunities for recreation and the more pleasant climate begin losing their charms for some, and they begin to think more positively of closer proximity to old friends and family members. So the early thinkers about migration got it right even for retirement migration. Streams beget counterstreams, and counterstreams are often negatively selective.

In Table 2, the 50 largest state-to-state migration streams from 1985 to 1990 are paired with their counterstreams.

Twenty of the featured pairings involve Florida, with

Florida the dominant partner (receiving the larger stream) in 18 of these exchanges. Both Georgia and North Carolina were dominant in their exchanges with Florida. There is speculation that the Florida-to-North Carolina stream includes persons from other states who have "tried" Florida, not found what they were looking for, and then moved to North Carolina. No doubt there are some such persons in the stream, but census data contains no migration history, so there is no way to determine the size of this segment.

Eight of the featured pairings involve California, with California the dominant partner in only two exchanges, with New York and Illinois. Arizona, Oregon, Nevada, Washington, Florida and Texas are all dominant in their exchanges with California.

Post-retirement Life Course And Migration

These stream patterns beg for an integrated explanation. No one factor can do the job, but put in the context of the life course of older persons, some of the patterns begin to make sense. Demographers routinely use a human development perspective for explaining migration patterns. However, they have seldom explored beyond nuclear family development and career mobility.[8] More recently, the developmental context of patterns of elderly interstate migration have been reported in demographic studies.[9] The nature of modern technology puts the kinship structures of older people under institutional pressures to make three basic types of

Table 2 — 50 Largest State-to-State Streams and Their Counterstreams, 1985-1990

Rank	Exchanges	Number	Rank	Exchanges	Number
1	NY → FL	104,019	26	FL → NC	8,841
	FL → NY	9,063		NC → FL	6,385
2	NJ → FL	41,315	27	IL → WI	8,568
	FL → NJ	4,173		WI → IL	3,066
3	MI → FL	32,058	28	IL → AZ	8,460
	FL → MI	6,712		AZ → IL	1,386
4	OH → FL	27,986	29	MA → NH	7,058
	FL → OH	8,707		NH → MA	1,167
5	PA → FL	27,567	30	NY → VA	6,972
	FL → PA	6,831		VA → NY	1,333
6	IL → FL	25,893	31	OR → WA	6,870
	FL → IL	5,148		WA → OR	5,762
7	MA → FL	25,450	32	TX → FL	6,787
	FL → MA	3,232		FL → TX	5,070
8	NY → NJ	23,903	33	VA → NC	6,102
	NJ → NY	7,716		NC → VA	2,901
9	CA → AZ	23,331	34	OK → TX	5,965
	AZ → CA	9,134		TX → OK	5,562
10	CA → OR	23,069	35	NJ → NC	5,871
	OR → CA	6,151		NC → NJ	374
11	CA → NV	21,389	36	NY → CT	5,689
	NV → CA	5,199		CT → NY	2,672
12	CT → FL	18,952	37	IL → IN	5,574
	FL → CT	1,810		IN → IL	2,172
13	CA → WA	16,689	38	NH → FL	5,504
	WA → CA	6,460		FL → NH	1,127
14	NJ → PA	14,820	39	CO → AZ	5,461
	PA → NJ	9,663		AZ → CO	2,031
15	CA → FL	13,407	40	AL → FL	5,217
	FL → CA	7,731		FL → AL	4,729
16	IN → FL	13,327	41	NY → AZ	5,116
	FL → IN	4,773		AZ → NY	821
17	NY → CA	11,695	42	MD → VA	5,109
	CA → NY	3,280		VA → MD	3,802
18	VA → FL	11,582	43	IL → MO	4,943
	FL → VA	3,897		MO → IL	3,282
19	FL → GA	11,533	44	LA → TX	4,874
	GA → FL	9,210		TX → LA	3,525
20	MD → FL	11,432	45	MI → AZ	4,857
	FL → MD	3,470		AZ → MI	1,329
21	NY → PA	10,404	46	NY → SC	4,794
	PA → NY	3,570		SC → NY	636
22	NY → NC	10,356	47	TX → AR	4,783
	NC → NY	1,083		AR → TX	2,599
23	CA → TX	10,134	48	ME → FL	4,726
	TX → CA	9,597		FL → ME	821
24	WI → FL	9,763	49	KY → FL	4,704
	FL → WI	1,737		FL → KY	2,253
25	IL → CA	9,136	50	NY → MA	4,680
	CA → IL	3,255		MA → NY	1,957

moves. One type follows closely after retirement. Another type is sometimes triggered when people experience moderate forms of disability. A third tends to occur when they have major forms of chronic disability. The pressure may be slight for the first type of move, but it may increase for the second and again for the third type.

When retirees have intact marriages, are relatively healthy and have enough retirement income, there are social pressures for some of them to relocate for lifestyle or amenity reasons.[10] Certain personal characteristics indicate a predisposition toward migration and influence its timing, but so do ties to the current community of residence and ties to other places. As Cuba demonstrated in his Cape Cod study, some retirees have planned their move for years and have vacationed at and visited their new location many times in anticipation of a move.[11] The reasons for relocation are complex and have to do with the attractiveness of amenities, friendship network maintenance and the ability to make a psychic move of identity from one place to another. At this stage of retirement, however, kinship functions can be managed over considerable distances, although it would be a mistake to assume that no recent retirees move closer to their children or other relatives.

The pressure for the second type of move occurs when people develop a disability that makes it difficult to carry out everyday household tasks, a situation often compounded by widowhood.[12] Migrants who move away from their children may choose to move to be near them again when they are disabled and widowed. The aggregate population profiles of migrants in the New York-to-Florida stream and Florida-to-New York counterstream seem to fit this interpretation.[13]

Limited kin resources is the motive for the third basic type of move, from more or less exclusive care by kin to institutional care.[14] Most movers of this type are not interstate migrants, but local movers.

The relevance of a developmental perspective for the geographical distribution of the elderly seems obvious. Movers of the first type tend to dominate the migration streams into amenity-rich destinations in popular receiving states such as Florida, Arizona and North Carolina. The counterstreams out of these states, although often much smaller than the streams, carry a much higher proportion of movers of the second type.

In this way, counterstreams become part of a system by which some migrants circulate in and out of destination states, depending upon the needs that are relevant to their life-course stage. It must be noted, however, that most migrants do not return. The actual proportion of migrants returning in the counterstream cannot be determined directly from census data.

Following this line of reasoning, the states that send many more migrants than they receive, like New York and California, may receive in the counterstreams a higher proportion of type-two movers than other states. States like Florida and Arizona, however, which are destinations rather than origins for most of their exchanges, probably benefit by receiving many more amenity migrants than other states. As states like Florida develop streams to other states, like those to North Carolina and Arizona, where Florida is primarily the sending state, the balance can begin gradually to change.

• • • • • • • • • • •

Streams of migrants develop over time. They are dynamic, growing and declining, and the types of migrants in those streams can come to change over time as well. The study of stream migration raises important marketing questions because it identifies the origin of migrants, where marketing can more effectively take place.

Interstate stream migration, like net migration, remains focused on states. Nonetheless, concentrations of retirees are not evenly distributed throughout a state, but are place specific. Therefore, in order to use migration information most effectively, it is important to know where within states migrants are accumulating. In Chapter 4 we will identify the major sending and receiving counties in the United States.

CHAPTER FOUR
MAJOR SENDING AND RECEIVING COUNTIES

Introduction

In 1970, the Census Bureau entered a geographical code into all of the records of individuals in the Public Use Microdata Sample. They called this code "county groups." The code identified a unit, usually composed of several counties, where the individual lived. The unit contained the census records of at least 250,000 people. Some whole states with small populations were counted as a single county group. In the largest cities, there were several units within a single metropolitan county. The name for the unit, "county groups," was not very descriptive. Another feature of the measure limited its usefulness: County groups were allowed to stray across state lines. Therefore, some county groups contained parts of two states.

Under contract with the National Institute on Aging, the author and a team of colleagues designed the technical specifications for a more useful microdata sample. The Census Bureau incorporated most of these recommendations into its microdata program in 1980.

In 1980, the Census Bureau reduced the size of the units from more than 250,000 to at least 100,000 persons and kept them within state boundaries. Unfortunately, it did not change the name of the unit. Now county groups, because they were smaller, could be even more numerous within a large metropolitan county. The improvements were welcomed by all microdata users, although many wished that the odd name had also been changed.

In 1990, the size and within-state boundary limitation of the units did not change, but the term "county group" was changed to Public Use Microdata Area. There are 1,726 PUMAs in the entire United States.

Because a PUMA must contain the census records of more than 100,000 persons, sparsely populated counties have to be grouped together. In these circumstances, the PUMAs are still county groups. Some PUMAs contain a county that holds a small city and an adjacent county; some split the city and its surrounding county into two PUMAs (Like Chicago and the rest of Cook County); some separate distinct economic or culture areas in one county. The PUMAs that split up most large cities can be put together to make up one unit equal to the metropolitan county. Occasionally, PUMAs cannot be converted precisely into counties or county groups. A few approximations were necessary.

It is important to work with a minimum common unit in describing migration, so counties, where they were subdivided, were reconstructed and used in this analysis. In some cases, county groups were the minimum unit of analysis.

It is important to note that where rural county groups are involved, the real destination of migrants is not likely to be spread evenly across all of the counties. If there is just one town located somewhere within five rural counties in which retirees are congregating, the town would have to be located in person, on the ground, and not with census data alone. In this case, census microdata is useful primarily by establishing the area within which to search.

One should also note that metropolitan counties in Sun Belt states will attract more migrants than most rural counties simply because they attract more people in general. There is more housing stock in cities, more places to live. Migrants to metropolitan counties often settle in the suburbs and rural parts of the county rather than downtown. By aggregating PUMAs to the county level, however, one loses sight of within-county variation.

Interstate Retirement Spots In the United States

The analysis of interstate migration to and from counties and county groups will follow the same general pattern used in the analysis of state migration flows in the second chapter. First, the major receiving and sending areas will be listed and briefly discussed. Second, areas with the greatest positive net migration — the surplus of in-migrants over out-migrants — will be identified. In-migration, out-migration and net migration is summarized for every county or county group in the country in Appendix B. Finally, two other rankings will be produced: destinations with the highest ratios of in-migrants to out-migrants and destinations with the highest ratios of out-migrants to in-migrants.

Major receiving counties and county groups — The most straightforward way of rating retirement destinations is simply to count noses. How many retirees moved into each area from out of state?

Two reminders should be posted at this point to avoid misinterpretation later. First, it should be clearly noted that popular destination states may have counties not listed here that contain large numbers of retirees from out of state. That is because our measures only pick up the recent migrants, not those who moved more than five years before the census. Second, a county that attracted large numbers of retirees from within the same state but few from out of state would not show up in our list at all. These tables reflect interstate migration only.

Table 1 lists the 100 counties or county groups receiving the most interstate migrants age 60+ from 1985 to 1990. Figure 1 shows the locations of each of these counties or county groups. As one would expect, Florida counties dominate the list, accounting for 28 percent. Furthermore, they are concentrated at the top of the list, 18 among the top 25 in Table 1. Having said this, the leading retirement county in the nation was Maricopa County, AZ, where Phoenix is located. From 1985 to 1990, an estimated 54,291 people over 60 moved to Maricopa County from some other state. This is a staggering number of older migrants entering a single county during a five-year period. It amounts to more than half of all (98,756) older migrants who moved into the

Table 1 — Major Destinations of Interstate Migrants Age 60+, 1985-1990

Rank	County or county group	State	# Received	Rank	County or county group	State	# Received
1	Maricopa	Arizona	54,291	51	Mecklenburg	North Carolina	5,415
2	Palm Beach	Florida	47,444	52	Duval	Florida	5,343
3	Broward	Florida	40,272	53	Cuyahoga	Ohio	5,252
4	Pinellas	Florida	35,065	54	Carbon, Monroe, Pike and Wayne	Pennsylvania	5,192
5	Clark	Nevada	30,865				
6	Lee	Florida	25,255	55	Henderson, Madison and Transylvania	North Carolina	5,178
7	Los Angeles	California	24,005				
8	Sarasota	Florida	22,225	56	Sacramento	California	5,172
9	Pasco	Florida	22,104	57	Shelby	Tennessee	5,028
10	Dade	Florida	21,305	58	Escambia and Santa Rosa	Florida	5,016
11	San Diego	California	20,155	59	Santa Clara	California	4,983
12	Pima	Arizona	18,182	60	Tarrant	Texas	4,906
13	Volusia	Florida	17,407	61	Monmouth	New Jersey	4,866
14	Polk	Florida	15,566	62	D.C.	D.C.	4,821
15	Brevard	Florida	14,621	63	Prince Georges	Maryland	4,816
16	Collier and Monroe	Florida	14,434	64	Fairfield	Connecticut	4,795
17	Hillsborough	Florida	14,036	65	Lane	Oregon	4,785
18	Riverside	California	13,644	66	Honolulu	Hawaii	4,772
19	Charlotte	Florida	13,134	67	Philadelphia	Pennsylvania	4,706
20	Manatee	Florida	13,043	68	Middlesex	New Jersey	4,687
21	Cook	Illinois	12,801	69	Hennepin	Minnesota	4,577
22	Lake	Florida	12,536	70	Benton and Madison	Arkansas	4,560
23	Marion	Florida	12,087	71	Clark	Washington	4,542
24	Hernando	Florida	11,685	72	Baxter, Boone, Carroll, Marion, Newton and Searcy	Arkansas	4,537
25	Citrus, Levy and Sumter	Florida	11,408				
26	Orange	California	11,313	73	Jackson	Oregon	4,529
27	King	Washington	11,217	74	Jackson	Missouri	4,491
28	Harris	Texas	10,705	75	Clallam, Jefferson and Mason	Washington	4,488
29	Orange	Florida	10,486	76	Fulton	Georgia	4,446
30	Douglas, Lyon, Storey, Washoe and Carson City*	Nevada	10,309	77	Pierce	Washington	4,425
				78	Barry, Christian, Dade, Dallas, Lawrence, McDonald, Polk, Stone, Taney and Webster	Missouri	4,364
31	Flagler, Putnam and St. Johns	Florida	9,527				
32	St. Lucie	Florida	9,023	79	Multnomah	Oregon	4,287
33	De Soto, Glades, Hardee, Hendry and Highlands	Florida	8,773	80	Hidalgo	Texas	4,198
				81	El Paso	Colorado	4,173
34	Coos, Curry, Douglas and Josephine	Oregon	8,387	82	Snohomish	Washington	4,125
				83	Bucks	Pennsylvania	4,109
35	Ocean	New Jersey	8,305	84	Rockingham	New Hampshire	4,036
36	La Paz and Mohave	Arizona	8,294	85	Oklahoma	Oklahoma	4,021
37	Montgomery	Maryland	7,705	86	Allegheny	Pennsylvania	4,017
38	Coconino and Yavapai	Arizona	7,456	87	Bergen	New Jersey	3,978
39	Indian River and Okeechobee	Florida	7,439	88	Hartford	Connecticut	3,971
40	Martin	Florida	7,124	89	New Haven	Connecticut	3,944
41	San Bernardino	California	6,897	90	Middlesex	Massachusetts	3,909
42	Fairfax, Falls Church* and Fairfax*	Virginia	6,582	91	Ramsey	Minnesota	3,903
				92	Gila and Pinal	Arizona	3,862
43	Bernalillo	New Mexico	6,402	93	Marion	Oregon	3,857
44	Dallas	Texas	6,053	94	De Kalb	Georgia	3,851
45	Bexar	Texas	5,879	95	Tulsa	Oklahoma	3,839
46	Horry	South Carolina	5,853	96	Franklin	Ohio	3,834
47	Wayne	Michigan	5,793	97	Ventura	California	3,814
48	St. Louis and St. Louis*	Missouri	5,770	98	Osceola	Florida	3,805
49	Baltimore and Baltimore*	Maryland	5,501	99	Hamilton	Ohio	3,799
50	Seminole	Florida	5,483	100	Washington	Oregon	3,787

*independent city

state. The star retirement spot in the United States is not in Florida.

Palm Beach County, FL, including West Palm Beach, placed second on the list, receiving 47,444 recent migrants, followed by Broward County, including Fort Lauderdale, which received 40,272 migrants. These two counties, located in southeast Florida north of Miami, together received 87,716 interstate migrants, but they accounted for only one-fifth (19.4 percent) of the 451,709 retirees that flooded into the Sunshine State between 1985 and 1990.

Unlike Maricopa County, Palm Beach and Broward counties do not maintain a migration monopoly in Florida. Pinellas County, including St. Petersburg, received 35,065 migrants. Lee County (25,255) contains Fort Myers and Sanibel Island. Sarasota County (22,225) includes the city of Sarasota. Pasco County (22,104), just north of Tampa, has no cities. Hernando County(11,685) is to Pasco's north. Citrus, Levy and Sumter counties (11,408) are north of Hernando. Dade County (21,305) contains Miami and Miami Beach. Volusia County (17,407) includes Daytona Beach. Polk County (15,566) includes Lakeland. The Kennedy Space Center is found in Brevard County (14,621). Collier and Monroe counties (14,434) include Naples and the Keys. Hillsborough County (14,036) includes Tampa. Charlotte County (13,134) is the location of Port Charlotte. Manatee County (13,043) includes Bradenton. Marion County (12,087) includes Ocala, an old central Florida resort town. Orange County (10,486) contains Lake Buena Vista, the home of Disney World and part of metropolitan Orlando. Osceola County (3,805) is immediately south of Orange County. Lake County (12,536) borders Orange County to the west. Flagler, Putnam and St. Johns counties (9,527) are between Jacksonville and Daytona Beach. St. Lucie County (9,023) includes Fort Pierce. De Soto, Glades, Hardee, Hendry and Highlands counties (8,773) are southern and inland. Indian River and Okeechobee counties (7,439) form a relatively less-developed area between St. Lucie and Brevard counties. Martin County (7,124), immediately north of Palm Beach County, lies between Lake Okeechobee and the Atlantic Ocean. Seminole County (5,483) contains the northern suburbs of Orlando. Duval County (5,343) includes Jacksonville. Escambia and Santa Rosa counties (5,016) are in the Panhandle near Mobile Bay.

Florida's frequent appearances on this list are not surprising. After all, Florida has received about a quarter of all older interstate migrants in each census migration period since 1960. What is surprising, however, is finding Phoenix leading the rankings and Clark County, NV, the home of Las Vegas, in fifth place in the 1990 Census. Nevada's southernmost county received 30,865 migrants.

There are several retirement counties in California that continued to attract substantial numbers of migrants in the five years ending in 1990. These were Los Angeles County (24,005); San Diego County (20,155); Riverside County (13,644), where Palm Springs is located; Orange County (11,313); San Bernardino County (6,897); Sacramento County (5,172); Santa Clara County (4,983), in the Bay Area; and Ventura County (3,814). Except for Santa Clara and Sacramento counties, all of the leading retirement destinations in California are in the southern part of the state, within a two-hour drive of Los Angeles.

The retirement counties in Arizona are, for the most part, located near cities as well. Maricopa County (54,291) includes Phoenix, Pima County (18,182) includes Tucson, and the combined La Paz and Mohave counties (8,294) are on the western boundary of the state, near California. Mohave County is across Lake Mead from Las Vegas, NV, and includes Lake Havasu City. Another two-county combination, Coconino and Yavapai counties (7,456), includes Flagstaff and Prescott. Gila and Pinal counties (3,862), which flank Maricopa County on the east, conclude the retirement spots in Arizona that appear among the top 100.

Nevada ranked 13th as a destination of interstate migrants, but Nevada's Clark County (30,865) ranked fifth. One other area in Nevada is listed, a county group made up of Douglas, Lyon, Storey and Washoe counties and Carson City (10,309). This county group includes Reno.

Bernalillo County (6,402), containing Albuquerque, is the only county in New Mexico that shows up among the top 100 retirement destinations. Nearly one-third (32.2 percent) of the 19,872 older migrants who entered New Mexico during the five years preceding 1990 settled here.

Texas, the fourth-ranking destination state, contains five counties among the top 100. Harris County (10,705), including Houston; Dallas County (6,053), including Dallas; Bexar County (5,879), including San Antonio; and Tarrant County (4,906), including Fort Worth, are the locations of the major Texas cities. The only other Texas listing is Hidalgo County (4,198), the site of McAllen, in the tropical tip of the state near the mouth of the Rio Grande. Retirees tend to flock to Texas' largest metropolitan areas.

The same pattern holds for the state of Oklahoma, where the two retirement counties are: Oklahoma County (4,021), including Oklahoma City; and Tulsa County (3,839), including Tulsa.

Turning our attention to the Pacific Northwest states of Oregon and Washington, we find quite a different pattern. Non-metropolitan counties abound. Six counties or county groups in Oregon appear among the top 100 retirement spots. Two are located just across the border from California. In the southwest corner of the state, the coastal county group contains Coos, Curry, Douglas and Josephine counties (8,387). The adjacent Jackson County (4,529) includes the city of Medford, located on Interstate 5, Oregon's major north-south artery. Interstate 5 also runs through Lane County (4,785), which includes Eugene and the University of Oregon; and Marion County (3,857), which includes Salem. The two other Oregon counties among the top 100 retirement spots are near the Washington border: Multnomah County (4,287), which includes Portland and a stretch of the Columbia River; and Washington County (3,787), immediately west of Portland.

The state of Washington attracts retirees to both urban and rural counties. The urban counties include: Clark County (4,542), across the state line from Portland; Pierce County (4,425), in which Tacoma is located; and Snohomish County (4,125), just north of Seattle. King County (11,217) includes Seattle itself. Clallam, Jefferson and Mason coun-

Figure 1 — Major Destinations of Interstate Migrants Age 60+, 1985-1990

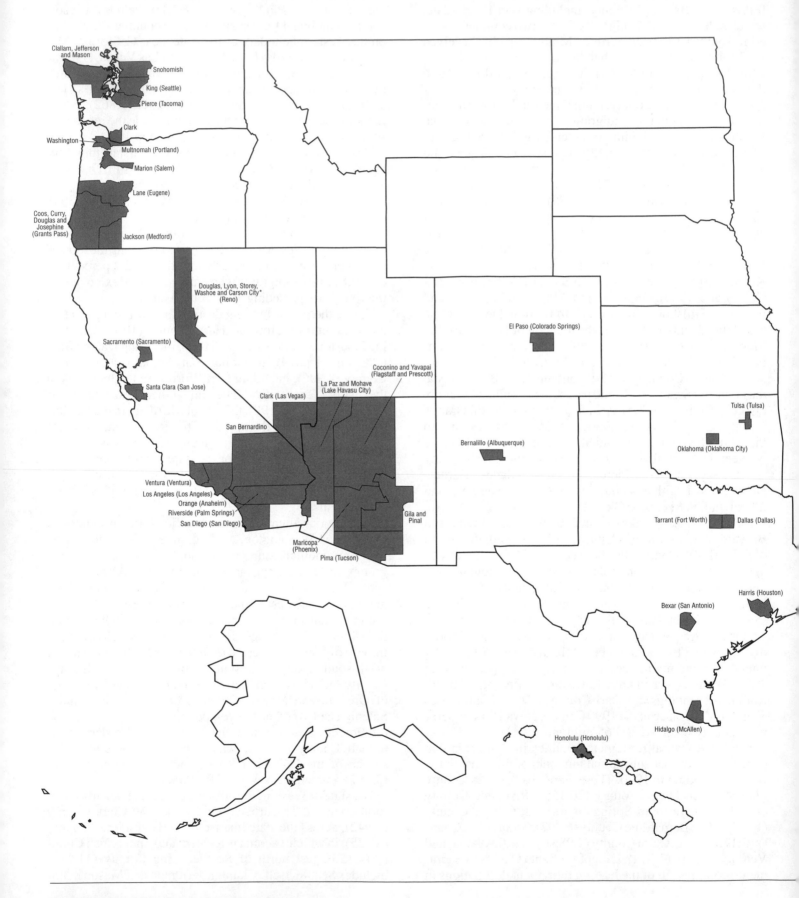

Hennepin (Minneapolis)
Ramsey (St. Paul)

Wayne (Detroit)

Cook (Chicago)

Cuyahoga (Cleveland)

Franklin (Columbus)

Allegheny (Pittsburgh)

Carbon, Monroe,
Pike and Wayne
Fairfield
Bucks
Bergen
Middlesex
Monmouth
Philadelphia (Philadelphia)
Montgomery
Ocean
New Haven

Rockingham
Middlesex
Hartford
(Hartford)

Jackson (Kansas City)

Hamilton
(Cincinnati)

St. Louis and
St. Louis*

Baltimore and Baltimore*
D.C.
Prince Georges
Fairfax,
Falls Church*
and Fairfax*

Barry, Christian,
Dade, Dallas,
Lawrence, McDonald,
Polk, Stone, Taney
and Webster

Baxter, Boone,
Carroll, Marion,
Newton and Searcy
Shelby (Memphis)

Henderson, Madison and
Transylvania

Benton
and Madison

Mecklenburg (Charlotte)

Fulton
(Atlanta)
De Kalb

Horry (Myrtle Beach)

Duval (Jacksonville)

Escambia
and Santa Rosa
(Pensacola)
Marion (Ocala)
Flagler, Putnam and St. Johns (St. Augustine)

Lake (Mount Dora)
Volusia (Daytona Beach)
Seminole
Orange (Orlando)
Polk (Winter Haven)
Brevard (Melbourne)
Osceola (Kissimmee)
Indian River and Okeechobee
St. Lucie
Martin

Citrus, Levy and Sumter

Hernando
Pasco (New Port Richey)
Pinellas (St. Petersburg and Clearwater)
Hillsborough (Tampa)
Manatee (Bradenton)
Sarasota (Sarasota)
Charlotte (Port Charlotte)
Lee (Fort Myers)

De Soto, Glades, Hardee, Hendry and Highlands
Palm Beach (West Palm Beach and Boca Raton)
Broward (Fort Lauderdale)

Collier and Monroe
(Naples and Key West)
Dade (Miami)

ties (4,488) are on the Olympic Peninsula.

The two listed counties in Georgia are Fulton (4,446) and De Kalb (3,851). Greater Atlanta sprawls across both counties.

South Carolina's only listing, Horry County (5,853), includes Myrtle Beach, a South Atlantic regional resort center.

North Carolina's two listings are: Mecklenburg County (5,415), including Charlotte; and Henderson, Madison and Transylvania counties (5,178), which include Hendersonville and Brevard.

There are two county groups in Arkansas. Benton and Madison counties (4,560) and Baxter, Boone, Carroll, Marion, Newton and Searcy counties (4,537) are located just south of the border with Missouri and include part of the Ozark Mountains.

North of that border, in Missouri, are Barry, Christian, Dade, Dallas, Lawrence, McDonald, Polk, Stone, Taney and Webster counties (4,364), containing much of the Missouri Ozarks. Branson, in Taney County, has become a major country music center comparable to Nashville, TN. The two additional Missouri listings in the top 100 are St. Louis County and the independent city of St. Louis (5,770) and Jackson County (4,491), including Kansas City, MO.

Four of the top 100 listings are in the Washington, DC, metropolitan area. The District of Columbia (4,821) is at the center of the cluster. One is in Virginia: the group containing Fairfax County and the independent cities of Fairfax and Falls Church (6,582), west of Washington. Two are in Maryland: Montgomery County (7,705), north of Washington; and Prince Georges County (4,816), east of Washington. Maryland also has a third entry on the list: Baltimore County and the independent city of Baltimore (5,501).

Pennsylvania's top destinations are not far from metropolitan areas. These are: Bucks County (4,109), north of Philadelphia bordering New Jersey; Philadelphia County (4,706), including the city of Philadelphia; Carbon, Monroe, Pike and Wayne counties (5,192), rural counties in the Pocono Mountains; and Allegheny County (4,017), which includes Pittsburgh.

In New Jersey, Ocean County (8,305), Monmouth County (4,866) and Middlesex County (4,687) are on the coast. They are long-standing retirement destinations. Bergen County (3,978), by contrast, is across from Yonkers, NY, in the Greater New York City bi-state metropolitan region.

Connecticut's three listings are all highly urbanized. Fairfield County (4,795) and New Haven County (3,944) are on the Atlantic Coast, and Hartford County (3,971) is inland.

Massachusetts' Middlesex County (3,909) contains the western suburbs of Boston and is the state's only appearance in the top 100.

Rockingham County (4,036), NH, contains the state's only stretch of Atlantic coastline and is the state's only mention on the list.

In Ohio, Cuyahoga County (5,252) contains Cleveland, Hamilton County (3,799) includes Cincinnati, and Franklin County (3,834) includes Columbus and Ohio State University.

In Illinois, Cook County (12,801) is Chicago's home.

Wayne County (5,793), MI, includes Detroit.

Hennepin County (4,577), which includes Minneapolis, and Ramsey County (3,903), which includes St. Paul, are Minnesota's two listings.

Honolulu County (4,772), HI, includes that state's capital city.

El Paso County (4,173), CO, includes Colorado Springs and the Air Force Academy.

Shelby County (5,028), TN, includes Memphis, the state's largest city.

Major sending counties and county groups — Exactly where do older migrants come from? Table 2 contains a listing of the top 100 sending counties and county groups. Figure 2 shows the locations of each of these counties or county groups.

Table 2 can be easily summarized. The listings in this table are rarely multiple counties; nearly all are single counties that contain major cities. From 1985 to 1990, more older migrants moved from Los Angeles County (59,516) than from any other.

We usually think of counties as containing cities. New York City, however, contains five counties, all on the top 100 list: Queens County (33,559), Kings County (28,606), New York County (14,155), Bronx County (11,230) and Richmond County (5,083). Several of New York City's suburban counties are also among the major sending counties: Nassau County (30,902), Suffolk County (20,111) and Westchester County (15,197). In the Hudson Valley bordering Connecticut, the Dutchess and Putnam county group (4,468) is also listed, as is Rockland County (4,329), bordering New Jersey. These could also be considered part of the Greater New York City suburban area. New York City does not stand alone, however. Other cities in the state also made the list. Erie County (8,505) contains Buffalo, and Monroe County (5,562) includes Rochester. It is easy to understand how New York state is the primary origin state for older migrants.

The state contributing the second largest number of migrants to the rest of the nation is California. From 1985-1990, more migrants left California than went to California. There are four Southern California coastal counties making the top 100 list, counting Los Angeles County (59,516). San Diego County (19,354) borders Mexico, and Orange County (19,404) and Ventura County (4,639) are part of Greater Los Angeles, to the south and north, respectively. Also listed are the contiguous Southern California desert counties of Riverside (8,304) and San Bernardino (8,322), and the San Francisco suburban counties of San Mateo (4,166), Santa Clara (8,283), Alameda (6,612) and Contra Costa (4,677). The final county, Sacramento (4,745), east of San Francisco, holds the state capital city by the same name. The pattern observed in New York of migration from the greater metropolitan areas of the largest cities holds also for California. Migration from the desert counties is different. These are not the suburbs of a large city. They are primarily retirement destinations.

The mixed pattern observed in California — migration out of large metropolitan counties and retirement destination counties or county groups — is repeated and exaggerated in

Table 2 — Major Origins of Interstate Migrants Age 60+, 1985-1990

Rank	County or county group	State	# Sent	Rank	County or county group	State	# Sent
1	Los Angeles	California	59,516	51	Hennepin	Minnesota	6,983
2	Cook	Illinois	53,945	52	Shelby	Tennessee	6,848
3	Queens	New York	33,559	53	Prince Georges	Maryland	6,751
4	Nassau	New York	30,902	54	Alameda	California	6,612
5	Kings	New York	28,606	55	Marion	Indiana	6,542
6	Suffolk	New York	20,111	56	Franklin	Ohio	6,372
7	Orange	California	19,404	57	Honolulu	Hawaii	6,283
8	San Diego	California	19,354	58	Hudson	New Jersey	6,275
9	Maricopa	Arizona	19,213	59	Pasco	Florida	6,215
10	Wayne	Michigan	18,531	60	Montgomery	Pennsylvania	6,188
11	Bergen	New Jersey	16,226	61	Lake	Illinois	6,157
12	Fairfield	Connecticut	15,551	62	Norfolk	Massachusetts	6,134
13	Westchester	New York	15,197	63	Macomb	Michigan	5,656
14	Pinellas	Florida	14,322	64	Sarasota	Florida	5,588
15	New York	New York	14,155	65	Passaic	New Jersey	5,565
16	Broward	Florida	13,458	66	Monroe	New York	5,562
17	Harris	Texas	12,791	67	Douglas, Lyon, Storey, Washoe and Carson City*	Nevada	5,525
18	Middlesex	Massachusetts	12,677				
19	Oakland	Michigan	12,316	68	Jackson	Missouri	5,420
20	Cuyahoga	Ohio	11,983	69	Hillsborough	Florida	5,249
21	Philadelphia	Pennsylvania	11,836	70	Volusia	Florida	5,192
22	Dade	Florida	11,322	71	Jefferson	Kentucky	5,144
23	Bronx	New York	11,230	72	Delaware	Pennsylvania	5,086
24	Baltimore and Baltimore*	Maryland	10,529	73	Richmond	New York	5,083
25	Allegheny	Pennsylvania	10,498	74	Orange	Florida	5,012
26	D.C.	D.C.	10,288	75	Suffolk	Massachusetts	4,979
27	Fairfax, Falls Church* and Fairfax*	Virginia	10,282	76	Lee	Florida	4,807
				77	Sacramento	California	4,745
28	Montgomery	Maryland	10,089	78	Worcester	Massachusetts	4,732
29	Du Page	Illinois	10,070	79	Bernalillo	New Mexico	4,712
30	Dallas	Texas	9,804	80	Denver	Colorado	4,690
31	Essex	New Jersey	9,645	81	Contra Costa	California	4,677
32	St. Louis and St. Louis*	Missouri	9,494	82	Ventura	California	4,639
33	Clark	Nevada	9,060	(Tie) 83	New Castle	Delaware	4,577
34	New Haven	Connecticut	8,920	(Tie) 83	Bristol	Massachusetts	4,577
35	Palm Beach	Florida	8,855	85	Summit	Ohio	4,548
36	Hartford	Connecticut	8,836	86	Bucks	Pennsylvania	4,528
37	Erie	New York	8,505	87	Tarrant	Texas	4,480
38	Union	New Jersey	8,488	88	Dutchess and Putnam	New York	4,468
39	Middlesex	New Jersey	8,468	89	Lucas	Ohio	4,457
40	King	Washington	8,422	90	Fulton	Georgia	4,411
41	San Bernardino	California	8,322	91	Multnomah	Oregon	4,393
42	Riverside	California	8,304	92	Camden	New Jersey	4,371
43	Santa Clara	California	8,283	93	Rockland	New York	4,329
44	Essex	Massachusetts	8,006	94	Barnstable, Dukes and Nantucket	Massachusetts	4,257
45	Monmouth	New Jersey	7,699				
46	Ocean	New Jersey	7,408	95	Johnson	Kansas	4,232
47	Morris	New Jersey	7,268	96	Hampden	Massachusetts	4,226
48	Pima	Arizona	7,053	97	San Mateo	California	4,166
49	Hamilton	Ohio	7,028	98	Burlington	New Jersey	4,121
50	Milwaukee	Wisconsin	6,985	99	Tulsa	Oklahoma	4,110
				100	Lake	Indiana	4,004

*independent city

Figure 2 — Major Origins of Interstate Migrants Age 60+, 1985-1990

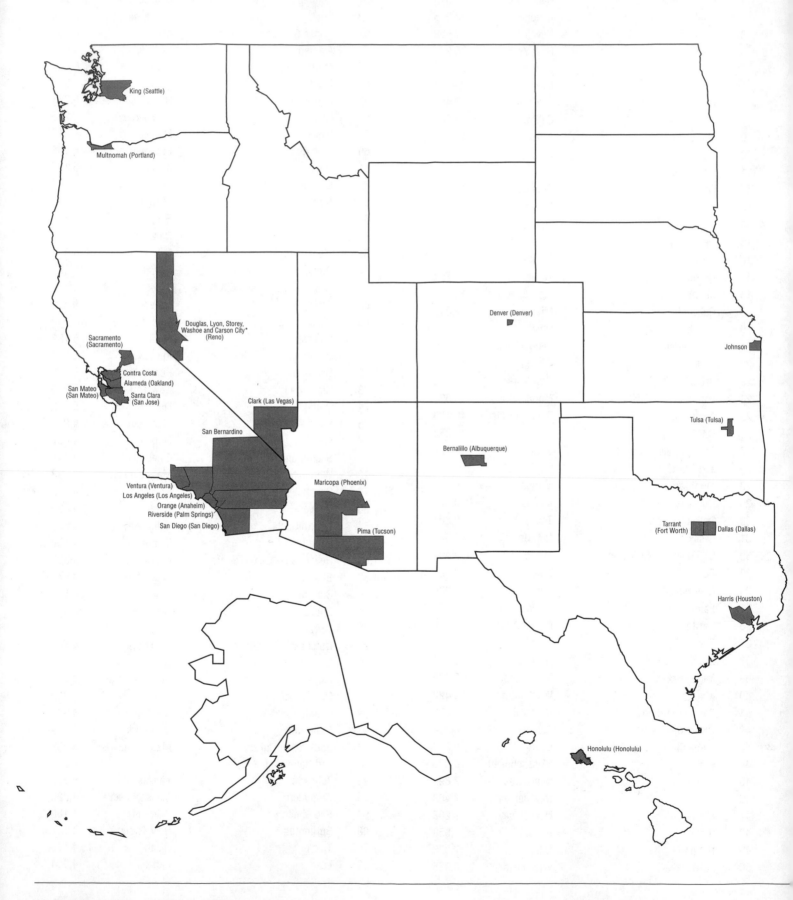

King (Seattle)

Multnomah (Portland)

Douglas, Lyon, Storey,
Washoe and Carson City*
(Reno)

Denver (Denver)

Johnson

Sacramento
(Sacramento)

Contra Costa
Alameda (Oakland)

San Mateo
(San Mateo)

Santa Clara
(San Jose)

Clark (Las Vegas)

Tulsa (Tulsa)

San Bernardino

Bernalillo (Albuquerque)

Ventura (Ventura)
Los Angeles (Los Angeles)
Orange (Anaheim)
Riverside (Palm Springs)
San Diego (San Diego)

Maricopa (Phoenix)

Pima (Tucson)

Tarrant
(Fort Worth)

Dallas (Dallas)

Harris (Houston)

Honolulu (Honolulu)

Hennepin
(Minneapolis)

Milwaukee
(Milwaukee)

Lake
Cook (Chicago)

Du Page

Lake (Gary)

Oakland
(Pontiac)

Macomb

Wayne
(Detroit)

Cuyahoga
(Cleveland)

Lucas (Toledo)

Marion
(Indianapolis)

Franklin
(Columbus)

Summit
(Akron)

Allegheny
(Pittsburgh)

Hamilton
(Cincinnati)

Jackson
(Kansas City)

St. Louis and
St. Louis*

Jefferson (Louisville)

Monroe
(Rochester)

Erie (Buffalo)

Hampden
(Springfield)

Dutchess
and Putnam

Westchester
Rockland

Bergen

Hudson

Passaic
Morris
Essex (Newark)
Union
Richmond (New York City)
Bucks
Montgomery
Delaware

Worcester

Middlesex
Essex
Suffolk (Boston)
Norfolk
Bristol

Barnstable, Dukes and
Nantucket (Cape Cod)

Hartford (Hartford)
New Haven
Fairfield

Suffolk
Nassau
Bronx (New York City)
Queens (New York City)
New York (New York City)
Kings (New York City)

Middlesex
Monmouth
Ocean
Burlington
Camden (Camden)
Philadelphia (Philadelphia)
New Castle

Montgomery

D.C.

Fairfax,
Falls Church*
and Fairfax*

Baltimore and Baltimore*

Prince Georges

Shelby (Memphis)

Fulton (Atlanta)

Volusia (Daytona Beach)

Pasco (New Port Richey)

Orange (Orlando)

Pinellas (St. Petersburg and Clearwater)

Hillsborough (Tampa)

Sarasota (Sarasota)

Lee (Fort Myers)

Palm Beach (West Palm Beach and Boca Raton)

Broward (Fort Lauderdale)

Dade (Miami)

* independent city

Major Sending and Receiving Counties   41

Florida. Florida is the third largest origin of older migrants, and 10 Florida counties appear among the top 100 origin areas. Most are bustling retirement destinations on the west coast of Florida. Three are in metropolitan southeast Florida, and only one is inland. The fact that separates Florida from California is that, without exception, all of the major origin counties in Florida are listed in Table 1 among the 100 major destination counties for retirement migration in the United States. The listings are: Pinellas County (14,322), Broward County (13,458), Dade County (11,322), Palm Beach County (8,855), Pasco County (6,215), Sarasota County (5,588), Hillsborough County (5,249), Volusia County (5,192), Orange County (5,012) and Lee County (4,807).

The New York pattern repeats itself in Illinois, the state ranking fourth as an origin of older migrants. Next to Los Angeles County, more older migrants originated in Cook County (53,945) than in any other county in the United States between 1985 and 1990. The other Illinois counties among the top 100 were both attached to Cook County and contain much of the suburban landscape of Greater Chicago. They are Du Page County (10,070) to the west, and Lake County (6,157) to the north.

New Jersey, the fifth-ranking sending state, presents the same mixed pattern seen in California. Of New Jersey's 11 counties listed among the top 100 origin counties, nine are primarily urbanized counties and two are retirement counties. On the New York state line, Hudson County (6,275), Bergen County (16,226) and Union County (8,488) are part of the Greater New York City Metropolitan Area. Camden County (4,371) and Burlington County (4,121) are the New Jersey suburban counties of Philadelphia. Monmouth County (7,699) and Ocean County (7,408) are on the Atlantic and are not parts of larger metropolitan complexes in the way the other counties are. They have a resort component. And Passaic (5,565), Morris (7,268), Essex (9,645) and Middlesex (8,468) counties are northern New Jersey metropolitan counties.

Pennsylvania, the sixth-leading origin state for older migrants, claims five counties among the top 100. They all contain urbanized areas. Four are connected to Philadelphia: Philadelphia County (11,836), Delaware County (5,086) to the southwest, Montgomery County (6,188) to the northwest and Bucks County (4,528) to the north. Allegheny County (10,498), which includes Pittsburgh, completes the collection.

Michigan ranked seventh as a sending state. Three of its counties appear among the leading origins of retirement migration, and all are in the Greater Detroit Metropolitan Area. They are Wayne County (18,531), Oakland County (12,316) and Macomb County (5,656).

Ohio, the eighth-ranked origin state, falls into the New York pattern along with the other northern tier states of Pennsylvania, Illinois and Michigan. All of Ohio's five listed counties contain large cities. Cuyahoga County (11,983) houses Cleveland, Cincinnati is located in Hamilton County (7,028), Franklin County (6,372) is the home of Columbus, Summit County (4,548) includes Akron and Lucas County (4,457) contains Toledo.

Texas is the ninth-leading contributor of older migrants.

The three counties from which the migrants came in sufficient numbers to merit entries on the list of the 100 major origin counties were: Harris County (12,791), where Houston is located; Dallas County (9,804), home to the city of the same name; and Tarrant County (4,480), which contains Fort Worth. All three are highly urbanized counties. The New York pattern is once again repeated.

Massachusetts ranked 10th as a sending state. Eight of its 14 counties are found among the 100 leading contributors of older migrants. Four are part of Greater Boston, two contain other cities and two are in southern Massachusetts retirement areas on the Atlantic. Greater Boston contains all or parts of Suffolk (4,979), Norfolk (6,134), Middlesex (12,677) and Essex (8,006) counties. Worcester County (4,732) includes the city of Worcester, and Hampden County (4,226) contains Springfield. The southern coastal county of Bristol (4,577) and the county group containing Barnstable, Dukes and Nantucket counties (4,257) contain no large cities. Barnstable County is Cape Cod. The mixed pattern, seen first in California and repeated in Florida and New Jersey, is also seen in Massachusetts.

The Washington, DC, metropolitan area lists among the top 100 the District of Columbia (10,288); Montgomery (10,089) and Prince Georges counties (6,751), MD; and a county group containing Fairfax County and the independent cities of Fairfax and Falls Church (10,282), VA. It fits the New York pattern.

Most of the leading origin counties in other states have populations of more than a quarter million, sometimes substantially more. In descending order of their out-migrating older population, they are: Maricopa County (19,213), AZ; Fairfield County (15,551), CT; Baltimore County and the independent city of Baltimore (10,529), MD; St. Louis County and the independent city of St. Louis (9,494), MO; Clark County (9,060), NV; New Haven County (8,920), CT; Hartford County (8,836), CT; King County (8,422), WA; Pima County (7,053), AZ; Milwaukee County (6,985), WI; Hennepin County (6,983), MN; Shelby County (6,848), TN; Marion County (6,542), IN; Honolulu County (6,283), HI; Douglas, Lyon, Storey and Washoe counties and the independent city of Carson City (5,525), NV; Jackson County (5,420), MO; Jefferson County (5,144), KY; Bernalillo County (4,712), NM; Denver County (4,690), CO; New Castle County (4,577), DE; Fulton County (4,411), GA; Multnomah County (4,393), OR; Johnson County (4,232), KS; Tulsa County (4,110), OK; and Lake County (4,004), IN.

What would cause the New York pattern of metropolitan out-migration to appear in some places and the California mixed pattern in others? The mix of migration motivations differs among migrants in different migration streams. Fuller discussion of this matter is provided when we consider the issue of return migration in Chapter 6.

Why should so many counties be both the origin and destination of large numbers of older migrants? It is obvious that there is considerable overlap between the major origin and destination areas listed in Tables 1 and 2. We like to think that counties are one or the other, but 55 counties or county groups are on both lists. Nearly all of the cities in Table 2 that are located in the Sun Belt are on both lists, and many of the counties containing large cities in the Northeast and Midwest are also on both lists. The county groups tend to be destinations only, although there are some exceptions. This overlap of top receiving and sending areas requires us to consider another approach to identifying the major substate destinations of retired migrants. This approach is net migration.

Most popular counties and county groups — The real estate agent and the housing developer would look at retirement spots in very different ways. The real estate agent might be concerned with how many retirees are moving into and out of the county because a house must be bought or sold for each. Tables 1 and 2 would provide real estate agents this kind of information. The home builder, however, is also interested in how many "surplus" retirees are moving into a destination, over and above those who are leaving. Assuming that retired interstate migrants predominate in the target area, such a number would give the builder some way of estimating new housing demand. Table 3 ranks the 100 most popular older migrant destinations on the basis of the net interstate migration they received between 1985 and 1990. Net migration is determined by subtracting out-migration from in-migration. Figure 3 shows where each of these counties or county groups are located.

In ranking the top 100 counties or county groups according to net retirement migration, the numbers range from 38,589 down to 1,071. Some counties containing larger cities were ranked lower in Table 3 than in Table 1 because they have high rates of in- and out-migration which cancel one another out. It is the net gain that is important in this comparison. In Florida, for example, Dade and Hillsborough counties dropped in ranking. Counties containing smaller cities ascended, and several groups of rural counties entered the list for the first time, usually found in the lower third of the rankings.

The largest number of counties or county groups in Table 3, once again, are in the state of Florida. Florida counties also have the greatest migrant surpluses, including 22 of the top 25 areas listed. Of the 100 ranked counties or county groups, 32 are located in Florida. In the descriptive listings below, the surplus migration in the destination counties between 1985 and 1990 will be indicated in parentheses.

Eight counties and two county groups are located on Florida's Atlantic Coast: Palm Beach County (38,589); Broward County (26,814); Volusia County (12,215); Brevard County (10,836); Dade County (9,983); Flagler, Putnam and St. Johns counties (7,990); St. Lucie County (7,681); Martin County (5,680); Indian River and Okeechobee counties (5,564); and Duval County (1,631).

None of the Gulf Coast counties or county groups increased their net migrant population by nearly 40,000 older people during the 1985-1990 period, as Palm Beach County did. Nonetheless, they did very well. The Gulf contains eight listed counties and five county groups. The exact location of the following counties or county groups was described earlier in this chapter: Pinellas County (20,743); Lee County (20,448); Sarasota County (16,637); Pasco County (15,889); Collier and Monroe counties (11,274); Charlotte County (11,248); Citrus, Levy and Sumter counties (9,745); Her-

nando County (9,704); Manatee County (9,373); Hillsborough County (8,787); and Escambia and Santa Rosa counties (2,736). Bay, Holmes and Washington counties (2,003) are in the Panhandle, and Bay County includes Panama City. Okaloosa and Walton counties (1,835) are between Panama City and Pensacola.

Perhaps surprising to some, Florida lists six counties and three county groups which are not primarily on the Atlantic or Gulf coasts. Their net numbers of migrants were not as large as either set of coastal counties, but were still appreciable. Polk County (11,849), Marion County (10,017), Lake County (9,249), De Soto, Glades, Hardee, Hendry and Highlands counties (7,183), Orange County (5,474), Seminole County (3,609) and Osceola County (2,874) were previously described. Bradford, Columbia, Dixie, Gilchrist, Hamilton, Lafayette, Madison, Suwannee, Taylor and Union counties (1,783) are sparsely populated farming counties that cut across the state from the Gulf to just north of Gainesville. Baker, Clay and Nassau counties (1,206) are all neighbors of Duval County, where Jacksonville is located.

After Florida, the largest number of counties or county groups in a single state in Table 3 are found in North Carolina, 12 in all. North Carolina differs from Florida in that most of the Tarheel State's retirement spots are groupings of non-metropolitan counties. Only four of the 12 are individual metropolitan counties, and eight are less populous county groups. Henderson, Madison and Transylvania counties (3,570) are in the Smoky Mountains of western North Carolina. Carteret, Craven, Jones and Pamlico counties (2,664) are on the other end of the state, on the Atlantic Coast. The Sandhills area of Anson, Montgomery, Moore and Richmond counties (2,604) includes Southern Pines and Pinehurst, a major national golfing center. Some metropolitan counties are listed in the top 100, such as Buncombe County (2,435), including Asheville; Mecklenburg County (2,121), including Charlotte; and Wake County (2,062), including Raleigh. Brunswick, Columbus and Pender counties (2,021) are just above the South Carolina line on the coastal plains surrounding New Hanover County (1,648), where Wilmington is located. Cherokee, Clay, Graham, Haywood, Jackson, Macon and Swain counties (1,558) are the state's westernmost counties, in the mountains, and Camden, Chowan, Currituck, Dare, Gates, Hyde, Pasquotank, Perquimans, Tyrrell and Washington counties (1,518) surround the Albemarle Sound and include the Outer Banks of North Carolina. Two central North Carolina county groups round out the list. Orange and Chatham counties (1,402) include Chapel Hill, home of the University of North Carolina. Cabarrus and Rowan counties (1,071) are in the Piedmont, just north of Charlotte. North Carolina's retirement spots are quite scattered, capitalizing on both mountainous and coastal amenities and scenic beauty, as well as inland golfing and lake settings.

Nine of Oregon's counties or county groups made the top 100 list in Table 3. The highest-ranked areas have already been described. They are: Coos, Curry, Douglas and Josephine counties (5,483); Jackson County (2,905); Lane County (2,793); Marion County (2,213); and Washington County (1,914). A non-metropolitan county group including Clat-

Table 3 — Most Popular Destinations of Migrants Age 60+, 1985-1990, Ranked by Net Migration

Rank	County or county group	State	# of In-migrants	# of Out-migrants	Net # Received
1	Palm Beach	Florida	47,444	8,855	38,589
2	Maricopa	Arizona	54,291	19,213	35,078
3	Broward	Florida	40,272	13,458	26,814
4	Clark	Nevada	30,865	9,060	21,805
5	Pinellas	Florida	35,065	14,322	20,743
6	Lee	Florida	25,255	4,807	20,448
7	Sarasota	Florida	22,225	5,588	16,637
8	Pasco	Florida	22,104	6,215	15,889
9	Volusia	Florida	17,407	5,192	12,215
10	Polk	Florida	15,566	3,717	11,849
11	Collier and Monroe	Florida	14,434	3,160	11,274
12	Charlotte	Florida	13,134	1,886	11,248
13	Pima	Arizona	18,182	7,053	11,129
14	Brevard	Florida	14,621	3,785	10,836
15	Marion	Florida	12,087	2,070	10,017
16	Dade	Florida	21,305	11,322	9,983
17	Citrus, Levy and Sumter	Florida	11,408	1,663	9,745
18	Hernando	Florida	11,685	1,981	9,704
19	Manatee	Florida	13,043	3,670	9,373
20	Lake	Florida	12,536	3,287	9,249
21	Hillsborough	Florida	14,036	5,249	8,787
22	Flagler, Putnam and St. Johns	Florida	9,527	1,537	7,990
23	St. Lucie	Florida	9,023	1,342	7,681
24	DeSoto, Glades, Hardee, Hendry and Highlands	Florida	8,773	1,590	7,183
25	Martin	Florida	7,124	1,444	5,680
26	Indian River and Okeechobee	Florida	7,439	1,875	5,564
27	Coos, Curry, Douglas and Josephine	Oregon	8,387	2,904	5,483
28	Orange	Florida	10,486	5,012	5,474
29	La Paz and Mohave	Arizona	8,294	2,846	5,448
30	Riverside	California	13,644	8,304	5,340
31	Douglas, Lyon, Storey, Washoe and Carson City*	Nevada	10,309	5,525	4,784
32	Coconino and Yavapai	Arizona	7,456	2,877	4,579
33	Horry	South Carolina	5,853	1,328	4,525
34	Seminole	Florida	5,483	1,874	3,609
35	Henderson, Madison and Transylvania	North Carolina	5,178	1,608	3,570
36	Clallam, Jefferson and Mason	Washington	4,488	1,179	3,309
37	Clark	Washington	4,542	1,319	3,223
38	Jackson	Oregon	4,529	1,624	2,905
39	Osceola	Florida	3,805	931	2,874
40	King	Washington	11,217	8,422	2,795
41	Lane	Oregon	4,785	1,992	2,793
42	Escambia and Santa Rosa	Florida	5,016	2,280	2,736
43	Hidalgo	Texas	4,198	1,482	2,716
44	Carbon, Monroe, Pike and Wayne	Pennsylvania	5,192	2,482	2,710
45	Carteret, Craven, Jones and Pamlico	North Carolina	3,435	771	2,664
46	Banks, Dawson, Forsyth, Franklin, Habersham, Hall, Hart, Lumpkin, Rabun, Stephens, Towns, Union and White	Georgia	3,522	871	2,651
47	Benton and Madison	Arkansas	4,560	1,938	2,622
48	Anson, Montgomery, Moore and Richmond	North Carolina	3,495	891	2,604
49	Buncombe	North Carolina	3,684	1,249	2,435
50	Beaufort, Colleton and Jasper	South Carolina	3,447	1,093	2,354

*independent city

Rank	County or county group	State	# of In-migrants	# of Out-migrants	Net # Received
51	Marion	Oregon	3,857	1,644	2,213
52	Baxter, Boone, Carroll, Marion, Newton and Searcy	Arkansas	4,537	2,360	2,177
53	Barry, Christian, Dade, Dallas, Lawrence, McDonald, Polk, Stone, Taney and Webster	Missouri	4,364	2,234	2,130
54	Mecklenburg	North Carolina	5,415	3,294	2,121
55	Snohomish	Washington	4,125	2,052	2,073
56	Wake	North Carolina	3,450	1,388	2,062
57	Yuma	Arizona	3,742	1,696	2,046
58	Brunswick, Columbus and Pender	North Carolina	2,787	766	2,021
59	Bay, Holmes and Washington	Florida	3,033	1,030	2,003
60	Bexar	Texas	5,879	3,885	1,994
61	Gila and Pinal	Arizona	3,862	1,901	1,961
62	Pierce	Washington	4,425	2,471	1,954
63	Sussex	Delaware	3,011	1,075	1,936
64	Washington	Oregon	3,787	1,873	1,914
65	Okaloosa and Walton	Florida	3,473	1,638	1,835
66	Cleburne, Fulton, Independence, Izard, Jackson, Sharp, Stone, Van Buren, White and Woodruff	Arkansas	3,607	1,808	1,799
(Tie) 67	Bradford, Columbia, Dixie, Gilchrist, Hamilton, Lafayette, Madison, Suwannee, Taylor and Union	Florida	2,662	879	1,783
(Tie) 67	Accomack, James City, Northampton, Poquoson*, Williamsburg* and York	Virginia	2,805	1,022	1,783
69	Bernalillo	New Mexico	6,402	4,712	1,690
70	Clatsop, Columbia, Lincoln and Tillamook	Oregon	2,850	1,162	1,688
71	Cameron	Texas	2,672	1,012	1,660
72	New Hanover	North Carolina	2,199	551	1,648
73	Duval	Florida	5,343	3,712	1,631
74	Clark, Garland, Hot Spring, Montgomery and Pike	Arkansas	3,229	1,630	1,599
75	Lancaster	Pennsylvania	3,067	1,496	1,571
76	Berkeley, Grant, Hampshire, Hardy, Jefferson, Mineral, Morgan and Pendleton	West Virginia	3,071	1,512	1,559
77	Cherokee, Clay, Graham, Haywood, Jackson, Macon and Swain	North Carolina	3,378	1,820	1,558
78	Camden, Chowan, Currituck, Dare, Gates, Hyde, Pasquotank, Perquimans, Tyrrell and Washington	North Carolina	2,487	969	1,518
79	Island, San Juan and Skagit	Washington	2,748	1,281	1,467
80	Pickens and Oconee	South Carolina	2,037	600	1,437
81	Hancock and Harrison	Mississippi	3,024	1,599	1,425
82	Orange and Chatham	North Carolina	1,824	422	1,402
83	Charleston	South Carolina	3,168	1,782	1,386
84	Cobb	Georgia	3,486	2,131	1,355
85	Benton and Linn	Oregon	2,094	750	1,344
86	Gwinnett	Georgia	2,394	1,064	1,330
87	Beaver, Garfield, Iron, Juab, Kane, Millard, Piute, Sanpete, Sevier, Washington and Wayne	Utah	2,436	1,110	1,326
88	Greene	Missouri	2,344	1,046	1,298
89	Clackamas	Oregon	2,987	1,697	1,290
90	Chatham	Georgia	2,720	1,439	1,281
91	Virginia Beach*	Virginia	3,330	2,084	1,246
92	Cumberland, Putnam and White	Tennessee	2,085	865	1,220
93	Baker, Clay and Nassau	Florida	2,210	1,004	1,206
94	Crook, Deschutes, Hood River, Jefferson, Sherman and Wasco	Oregon	2,547	1,343	1,204
95	Baldwin and Escambia	Alabama	2,213	1,025	1,188
96	Rockingham	New Hampshire	4,036	2,860	1,176
97	Caroline, Cecil, Kent, Queen Annes and Talbot	Maryland	3,029	1,868	1,161
98	Delta and Mesa	Colorado	2,448	1,334	1,114
99	Campbell, Claiborne, Cocke, Hamblen, Loudon, Monroe, Morgan, Roane and Scott	Tennessee	2,361	1,279	1,082
100	Cabarrus and Rowan	North Carolina	1,644	573	1,071

Island, San Juan and Skagit

Clallam, Jefferson and Mason

Snohomish

King (Seattle)

Pierce (Tacoma)

Clark / Marion (Salem)
Clackamas

Washington

Clatsop, Columbia, Lincoln and Tillamook

Crook, Deschutes, Hood River, Jefferson, Sherman and Wasco

Benton and Linn

Lane (Eugene)

Coos, Curry, Douglas and Josephine (Grants Pass)

Jackson (Medford)

Douglas, Lyon, Storey, Washoe and Carson City* (Reno)

Beaver, Garfield, Iron, Juab, Kane, Millard, Piute, Sanpete, Sevier, Washington and Wayne

Delta and Mesa

Clark (Las Vegas)

Coconino and Yavapai (Flagstaff and Prescott)

Bernalillo (Albuquerque)

La Paz and Mohave

Riverside (Palm Springs)

Gila and Pinal

Yuma

Maricopa (Phoenix)

Pima (Tucson)

Bexar (San Antonio)

Hidalgo (McAllen)

Cameron (Brownsville and Harlingen)

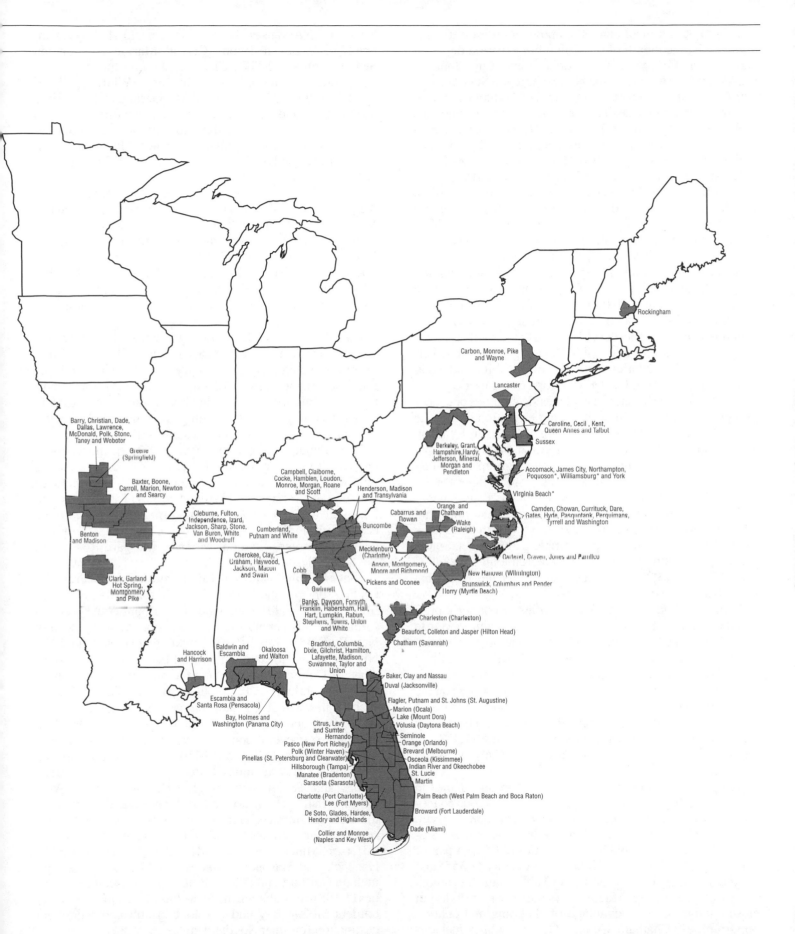

Barry, Christian, Dade,
Dallas, Lawrence,
McDonald, Polk, Stone,
Taney and Webster

Greene
(Springfield)

Baxter, Boone,
Carroll, Marion, Newton
and Searcy

Benton
and Madison

Cleburne, Fulton,
Independence, Izard,
Jackson, Sharp, Stone,
Van Buren, White
and Woodruff

Cumberland,
Putnam and White

Clark, Garland
Hot Spring,
Montgomery
and Pike

Cherokee, Clay,
Graham, Haywood,
Jackson, Macon
and Swain

Campbell, Claiborne,
Cocke, Hamblen, Loudon,
Monroe, Morgan, Roane
and Scott

Henderson, Madison
and Transylvania

Buncombe

Cobb

Gwinnett

Banks, Dawson, Forsyth
Franklin, Habersham, Hall,
Hart, Lumpkin, Rabun,
Stephens, Towns, Union
and White

Mecklenburg
(Charlotte)

Anson, Montgomery,
Moore and Richmond

Pickens and Oconee

Cabarrus and
Rowan

Orange and
Chatham

Wake
(Raleigh)

Berkeley, Grant,
Hampshire, Hardy,
Jefferson, Mineral,
Morgan and
Pendleton

Carbon, Monroe, Pike
and Wayne

Lancaster

Caroline, Cecil , Kent,
Queen Annes and Talbot

Sussex

Accomack, James City, Northampton,
Poquoson*, Williamsburg* and York

Virginia Beach*

Camden, Chowan, Currituck, Dare,
Gates, Hyde, Pasquotank, Perquimans,
Tyrrell and Washington

Carteret, Craven, Jones and Pamlico

New Hanover (Wilmington)

Brunswick, Columbus and Pender

Horry (Myrtle Beach)

Charleston (Charleston)

Beaufort, Colleton and Jasper (Hilton Head)

Chatham (Savannah)

Rockingham

Hancock
and Harrison

Baldwin and
Escambia

Okaloosa
and Walton

Escambia and
Santa Rosa (Pensacola)

Bay, Holmes and
Washington (Panama City)

Bradford, Columbia,
Dixie, Gilchrist, Hamilton,
Lafayette, Madison,
Suwannee, Taylor and
Union

Baker, Clay and Nassau

Duval (Jacksonville)

Flagler, Putnam and St. Johns (St. Augustine)

Marion (Ocala)

Lake (Mount Dora)

Volusia (Daytona Beach)

Citrus, Levy
and Sumter

Hernando

Pasco (New Port Richey)

Polk (Winter Haven)

Pinellas (St. Petersburg and Clearwater)

Hillsborough (Tampa)

Manatee (Bradenton)

Sarasota (Sarasota)

Seminole

Orange (Orlando)

Brevard (Melbourne)

Osceola (Kissimmee)

Indian River and Okeechobee

St. Lucie

Martin

Charlotte (Port Charlotte)

Lee (Fort Myers)

De Soto, Glades, Hardee,
Hendry and Highlands

Collier and Monroe
(Naples and Key West)

Palm Beach (West Palm Beach and Boca Raton)

Broward (Fort Lauderdale)

Dade (Miami)

* independent city

Major Sending and Receiving Counties   47

sop, Columbia, Lincoln and Tillamook counties (1,688) is bounded by the mouth of the Columbia River on the north and the Pacific on the west. Benton and Linn counties (1,344) include Corvallis, the home of Oregon State University. Clackamas County (1,290), south of Portland, provides the urban proximity desired for many interstate migrants seeking small-town lifestyles. Crook, Deschutes, Hood River, Jefferson, Sherman and Wasco counties (1,204) are east of Portland and extend southward from the Columbia River.

The six Arizona counties and county groups in the top 100 are easy to describe. Phoenix is in Maricopa County (35,078), which is second only to Palm Beach County, FL, in net migration. Every county or county group that borders Maricopa County made the list, and no county or county group that does not touch Maricopa County is included. West of Phoenix is the county group consisting of La Paz and Mohave counties (5,448); La Paz touches Maricopa on the west. Yuma County (2,046) is south of La Paz County and also touches Maricopa on the west. Pima County (11,129) contains Tucson and borders Maricopa to the south. Coconino and Yavapai counties (4,579) are grouped together. Yavapai borders Maricopa to the north. Gila and Pinal counties (1,961) both border Maricopa to the east.

The state of Washington also places six counties or county groups in the top 100 in terms of net migration during the 1985-1990 period. The county group of Clallam, Jefferson and Mason counties (3,309) is located on the Olympic Peninsula, west of Puget Sound. A county group containing Island, San Juan and Skagit counties (1,467), three Pacific Coast counties north of Seattle, is ranked. King County (2,795) contains Seattle itself, and the two counties that flank it, Snohomish County (2,073) to its north and Pierce County (1,954) to its south, complete the Puget Sound collection of retirement counties. The remaining county is Clark County (3,223), located just across the Columbia River from Portland.

South Carolina contains four counties or county groups listed in Table 3. Horry County (4,525), containing Myrtle Beach, leads the list. Beaufort, Colleton and Jasper counties (2,354) are coastal counties south of Charleston. Hilton Head Island is in Beaufort County. Charleston County (1,386) includes the city of Charleston and is located on the Atlantic Coast. Georgetown County is the lone South Carolina coastal county not appearing in Table 3. The county group containing Pickens and Oconee counties (1,437), in the Smoky Mountains, was the only South Carolina listing far from the Atlantic Coast.

Georgia boasts four counties or county groups on the top 100 list. The highest ranking goes to a mountainous county group north of Atlanta, including Banks, Dawson, Forsyth, Franklin, Habersham, Hall, Hart, Lumpkin, Rabun, Stephens, Towns, Union and White counties (2,651). A pair of counties just outside of Atlanta, Cobb County (1,355) and Gwinnett County (1,330), appear in Table 3, just far enough away from the big city to facilitate a small-town lifestyle, but close enough to take advantage of shopping and cultural opportunities. Chatham County (1,281), which includes Savannah, also appears on the list.

The Ozark regional retirement area includes Arkansas and Missouri. In Arkansas, there are Benton and Madison counties (2,622); Baxter, Boone, Carroll, Marion, Newton and Searcy counties (2,177); Cleburne, Fulton, Independence, Izard, Jackson, Sharp, Stone, Van Buren, White and Woodruff counties (1,799); and Clark, Garland, Hot Spring, Montgomery and Pike counties (1,599). To the north, Greene County (1,298), MO, including Springfield, makes the list. Barry, Christian, Dade, Dallas, Lawrence, McDonald, Polk, Stone, Taney and Webster counties (2,130), MO, line the Arkansas border.

Two of the three Texas counties in Table 3 are located in the Rio Grande Valley. Hidalgo County (2,716) includes McAllen. Cameron County (1,660), at the mouth of the Rio Grande, contains Brownsville. The third Texas listing is Bexar County (1,994), which includes San Antonio.

Representing Nevada in Table 3 are Clark County (21,805), which includes Las Vegas, and county group Douglas, Lyon, Storey and Washoe counties and Carson City, an independent city (4,784).

The other states with two listings each are Pennsylvania, Virginia and Tennessee. Lancaster County (1,571) is found in Pennsylvania's Amish country, and Carbon, Monroe, Pike and Wayne counties (2,710) are in the Pocono Mountains. Virginia's two listings are both found on the Atlantic Coast: a county group containing Accomack, James City, Northampton and York counties along with the independent cities of Poquoson and Williamsburg (1,783); and the independent city of Virginia Beach (1,246). Tennessee's entries on Table 3 are mountainous county groups. One includes Cumberland, Putnam and White counties (1,220), between Nashville and Knoxville. The other rings Knoxville on the east, north and west, and includes Campbell, Claiborne, Cocke, Hamblen, Loudon, Monroe, Morgan, Roane and Scott counties (1,082).

The remaining listings in Table 3 are scattered across the country, one per state. New Mexico's sole listing is Bernalillo County (1,690), which includes Albuquerque. In California, the only county listed is Riverside (5,340). The only New England county listed is Rockingham County (1,176), NH. Delta and Mesa counties (1,114) are on the western slope of Colorado, and include Grand Junction. A county group in southwest Utah includes Beaver, Garfield, Iron, Juab, Kane, Millard, Piute, Sanpete, Sevier, Washington and Wayne counties (1,326). Sussex County (1,936), DE, encompasses several popular Atlantic Coast beach resorts, including Rehoboth Beach. A Maryland county group by the Chesapeake Bay includes Caroline, Cecil, Kent, Queen Annes and Talbot counties (1,161). The strip of West Virginia flanked by Maryland on the north and Virginia on the south also attracts interstate migrants. This mountainous county group includes Berkeley, Grant, Hampshire, Hardy, Jefferson, Mineral, Morgan and Pendleton counties (1,559). Hancock and Harrison counties (1,425), in Mississippi, include Gulfport and Biloxi. Baldwin and Escambia counties (1,188), in Alabama, make the top 100. Baldwin County borders Mobile Bay and is a long-established retirement destination for other Southern states.

Destinations with the highest ratios of in-migrants to out-migrants — Now that the logic of positive net (or surplus) migration has been illustrated in Table 3, it is important to take one more step in examining the attractiveness of retirement migration spots within states.

When we rely only on the number of in-migrants to designate the importance of a retirement destination, we are trapped by geography. As noted earlier, cities will receive relatively larger numbers of migrants of all ages. The majority of interstate migrants age 60 and over move from one metropolitan area to another, although they often step down in the size of the metropolitan area. Only a minority actually move from metropolitan to non-metropolitan locations. The older migrants into cities distribute themselves throughout the city's residential areas. These migrants blend in with the rest of the population. Most do not call attention to themselves because they do not concentrate in particular places. As a result, large cities seem much less like retirement destinations than smaller cities or towns do, where retirees come in smaller numbers but have a higher degree of concentration and visibility.

The ratio of in-migrants to out-migrants is a good tool for illuminating even smaller places whose older populations are growing due to interstate migration. It simply tells how many older migrants moved in for every one who moved out during the 1985-1990 period. An index of 4.0 means that four migrants moved in for each one who moved out. A ranking of the 100 highest ratio counties or county groups is found in Table 4. The size of the migration flow is not an issue in this table; there is no bottom limit on size. It may be helpful, therefore, to keep in mind that if an area ranked in Table 4 cannot be found in Table 1, it received fewer than 3,787 interstate in-migrants between 1985 and 1990. Areas with small numbers of migrants can still be very popular in the sense captured by the index.

The county or county group with the highest ratio of in-migrants to out-migrants in the United States is Pitt County, NC, including Greenville. During the last census migration period, it received 7.45 older migrants for each one who left. Pitt County illustrates the fact that relatively small amounts of migration can produce a large index score. Between 1985 and 1990, 723 interstate migrants age 60+ moved into Pitt County and 97 moved out. Pitt County does not appear in Tables 1 or 3.

Not all areas in Table 4 receive small numbers of migrants, however. Charlotte County, containing Port Charlotte, FL, had a ratio of 6.96, nearly as high as that of Pitt County. During the same five-year period, Charlotte County received 13,134 interstate migrants and lost 1,886.

Florida listings dominate this ranking just as they dominate all other comparisons concerning retirement migration. More than one-quarter (27 percent) of the listings in Table 4 are in Florida. In the migration arena, Florida is a blue-chip state containing plenty of high growth markets that are still perking. Of the 10 areas that received more than five times the number of their older out-migrants, nine were in Florida.

North Carolina is the only state that rivals Florida, with 22 listings. There are eight listings from Tennessee, seven each from South Carolina and Texas, six from Oregon, four each from Arizona, Georgia and Virginia, and three each from Kentucky and Washington. Arkansas, Delaware, Minneso-

ta, Mississippi and Nevada have one listing each.

It is instructive to pause and notice the states and regions that are missing from Table 4. There are no listings from the New England states or south to New Jersey. There are none in the Middle Atlantic states. There are none in the Industrial Midwest, except for one in Minnesota. There are none in the mountain states north of Arizona and Nevada. And there is a conspicuous absence in the Pacific region: California has no listings. There may be retirement spots in all of these regions, but the ratio of in-migration to out-migration is not high.

These are the seeds of future retirement development. Will the Southern states overtake Florida? The honest answer has to be, "Not anytime soon." Concerning retirement migration, Florida is a sequoia with seedlings growing at its base. It will not be fighting for sun for a very long time. But the growth of retirement spots at so many places throughout the Southern region is encouraging for those who look to retirement migration as an economic development strategy in the Sun Belt states.

A final point. Where is that top 100 listing in Minnesota, exactly? It includes six non-metropolitan counties: Dodge, Goodhue, Le Sueur, Rice, Steele and Waseca. They are located in the southeastern part of the state, south of the Twin Cities and not far from Rochester and the Mayo Clinic. Between 1985 and 1990, 732 older interstate migrants settled in this county group, and 287 left it.

Destinations with the highest ratios of out-migrants to in-migrants — A county with many more out-migrants than in-migrants would be considered unpopular in the context of interstate retirement migration. It is important to realize, however, that unpopular states may also harbor regional retirement centers and popular summer vacation spots. Just as retirement destinations are spread unevenly over popular states, the counties that lose far more older migrants than they receive are not spread uniformly over the major sending states either. Put another way, if popular states are not uniformly popular, then neither are unpopular states uniformly unpopular. Popularity and unpopularity are mixed, in some proportion, in most states.

In Table 5 the ratio is reversed. It now tells how many older migrants moved out for each one that moved in. The county or county group with the highest ratio of out-migrants to in-migrants is Nassau County, NY, which lost 12.4 migrants for each one it received. All of the 100 counties or county groups listed lost at least 2.24 times as many older interstate migrants as they received between 1985 and 1990. These are not necessarily sending the largest number of migrants to other states; those areas are listed in Table 2.

This ratio is designed to answer the question "Where are the places that far more people want to leave in retirement than want to enter?" These are the areas, large and small, where there is practically no in-migration of retirees as compared with the relative flood of out-migration.

The counties and county groups in Table 5 tend to be located outside the Sun Belt. The exceptions are four unpopular counties or county groups in Mississippi and Louisiana.

New York ranks first in the number of listings in Table 5 with 26, Michigan ranks second with 16, and New Jersey

Table 4 — Counties or County Groups with the Highest Ratios of In-migrants to Out-migrants Age 60+, 1985-1990

Rank	County or county group	State	In-migrants per Out-migrant
1	Pitt	North Carolina	7.45
2	Charlotte	Florida	6.96
3	Citrus, Levy and Sumter	Florida	6.86
4	St. Lucie	Florida	6.72
5	Flagler, Putnam and St. Johns	Florida	6.20
6	Hernando	Florida	5.90
7	Marion	Florida	5.84
8	De Soto, Glades, Hardee, Hendry and Highlands	Florida	5.52
9	Palm Beach	Florida	5.36
10	Lee	Florida	5.25
11	Martin	Florida	4.93
12	Johnston and Lee	North Carolina	4.90
13	Breckinridge, Grayson, Larue, Marion, Nelson and Washington	Kentucky	4.62
14	Collier and Monroe	Florida	4.57
15	Comal, Guadalupe, Karnes and Wilson	Texas	4.49
16	Carteret, Craven, Jones and Pamlico	North Carolina	4.46
17	Horry	South Carolina	4.41
18	Hays, Bastrop, Caldwell, Fayette, Lee and Milam	Texas	4.38
19	Orange and Chatham	North Carolina	4.32
20	Calhoun, Franklin, Gadsden, Gulf, Jackson and Liberty	Florida	4.30
21	Harnett and Sampson	North Carolina	4.22
22	Polk	Florida	4.19
23	Osceola	Florida	4.09
24	Banks, Dawson, Forsyth, Franklin, Habersham, Hall, Hart, Lumpkin, Rabun, Stephens, Towns, Union and White	Georgia	4.04
25	New Hanover	North Carolina	3.99
26	Sarasota	Florida	3.98
27	Indian River and Okeechobee	Florida	3.97
28	Anson, Montgomery, Moore and Richmond	North Carolina	3.92
29	Brevard	Florida	3.86
(Tie) 30	Lake	Florida	3.81
(Tie) 30	Clallam, Jefferson and Mason	Washington	3.81
32	Union and Stanly	North Carolina	3.75
33	Brunswick, Columbus and Pender	North Carolina	3.64
34	Franklin, Granville, Person, Vance and Warren	North Carolina	3.60
35	Pasco	Florida	3.56
36	Manatee	Florida	3.55
37	Clark	Washington	3.44
38	Clark	Nevada	3.41
39	Pickens and Oconee	South Carolina	3.40
40	Volusia	Florida	3.35
41	Davie, Stokes, Surry and Yadkin	North Carolina	3.26
42	Allendale, Bamberg, Barnwell, Calhoun, Hampton and Orangeburg	South Carolina	3.24
43	Henderson, Madison and Transylvania	North Carolina	3.22
44	Alleghany, Ashe, Avery, Mitchell, Watauga, Wilkes and Yancey	North Carolina	3.19
45	Clay, Jackson, Knox, Laurel and Rockcastle	Kentucky	3.17
46	Beaufort, Colleton and Jasper	South Carolina	3.15
47	Bradford, Columbia, Dixie, Gilchrist, Hamilton, Lafayette, Madison, Suwannee, Taylor and Union	Florida	3.03
48	Broward	Florida	2.99
49	Clarendon, Georgetown and Williamsburg	South Carolina	2.97
50	Buncombe	North Carolina	2.95

*independent city

Rank	County or county group	State	In-migrants per Out-migrant
51	Bay, Holmes and Washington	Florida	2.94
(Tie) 52	Seminole	Florida	2.93
(Tie) 52	Forrest, Lamar and Perry	Mississippi	2.93
54	La Paz and Mohave	Arizona	2.91
55	Coos, Curry, Douglas and Josephine	Oregon	2.89
56	Bledsoe, Grundy, Marion, Meigs, Polk, Rhea and Sequatchie	Tennessee	2.88
57	Cabarrus and Rowan	North Carolina	2.87
(Tie) 58	Hidalgo	Texas	2.83
(Tie) 58	Maricopa	Arizona	2.83
(Tie) 60	Sussex	Delaware	2.80
(Tie) 60	Brazos	Texas	2.80
(Tie) 62	Benton and Linn	Oregon	2.79
(Tie) 62	Jackson	Oregon	2.79
(Tie) 62	Alexander, Burke and Caldwell	North Carolina	2.79
65	Anderson	South Carolina	2.76
66	Accomack, James City, Northampton, Poquoson*, Williamsburg* and York	Virginia	2.74
67	Allen, Barren, Butler, Edmonson, Hart, Metcalfe and Monroe	Kentucky	2.71
68	Hillsborough	Florida	2.67
69	Rutherford	Tennessee	2.66
70	Randolph	North Carolina	2.65
71	Cameron	Texas	2.64
72	Whatcom	Washington	2.61
73	Coconino and Yavapai	Arizona	2.59
(Tie) 74	Bartow, Gordon, Haralson and Paulding	Georgia	2.58
(Tie) 74	Pima	Arizona	2.58
(Tie) 76	Roanoke* and Salem*	Virginia	2.57
(Tie) 76	Camden, Chowan, Currituck, Dare, Gates, Hyde, Pasquotank, Perquimans, Tyrrell and Washington	North Carolina	2.57
78	Camp, Rains, Upshur, Van Zandt and Wood	Texas	2.56
(Tie) 79	Anderson, Grainger, Jefferson and Union	Tennessee	2.55
(Tie) 79	Dodge, Goodhue, Le Sueur, Rice, Steele and Waseca	Minnesota	2.55
81	Greene, Hancock, Hawkins, Johnson and Unicoi	Tennessee	2.53
82	Wake	North Carolina	2.49
(Tie) 83	Wayne	North Carolina	2.48
(Tie) 83	Essex, Gloucester, King and Queen, King William, Lancaster, Mathews, Middlesex, Northumberland, Richmond and Westmoreland	Virginia	2.48
(Tie) 83	Nash and Wilson	North Carolina	2.48
(Tie) 86	Clatsop, Columbia, Lincoln and Tillamook	Oregon	2.45
(Tie) 86	Pinellas	Florida	2.45
88	Appling, Bulloch, Candler, Evans, Jeff Davis, Tattnall, Toombs and Wayne	Georgia	2.44
(Tie) 89	Bradley and McMinn	Tennessee	2.41
(Tie) 89	Cumberland, Putnam and White	Tennessee	2.41
91	Lane	Oregon	2.40
92	Lincoln and Iredell	North Carolina	2.39
93	Sumter	South Carolina	2.38
(Tie) 94	Benton and Madison	Arkansas	2.35
(Tie) 94	Williamson	Texas	2.35
(Tie) 94	Marion	Oregon	2.35
97	Clarke, Jackson, Madison, Oconee and Oglethorpe	Georgia	2.33
98	Blount and Sevier	Tennessee	2.31
(Tie) 99	Chesterfield	Virginia	2.30
(Tie) 99	Sumner	Tennessee	2.30

Table 5 — Counties or County Groups with the Highest Ratios of Out-migrants to In-migrants Age 60+, 1985-1990

	Rank	County or county group	State	Out-migrants per In-migrant
	1	Nassau	New York	12.40
	2	Queens	New York	12.26
	3	Kings	New York	10.53
	4	Bronx	New York	9.99
	5	Westchester	New York	7.56
(Tie)	6	Suffolk	New York	6.53
(Tie)	6	Richmond	New York	6.53
	8	Schenectady	New York	6.40
	9	Bay	Michigan	5.52
	10	St. Clair	Michigan	5.13
	11	Clark, Finney, Ford, Grant, Gray, Greeley, Hamilton, Haskell, Hodgeman, Kearny, Lane, Meade, Morton, Ness, Scott, Seward, Stanton, Stevens and Wichita	Kansas	5.09
	12	Rockland	New York	5.04
	13	Union	New Jersey	4.84
	14	Essex	New Jersey	4.70
	15	New York	New York	4.68
	16	Kane	Illinois	4.48
	17	Oswego	New York	4.31
	18	Lake	Illinois	4.25
(Tie)	19	Cook	Illinois	4.21
(Tie)	19	Morris	New Jersey	4.21
	21	Dutchess and Putnam	New York	4.18
	22	Iberia, St. Martin and St. Mary	Louisiana	4.11
	23	Bergen	New Jersey	4.08
	24	Passaic	New Jersey	3.84
	25	Norfolk	Massachusetts	3.79
	26	Warren and Sussex	New Jersey	3.75
	27	Ulster	New York	3.66
	28	Oakland	Michigan	3.61
(Tie)	29	Will and Grundy	Illinois	3.49
(Tie)	29	Du Page	Illinois	3.49
	31	Alger, Chippewa, Delta, Luce, Mackinac and Schoolcraft	Michigan	3.46
	32	Niagara	New York	3.45
	33	Essex	Massachusetts	3.36
	34	Chemung and Schuyler	New York	3.32
	35	Macomb	Michigan	3.26
(Tie)	36	Fairfield	Connecticut	3.24
(Tie)	36	Middlesex	Massachusetts	3.24
	38	Muskingum and Perry	Ohio	3.22
	39	Wayne	Michigan	3.20
	40	Chautauqua	New York	3.19
	41	Polk	Iowa	3.10
(Tie)	42	Clare, Gratiot and Isabella	Michigan	3.02
(Tie)	42	Lewis and St. Lawrence	New York	3.02
(Tie)	44	Arenac, Gladwin, Iosco, Ogemaw and Roscommon	Michigan	3.01
(Tie)	44	Orleans	Louisiana	3.01
	46	Erie	New York	2.99
	47	Hudson	New Jersey	2.98
	48	Clinton and Eaton	Michigan	2.95
	49	Tolland	Connecticut	2.93
	50	Kent	Rhode Island	2.92

Rank	County or county group	State	Out-migrants per In-migrant
51	Logan, Simpson and Warren	Kentucky	2.91
52	Plymouth	Massachusetts	2.89
53	Hunterdon	New Jersey	2.86
54	Onondaga	New York	2.78
55	Cloud, Ellsworth, Jewell, Lincoln, Mitchell, Ottawa, Republic, Saline and Washington	Kansas	2.71
56	Somerset	New Jersey	2.68
57	Rock Island	Illinois	2.67
(Tie) 58	Kalamazoo	Michigan	2.66
(Tie) 58	Ingham	Michigan	2.66
(Tie) 60	Allegheny	Pennsylvania	2.61
(Tie) 60	Kendall and De Kalb	Illinois	2.61
(Tie) 60	Peoria	Illinois	2.61
(Tie) 63	Winnebago	Wisconsin	2.58
(Tie) 63	Champaign, Logan and Shelby	Ohio	2.58
(Tie) 63	Delaware and Sullivan	New York	2.58
66	Lucas	Ohio	2.56
(Tie) 67	Fairbanks North Star, Juneau, Kenai Peninsula, Ketchikan Gateway, Matanuska-Susitna and Sitka	Alaska	2.55
(Tie) 67	Jackson	Michigan	2.55
(Tie) 69	Bolivar, Humphreys, Issaquena, Sharkey, Sunflower and Washington	Mississippi	2.54
(Tie) 69	Ozaukee and Washington	Wisconsin	2.54
(Tie) 71	Anchorage	Alaska	2.52
(Tie) 71	Philadelphia	Pennsylvania	2.52
73	Fulton and Herkimer	New York	2.49
(Tie) 74	Acadia and Vermilion	Louisiana	2.48
(Tie) 74	Los Angeles	California	2.48
(Tie) 76	Kent	Michigan	2.47
(Tie) 76	Middlesex	Connecticut	2.47
78	Bristol	Massachusetts	2.45
79	Albany	New York	2.44
80	Hampden	Massachusetts	2.43
81	Lake	Ohio	2.41
82	Waukesha	Wisconsin	2.39
83	Washtenaw	Michigan	2.38
(Tie) 84	Saginaw	Michigan	2.37
(Tie) 84	Mahoning	Ohio	2.37
86	Milwaukee	Wisconsin	2.36
(Tie) 87	San Francisco	California	2.35
(Tie) 87	Chenango and Madison	New York	2.35
(Tie) 89	Genesee, Orleans and Wyoming	New York	2.33
(Tie) 89	Greene	Ohio	2.33
91	Athens, Hocking, Meigs and Vinton	Ohio	2.32
92	Cedar, Clinton, Delaware, Dubuque and Jackson	Iowa	2.30
(Tie) 93	Mercer	Pennsylvania	2.29
(Tie) 93	Santa Cruz	California	2.29
(Tie) 95	Cuyahoga	Ohio	2.28
(Tie) 95	Livingston	Michigan	2.28
97	Cortland, Tioga and Tompkins	New York	2.27
(Tie) 98	New Haven	Connecticut	2.26
(Tie) 98	Monroe	New York	2.26
100	Baca, Bent, Cheyenne, Crowley, Kiowa, Kit Carson, Lincoln, Logan, Morgan, Otero, Phillips, Prowers, Sedgwick, Washington and Yuma	Colorado	2.24

third with nine. Ohio and Illinois are each listed eight times. Massachusetts is listed six times and Wisconsin and Connecticut four. California, Louisiana and Pennsylvania have three listings. Kansas, Iowa and Alaska appear twice, and a single listing exists for Mississippi, Rhode Island, Kentucky and Colorado

Noted in Table 2 was the fact that the major sending areas tend to contain large cities. The surprise in Table 5 is that there are several non-metropolitan county groups that are as "unpopular" as the counties containing large cities. There are 19 sparsely populated counties in the southwestern corner of Kansas that lost 5.09 times as many residents to interstate migration as they received. There is a strong Northern European ancestry evident in these counties. Iberia, St. Martin and St. Mary parishes (counties) in Louisiana, southwest of New Orleans, are dominated culturally by descendants of French Canadian immigrants expelled by the British from Nova Scotia before Louisiana statehood. They lost 4.11 times as many older citizens to interstate out-migration as they received. Finally, the Mississippi Delta counties of Bolivar, Humphreys, Issaquena, Sharkey, Sunflower and Washington lost 2.54 migrants to other states for each that moved in. A high proportion of the citizens of these counties are African Americans. There may be an ethnic basis underlying some rural out-migration in old age.

The non-metropolitan county group of Alger, Chippewa, Delta, Luce, Mackinac and Schoolcraft counties, in upper Michigan between Lake Michigan and Lake Superior, lost 3.46 times as many older residents to interstate migration as it gained during the last census migration period. Two non-metropolitan county groups in rural central Michigan lost about three for each one they gained. One contains Clare, Gratiot and Isabella counties; the other contains Arenac, Gladwin, Iosco, Ogemaw and Roscommon counties. The southeast Ohio non-metropolitan county group of Athens, Hocking, Meigs and Vinton counties lost 2.32 older residents for each one received. A north-central Kansas county group containing Cloud, Ellsworth, Jewell, Lincoln, Mitchell, Ottawa, Republic, Saline and Washington counties lost 2.71 older residents for each they received. The sparsely populated eastern prairie counties of Colorado, including Baca, Bent, Cheyenne, Crowley, Kiowa, Kit Carson, Lincoln, Logan, Morgan, Otero, Phillips, Prowers, Sedgwick, Washington and Yuma counties, form a county group that lost 2.24 older citizens for each one that entered.

Retirement out-migration, in the absence of other information, is usually assumed to be from metropolitan counties. These are the places of economic opportunity. More city retirees can afford to move and more have been geographically mobile during their working years. It is clear from Table 5, however, that although metropolitan counties may dominate the list of unpopular counties, there are some very sparsely populated areas of Midwestern states that are not popular with retirees. The exceptions to general patterns are memorable and sometimes important. In Table 2, the non-metropolitan areas with substantial out-migration tended to be tourist counties that have accumulated retirees in the past. That is not always the case with the non-metropolitan areas in Table 5.

Attention should not be diverted unnecessarily from the central character of unpopular retirement places, however. On the whole, they are in the Northeast and Midwest, California being the major exception, and are often the state's major city, adjacent suburban counties, and counties including some of the minor cities of the state. The least popular major cities are New York City, Boston, Philadelphia, Newark, Cleveland, Chicago, Detroit, New Orleans, Milwaukee, Los Angeles and San Francisco. The least popular smaller cities include Buffalo and Schenectady, NY; Springfield, MA; New Haven, CT; Pittsburgh, PA; Toledo and Youngstown, OH; Peoria and Rock Island, IL; Grand Rapids, Lansing, Kalamazoo, Ann Arbor, Saginaw, Jackson, St. Clair and Bay City, MI; Des Moines, IA; Santa Cruz, CA; and Anchorage, AK.

When considering the specific locations of concentrations of older migrants, it is important to remember that the picture is constantly changing. New locations are arising all the time. This observation is obvious in North Carolina where "popular" destinations, in their embryonic form, are popping up all over. It is not really possible to predict very far ahead in these developments.

Speculation, however, is fun. Cheryl Russell speculates a great deal about the future aging of the baby boom generation in her book "The Master Trend."[2] As she gazes deep into her crystal ball, Russell predicts a polarization of income among baby boomers with both ends of the income spectrum stretching, producing both a larger affluent and a larger near-poverty subpopulation when the boomers reach retirement age. She feels that when the affluent baby boomers retire after 2020, they will be less likely to settle in the crowded retirement areas of today. They do not have a strong history of following the crowd. Instead, there will be lots of new retirement havens created in areas near, but not in, the old ones. She observes that baby boomers formed the exurbs, long-distance commuting suburbs from work (the young New York professionals living in Connecticut, for example). The same pattern may hold for retirement living, moving the new retirees out beyond the familiar settlements. Russell says that "the states that will boom when baby boomers retire are Vermont, Virginia, South Carolina, New Mexico, Nevada, Oregon and Washington." As we have seen, this process is not waiting for the baby boomers to arrive in 20 years, it is happening now. There are top destination counties or county groups in all but one of these states. She only missed on Vermont, a state to watch in the future.

• • • • • • • • • • •

The connection between origin and destination, the stream, promotes the continuity and growth of the retirement destination. The major sending and receiving retirement counties in the United States have been identified in this chapter. In Chapter 5, the major migration streams will be considered, providing the context for a discussion of pinpoint migration marketing.

CHAPTER FIVE
COUNTY-TO-COUNTY STREAMS

Introduction

It is clear from the discussion in Chapter 3 that many states contribute older migrants to the state of Florida, and that retirees leave California for its contiguous states of Arizona, Nevada and Oregon. However, state-to-state streams are not geographically focused enough for some marketers. County-to-county migration streams may be more useful.

From a demographic point of view, migration streams are important because they keep the flow of migrants coming. It is conceivable that thousands of migrants could move to a county from numerous origins, and that, when they arrived, no one would know anyone else who lives there. Boom towns during the westward expansion experienced this kind of in-migration. Boom towns declined as quickly as they grew. The maps of Western states are dotted with their carcasses. There were no migration streams to sustain their growth.

When people for whom a retirement move is a real possibility know friends or relatives who have moved to a potential destination, an emotional connection is made to the place because it is associated with someone who is esteemed. As knowledge and positive feelings about the place increase, the chance of a move to that site also increases. As this process repeats itself hundreds of times, the stream begins to flow. Stream migration has definite implications for the future. Locating the retirement counties that are the most likely to continue to grow, therefore, requires knowledge about county-to-county migration streams.

A national portrait of county-to-county retirement migration has never before been produced. It appears for the first time on the pages of this book. A first look at these geographic patterns is very exciting, but it also carries a burden. Little research literature exists that would prepare our expectations. The only exception is Richard Ormrod's study of inter-PUMA migration within California between 1975 and 1980, cited in Chapter 4. He noted that retirement migration within California tended to be from north to south, as it is among interstate migrants in the United States as a whole. Not only is research essentially silent on interstate stream migration of retirees between counties, but there is also little theory that would guide speculation on the subject. Do retirees from the Bronx move to Palm Beach or to the Jersey Shore? There is no basis on which to make an educated guess.

This chapter focuses on the 100 largest streams between counties or county groups. Each of these streams carried 640 or more migrants during the 1985-1990 migration period. One thousand streams each contained at least 176 migrants, and perhaps another thousand streams contained fewer. The largest streams are most likely to perpetuate themselves into the future. For this reason, the analysis is limited to them.

Several questions will be addressed in this chapter. First, how large are the largest streams, and are there any noticeable differences between the largest and smallest streams on the list?

Second, do sending counties or county groups tend to send streams only to one state or several? That is, how narrowly do they focus their collective streams?

Third, what are the patterns of stream reception? That is, how do receiving counties or county groups in the same state differ in terms of the streams they receive? Do they attract streams from the same or from different out-of-state areas?

In order to answer the first question, the streams must be ranked. The ranking is found in Table 1.

How Big Are the Largest Streams?

As noted in Table 1, the single largest stream between two counties (7,519 migrants) is not between New York and South Florida. Instead, it is between Los Angeles County, CA, and Clark County, NV, the location of Las Vegas. However, seven of the top 10 streams are from New York to South Florida.

When the top 10 and the bottom 10 streams are compared, another generalization is evident. The largest migration streams emanate from counties containing the largest cities (Los Angeles, New York and Chicago). Many of the smallest streams are from suburban counties adjacent to Philadelphia, New York City and Washington, DC. Florida counties dominate the destinations at both ends of the chart, but smaller streams are split between South Florida and west Florida. Table 2 reorders the county-to-county streams by origin state so patterns can be established.

Which Counties or County Groups Send Large Streams?

New York — Between 1985 and 1990, 35 of the top 100 migration streams in the United States originated in New York state. Each of the origin counties was in or near New York City. The city contains five counties, which together account for 19 of the streams: Queens (8), Kings (6), New York (2), Bronx (2) and Richmond (1). Queens and Kings dominate the streams from the city. Similarly, there are some suburban counties that originate more large streams than others. Nassau (6) and Suffolk (6) counties on Long Island send the most. Westchester County (3) near Connecticut and Rockland County (1) near New Jersey, complete the New York picture. Older migrants may originate in many places in the state. Only the counties associated directly or as suburban neighbors with New York City, however, send large streams of retirees to specific other counties out of state.

California — Los Angeles County dominates California's sending scene, originating 11 streams to counties or county groups in other states. Los Angeles cannot match New York City's 19 streams, but there is certainly nothing

Table 1 — Largest County-to-County Streams of Interstate Migrants Age 60+, 1985-1990

Rank	Destination County & State	Origin County & State	# of Migrants
1	Clark County, Nevada	Los Angeles County, California	7,519
2	Broward County, Florida	Queens County, New York	4,860
3	Palm Beach County, Florida	Nassau County, New York	4,755
4	Palm Beach County, Florida	Queens County, New York	3,414
5	Broward County, Florida	Kings County, New York	3,392
6	Maricopa County, Arizona	Cook County, Illinois	3,024
7	Broward County, Florida	Nassau County, New York	2,859
8	Maricopa County, Arizona	Los Angeles County, California	2,815
9	Palm Beach County, Florida	Kings County, New York	2,467
10	Dade County, Florida	Queens County, New York	2,348
11	Palm Beach County, Florida	Westchester County, New York	2,031
12	Dade County, Florida	Hudson County, New Jersey	2,022
13	Prince Georges County, Maryland	D.C.	1,911
14	Clark County, Nevada	Orange County, California	1,778
15	Douglas, Lyon, Storey and Washoe counties, Nevada	Los Angeles County, California	1,718
16	Lake County, Indiana	Cook County, Illinois	1,690
17	Ocean County, New Jersey	Kings County, New York	1,686
18	Montgomery County, Maryland	D.C.	1,602
19	Dade County, Florida	Kings County, New York	1,599
20	La Paz and Mohave counties, Arizona	Los Angeles County, California	1,545
21	Palm Beach County, Florida	Bergen County, New Jersey	1,499
22	Pinellas County, Florida	Cook County, Illinois	1,478
23	Rockingham County, New Hampshire	Essex County, Massachusetts	1,459
24	Palm Beach County, Florida	Suffolk County, New York	1,446
25	Broward County, Florida	Suffolk County, New York	1,407
26	Dade County, Florida	Los Angeles County, California	1,404
27	Los Angeles County, California	Cook County, Illinois	1,399
(Tie) 28	Coos, Curry, Douglas and Josephine counties, Oregon	Los Angeles County, California	1,356
(Tie) 28	King County, Washington	Los Angeles County, California	1,356
30	Dade County, Florida	New York County, New York	1,318
(Tie) 31	Camden County, New Jersey	Philadelphia County, Pennsylvania	1,239
(Tie) 31	Monmouth County, New Jersey	Kings County, New York	1,239
33	Clark County, Nevada	Cook County, Illinois	1,229
34	Broward County, Florida	Cook County, Illinois	1,182
35	Pasco County, Florida	Nassau County, New York	1,180
36	Broward County, Florida	Westchester County, New York	1,168
37	Coahoma, De Soto, Panola, Quitman, Tallahatchie, Tate and Tunica counties, Mississippi	Shelby County, Tennessee	1,167
38	Johnson County, Kansas	Jackson County, Missouri	1,157
39	Maricopa County, Arizona	Orange County, California	1,152
40	Coconino and Yavapai counties, Arizona	Los Angeles County, California	1,148
41	Middlesex County, New Jersey	Queens County, New York	1,140
42	Broward County, Florida	Bronx County, New York	1,136
43	Palm Beach County, Florida	Middlesex County, Massachusetts	1,125
44	Cape May and Salem counties, New Jersey	Philadelphia County, Pennsylvania	1,074
45	Hillsborough County, New Hampshire	Middlesex County, Massachusetts	1,062
46	Palm Beach County, Florida	New York County, New York	1,047
47	Broward County, Florida	Bergen County, New Jersey	1,035
48	Middlesex County, New Jersey	Kings County, New York	1,034
49	Palm Beach County, Florida	Bronx County, New York	1,030
50	Pasco County, Florida	Suffolk County, New York	1,014

Rank	Destination County & State	Origin County & State	# of Migrants
51	Pasco County, Florida	Cook County, Illinois	985
52	Pasco County, Florida	Queens County, New York	984
53	Ocean County, New Jersey	Queens County, New York	982
54	Pima County, Arizona	Los Angeles County, California	948
55	La Paz and Mohave counties, Arizona	Orange County, California	935
56	Sarasota County, Florida	Cook County, Illinois	928
57	Maricopa County, Arizona	Denver County, Colorado	898
58	Clark County, Nevada	San Bernardino County, California	892
59	Lee County, Florida	Cook County, Illinois	885
60	Ramsey County, Minnesota	Cloud, Ellsworth, Jewell, Lincoln, Mitchell, Ottawa, Republic, Saline and Washington counties, Kansas	883
61	Pinellas County, Florida	Wayne County, Michigan	867
62	Maricopa County, Arizona	Hennepin County, Minnesota	854
63	Fairfield County, Connecticut	Westchester County, New York	848
64	Clark and Floyd counties, Indiana	Jefferson County, Kentucky	838
65	Lane County, Oregon	Los Angeles County, California	836
66	Palm Beach County, Florida	Fairfield County, Connecticut	825
67	Los Angeles County, California	Harris County, Texas	810
68	Dade County, Florida	Cook County, Illinois	798
69	Dade County, Florida	Union County, New Jersey	795
70	Palm Beach County, Florida	Hartford County, Connecticut	794
71	Hernando County, Florida	Nassau County, New York	787
72	Palm Beach County, Florida	Rockland County, New York	786
73	San Diego County, California	Cook County, Illinois	780
74	Palm Beach County, Florida	Cook County, Illinois	763
75	Maricopa County, Arizona	Oakland County, Michigan	760
76	Palm Beach County, Florida	Monmouth County, New Jersey	753
77	Hernando County, Florida	Cook County, Illinois	733
78	Jackson County, Oregon	Los Angeles County, California	731
79	La Paz and Mohave counties, Arizona	San Diego County, California	722
(Tie) 80	Palm Beach County, Florida	Essex County, New Jersey	720
(Tie) 80	Broward County, Florida	Essex County, New Jersey	720
82	Douglas, Lyon, Storey and Washoe counties and Carson City*, Nevada	Santa Clara County, California	717
83	San Diego County, California	Maricopa County, Arizona	716
84	Pinellas County, Florida	Suffolk County, New York	710
85	Monmouth County, New Jersey	Queens County, New York	707
86	Burlington County, New Jersey	Philadelphia County, Pennsylvania	703
(Tie) 87	Jackson County, Missouri	Johnson County, Kansas	694
(Tie) 87	Ocean County, New Jersey	Nassau County, New York	694
89	Ramsey County, Minnesota	Clark, Finney, Ford, Grant, Gray, Greeley, Hamilton, Haskell, Hodgeman, Kearny, Lane, Meade, Morton, Ness, Scott, Seward, Stanton, Stevens and Wichita counties, Kansas	693
90	Palm Beach County, Florida	Montgomery County, Pennsylvania	689
91	Ocean County, New Jersey	Richmond County, New York	687
92	Broward County, Florida	New Haven County, Connecticut	679
93	Pinellas County, Florida	Queens County, New York	672
94	Pinellas County, Florida	Nassau County, New York	662
95	Riverside County, California	Cook County, Illinois	659
96	Suffolk County, Massachusetts	Hancock, Penobscot and Piscataquis counties, Maine	656
97	St. Lucie County, Florida	Suffolk County, New York	649
98	Hernando County, Florida	Suffolk County, New York	648
99	D.C.	Prince Georges County, Maryland	643
100	Broward County, Florida	Philadelphia County, Pennsylvania	640

*independent city

Table 2 — Largest County-to-County Streams of Interstate Migrants Age 60+, by Origin County, 1985-1990

Rank	Destination County & State	Origin County & State	# of Migrants
New York			
2	Broward County, Florida	Queens County, New York	4,860
4	Palm Beach County, Florida	Queens County, New York	3,414
10	Dade County, Florida	Queens County, New York	2,348
41	Middlesex County, New Jersey	Queens County, New York	1,140
52	Pasco County, Florida	Queens County, New York	984
53	Ocean County, New Jersey	Queens County, New York	982
85	Monmouth County, New Jersey	Queens County, New York	707
93	Pinellas County, Florida	Queens County, New York	672
3	Palm Beach County, Florida	Nassau County, New York	4,755
7	Broward County, Florida	Nassau County, New York	2,859
35	Pasco County, Florida	Nassau County, New York	1,180
71	Hernando County, Florida	Nassau County, New York	787
(Tie) 87	Ocean County, New Jersey	Nassau County, New York	694
94	Pinellas County, Florida	Nassau County, New York	662
5	Broward County, Florida	Kings County, New York	3,392
9	Palm Beach County, Florida	Kings County, New York	2,467
17	Ocean County, New Jersey	Kings County, New York	1,686
19	Dade County, Florida	Kings County, New York	1,599
(Tie) 31	Momouth County, New Jersey	Kings County, New York	1,239
48	Middlesex County, New Jersey	Kings County, New York	1,034
11	Palm Beach County, Florida	Westchester County, New York	2,031
36	Broward County, Florida	Westchester County, New York	1,168
63	Fairfield County, Connecticut	Westchester County, New York	848
24	Palm Beach County, Florida	Suffolk County, New York	1,446
25	Broward County, Florida	Suffolk County, New York	1,407
50	Pasco County, Florida	Suffolk County, New York	1,014
84	Pinellas County, Florida	Suffolk County, New York	710
97	St. Lucie County, Florida	Suffolk County, New York	649
98	Hernando County, Florida	Suffolk County, New York	648
30	Dade County, Florida	New York County, New York	1,318
46	Palm Beach County, Florida	New York County, New York	1,047
42	Broward County, Florida	Bronx County, New York	1,136
49	Palm Beach County, Florida	Bronx County, New York	1,030
72	Palm Beach County, Florida	Rockland County, New York	786
91	Ocean County, New Jersey	Richmond County, New York	687
California			
1	Clark County, Nevada	Los Angeles County, California	7,519
8	Maricopa County, Arizona	Los Angeles County, California	2,815
15	Douglas, Lyon, Storey and Washoe counties and Carson City*, Nevada	Los Angeles County, California	1,718
20	La Paz and Mohave counties, Arizona	Los Angeles County, California	1,545
26	Dade County, Florida	Los Angeles County, California	1,404
(Tie) 28	Coos, Curry, Douglas and Josephine counties, Oregon	Los Angeles County, California	1,356
(Tie) 28	King County, Washington	Los Angeles County, California	1,356
40	Coconino and Yavapai counties, Arizona	Los Angeles County, California	1,148
54	Pima County, Arizona	Los Angeles County, California	948
65	Lane County, Oregon	Los Angeles County, California	836
78	Jackson County, Oregon	Los Angeles County, California	731
14	Clark County, Nevada	Orange County, California	1,778
39	Maricopa County, Arizona	Orange County, California	1,152
55	La Paz and Mohave counties, Arizona	Orange County, California	935
58	Clark County, Nevada	San Bernardino County, California	892
82	Douglas, Lyon, Storey and Washoe counties and Carson City*, Nevada	Santa Clara County, California	717
79	La Paz and Mohave counties, Arizona	San Diego County, California	722
Illinois			
6	Maricopa County, Arizona	Cook County, Illinois	3,024
16	Lake County, Indiana	Cook County, Illinois	1,690
22	Pinellas County, Florida	Cook County, Illinois	1,478
27	Los Angeles County, California	Cook County, Illinois	1,399
33	Clark County, Nevada	Cook County, Illinois	1,229
34	Broward County, Florida	Cook County, Illinois	1,182

*independent city

Rank	Destination County & State	Origin County & State	# of Migrants
51	Pasco County, Florida	Cook County, Illinois	985
56	Sarasota County, Florida	Cook County, Illinois	928
59	Lee County, Florida	Cook County, Illinois	885
68	Dade County, Florida	Cook County, Illinois	798
73	San Diego County, California	Cook County, Illinois	780
74	Palm Beach County, Florida	Cook County, Illinois	763
77	Hernando County, Florida	Cook County, Illinois	733
95	Riverside County, California	Cook County, Illinois	659

New Jersey

Rank	Destination County & State	Origin County & State	# of Migrants
12	Dade County, Florida	Hudson County, New Jersey	2,022
21	Palm Beach County, Florida	Bergen County, New Jersey	1,499
47	Broward County, Florida	Bergen County, New Jersey	1,035
69	Dade County, Florida	Union County, New Jersey	795
76	Palm Beach County, Florida	Monmouth County, New Jersey	753
(Tie) 80	Palm Beach County, Florida	Essex County, New Jersey	720
(Tie) 80	Broward County, Florida	Essex County, New Jersey	720

Pennsylvania

Rank	Destination County & State	Origin County & State	# of Migrants
(Tie) 31	Camden County, New Jersey	Philadelphia County, Pennsylvania	1,239
44	Cape May and Salem counties, New Jersey	Philadelphia County, Pennsylvania	1,074
86	Burlington County, New Jersey	Philadelphia County, Pennsylvania	703
100	Broward County, Florida	Philadelphia County, Pennsylvania	640
90	Palm Beach County, Florida	Montgomery County, Pennsylvania	689

Massachusetts

Rank	Destination County & State	Origin County & State	# of Migrants
23	Rockingham County, New Hampshire	Essex County, Massachusetts	1,459
43	Palm Beach County, Florida	Middlesex County, Massachusetts	1,125
45	Hillsborough County, New Hampshire	Middlesex County, Massachusetts	1,062

Kansas

Rank	Destination County & State	Origin County & State	# of Migrants
60	Ramsey County, Minnesota	Cloud, Ellsworth, Jewell, Lincoln, Mitchell, Ottawa, Republic, Saline, and Washington counties, Kansas	883
89	Ramsey County, Minnesota	Clark, Finney, Ford, Grant, Gray, Greeley, Hamilton, Haskell, Hodgeman, Kearny, Lane, Meade, Morton, Ness, Scott, Seward, Stanton, Stevens and Wichita counties, Kansas	693
(Tie) 87	Jackson County, Missouri	Johnson County, Kansas	694

Connecticut

Rank	Destination County & State	Origin County & State	# of Migrants
66	Palm Beach County, Florida	Fairfield County, Connecticut	825
70	Palm Beach County, Florida	Hartford County, Connecticut	794
92	Broward County, Florida	New Haven County, Connecticut	679

District of Columbia

Rank	Destination County & State	Origin County & State	# of Migrants
13	Prince Georges County, Maryland	D.C.	1,911
18	Montgomery County, Maryland	D.C.	1,602

Michigan

Rank	Destination County & State	Origin County & State	# of Migrants
61	Pinellas County, Florida	Wayne County, Michigan	867
75	Maricopa County, Arizona	Oakland County, Michigan	760

Tennessee

Rank	Destination County & State	Origin County & State	# of Migrants
37	Coahoma, De Soto, Panola, Quitman, Tallahatchie, Tate and Tunica counties, Mississippi	Shelby County, Tennessee	1,167

Missouri

Rank	Destination County & State	Origin County & State	# of Migrants
38	Johnson County, Kansas	Jackson County, Missouri	1,157

Colorado

Rank	Destination County & State	Origin County & State	# of Migrants
57	Maricopa County, Arizona	Denver County, Colorado	898

Minnesota

Rank	Destination County & State	Origin County & State	# of Migrants
62	Maricopa County, Arizona	Hennepin County, Minnesota	854

Kentucky

Rank	Destination County & State	Origin County & State	# of Migrants
64	Clark and Floyd counties, Indiana	Jefferson County, Kentucky	838

Texas

Rank	Destination County & State	Origin County & State	# of Migrants
67	Los Angeles County, California	Harris County, Texas	810

Arizona

Rank	Destination County & State	Origin County & State	# of Migrants
83	San Diego County, California	Maricopa County, Arizona	716

Maine

Rank	Destination County & State	Origin County & State	# of Migrants
96	Suffolk County, Massachusetts	Hancock, Penobscot and Piscataquis counties, Maine	656

Maryland

Rank	Destination County & State	Origin County & State	# of Migrants
99	D.C.	Prince Georges County, Maryland	643

to rival Los Angeles in other Sun Belt states. Orange County (3) and San Bernardino County (1) are neighbors to Los Angeles on the south and east, respectively. San Diego County (1) borders Orange County immediately to the south. Santa Clara County (1) includes San Jose and is located in the Bay Area, south of San Francisco. It is the only county outside Southern California that sends a large stream of older migrants to another state.

Illinois — Cook County, Chicago's home, is the only county in the state that sends large migration streams to places in other states. Furthermore, it sends 14 of them, second only to New York City as an origin of interstate migration streams.

New Jersey — Interstate streams originate from five of New Jersey's counties. All of the counties — Hudson (1), Bergen (2), Union (1), Monmouth (1) and Essex (2) — are located in the northern region of the state associated with the Greater New York Metropolitan Area.

Pennsylvania — Philadelphia, like New York City, Chicago and Los Angeles, monopolizes the sending of migration streams from the state of Pennsylvania. Four of the five streams originate in Philadelphia County, the city's location, and one comes from Montgomery County, an adjacent suburban county.

Massachusetts — The two northern suburban counties of Boston, Essex (1) and Middlesex (2), originate the state's only large migration streams to places in other states.

Kansas — Kansas does not fit the pattern where streams come from cities or their suburban counties. Of its three major streams, two originate from sparsely populated county groups and one originates from suburban Kansas City. Perhaps the most unusual area from which a large migration stream embarks for an out-of-state location is made up of 19 counties in the southwest corner of Kansas, bordering Oklahoma to the south and Colorado to the west. The counties sit like a stack of blocks, four counties tall and five wide, filled with small towns and prairie. They are Clark, Finney, Ford, Grant, Gray, Greeley, Hamilton, Haskell, Hodgeman, Kearny, Lane, Meade, Morton, Ness, Scott, Seward, Stanton, Stevens and Wichita counties. They are the polar opposite of New York City, Chicago or Los Angeles. Also in Kansas, from the Nebraska border southward to Salina, there is another series of somewhat more populous counties that constitutes a major sending county group. This county group consists of Cloud, Ellsworth, Jewell, Lincoln, Mitchell, Ottawa, Republic, Saline and Washington counties. Finally, Johnson County, containing the southwestern suburbs of Kansas City, originates a major stream of out-of-state migrants.

Connecticut — Three counties in Connecticut dispatch large streams. They are Fairfield (1), Hartford (1) and New Haven (1) counties. Fairfield County houses many New York exurbanites, and Hartford and New Haven counties are also highly urbanized.

The District of Columbia — The federal district that accommodates the nation's capital routes two large streams to out-of-district locations.

Michigan — The two counties that originate large migration streams from Michigan are Wayne (1) and Oakland (1).

Detroit is located in Wayne County and Oakland is its adjacent suburban neighbor. The metropolitan character of large stream out-migration is again illustrated.

Nine states each generate a single large stream to an out-of-state location. All but one of these streams are from single metropolitan counties. Shelby County, TN, contains Memphis. Jackson County, MO, contains part of Kansas City. Denver County, CO, contains the city of Denver. Hennepin County, MN, contains Minneapolis. Jefferson County, KY, contains Louisville. Harris County, TX, contains Houston. Maricopa County, AZ, contains Phoenix. Prince Georges County, MD, contains some of Washington's suburban fringe, as well as much larger areas of farmland and small towns.

Hancock, Penobscot and Piscataquis counties, ME, compose a highly forested county group that originates a major stream of retirees. The city of Bangor is located in southern Penobscot County.

The overall pattern is one of metropolitan out-migration, this time in the context of sending forth migration streams to specific other counties or county groups.

The pattern holds in all but a very small number of cases, notably in Kansas and Maine.

How Do Sending Counties Direct Their Streams?

Out-migration, at least when it comes to large migration streams, is a metropolitan phenomenon with few exceptions. How are streams directed? Do they focus narrowly on destinations near one another? Are they split between nearby regional destinations and national destinations farther away? Or are they sent in all directions, like an explosion, to areas in each major retirement state? Rather than delineating the experience of each sending state, this part of the analysis will be divided into three distinct patterns. The first will be called the New York City pattern; the second, the Los Angeles pattern; and the third, the Chicago pattern. These cities and their adjacent suburban counties originate nearly two-thirds of the top 100 retirement streams.

The New York City Pattern — The New York City pattern is defined as having a favorite national destination and a favorite regional destination. All of the counties associated with the Greater New York City Metropolitan Area send streams to one, the other, or both of these destinations. The choice is relatively limited in that sense, although there is some variation within the destination states.

New York has a long-standing love affair with the state of Florida as a distant national retirement destination. Wealthy New York families had winter homes near St. Augustine, FL, before Henry Flagler built his railroad to Palm Beach in the 1890s. In 1896 the railroad reached Miami, tying it to the outside world. Finally, after two hurricanes, the overseas railroad reached Key West in 1912.[1] Flagler also built large resort hotels near the railheads at these spots to give passengers a reason for their trip. Flagler, a retired Standard Oil executive turned railroad builder, is credited with opening the lower half of the state to settlement, and is therefore considered a state hero of major magnitude.

The New York social elite established the value of Florida for winter vacationing in the city's collective consciousness before railroads made it accessible to the middle class. By the time automobiles and highways opened the state to a larger segment of the population, it was a widely valued location. New Yorkers' interest in Florida is so culturally embedded and long-standing, and its migration streams so deeply entrenched, that it is difficult to imagine the circumstances that could cause a major short-term reversal of this pattern. There is some truth to the old maxim that Miami is as far south as one can go without leaving New York.

The history of New York's interest in the Jersey Shore is only somewhat more recent, but less elite in its origin. Before 1910, the nation's large cities were connected primarily by rail or waterways. When automobiles began pouring off assembly lines, cities could expand outward much more rapidly and paved roads began to connect cities with their immediate neighbors.[2] This was the time, in the 1920s, when Sunday drives became a favorite family recreational activity for car owners, and the Jersey Shore became a popular recreational spot for New Yorkers.[3] The first divided highway was proposed in New Jersey in 1927.[4] The rail line from Philadelphia to Atlantic City and Cape May carried heavy traffic to seaside recreation resorts in the 1930s.[5] The retirement migration streams to New Jersey are many decades old. As New Jersey has become more populous and urbanized, this regional destination has lost some of its attractiveness; but it still attracts retirees from New York and is likely to continue to do so in the future.

The streams from each New York county are grouped by county of origin in Table 2. Only Florida and New Jersey are destinations, with one minor exception: A stream of migrants from Westchester County moves to adjacent Fairfield County in Connecticut. Retired New Yorkers move to many states, but the largest streams of migrants move to Florida and New Jersey.

Some other cities follow the New York City pattern. Philadelphia, for example, divides its large streams between these same two states, but favors New Jersey over Florida. Likewise, Massachusetts follows a modified New York pattern, substituting New Hampshire for New Jersey.

The Los Angeles Pattern — The Los Angeles pattern is very different from that of New York City. From 1985 to 1990, Los Angeles County sent nine large streams of retirees to its adjacent states: Arizona, Nevada and Oregon. One stream went to Washington and one stream went to Dade County, FL. Adjacency, therefore, is the heart of the Los Angeles out-migration pattern.

Compared to the Empire State, Los Angeles is a relative newcomer to the role of originating large retirement streams. California could not receive major infusions of migrants of any age until the highways were built in the 1930s.[6] The film industry, located primarily in Southern California, tended to glamorize California and enhanced its ability to attract migrants.[7] The drought in the Great Plains states, particularly Oklahoma, early in the 1930s, spurred a major wave of migration to the Pacific Coast.[8] In the 1940s, California became important to the Pacific Theatre of World War II and many of the GIs, once exposed to the state, moved to

California after the war.[9] These waves of growth starting in the 1930s and 1940s led Southern California to begin producing large crops of retirees during the past two decades. Migration came easily to California retirees. Owing perhaps to its settlement history, the Southern California culture seems to value mobility. Turnpikes existed in the East; California built freeways.[10] Population movement is part of its cultural landscape.[11]

One major difference between Los Angeles and New York or Chicago is the climate. Southern California's dry, warm climate is arguably the best in America. Migrants leave to avoid congestion, pollution, high cost of living, crime and other big-city problems. But, many move within the region to retain the agreeable climate and the lifestyle it affords. They do not move farther away because their needs are met nearby.

Some other cities follow the Los Angeles pattern. The large retirement migration streams from Washington, DC, terminate in Maryland counties. In Kentucky and Tennessee, large streams go from Louisville and Memphis to county groups immediately across the state line in the adjoining state.

The Chicago Pattern — From Chicago's vantage point, the popular Sun Belt destination states all seem about the same distance away, thus they are all fair game. New York loves Florida, but Chicago plays the field.

Chicago housed the stockyards for the nation. Some residents believe that all trails lead eventually to Chicago, whether on the range, rail or water.[12] Chicago provided farm machinery to the Midwestern states and the whole Midwest became its psychological hinterland. It was the mail order retailer to the nation through Marshall Field and Sears Roebuck. O'Hare International Airport is not just a regional hub but the nation's largest airport and gateway to the world.

Chicago is in Cook County, which sends large migration streams to Arizona, Florida, Nevada, California and Indiana. It sends the largest and longest stream to each of the three counties in Southern California that receive large streams from out of state. Furthermore, if one compares Cook County with any single county in New York, Cook sends large streams to more Florida counties than its nearest New York competitor. Suffolk County (on Long Island) dispatches large streams to six Florida counties, more than any other New York county. Cook originates streams to eight Florida counties.

The only other city that follows Chicago's pattern is in Michigan. Two counties in metropolitan Detroit originate streams. The one from Wayne County connects with Pinellas County, FL. The one from Oakland County goes to Maricopa County, AZ.

Which Counties or County Groups Receive Large Streams?

Florida — Nearly half (49) of the top 100 retirement migration streams are destined for Florida counties. They account for the stability of Florida as the leading destination state over the past four census decades, from 1960 to 1990. Chapter 4 reported that during the 1985-1990 migration period, Palm Beach County, FL, held onto a greater

Table 3 — Largest County-to-County Streams of Interstate Migrants Age 60+, by Destination County, 1985-1990

Rank	Destination County & State	Origin County & State	# of Migrants
Florida			
3	Palm Beach County, Florida	Nassau County, New York	4,755
4	Palm Beach County, Florida	Queens County, New York	3,414
9	Palm Beach County, Florida	Kings County, New York	2,467
11	Palm Beach County, Florida	Westchester County, New York	2,031
21	Palm Beach County, Florida	Bergen County, New Jersey	1,499
24	Palm Beach County, Florida	Suffolk County, New York	1,446
43	Palm Beach County, Florida	Middlesex County, Massachusetts	1,125
46	Palm Beach County, Florida	New York County, New York	1,047
49	Palm Beach County, Florida	Bronx County, New York	1,030
66	Palm Beach County, Florida	Fairfield County, Connecticut	825
70	Palm Beach County, Florida	Hartford County, Connecticut	794
72	Palm Beach County, Florida	Rockland County, New York	786
74	Palm Beach County, Florida	Cook County, Illinois	763
76	Palm Beach County, Florida	Monmouth County, New Jersey	753
(Tie) 80	Palm Beach County, Florida	Essex County, New Jersey	720
90	Palm Beach County, Florida	Montgomery County, Pennsylvania	689
2	Broward County, Florida	Queens County, New York	4,860
5	Broward County, Florida	Kings County, New York	3,392
7	Broward County, Florida	Nassau County, New York	2,859
25	Broward County, Florida	Suffolk County, New York	1,407
34	Broward County, Florida	Cook County, Illinois	1,182
36	Broward County, Florida	Westchester County, New York	1,168
42	Broward County, Florida	Bronx County, New York	1,136
47	Broward County, Florida	Bergen County, New Jersey	1,035
(Tie) 80	Broward County, Florida	Essex County, New Jersey	720
92	Broward County, Florida	New Haven County, Connecticut	679
100	Broward County, Florida	Philadelphia County, Pennsylvania	640
10	Dade County, Florida	Queens County, New York	2,348
12	Dade County, Florida	Hudson County, New Jersey	2,022
19	Dade County, Florida	Kings County, New York	1,599
26	Dade County, Florida	Los Angeles County, California	1,404
30	Dade County, Florida	New York County, New York	1,318
68	Dade County, Florida	Cook County, Illinois	798
69	Dade County, Florida	Union County, New Jersey	795
22	Pinellas County, Florida	Cook County, Illinois	1,478
61	Pinellas County, Florida	Wayne County, Michigan	867
84	Pinellas County, Florida	Suffolk County, New York	710
93	Pinellas County, Florida	Queens County, New York	672
94	Pinellas County, Florida	Nassau County, New York	662
35	Pasco County, Florida	Nassau County, New York	1,180
50	Pasco County, Florida	Suffolk County, New York	1,014
51	Pasco County, Florida	Cook County, Illinois	985
52	Pasco County, Florida	Queens County, New York	984
71	Hernando County, Florida	Nassau County, New York	787
77	Hernando County, Florida	Cook County, Illinois	733
98	Hernando County, Florida	Suffolk County, New York	648
56	Sarasota County, Florida	Cook County, Illinois	928
59	Lee County, Florida	Cook County, Illinois	885
97	St. Lucie County, Florida	Suffolk County, New York	649
New Jersey			
17	Ocean County, New Jersey	Kings County, New York	1,686
53	Ocean County, New Jersey	Queens County, New York	982
(Tie) 87	Ocean County, New Jersey	Nassau County, New York	694
91	Ocean County, New Jersey	Richmond County, New York	687
(Tie) 31	Monmouth County, New Jersey	Kings County, New York	1,239
85	Monmouth County, New Jersey	Queens County, New York	707
41	Middlesex County, New Jersey	Queens County, New York	1,140
48	Middlesex County, New Jersey	Kings County, New York	1,034
(Tie) 31	Camden County, New Jersey	Philadelphia County, Pennsylvania	1,239

Rank	Destination County & State	Origin County & State	# of Migrants
44	Cape May and Salem counties, New Jersey	Philadelphia County, Pennsylvania	1,074
86	Burlington County, New Jersey	Philadelphia County, Pennsylvania	703
Arizona			
6	Maricopa County, Arizona	Cook County, Illinois	3,024
8	Maricopa County, Arizona	Los Angeles County, California	2,815
39	Maricopa County, Arizona	Orange County, California	1,152
57	Maricopa County, Arizona	Denver County, Colorado	898
62	Maricopa County, Arizona	Hennepin County, Minnesota	854
75	Maricopa County, Arizona	Oakland County, Michigan	760
20	La Paz and Mohave counties, Arizona	Los Angeles County, California	1,545
55	La Paz and Mohave counties, Arizona	Orange County, California	935
79	La Paz and Mohave counties, Arizona	San Diego County, California	722
40	Coconino and Yavapai counties, Arizona	Los Angeles County, California	1,148
54	Pima County, Arizona	Los Angeles County, California	948
Nevada			
1	Clark County, Nevada	Los Angeles County, California	7,519
14	Clark County, Nevada	Orange County, California	1,778
33	Clark County, Nevada	Cook County, Illinois	1,229
58	Clark County, Nevada	San Bernardino County, California	892
15	Douglas, Lyon, Storey and Washoe counties, Nevada	Los Angeles County, California	1,718
82	Douglas, Lyon, Storey and Washoe counties, Nevada	Santa Clara County, California	717
California			
27	Los Angeles County, California	Cook County, Illinois	1,399
67	Los Angeles County, California	Harris County, Texas	810
73	San Diego County, California	Cook County, Illinois	780
83	San Diego County, California	Maricopa County, Arizona	716
95	Riverside County, California	Cook County, Illinois	659
Oregon			
(Tie) 28	Coos, Curry, Douglas and Josephine counties, Oregon	Los Angeles County, California	1,356
65	Lane County, Oregon	Los Angeles County, California	836
78	Jackson County, Oregon	Los Angeles County, California	731
Maryland			
13	Prince Georges County, Maryland	District of Columbia	1,911
18	Montgomery County, Maryland	District of Columbia	1,602
New Hampshire			
23	Rockingham County, New Hampshire	Essex County, Massachusetts	1,459
45	Hillsborough County, New Hampshire	Middlesex County, Massachusetts	1,062
Minnesota			
60	Ramsey County, Minnesota	Cloud, Ellsworth, Jewell, Lincoln, Mitchell, Ottawa, Republic, Saline and Washington counties, Kansas	883
89	Ramsey County, Minnesota	Clark, Finney, Ford, Grant, Gray, Greeley, Hamilton, Haskell, Hodgeman, Kearny, Lane, Meade, Morton, Ness, Scott, Seward, Stanton, Stevens and Wichita counties, Kansas	693
Indiana			
16	Lake County, Indiana	Cook County, Illinois	1,690
64	Clark and Floyd counties, Indiana	Jefferson County, Kentucky	838
Washington			
(Tie) 28	King County, Washington	Los Angeles County, California	1,356
Mississippi			
37	Coahoma, De Soto, Panola, Quitman, Tallahatchie, Tate and Tunica counties, Mississippi	Shelby County, Tennessee	1,167
Kansas			
38	Johnson County, Kansas	Jackson County, Missouri	1,157
Connecticut			
63	Fairfield County, Connecticut	Westchester County, New York	848
Missouri			
(Tie) 87	Jackson County, Missouri	Johnson County, Kansas	694
Massachusetts			
96	Suffolk County, Massachusetts	Hancock, Penobscot and Piscataquis counties, Maine	656
District of Columbia			
99	D.C.	Prince Georges County, Maryland	643

surplus of older migrants (when out-migrants are subtracted from in-migrants) than any other county in the United States, more than 38,000. It should not be surprising, therefore, to find that Palm Beach County receives the largest number of large migration streams from out-of-state counties, 16 in all. It receives more large streams than any single county sends.

The larger streams to Palm Beach County approach almost entirely from the Northeast, predominately from New York City and its suburban counties. The states of New Jersey (Bergen, Monmouth and Essex counties), Pennsylvania (Montgomery County), Connecticut (Fairfield and Hartford counties) and Massachusetts (Middlesex County) also send streams to Palm Beach County. The only stream from outside this five-state area comes from Cook County, IL, and it is one of the smaller of these large streams.

After Palm Beach County comes Broward County (11), Dade County (7), Pinellas County (5), Pasco County (4), Hernando County (3), Sarasota County (1), Lee County (1) and St. Lucie County (1).

Broward County, FL, receives fewer large streams than Palm Beach County, but the regional profile of streams is very similar. Large streams come from New York City and its suburban counties and counties in three adjacent states: Bergen and Essex counties, NJ; Philadelphia County, PA; and New Haven County, CT. Again, the only stream from outside the region is from Cook County, IL.

Dade County, FL, has a much more complex population mix than Broward or Palm Beach counties. Miami has a considerably larger central city than Fort Lauderdale or West Palm Beach. It attracts large migration streams from New York City, from Hudson and Union counties, NJ, and from Cook County, IL. But it picks up an additional stream from a third part of the nation — Los Angeles County. Between 1985 and 1990, 1,404 older migrants moved from Los Angeles to Miami.

In Florida, there is a widely held belief that the Atlantic Coast attracts migrants primarily from the Middle Atlantic and New England states, and that the Gulf Coast attracts migrants primarily from the East and West North Central states. There is a reason for these expectations. Interstate 75, the concrete ribbon that moves down the west coast of Florida, from Tampa southward, also connects Tampa to the Midwest. Interstate 95, the thoroughfare that follows the east coast of Florida from Jacksonville to Miami, connects Florida to New York.

An analysis of the major streams in Table 3 suggests that this popular myth is in need of revision. It is true that Florida's east coast is overwhelmingly supplied by counties in the Middle Atlantic and New England regions. Out of 35 total streams to the east coast of Florida, 31 are from the Middle Atlantic or New England, three are from the East North Central region and one is from California. But out of 14 total streams to the west coast of Florida, eight are from the Middle Atlantic or New England and six are from the East North Central region. If these large streams are indicative of total retirement migration, and they should be, Florida's Gulf Coast depends at least as heavily on the Middle Atlantic and New England for its retirees as it does on the East and West North Central regions.

It is sometimes said that Florida is like a test tube; it fills from the bottom up. From World War II through the 1960s, Miami Beach and the rest of Dade County were the major focus of elderly migration. The area's major rival was St. Petersburg on the Gulf Coast. In the 1970s, Miami changed, as it became the "Capital of the Caribbean." Many large American companies set up Latin American division headquarters in Coral Gables during this period, and Spanish came to be Miami's second language. Retirement migration became Miami's second engine for economic growth.[13]

During this period, housing construction around Fort Lauderdale, north of Miami, accelerated and Broward County rapidly became South Florida's leading retirement destination.[14] During the 1980s, a second shift seems to have occurred. Broward County continued to expand its retirement housing market, although its rate of growth slowed. Palm Beach County, to its north, overtook it as the most rapidly growing retirement destination during this period. Some in Florida expect this trend to continue in the future as Palm Beach becomes more crowded than retirees prefer. When this happens, counties just to the north may begin to rapidly expand, continuing the growth up the Atlantic Coast.

The leading recipient of large migration streams on the Gulf is still Pinellas County (5), which includes St. Petersburg. The second leading destination is Pasco County (4), the county immediately north of St. Petersburg and Tampa that has developed almost entirely as a retirement destination with only small towns. Hernando County, just north of Pasco, rapidly expanded during the 1980s. The "test tube" continues to fill. Sarasota and Lee counties, south of Tampa but not adjacent to it, received one large migration stream each during the period.

New Jersey — The coastal counties of Monmouth, Ocean, Atlantic and Cape May, and the Delaware Bay counties of Cumberland and Salem, have provided summer resorts to the New York and Philadelphia populations for most of this century and have developed substantial retirement industries as a result. These retirement counties are not well known nationally. When New Jersey is mentioned as a regional retirement state outside of New York and Pennsylvania, eyebrows usually rise.

New Jersey counties receive 11 large retirement migration streams. The leader is Ocean County (4), as one would expect, followed by Monmouth County (2), Middlesex County (2), Camden County (1), Burlington County (1) and the county group of Cape May and Salem counties (1).

As reported in Table 3, New Jersey receives migration streams from only the adjacent states of New York and Pennsylvania. It is clearly a regional destination. Furthermore, it attracts large streams of retirees from only two areas, New York City and its suburbs and Philadelphia. These two areas, however, send their streams to different parts of the state. Ocean County receives streams from three of the five New York City counties (Kings, Queens and Richmond), and from Nassau County. Only Manhattan (New York County) and the Bronx (Bronx County) fail to contribute as many as 640 migrants to Ocean County. Manhattan retirees prefer Dade and Palm Beach counties,

FL. Bronx retirees tend to choose Palm Beach and Broward counties, FL.

Streams also attach the New York City counties to northern New Jersey: Middlesex County and Monmouth County attract from Kings and Queens counties. Camden and Burlington counties are across the state line from Philadelphia and they receive streams of migrants from Philadelphia. The county group including the coastal counties of Cape May and Salem also receives a stream of retirees from Philadelphia.

Do migration destination counties in the same state recruit from different areas? The evidence for differential recruitment is weaker in Florida than it is in New Jersey. New York City and Philadelphia divide up the New Jersey territory, addressing their major migrant streams differently.

Another stream pattern is now evident. It involves a move across state lines away from a large city, but not very far away. The moves from Philadelphia to Camden and Burlington counties in New Jersey are examples of this pattern, as are the moves from New York City to the northern New Jersey counties. This is a pattern common in regional retirement centers, a search for the best of both worlds.

Arizona — The destination state most like Florida in its appeal to retirees, although much smaller in population, is the desert state of Arizona. Four counties or county groups attract large streams, but Maricopa County, which includes Phoenix, Tempe, Arizona State University, Mesa, Scottsdale and Sun City, is in a class by itself, attracting six of the 11 large out-of-state streams. The county group composed of La Paz and Mohave counties, which borders the western side of the state, near California and southern Nevada, receives three large streams. Hoover Dam and Lake Mead stand between Mohave County and Las Vegas, a few miles away. Lake Havasu City is located in southern Mohave County. There are two remaining streams. One enters Coconino and Yavapai counties, a county group north of Maricopa, and the other enters Pima County, south of Maricopa, which includes Tucson and the University of Arizona.

Maricopa County shares with Dade County, FL, an attachment to large migration streams from several distant states. Its largest streams come from major cities such as Chicago, Los Angeles, Denver, Minneapolis and Detroit, and their suburbs. No streams are from New England or the Middle Atlantic states. The western county group containing La Paz and Mohave counties, on the California border, attracts streams from three Southern California counties: Los Angeles County, Orange County and San Diego County. Only Los Angeles County sends major streams to the two other Arizona areas that appear in Table 3. Southern California is to Arizona what New York is to Florida.

Nevada — Six large migration streams enter Nevada from counties in other states. Four arrive in Clark County, which contains Las Vegas. Two enter a county group that includes Douglas, Lyon, Storey and Washoe counties and Carson City, an independent city. Douglas and Washoe border Lake Tahoe, and Reno is located in Washoe County.

Five of the six large migration streams entering Nevada are from California. One stream is from Chicago, to Clark County. Los Angeles and its neighbors clearly dominate the Nevada streams. Migration streams arrive in Clark County from three Southern California counties: Los Angeles, Orange and San Bernardino counties. Streams from Los Angeles County and Santa Clara County enter the county group consisting of Douglas, Lyon, Storey and Washoe counties and Carson City.

California — The state receives five large streams, all into Southern California. Two enter Los Angeles County, two enter San Diego County and one enters Riverside County, where Palm Springs is located.

Los Angeles receives large streams from Chicago and Houston. San Diego receives large streams from Chicago and Phoenix, and Riverside County receives a large stream from Chicago. Once again, Chicago retirees move in large streams to the leading retirement destinations in Florida, Arizona and California. They seem ubiquitous. No large migration streams reach California counties from New England or the Middle Atlantic states.

Oregon — Three large streams flow into Oregon. Two receiving areas border California: the county group consisting of Coos, Curry, Douglas and Josephine counties; and the adjacent Jackson County. The third receiving area is Lane County, which includes the city of Eugene and the University of Oregon. All three large streams are from Los Angeles County.

All of the states mentioned thus far are established retirement migration destinations. There are a number of other states, which are rarely thought of as retirement destinations, that receive one or two large streams of older migrants.

Maryland — Two large streams enter Maryland. One goes to Montgomery County, north of Washington, DC, and the other enters Prince Georges County, east of Washington, DC. Both streams come from Washington, DC.

New Hampshire — Two New Hampshire counties receive large streams of older migrants. One is Rockingham County, which includes the state's only stretch of Atlantic Coast and the city of Portsmouth. The other is Hillsborough County, which sits on the Massachusetts state border. Both streams to New Hampshire come from metropolitan suburbs of Boston.

Minnesota — The only county in Minnesota to receive a large stream of retired migrants receives two of them. It is Ramsey County, and contains St. Paul, the state's capital city. The two county groups from north-central and southwestern Kansas, described in an earlier section of this chapter, send their large streams of retirees to Ramsey County. Other than the migration streams from Los Angeles County to western Nevada, Oregon and Washington, these two Minnesota streams are the only ones that move northward. They are, in other words, the only streams outside the Sun Belt region that move northward to a non-contiguous state.

Indiana — Two areas in Indiana receive streams of older migrants. Lake County is located near the Illinois line in the northwestern corner of the state. The other receiving area, located on the Kentucky border, contains Clark and Floyd counties.

Indiana is not a regional retirement center. The pattern that was noted in New Jersey, whereby Philadelphia migrants formed large streams to Camden and Burlington counties across the state line, is repeated in Indiana. Cook County residents form a major stream into Lake County, IN, just across the state line. And in the south, Louisville residents move across the state line into a county group including Clark and Floyd counties.

Madame Francoise Cribier, a French geographer, described the pattern of workers moving from the provinces surrounding Paris to the big city to work, and after retirement returning to their home provinces. Some migration out of large cities to surrounding counties may represent this type of migration. On the other hand, as noted in the discussion of New Jersey, such migration patterns could also represent the principle of moving to a place where a more relaxed small-town lifestyle is possible, but not far from the city and its commercial, medical and cultural opportunities. These two forms of migration may be artificially differentiated, for there are no doubt many migrants who could check both boxes.

The remaining seven receiving areas are each located in different states and the District of Columbia. Each receives one migration stream from another state. King County, WA, includes the city of Seattle and receives a stream from Los Angeles. In northwest Mississippi, there is a county group containing Coahoma, De Soto, Panola, Quitman, Tallahatchie, Tate and Tunica counties. It borders the Tennessee line and receives migrants from Shelby County, TN, which includes Memphis, in a repeat of the pattern noted above.

Fairfield County, CT, borders suburban New York City and receives its stream from that area. The stream may include suburban New Yorkers who, in retirement, are finally becoming the exurbanites that they wanted to be while they were working. Some, no doubt, are returning to hometowns where they had lived before moving to New York earlier in their lives.

Johnson County, KS, includes suburban Kansas City. Jackson County, MO, includes the Missouri part of Kansas City and the city of Independence. These two neighboring counties exchange streams.

Kansas City provides a wonderful example of the kinds of exchanges that are likely to happen when a city straddles a state line. In Kansas City, State Line Road separates Kansas from Missouri. A simple relocation in the city, not necessarily to an address any greater distance from shopping, medical care or church, may be recorded as an interstate move and makes one a migrant. Some of the migrants in this stream are making genuine retirement moves. It would not be possible, however, to separate the real migrants from the local movers using census microdata.

Suffolk County, MA, includes the city of Boston and receives a stream from a county group composed of Hancock, Penobscot and Piscataquis counties, ME. This large stream moves in the right direction, southward, but retirement migration is usually away from large cities, not into them. It is possible that this stream includes in it many retired Bostonians who, in their advancing years, can no longer cope with Maine winters and are returning home. There is no way directly to uncover motivations when using census data. Boston, however, seems an unlikely place to end the trip. It is not well known as a regional retirement destination. There does exist a minority of retirees who move from non-metropolitan to metropolitan locations.[15] Perhaps they are concentrated in this stream.

Finally, the nation's capital receives a stream from Prince Georges County, MD, its suburban neighbor.

The areas that receive several migration streams from other states are obvious and expected retirement destinations. Those that receive very few streams are much less typical. Rarely are they located in Sun Belt states, and often they include either several sparsely populated counties or a large city.

The Weird and the Wonderful

Generalizations derived from examining the large retirement migration streams in the United States do not seem so surprising upon reflection. Why should most of the streams not originate in the large cities and their suburban counties? Persons retiring in these environments have often had greater economic opportunities than small-town residents. It is for economic opportunities, perhaps, that migration early in life tends to move from smaller to larger population centers.[16] Those who never leave their hometowns are less likely to have conquered the uncertainties that moving involves in the first place, and certainly are less likely to move when they retire.[17]

In this context, it is understandable that small-town Kansans in the prairie counties near Colorado and Oklahoma would want to escape the cold fronts that pour down the Great Plains from Canada in the wintertime, chilling the bones, slicking the pavement and covering the sidewalks. What would motivate them to create a large retirement stream from this setting to St. Paul, MN? Did they go to St. Paul to attend a performance of Garrison Keeler's "A Prairie Home Companion" never to return to the prairie? Is there an ethnic dimension to their migration? Do they include large numbers of Scandinavian-Americans seeking a more hospitable cultural climate in Minnesota? Without this or some other explanation, their move would seem to be in the wrong geographical direction. It certainly seems counter-intuitive, considering the dominance of the Sun Belt migration pattern.

• • • • • • • • • •

Chapter 6 will ponder a special type of retirement migration, one referred to by gerontological demographers and others as "return migration."

CHAPTER SIX
SPECIAL TYPES: RETURNING TO ONE'S HOME STATE

Introduction

"Carry me back to old Virginny,
There's where the cotton and the corn and taters grow....
No place on earth do I love more sincerely
Than old Virginny, the state where I was born."
– James A. Bland

The familiar words of this old song speak of the nostalgia which was once thought to be strong among retired people, motivating much of their interstate migration. Return migration — moving back to one's state of birth — was thus assumed to be substantial. But retirement migration on the whole, as seen in Chapters 2 and 3, may be better described by tunes such as "Moon Over Miami," "Do You Know the Way to San Jose," and "By the Time I Get to Phoenix." Older migrants, collectively, seem attracted to states not only with a pleasant winter climate but also with a relatively large tourism industry.

How common among older migrants is returning to one's state of birth? Do some states attract back more of their native sons and daughters than other states, and if so, are there regional preferences? Is regional attractiveness compounded by an ethnic connection? Finally, are there different types of return migration? These are some of the questions addressed in this chapter.

How Common is Returning to One's State of Birth?

What is currently known about the return migration of retirees is found in the writings of a handful of researchers over the past two decades. The earliest of these was Professor William Serow from Florida State University, who discovered in 1978 that 20 percent of all interstate migrants are returning to their state of birth.[1] This observation holds for both the older and the general populations, so retirees are not more likely than younger people to move to their state of birth. Furthermore, Serow argues, because there are fewer older people available to move anywhere, and because they are less likely to move in any case than younger people, older return migrants are in a small minority among the total pool of persons moving to their state of birth. This finding squashed the old myths that retirees are much more likely to be going home, and that most people returning home are retirees. People of retirement age clearly do not dominate return migration in either sense. Serow's primary measure of return migration was derived by dividing the number of return migrants by the total number of migrants entering each state (RM/TM).

In 1979, Longino responded that when seeking to determine the rate at which retirees return home, one should not base the rate on the total retiree migrant population, but rather on those who are living outside their state of birth when the migration decision is made.[2] It is not reasonable to include those living in their state of birth when they decide to move; they could not be return migrants because they are not "at risk" of becoming return migrants. When the proportion was recalculated using Longino's return migration quotient (RMQ), for the same census period, the proportion of return migrants rose from one-fifth to one-third. That is a sizeable proportion.

Finally, Professor Andrei Rogers, from Colorado University, chastised both previous researchers for studying "snapshots" frozen at the time of the census, and not considering return migration as a dynamic process that changes over time.[3] When he looked at return migration over several decades and made projections into the future, Rogers' research concluded that retirees tended to return to their states of birth at lower rates than younger migrants and that the gap is growing, demonstrating once again that retirees do not have a corner on the return migration market.

By the time of the 1990 Census, no serious researchers expected return migration to dominate the retirement migration picture. In fact, return migration as a percentage of total migration is on the decline. Serow had shown, using 1970 data, that 20.3 percent of older migrants were returning to their state of birth. The 1980 figure was 18.6 percent. In 1990 the comparable figure declined further to 17.5 percent.

Does this picture of declining return migration hold also when retirees moving out of their home states (and therefore not at risk of being return migrants) are excluded from the formula? In 1970, 33.3 percent of the remaining migrants were returning home. In 1990 the proportion had declined to 25.5 percent. It is not possible to directly estimate the percentage for 1980, but it is reasonable to assume that it was somewhere between the 1970 and 1990 figures. As Rogers would surely remind us, return migration is a dynamic process, changing over time.

Do Return Migrants Have Regional Preferences?

All of the reports of older return migrants noted above have found that some states and regions are more popular to return migrants than others. Using Serow's RM/TM and Longino's RMQ, two measures of return migration, the 1990 comparisons of states and regions are provided in Table 1.

As noted at the bottom of the RMQ column, 25.5 percent of the national interstate migrating older population residing outside their state of birth in 1985 returned by 1990. Therefore, that percentage was chosen as the break point between a high incidence and a low incidence of return migration to states. State-to-state variation is substantial, with West Virginia attracting back nearly two-thirds (64.4 percent) of its potential return migrants, while Nevada, Arizona, Florida and Alaska attracted less than 4 percent of their potential

Table 1— Volume and Rate of Return Migration, Plus Net Migration, Migrants Age 60+, 1985-1990

State or Region	Return Migrants	Total In-migrants	RM/TM	RMQ	Net Migrants
Maine	2,938	11,929	24.6	35.1	1,395
New Hampshire	1,814	15,058	12.0	21.8	2,273
Vermont	1,103	5,916	18.6	27.1	469
Massachusetts	8,128	23,796	34.2	42.8	-32,941
Rhode Island	1,468	5,842	25.1	34.5	-3,447
Connecticut	2,999	17,351	17.3	25.4	-24,821
New England	**18,450**	**79,892**	**23.1**	**33.0**	**-57,072**
New York	17,328	42,802	40.5	48.6	-179,979
New Jersey	6,659	49,176	13.5	23.4	-57,380
Pennsylvania	24,101	57,538	41.9	55.6	-21,365
Middle Atlantic	**48,088**	**149,516**	**32.2**	**44.7**	**-258,724**
Ohio	16,215	44,459	36.5	48.3	-29,812
Indiana	10,907	31,405	34.7	47.3	-7,021
Illinois	14,646	36,897	39.7	50.1	-70,239
Michigan	10,349	31,885	32.5	42.1	-42,776
Wisconsin	7,589	23,030	33.0	47.8	-8,145
East North Central	**59,706**	**167,676**	**35.6**	**47.3**	**-157,993**
Minnesota	6,974	19,370	36.0	46.1	-4,588
Iowa	5,953	11,669	51.0	62.7	-9,293
Missouri	11,471	35,251	32.5	42.9	737
North Dakota	1,190	3,140	37.9	53.8	-1,180
South Dakota	1,596	4,141	38.5	54.1	-1,103
Nebraska	3,745	9,852	38.0	47.2	-942
Kansas	5,355	16,492	32.5	42.3	-7,152
West North Central	**36,284**	**99,915**	**36.3**	**47.0**	**-23,521**
District of Columbia	581	4,821	12.1	15.3	-5,467
Delaware	676	8,026	8.4	14.7	1,681
Maryland	4,342	32,428	13.4	18.3	-8,905
Virginia	9,159	46,554	19.7	26.8	3,859
West Virginia	6,631	12,919	51.3	64.4	-17
North Carolina	15,474	64,530	24.0	33.0	38,094
South Carolina	6,411	34,251	18.7	27.1	18,236
Georgia	10,853	44,475	24.4	33.8	16,000
Florida	5,826	451,709	1.3	2.5	323,148
South Atlantic	**59,953**	**699,713**	**8.6**	**14.4**	**386,629**
Kentucky	10,273	21,770	47.2	58.2	1,326
Tennessee	11,055	36,306	30.4	42.2	10,173
Alabama	10,215	25,336	40.3	50.5	5,765
Mississippi	7,908	17,637	44.8	57.4	4,484
East South Central	**39,451**	**101,049**	**39.0**	**50.7**	**21,748**
Arkansas	7,551	29,848	25.3	35.8	11,394
Louisiana	4,728	14,004	33.8	45.6	-7,433
Oklahoma	9,573	23,572	40.6	51.0	2,498
Texas	16,602	78,117	21.3	29.7	8,261
West South Central	**38,454**	**145,541**	**26.4**	**36.2**	**14,720**
Montana	1,184	6,140	19.3	25.4	-1,086
Idaho	1,592	10,832	14.7	18.6	627
Wyoming	766	4,207	18.2	23.2	-2,284
Colorado	3,393	30,672	11.1	15.0	1,857
New Mexico	1,482	19,872	7.5	9.9	5,174
Arizona	1,383	98,756	1.4	2.1	60,476
Utah	3,130	10,751	29.1	36.3	2,603
Nevada	436	43,131	1.0	1.3	26,938
Mountain	**13,366**	**224,361**	**6.0**	**8.3**	**94,305**
Washington	5,598	47,484	11.8	14.6	18,139
Oregon	3,804	43,996	8.6	10.7	21,219
California	9,152	131,514	7.0	9.6	-55,726
Alaska	60	2,395	2.5	3.3	-3,442
Hawaii	870	8,053	10.8	14.5	-282
Pacific	**19,484**	**233,442**	**8.3**	**11.0**	**-20,092**
United States	**333,236**	**1,901,105**	**17.5**	**25.5**	

return migrants. Figure 1 illustrates state variation in attraction of older return migrants from 1985-1990.

At the bottom of the RM/TM column, we find that 17.5 percent of all older in-migrants returned to their state of birth between 1985 and 1990. As with the RMQ, the RM/TM varies widely from state to state. Return migrants as a percentage of all older in-migrants ranged from about 51 percent in West Virginia and Iowa to about 1 percent in Nevada, Florida and Arizona.

There are many ways to make sense of these and related measures. Perhaps the most straightforward way is to compare states that do well at attracting migrants, and those that do well at attracting return migrants. The two populations are not the same. It is quite possible to do well with one group but not the other.

As a measure of overall attractiveness to older migrants, net migration will be used. This measure, derived by subtracting out-migrants from in-migrants for the period from 1985 to 1990, has two advantages. First, it cuts the list of states in half because almost as many states have a net gain as have a net loss. Second, it does not penalize small states that cannot compete in absolute numbers with the large destination states, but nonetheless could have a strong net surplus. The reader may wish to refer to Table 4 in Chapter 2 for the ranking on this measure, although the net numbers are shown here in Table 1.

As a measure of return migration by older migrants, the RMQ is used. States are divided into two categories, above- or below-average RMQ.

A few states fall near the middle of the distribution on both of these measures, reducing confidence in their placement. The placement of states with only a tiny handful of surplus migrants should be given less weight also because the return migrants could be accounting for the net surplus. Most states, however, are clearly above or below the mean on each measure.

The purpose of this exercise is not to examine individual states but to ask if there is a regional pattern in the nation, some regions favoring return migration more than others. Figure 2 illustrates the national picture.

States attracting migrants in gen-

Figure 1 — State Variation in Attraction of Return Migrants Age 60+, 1985-1990

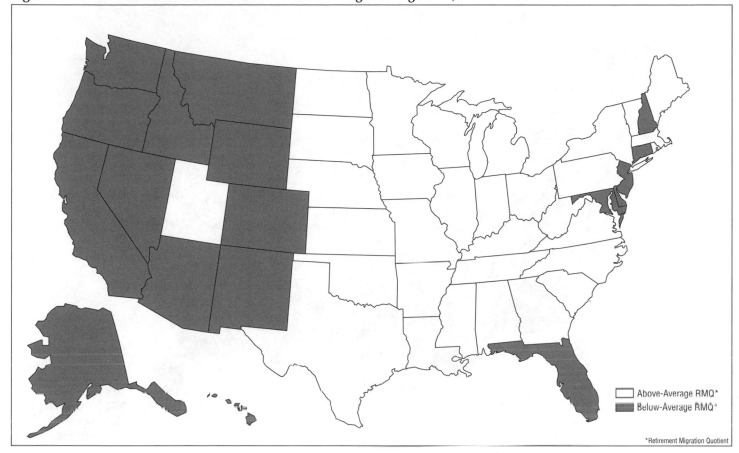

Above-Average RMQ*
Below-Average RMQ^

*Retirement Migration Quotient

eral and return migrants too — Many states that are popular destinations for older interstate migrants in general also tend to attract a high percentage of return migrants. States with a positive net migration and an above-average RMQ are: North Carolina, South Carolina, Georgia, Arkansas, Tennessee, Texas, Oklahoma, Alabama, Mississippi, Virginia, Kentucky, Maine, Vermont, Missouri and Utah.

Return migrants tend to flow more freely into those states that once flew the Stars and Bars above their statehouses. The East South Central division, in particular, attracts a high proportion of return migrants.

About half of the states in this category offer warmer climates and salt water. Most have a strong geographical identity. Utah has a unique religious history. The Deep South and New England are historically rural states with strong cultural bases where roots go deep . In many of these states there is a cost-of-living advantage for migrants, as well. Although the cost of living differential is attractive in the short run, there are no doubt other hidden advantages. Returning to a state that has maintained a relatively strong regional identity and rural cultural base may be an emotionally comfortable experience for many of those born in the South between the two World Wars. It is obvious at a glance, however, that some of the leading retirement destination states are not on this list.

States attracting migrants in general, but not attracting return migrants — Some states do a better job at drawing migrants in general than their native sons and daughters. This is reflected in a positive net migration, but

a lower than average RMQ. Several of these states have been mentioned repeatedly as leading retirement destinations. Florida has dominated retirement migration for four decades, but from 1985-1990 it did not do well in attracting back older native Floridians who were on the move. Arizona, Nevada, Oregon and Washington receive much of California's retirement out-migration. They are also prominent on lists of attractive destination states, but lower than average numbers of return migrants moved to these states in the last migration period. The mountain states of New Mexico, Colorado and Idaho also fall into this category, as do New Hampshire and Delaware. They are attractive to outsiders, but not necessarily to migrants who were born there.

States not attracting migrants in general, but still attracting return migrants — Some states have a negative net migration though they attract more than the national average percentage of return migrants. The states are: Massachusetts, Rhode Island, New York, Pennsylvania, West Virginia, Ohio, Indiana, Illinois, Michigan, Wisconsin, Minnesota, Iowa, North Dakota, South Dakota, Nebraska, Kansas and Louisiana. Most of these states have a colder climate that may help to motivate out-migration to the Sun Belt. One point seems clear from Figure 2: It is not climate that primarily motivates migrants to return to their states of birth. Many Northern states seem to do about as well as Southern states.

States attracting neither migrants in general nor return migrants — Some states have a negative net migration and attract less than the national average percentage of

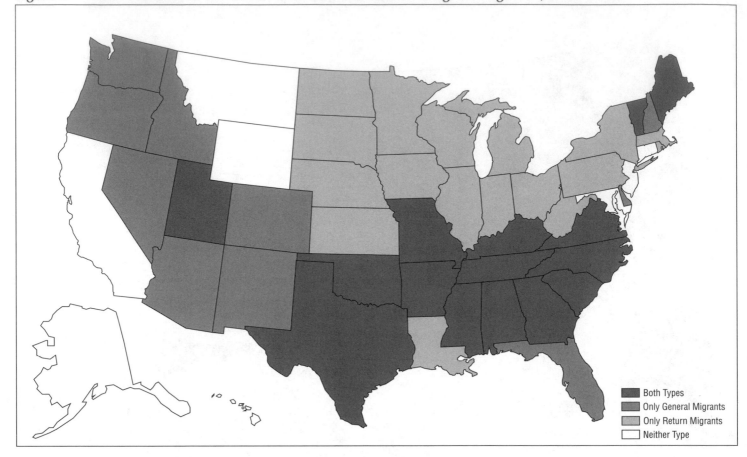

Both Types
Only General Migrants
Only Return Migrants
Neither Type

return migrants. These states are: Connecticut, New Jersey, Maryland, Montana, Wyoming, California, Alaska and Hawaii, plus the District of Columbia. The mountain states and New Jersey are only marginally low in attracting return migrants. It is California and the distant states of Alaska and Hawaii that epitomize this final type.

Do return migrants have regional preferences? Apparently they do. However, return migrants are not automatically attracted back to the states that are the most attractive to other interstate retirees. The states that attract them back are found in and outside the Sun Belt. They have positive and negative net migration patterns. The dimensions that may underlie this regional preference pattern will be discussed later in this chapter.

Do States Change Over Time in Their Attractiveness to Return Migrants?

States seem to change gradually in their ability to attract older interstate migrants. Is this pattern also evident with regard to return migrants? The RMQ was first used with data from the 1965-1970 migration period. It was not used again until the recent 1985-1990 period. Changes over the twenty-year period, between 1970 and 1990, are displayed in Table 2. It should be noted that the census microdata was a 1 percent sample of census records in 1970, and a 5 percent sample in 1990.

State change is inevitable when retirement return migration declined from one-third to one-quarter between 1970 and 1990 for the nation as a whole. One would expect all

states to lose their hold on return migrants. This did not happen. The RMQ actually increased in more than half (28) of the states. Change, therefore, was dramatic.

Furthermore, there are regional shifts in return migration. In the East North Central, West North Central and East South Central regions, all states increased their intake of potential return migrants. Four of six states in the New England region increased their RMQ. In the Middle Atlantic region, New York and Pennsylvania increased and New Jersey declined. Many of the states that send the most migrants to the Sun Belt have increased their RMQ.

In 1970 it could be said that the census divisions attracting the greatest share of their potential return migrants were found in the Sun Belt. The RMQ scores for New England and the two North Central regions in 1970 were between 22.8 percent and 29.4 percent. The South Atlantic and the two South Central divisions, by contrast, had RMQ scores between 36.6 percent and 50.6 percent. The Pacific division received more than half of its potential return migrants.

The picture had nearly reversed by 1990. The increase in return migration to the Northern states was paralleled by a decline in return migration in the South Atlantic, West South Central, Mountain and Pacific regions. The only exception to the trend was the East South Central region, where Kentucky, Tennessee, Alabama and Mississippi attracted more of their native sons and daughters on the move.

Decline in RMQ was precipitous for major receiving states. Florida fell from 81.2 percent to 2.5 percent. Arizona fell from 50 percent to 2.1 percent and Nevada dropped from

Table 2 — Return Migration, Migrants Age 60+, 1965-1970 and 1985-1990

State or Region	RMQ 1965-1970	RMQ 1985-1990
Maine	26.5	35.1
New Hampshire	42.9	21.8
Vermont	25.8	27.1
Massachusetts	26.4	42.8
Rhode Island	29.0	34.5
Connecticut	37.7	25.4
New England	**29.4**	**33.0**
New York	25.5	48.6
New Jersey	42.1	23.4
Pennsylvania	29.5	55.6
Middle Atlantic	**29.7**	**44.7**
Ohio	32.4	48.3
Indiana	26.1	47.3
Illinois	26.2	50.1
Michigan	28.9	42.1
Wisconsin	25.4	47.8
East North Central	**27.9**	**47.3**
Minnesota	22.5	46.1
Iowa	21.1	62.7
Missouri	29.4	42.9
North Dakota	18.2	53.8
South Dakota	14.8	54.1
Nebraska	21.6	47.2
Kansas	18.7	42.3
West North Central	**22.8**	**47.0**
District of Columbia	26.7	15.3
Delaware	57.1	14.7
Maryland	52.2	18.3
Virginia	45.8	26.8
West Virginia	33.6	64.4
North Carolina	54.0	33.0
South Carolina	56.3	27.1
Georgia	48.8	33.8
Florida	81.2	2.5
South Atlantic	**50.6**	**14.4**
Kentucky	29.0	58.2
Tennessee	38.0	42.2
Alabama	42.0	50.5
Mississippi	41.9	57.4
East South Central	**36.6**	**50.7**
Arkansas	36.4	35.8
Louisiana	52.4	45.6
Oklahoma	33.6	51.0
Texas	51.5	29.7
West South Central	**43.0**	**36.2**
Montana	22.2	25.4
Idaho	10.7	18.6
Wyoming	0.0	23.2
Colorado	23.2	15.0
New Mexico	19.0	9.9
Arizona	50.0	2.1
Utah	51.5	36.3
Nevada	50.0	1.3
Mountain	**25.9**	**8.3**
Washington	57.9	14.6
Oregon	56.3	10.7
California	54.7	9.6
Alaska	0.0	3.3
Hawaii	100.0	14.5
Pacific	**55.7**	**11.0**
United States	**33.3**	**25.5**

50 percent to 1.3 percent. California, which shifted from a receiving to a major sending state over the past decade, declined dramatically as well, from 54.7 percent to 9.6 percent.

There are dynamic processes underlying changes in return migration over time. Some of these will be explored in this chapter.

Does Ethnic Enclave Settlement Explain Regional Differences in Return Migration?

It is clear that no single scheme can fully explain return migration. Nonetheless, there is a popular ethnic explanation for return to the South and Southwest that should be examined. It concerns the return migration of African Americans and Hispanics. Regional return migration, it is said, involves a historical work cycle. Industrial states recruit workers from rural parts of the country. Streams of workers continue to tie these sending and receiving states together. However, over time, return migration streams develop that carry some of the retired workers back to their states of birth. These return streams build in a delayed but roughly proportional response to the earlier stream development for work. Rogers insisted that return migration must be understood in the context of the complex rhythms of rising and falling stream migration throughout the life course. This pattern has been suggested with regard to African-American and Hispanic retirement migration.

Return migration among African Americans — After the turn of the century the stream of European immigrants began to ebb. The industrial labor force had grown dependent on European ethnics and now experienced acute shortages of unskilled labor. Migration streams of Southeastern African Americans grew as people moved to the Northern cities of Boston, Detroit, New York and Philadelphia.[4]

In the rural South, economic circumstances worsened for African Americans at the beginning of the century. Agricultural machines, low cotton prices and the boll weevil increased unemployment and poverty for rural African Americans. These stressful economic conditions were intensified in the 1930s by a worldwide economic depression. The volume of migration slowed, but African Americans continued to leave their rural Southern homes for urban destinations in the Northeastern and North Central cities of the nation, mainly because the metropolitan areas provided more relief programs for the poor.[5] In Texas and Oklahoma, the dust storms further aggravated bleak economic conditions. Thus many African Americans from the dust bowl states, joined by others from Louisiana and Arkansas, started a new migrant stream to California.[6]

These migration streams continued into the 1970s, with a net out-migration of Southern African Americans to Northern and Western cities. African Americans from the Southern coastal states migrated to cities and neighborhoods in the Northeast. Those in the East South Central region migrated toward the industrial cities of the East North Central region, particularly Chicago and Detroit. A significant migration stream from the Deep South moved westward to California.

Since 1960, however, there has been a migration turnaround in the South. African Americans who left the South and migrated northward and westward are now returning to the region.[7] This turnaround coincided with improving economic conditions in the South and a relative decline in Northern growth rates.[8] In 1950 the average family income of Southern families was only 78 percent of the national average. By 1980 the average Southern family income had climbed to 91 percent of the national average. The economic profiles of both African Americans and whites improved in the "New South." The civil rights movement — particularly civil rights legislation and affirmative action — significantly impacted the day-to-day lives of African Americans in the South, reducing the effect of racial discrimination in employment, education and political participation, especially in urbanized areas.[9] Relative racial tolerance and increased economic opportunities pulled many African Americans to the Southern states. This may explain the increased proportion of African Americans living in the South from 1980 to 1988, the first rise in this century.

In addition to family ties and past experience, a cost-of-living advantage is another reason that the South may be attractive to older African-American migrants.

African-American migration history and other reasons mentioned above lead us to three expectations: that interregional moves will be strong among African-American migrants of retirement age; that the South will be the primary recipient of regional migration streams of retired African Americans; and that return migration should be especially strong into the states of the Old South. In a study of African-American retirement migration, based on the 1980 Census, the author confirmed all three of these expectations.[10] Except for the South, the incidence of interstate moves within regions is relatively low. A majority of older blacks who make interstate moves are moving into Southern states. Using the return migration measure RM/TM, eight states have high concentrations of 50 percent or more return migrants among their older African-American in-migrants: West Virginia (67 percent), North Carolina (62 percent), South Carolina (85 percent), Georgia (70 percent), Alabama (71 percent), Mississippi (88 percent), Arkansas (76 percent) and Louisiana (64 percent). With the exception of West Virginia, all had been Confederate states.

African-American retirement migration to the South may decline in the future as the proportion of Southern-born African Americans living outside the South dwindles over time. Popular retirement destinations may increasingly attract African-American migrants in the future. Secondhand nostalgia may not be enough to motivate retiring African Americans who were born outside the South to return to their ancestral homes.

Return migration among Hispanics — When considering retirement migration among Hispanics, the starting point is not historical patterns of labor force migration, but simply the size and growth of this extraordinary subpopulation. Population growth itself provides a second dynamic process to return migration. Although Hispanics make up the second largest of the minority groups (just behind African Americans), they may either equal or outnumber African Americans by the year 2000 if the present rates of fertility and immigration continue.[11] Because of their high fertility rate, the Hispanic population is expected to grow much more rapidly than the American population in general. This expectation should hold doubly for the older population. A recent study by the Chairman of the House Select Committee on Aging includes Census Bureau projections that the rate of growth among older Hispanics will be 4.5 times as great as that of the entire aged population from 1987 to the year 2000.[12]

In 1980, 85 percent of all Hispanics resided in just nine states: California, Texas, New York, Florida, Illinois, New Jersey, New Mexico, Arizona and Colorado. Comparing these figures with those of the 1970 Census, the trend has been toward greater geographical concentration.[13]

This trend becomes clearer when regional comparisons are made for Hispanics as a whole and for the three largest subgroups: Mexicans, Puerto Ricans and Cubans. More than half of all Hispanics reside in the Southwest, with high concentrations in California and Texas. The Northeast is next, with high concentrations in New York and New Jersey, while Florida houses the next largest of the major regional concentrations. Although recent growth trends are beginning to alter the pattern of U.S. Hispanic concentrations, the three major Hispanic groups are presently concentrated in border states or in states that historically have served as major ports of entry into the United States. More specifically, Mexican Americans have been highly concentrated in Southern California and Texas.

Puerto Ricans, by contrast, have been disproportionately concentrated in New York and New Jersey since 1917, when they were granted citizenship. Only 6 percent of Puerto Ricans live inland, settling mainly in the Chicago area. Of the three Hispanic groups, Cubans, having emigrated from Cuba in successive waves from 1950 to 1980, remain the most highly concentrated of all Hispanic groups, residing mainly in Miami. The choice of Cubans to remain in South Florida may be explained by the comparable climate and geographical proximity to Cuba.

The social significance of this ethnic enclave phenomenon cannot be overstated. On the one hand, it provides the basic demographic framework for the maintenance of group cohesion and identity through the reinforcement of cultural values and ethnic norms. On the other hand, it serves to heighten the nation's awareness of Hispanics as an influential ethnic and political force. Whether one examines interstate migration or migration to the United States from abroad, the existing Hispanic enclaves should act as "ethnomagnets" drawing persons of similar ethnic subgroups together and forming a clearly defined migration system. One would expect, therefore, to find three distinct patterns of Hispanic retirement migration, one each for the Mexicans, Puerto Ricans and Cubans.

The geographical concentration of Hispanics is attractive to older migrants because it facilitates a comfortable and familiar lifestyle. Family members follow earlier family members. The draw of culture and family ties, therefore, shape clearly distinguishable regional migration patterns among the separate Hispanic subgroups.

In another study, using 1980 Census microdata, the author examined the retirement migration of the three Hispanic subpopulations, expecting to find significant amounts of return migration only among the older Mexican population due to its greater generational depth.[14] First, there were three distinct migration systems for the three Hispanic groups. Cubans tended to move to Florida, Puerto Ricans to New York and Mexicans to the Southwest states, as expected. Older Mexican migrants were the most likely of the three Hispanic groups to return to their state of birth. If all migrants born outside the United States could have been excluded from the data, the rate of return migration would have exceeded that of the population of older non-Hispanic migrants, owing to the small number of states between which Hispanics tend to move.

Because of the geographical enclaves of Hispanic Americans, as the population ages, those who left the enclaves to work in other cities and states will tend to return in high proportions. The regional return migration experience of African Americans, therefore, is likely to be repeated in the future by older Hispanics, reinforcing the retirement migration trends to the states in which their home bases are located.

Ethnic return migration focuses on the Sun Belt because many African Americans were reared in the South and because Mexican and Cuban Americans first settled in the Sun Belt. No doubt, when Asian retirement migration is studied, the strong settlement pattern in the Pacific rim states will result in high return migration to that region.

Ethnic enclave settlement does not "explain" regional differences in return migration because the overwhelming majority of older migrants are not of ethnic origin. Rather, it tends to compound trends that are already present among the majority migrants.

Are There Subtypes of Return Migration Underlying Regional Differences?

To sort out some of the reasons for regional differences in return migration, it is necessary to look at the characteristics of migrants returning to the different parts of the United States.

Only two studies have directly attempted to describe the population characteristics of older interstate return migrants. The first was a study by the author published in 1979.[15] This study showed that return migrants age 60 and over were less well off in terms of educational background and economic characteristics, relative to non-return migrants, in the 1965-1970 migration period. In addition, return migrants were less likely to be married and living independently and more likely to be female, widowed and younger.

The other study, by William Serow and Douglas Charity, captured a similar picture of older return migrants using 1980 Census data.[16] They found that return migration rates were higher, in aggregate, among females, among persons age 65-74 rather than 75+, and among persons who were not currently married. Although there is general consistency in these two sets of findings, they throw little light on the nature of elderly return migration. Two competing models of the phenomenon exist in the literature. We term these models "provincial" (a subset of amenity migration) and "counterstream" (a subset of dependency migration).

Provincial return migration — African-American return migration, as described in the earlier section, illustrates this concept. The portrait of migration for a job when one is young, ultimately followed by a return to one's roots after retirement, has appealed to migration theorists. The advantages are obvious: The retiree gains a lower cost of living in a location where the world-wise experience and greater retirement income give the retiree a higher status than relatives who never left. This pattern was described nearly 15 years ago by the French geographer Francoise Cribier as "provincial return migration." [17]

Cribier described an interview she conducted during one of her migration studies:

"A retired respondent had just moved to a village on the outskirts of Paris. He spoke to me of his coming to Paris 40 years earlier and of his Parisian life before retirement. Among the reasons he gave for moving were health and love for the countryside — especially its tranquility — which was true. But in his disenchanted discourse on the Paris of today, he saw the Parisians as young, employed people and in Paris he could only be an old-timer. Paris was no longer what it had been for him. I understood then that moving to the village as a retired Parisian, he had found a way of remaining a Parisian forever." (p. 263)

Dexter Burley provided an exotic example of return retirement migration.[18] In their youth, the Dorze weavers of Ethiopia migrate to Addis Ababa, where they specialize in weaving and occupy the same neighborhood. When they retire, they migrate back to the Gamu Highlands, where they have much higher social status and greater relative economic advantages than would have otherwise been possible.

Research has consistently confirmed that the characteristics of migrants over age 60, on the whole, are positive as compared with those their age who have not moved, indicating a relatively high level of financial independence.[19] Collectively, these migrants are younger, married homeowners with more education; amenity migrants prevail.[20] Consequently, they tend to rejuvenate and enrich the older populations in areas to which they move.

If all return migrants are provincial return migrants, and if provincial migrants are a variety of amenity migrants, then their demographic characteristics should match the profile of amenity migrants. Unfortunately, they do not. The studies cited above, by Longino and Serow and associates, demonstrate that return migrants, in aggregate, are slightly more dependent, economically and socially, than non-return migrants of the same age. This brings us to the second major model of return migration, what has been termed the counterstream return migration pattern.

Counterstream return migration — As first discussed in Chapter 3, this approach would interpret elderly return migration as part of a cyclical migration process after retirement. Some recent theoretical perspectives focus on the life course of migrants and emphasize the triggering mechanisms associated with life events and probabilities.[21] Eugene Litwak, who teaches at Columbia University, and the author have argued that persons who move after retirement may be motivated differently depending upon their level of functional health. Three basic types of moves are involved, and they are most likely to be triggered by different events. The first occurs when people experience retirement, the second when moderate forms of disability appear, and the third when there are major forms of chronic disability. The second and third types of moves would be classified as dependency moves.

Thus, consistent with life course theories of elderly migration, return migrants would have higher mean ages than non-return migrants. The studies of the characteristics of older return migrants find, however, that return migrants are slightly younger, in the aggregate, than non-return migrants. Neither the provincial return migration model nor the counterstream migration model consistently explains this finding.

Regional return migration — Retirement migration in the United States has a regional character because of important regional differences in climate and cost of living — factors that figure into the destination decision of amenity migrants.[22] It also has a strong regional bias because elderly amenity migrants tend to move to locations where they have vacationed and visited in their past, and vacationing regions usually have strong climatic and lifestyle advantages.

Early studies showed that the proportion of older migrants returning to their states of birth varied greatly between regions, a point confirmed again in Table 1.[23] In studies of ethnicity and migration, where return migration is an important factor in directing the streams, regional differences are also pronounced.

In addition, a comparison of streams and counterstreams between pairs of sending and receiving states also provides a key to understanding the regional nature of return migration. As discussed in Chapter 3, counterstreams carrying elderly migrants out of Florida contain much higher proportions of return migrants than do the streams into Florida, a finding reported a decade ago by the author.[24] Florida counterstream out-migrants, collectively, had higher indicators of dependency and need than did in-migrants to Florida from the same exchange partners. Counterstream migrants were generally older, more often widowed, and less often living independently than migrants in the much larger stream to Florida. This fact was taken as evidence for the life course migration theory. It strongly suggested that counterstream return migration is a type of dependency migration and may be strong in those streams from the Sun Belt states in the South and West to the regions from which so many retired migrants originate — the North Central region and the Northeast. If these speculations are true, then the return migrants in northward-bound interregional streams should have higher indicators of need for assistance than those in other such streams.

Reviewing the two return migration models in light of clear regional differences may offer a way to solve the puzzle of return migrant characteristics. Because provincial return migration is a less affluent variety of amenity migration, we expect return migrants to be less positively selected than non-return migrants in the Sun Belt regional streams. On the other hand, because counterstream return migration is a type of dependency migration, we expect return migrants to the Midwest region and Northeast to be a more dependent population than non-return migrants.

Hoping to solve the puzzle, the author and Serow compared only return migrants in the different regions, using 1980 Census data.[25] When profiled as a whole, return migrants over age 60 seem to be a slightly more dependent segment of the older migrant population. In 1980, they were older and more residentially dependent than non-return migrants. However, when regional variations are considered, this generalization breaks down. Interstate return migrants who moved within regions were not very different from one another. However, interregional return migrants into the Northeast and Midwest were far older, more often widowed, less likely to be living independently and more likely to be institutionalized than interregional return migrants into the South and West. This finding supports the expectations of counterstream return migration to the Midwest and Northeast and provincial return migration to the South and West.

Perhaps returning to one's state of birth is overemphasized in discussions of counterstream migration. Conceivably it is not a return to one's state of birth that is at issue among counterstream migrants, but rather a return from a Sun Belt retirement move to an earlier place of residence, regardless of whether one was born there. The absence of a detailed migration history in the decennial census or any other representative sample of the nation's population makes it impossible to state with any precision how long any one individual actually lived in his or her state of birth or at any other location. It is known, for example, that the share of one's lifetime spent in the state of birth varies widely among states, from 59.5 percent for those born in Texas to less than 20 percent among natives of Alaska or the District of Columbia.[26] One's informal support system, composed of close friends and children, may more often be located at one's adult state of birth. Were truly longitudinal data on residential histories available for individuals, the concept of return migration might well be better formulated in terms of that location where the migrant had spent the significant portion of his or her life, rather than the state-of-birth proxy used here and elsewhere.

The regions that have been heavily impacted by general migration after World War II, such as the West, may be more likely than other regions to receive older in-migrants who, although not born there, had come there when they were young and thus spent their youth in the region. Some and perhaps many migrants are returning not to their places of birth but to the residences of their youth, although they get labeled as "non-return" migrants.

• • • • • • • • • • •

Return migrants possess a historical link to the destination state. There is a second special type of migrant considered in the next chapter that maintains their connection both to their origin and destination communities. They are dual-community residents. If their home base is in the North and they spend the colder part of the year in a Sun Belt state, they will be called "snowbirds."

CHAPTER SEVEN
SPECIAL TYPES: SNOWBIRDS

Introduction

Each autumn, as the arctic air descends deeper into the United States, many species of waterfowl start their southern migration. Some of them journey to Florida, where ornithologists have gathered precise data on the number of species, their settlement patterns, length of stay in various locations, changes in migration patterns over time and the ecosystems that support them. This data is used to justify various federal and state regulations designed to protect these seasonal migrants. Only recently have geographers, demographers and gerontologists assembled data on a different type of seasonal resident from the Northern states to Texas, Arizona and Florida, the species Homo sapiens, popularly known as the "snowbird." In demographic parlance, they are seasonal migrants.

The purpose of examining special types of migration is to expand our understanding of migration motivation. Return migration as a special type of retirement migration was reviewed in Chapter 6. Return migrants hear the call of other times and places and respond to it. Seasonal migrants, however, teeter on the bridge between being a permanent resident of one place and becoming a permanent resident of another. Seasonal migration is a lens through which the anatomy of a move can be examined and understood. The insights gained in the study of seasonal migration are amply applicable to retirement migration in general.[1] This chapter focuses on the seasonal migration segment of the retirement migration market.

Profiling Seasonal Migrants

The Census Bureau does not directly attempt to measure seasonal migration. In fact, even if census forms are forwarded to one's vacation home, where they are completed and mailed back, the form is counted as though it had been filled out at one's usual residence.

The Census Bureau produced a report after the 1980 Census on persons who said their usual residence was elsewhere (UREs).[2] Many of them may have been seasonal migrants. The usual state of residence was cross-classified with the temporary residence at the time of the census, producing a matrix of non-permanent migration streams. In April 1980, the census counted nearly half a million non-permanent residents, approximately half of whom were in Florida. Some migrant characteristics, including age, were reported as state averages. It is obvious where snowbirds roost just from examining the state averages. The mean age of the "UREs" was higher in Florida and Arizona than in other states. Although this report has been used in some gerontological research, the findings represent a clouded vision at best. The first problem is that snowbirds are mixed with migrant farm workers, construction workers and others whose work takes them away from home for weeks or months at a time. The second problem is that the census may have underestimated seasonal retirement migration, because many snowbirds are home by April 1.[3]

There have been several surveys of seasonal migrants, however, that provide snapshots of snowbirds at their destinations. The surveys have been conducted in Texas, Arizona and Florida. In addition, one survey was conducted in upstate New York when migrants had returned home. These surveys provide very important information, but they are not able to present a national picture. They tend to focus on the characteristics of migrants and general reasons for their move.

Some studies have used clever approaches to finding out about retired seasonal migrants. One study in Arizona used *Woodall's Campground Directory*[4] of RV parks and resorts to estimate the national distribution of seasonal migrants, and it used the home state listing in the directories of RV parks to study the migration patterns of those who winter in Phoenix.[5] Because nobody knows how many retired seasonal migrants there are, it is difficult to know how best to sample them.

The first published report on Canadian seasonal migrants in Florida was based on an ethnographic study of 240 people who wintered in the northwestern Panhandle area of Florida.[6] It is a largely narrative characterization of this small seasonal population.

In 1986, the Canadian Embassy in Washington, DC, in cooperation with the International Exchange Center on Gerontology, commissioned a study of Canadian winter residents of Florida. A team of Canadian and Florida gerontologists, including the author, designed a mail survey to focus on the use of health care and other services in Florida while Canadians were wintering there. The mailing list consisted of subscribers to an English-language newspaper published in Florida for Canadians wintering in the Sunshine State. A later survey, replicating the questionnaire, was conducted on a sample of French-speaking Canadians in Florida. The research team included Dr. Victor Marshall and Joanne Daciuk from the University of Toronto; Dr. Larry Mullins from the University of South Florida; Dr. Richard Tucker, the team leader, from the University of Central Florida; and the author.

Researchers have been forced to conduct local surveys in order to study seasonal migrants. The surveys are accumulating and beginning to be compared, thereby providing a broader national picture. Information about the migration decision (to move seasonally, to settle down permanently or to return home permanently) is much more abundant in these surveys than in census data.

Results of local surveys have shown that seasonal migrants are overwhelmingly white and retired. They are healthy, married couples in their mid- to late 60s with higher levels of income and education than the older population in general.

A 1988 survey of seasonal residents in Phoenix recreational vehicle parks characterized them as being of predominantly middle to upper-middle income. Sixty percent had incomes between $20,000 and $50,000. One-fifth had lower and one-fifth had higher incomes than the broad middle category.[7]

One recent study compared samples of Canadians who wintered in Florida with U.S. citizens who winter in the Rio Grande Valley of Texas (Hidalgo County).[8] The similarities between the two were impressive. More than 90 percent of both groups were married couples, the remainder being widowed. The average age of U.S. citizens was a little younger (66.9 years) than that of Canadians (68.9 years). The snowbirds had a mean of about 12 years of formal education and three children, regardless of their origin. Canadians, collectively, had somewhat higher incomes, after considering exchange rates, perhaps because they were less often fully retired (77.9 percent vs. 84.4 percent). Compared to their U.S. counterparts, Canadians more often held professional, technical or managerial jobs (34.9 percent vs. 26.2 percent) and other white collar occupations (32.1 percent vs. 19.7 percent) and were less likely to be craftsmen (7.4 percent vs. 20.6 percent), semiskilled and service workers and farmers (8.7 percent vs. 16.8 percent). High proportions in both groups were homeowners.

Both U.S. and Canadian snowbirds were in very good health, although a higher proportion of Canadians (85 percent vs. 80 percent) assessed their health as good or excellent, and they had lower rates of chronic conditions than U.S. seasonal migrants. Snowbirds in Texas had high mental health ratings; comparable data were unavailable for the Canadians in Florida. How typical these seasonal migrants were of all such migrants from their countries is not known, although the Arizona snowbird studies also came to the same conclusion that seasonal migrants are an advantaged group, as compared to all persons their age.[9]

Nonetheless, there is economic variation among seasonal migrants. Anecdotal evidence has been reported about some Canadians with more modest means who migrate in the winter to the Panhandle of Florida and to Myrtle Beach, SC. The lower "off-season" rates make wintering in these locations relatively inexpensive but provide a large climatic advantage over Canada during the winter.[10]

Seasonal migrants have the relative youth, spouses and economic independence associated with amenity migration. A recently published study even allows us to examine, for the first time, some of the spatial dimensions of their movement patterns.

The Migration Patterns Of Seasonal Migrants

Kevin McHugh and Robert Mings, geographers from Arizona State University, were the first to map the older migration streams of seasonal migrants, even to one location. They derived information on 8,587 households from the resident directories of 10 Phoenix RV resorts. The entries contained the migrants' home states. They concentrated on those state streams that made up at least 4 percent of the total.

One pattern that emerged was seasonal migration from distant Northern states. California and Colorado, which touches Arizona at its northeast tip, were the only contiguous states that sent migrants in large numbers. The others were Oregon, Washington, North Dakota, Minnesota, Iowa, Illinois and Michigan, with the heaviest flows coming from Washington, Minnesota and Iowa. There were two Canadian provinces that contributed sizable streams to the Phoenix RV resorts: British Columbia and Alberta, north of the states of Washington, Idaho and Montana. Each of these states contributed permanent migrants to Arizona as well.

By combining their directory counts with the population characteristics in the states and provinces, McHugh and Mings were able to estimate the rates (per 1,000) of seasonal migration to Phoenix of the populations age 55-70 in each of the origins. The propensity to seasonally migrate to Arizona, using this measure, was highest in the northern plains and mountain states and bordering Canadian provinces: North Dakota (28.7), Montana (16.6), Wyoming (16.3), Saskatchewan (13.2), Alberta (11.2), Washington (11.1) and South Dakota (10.9). Selective out-migration rates from certain communities in these states and provinces may have been much higher.

The fact that flows to Arizona dropped off the farther east one goes reflects the intervening opportunities of Texas and Florida, also popular seasonal destinations. The fact that winter migration to Arizona dropped off the farther south one goes reflects a narrowing of the difference between the winter temperature in Arizona and at the origin. Climate is apparently a very strong factor in motivating seasonal migration. Furthermore, McHugh and Mings noted that some RV resorts tended to have high numbers of migrants from certain states and provinces. This observation implies that the network recruitment process is at work even among seasonal migrants.

A recent review of Canadian retirement migration estimated that seasonal migration within Canada or to the United States is more common than permanent migration within Canada.[11] This expectation has been supported by the assessments of Statistics Canada, the census bureau of Canada.[12] Based on their estimates, the total number of older Canadian seasonal migrants in Florida alone is a quarter million.[13] Many older Canadians from the western, prairie provinces (Alberta, Saskatchewan and Manitoba) engage in seasonal migration to Arizona, Nevada, California and Hawaii.

English-speaking Canadians bound for Florida concentrate on the west coast, near St. Petersburg, and the French-speaking Canadians settle primarily on the east coast, north of Miami.[14] The pattern implies that the two are distinct cultural communities with separate identities. Similar ethnic migration patterns are discussed in Chapter 6. The South Florida area of settlement has a long French-Canadian history, dating back to the 1930s. Even in 1946, the Miami area reported 4.6 percent of its population as French Canadians, primarily from Quebec. By the 1960s, a growing tourism industry had emerged catering to French Canadians, with many of the motels and restaurants owned and operated by migrants from Quebec.[15]

The trails that bring snowbirds south to Arizona or Florida are not strange or innovative. They follow the Sun Belt regional pattern discussed in Chapter 2 of this book. Perhaps the primary difference between seasonal and permanent migrants is that seasonal migrants sometimes travel farther, implying that the climatic change may be more important to them than to permanent migrants. The northward seasonal pattern from Florida and the desert states to cooler mountainous locations in North Carolina and New England in the east and to Colorado in the west have not yet been studied. Nevertheless, in the wintertime, Sun Belt migration patterns dominate.

Counterstream migration, discussed in Chapter 3, demonstrates the less permanent side of what demographers refer to as permanent migration. Seasonal migration is impermanent by nature. Exploring the concept of relative permanence in seasonal migration throws considerable light on the issue in general. Surveys have provided quite useful information on the subject, going far beyond the guesswork employed in discerning the tea leaves of migrant characteristics available in census records.

The Issue of Permanence

The U.S. Census assumes that one's "usual place of residence" is not temporary. In reality, much of the migration among older people may be temporary.[16] One study surveyed older people in upstate New York and found that 14 percent of the sample had spent part of the previous year wintering in another state, usually in the Southern rim states and particularly in the Southeast.[17] Estimates of the average length of stay, also derived from various surveys, range from 6.7 months in Florida trailer parks[18] to 4.7 months in lower Rio Grande Valley of Texas.[19] The consensus among researchers today puts the average stay at about five months, the majority staying five or six months. Most arrive before Christmas and are gone by May.

Seasonal migration may begin as an extension of vacationing patterns. The stay is gradually lengthened and then more affordable accommodations are sought by purchasing a cottage, mobile home or RV. Previous vacationing by Canadian snowbirds in Florida before buying a residence was common. Many had a long history of progressively more lengthy visits to Florida.[20] Seasonal migration was seen as a process. The length of the visit, however, had a definite limit for Canadians. Migrants tended to stay for five months because they would lose their Canadian medicare benefits if they spent more than six months abroad each year.[21]

A good deal of research has been devoted to the question of whether seasonal migration is only a stage, a precursor to a permanent move. The scholar who has pursued this issue with the most devotion is Kevin McHugh.[22] He points out that only three studies have asked temporary migrants how they felt about a permanent move. These studies in Texas and Arizona found that between 21 percent and 30 percent of seasonal visitors were considering a more permanent move. Expectations do not predict behavior very well; there are too many contingencies that intervene. Nonetheless, what are those factors that predict the expectations of turning seasonal migration into a permanent move? In keeping with the conceptual framework discussed earlier in this chapter, McHugh found that snowbird expectations of eventual permanent migration were closely related to strength of place ties to their origin, what has been called "moorings." As long as the place ties to the home community are strong, McHugh argues, seasonal migration becomes a "substitute" for permanent migration. It captures the advantages of climate and amenity improvements during the winter, without the disadvantages of cutting ties to the home community. As place ties to the origin community weaken and place ties to the seasonal host community strengthen, there is a clearly perceptible shift in expectations toward becoming a permanent migrant. Under these circumstances, seasonal migration comes to be seen as a precursor to a permanent move.

The theoretical evolution from seasonal to permanent migrant, for those who make this transition, is ripe with scholarly speculation. Certainly there must be enough of these migrants who can be located and studied. An image was used earlier of migrants teetering on a bridge between moving permanently to the destination or giving up seasonal migration and staying permanently at the origin. One factor that works strongly against developing robust place ties at the destination is the impermanence of the migrant community itself. Migrants may be more likely to develop ties with the floating and kaleidoscopic migrant community than with the permanent host community and its institutions. The psychological transition from visitor to permanent resident is very difficult to achieve in a community of visitors. Also, the seasonal migrant community in the winter is constantly changing. New snowbirds come each year and some repeaters stop coming. The turnover in the community works against the development of strong place ties and serves as a constant reminder that someday the time may come when the migrant will be forced to forego the winter visit. Consequently, the age of the migrant or the number of years into the process begins working against a permanent move.

McHugh concluded that younger seasonal migrants who increase their stays to more than six months and who have family members and close friends living permanently at the destination are the most likely to expect to do the same themselves. Otherwise, there is a strong devotion among seasonal migrants to the snowbirding lifestyle, to the culture they create and re-create time and again, which is qualitatively different from permanent migration.

The tendency of most observers is to rely almost entirely on the concept of place ties, or moorings, when considering the issue of permanence. On second examination, however, the standing of resources is often elevated to critical status in triggering events that resolve the pull between the two places and precipitate a more permanent move in one direction or the other.

Place Ties and Resources

Much emphasis has been given to place ties as the primary ingredient in moving the vehicle forward or backward across the bridge of seasonal migration. It is the gravitational force in the equation. However, economic, health and psychic resources are equally important. In one study of Arizona snowbirds, McHugh found that age worked against eventual permanent migration, or at least the expectation of migration.[23] The reason for this conclusion is that with increasing age there is also an increased likelihood of fluctuations in major resources that make seasonal migration a practical possibility. The rigors of such a life become less endurable eventually. Health failures become more likely with age. Financial robustness is stronger earlier than later in retirement, particularly for lower-middle-class retirees. Seasonal migration is postponed and finally terminated, not because of a weakening of place ties at the destination, but reluctantly because of the instability of resources.

Joanne Daciuk and Victor Marshall, from the University of Toronto, examined the Canadian snowbird data in a way complementary to McHugh. They found that there is an important difference in health status between migrants who expected to stop their seasonal moves and those who expected to continue. Not surprisingly, those with serious illnesses such as cancer did not expect to be able to continue. The same was true for persons with increasing arthritic conditions which made it difficult to drive long distances. Having a medical emergency in Florida also increases expectations that migration will soon end. Those who have a less optimistic view of the American medical system are more greatly deterred than those who are more optimistic.

Canadian seasonal migrants are very conscious of health issues. Prior to leaving Canada, most visit a Canadian doctor for a checkup, stock up on prescription drugs and enroll in a private health-insurance plan to supplement their provincial health plan, just as U.S. seasonal migrants to Mexico would do.[24]

Place ties and resources are now commonly considered in analyzing migration decisions. A final concept, person ties, deserves some status in the mix of motivating factors impacting the decision to move.

Person Ties

How important are person ties in maintaining seasonal migration? Part of the answer may be found in the research on snowbirds, particularly the Canadian study.

A majority of Canadians in Florida hold long-term leases in mobile home communities. Returning to the same home year after year seems to foster integration into snowbird communities.

A minority of Canadian snowbirds, about 13 percent or as many as 20 percent (depending upon the overlap of categories), have family members living permanently in Florida, so they move away from their Canadian family and toward their Florida family when they winter. Seventy percent have close friends living permanently in Florida and within 50 miles of their winter home. Person ties, to friends, are very common.[25] In addition, there is an active stream of visitors from Canada for a large proportion of snowbirds. More than one-third (38 percent) have been visited during the winter by a child and a similar proportion (39 percent) expect such a visit before their return to Canada. More than one-fifth (22 percent) have been visited by a sibling and a similar proportion (20 percent) expect to be visited before they return. One

respondent on this survey wrote on the back page "Do we miss our Canadian friends? You don't realize how many friends you have until you own a place in Florida, especially in the winter." Loneliness was hardly a problem.[26]

There may be a relationship between permanent international migration and seasonal migration. In 1980, there were 833,920 native-born Canadians living in the United States. Many (84 percent) of these migrants had become naturalized U.S. citizens. Thirty-nine percent were 60 years of age or older. Florida is the only distant state from the Canadian border on the Atlantic Coast that attracts Canadian expatriates in large numbers. Although nearly half of those who had moved to Florida were over 60 years old, most moved to the United States in their early and middle adulthood, and then moved to Florida after retirement. It is possible that permanent Florida residents who were born in Canada attract the seasonal migrants, or perhaps Canadian snowbirding relatives attract former Canadians to retire in Florida.[27]

There is no doubt that person ties play an important role in the mental health of migrants, and in their migration motivation and location selection. There are also ties to other migrants that should be considered. Seasonal migration has some of the markings of a nomadic cultural phenomenon, a movable feast.

Seasonal Migrants and Lifestyle

McHugh and Mings, in their study of seasonal migrants to RV resorts in Phoenix, remind us that the culture of snowbirds is a movable feast. The RV resorts of today are a far cry from the old "trailer courts" of three decades ago. Business has already targeted one segment of the retirement market very well, those interested in seasonal recreational travel. The growth of planned, large-scale RV resorts in Phoenix goes back to the 1960s, and has been a major local growth industry during the last two decades.

These planned resorts are like winter camps for elders. They have many recreational facilities and group-oriented programs. Organized sports teams compete in league play. Local dining, shopping and sightseeing trips are organized by resorts. In McHugh and Mings' study, 40 percent of seasonal migrants had taken recent trips to such places as the Grand Canyon, Las Vegas, San Diego, Santa Fe, Lake Havasu City and several locations in Mexico. They used their winter home in Phoenix as a "home base" from which to explore.

In physical appearance, these resorts look much like suburban tract housing with their regular streets, standard-sized lots and similarity in the external appearance of dwellings. For added security, many are walled communities with entrance gates and security personnel. Sometimes residents wear "badges" so that outsiders are quickly identified. Crime is extremely low in these communities.

The average stay of winter visitors in Phoenix is five months, the same as the average stay for Canadian snowbirds in Florida. There are many couples who visit the same location year after year, building a network of friends from among the other seasonal migrants. Returning to the RV resort is happily anticipated in the same way that college students look forward to returning to school after a summer vacation to see their friends and engage in enjoyable campus activities. They not only have fun things to do, but friends who value these activities with whom to share them.

The dialogue among researchers concerning whether seasonal migration is part of a process leading to permanent migration has concluded that seasonal migration generates its own lifestyle and culture, different from that of permanent migrants but equally valuable in its own right. Once having adopted the lifestyle, seasonal migration is likely to last for several years, finally interrupted and reluctantly terminated by a fluctuation or decrease in necessary resources. There are some who do settle down and stay, but those are often people who have strong person ties and place ties to the host community. They have family members and others living permanently nearby who tend to anchor them.

In an informal analysis of the Canadian snowbirds in Florida, a colleague and the author distinguished a large cluster of migrants who seemed to form a special type of seasonal migration. They justified their mobility primarily as an opportunity to be with migrating friends from Canada. They were nomadic in the sense that their social ties were fundamentally with the same migrants in the communities they shared at both ends of the move. Their ties were not to places but to the migrating community itself. These important person ties were part of the movable feast.

• • • • • • • • • • •

In Chapter 8, we will consider retirement migration to regional destinations.

CHAPTER EIGHT
SPECIAL TYPES: REGIONAL RETIREMENT DESTINATIONS

Introduction

All states have vacation spots where residents in nearby towns and cities travel an hour or two for a pleasant day of hiking, swimming, boating or fishing, often with their families. Outdoor recreational sites — such as state parks — arise first in response to demand from within the state. Many of these vacation spots find cottages appearing along the shoreline or in places with inspiring views, and later these cottages come to house retirees for a part of the year. If the infrastructure is present for community life to exist, and if the cottages can be summerized or winterized for the off-season, then some of these retirees will choose to live year-round in their former vacation home. As this happens, a retirement destination forms. There are a handful of such vacationing places in every state, and nearly every state has one or two spots where stays longer than usual vacationing visits have already begun to take hold.

When tourists begin to arrive from out of state, a vacation spot is on its way to becoming a destination for some interstate retirees, for the same reasons that vacationers from within state move to these places. A six-to-eight hour drive seems to limit the distance most families are willing to travel for a vacation, especially if there are children. For that reason out-of-state tourists, in all but tropical and desert America, seem to be drawn most heavily from neighboring states. The informal wisdom of most observers is that if the natural course is allowed to take place, unhurried by development and promotion activities, there is a lag of about 15 years between the time that out-of-state tourists become a substantial minority of visitors to the time that out-of-state retirement migration becomes noticeable. As this process unfolds, regional retirement destinations form, areas with strong regional visibility but without very strong national visibility.

The study of retirement migration should not be limited to the destinations that attract large numbers of interstate migrants from faraway states, the so-called "national destinations." It is true that these areas are in high profile; they are known nationally as good places to live during retirement. However, just as many interstate migrants are moving much shorter distances. It is a shame that regional retirement migration has been nearly overlooked by researchers until recently.

Demographic Studies Of Regional Migration

Studies of regional migration of older persons are not common because of the type of data available to, and the resulting macro-perspective assumed by, demographers. Demographic research relies almost exclusively on large national data sets, produced primarily by the Bureau of the Census and the Bureau of Labor Statistics. These standard government surveys provide a national picture. The picture is like the view from an airplane 30,000 feet above the ground, a broad view. It is only when the national picture is clearly established that demographers tend to move to lower levels of geographic analysis.

Still, there are several noteworthy examples of regional research on elderly migration that have employed demographic data and methods. One study, for example, used county-level net migration data from 1970 and 1980 in the upper Midwest to identify a rural "resort belt" across north central Minnesota and upper Wisconsin and Michigan that attracts retired people from within the region but not necessarily from out of state.[1] The other Midwestern regional migration area mentioned was in the Ozarks, largely in southern Missouri and northern Arkansas.

A second study took county net migration analysis a step further to show how retirement migration has changed over time in the New England region.[2] This study identified those counties that had a positive net migration rate for persons 65-74 and 75 and over from 1930 to 1980. For the most part, these counties primarily attracted younger retirees; they were the locations of long-standing recreation and retirement areas and were distinguished by a high percentage of elderly residents, small city size and low population density. Further, these counties had high levels of family income and tourist employment and low levels of agricultural employment. Nearly all were on the water between Rhode Island and Maine. Barnstable County, MA, was one of these.

As with the Midwestern county study, there was no way of telling how many or what proportion of retirees who moved to these New England retirement counties came from the same state or from other states.

A third investigation provides an example of migration census studies that use data on individuals rather than counties. That study used census microdata, the kind of data used in most of the tables in this book. The purpose of the study was to determine the intercounty migration patterns of older migrants in California.[3] Because California is so large and populous, it is being discussed here as a retirement region within itself. Older Californians who moved between 1975 and 1980 tended to come from three source regions: northern California, the San Francisco Bay Area and Los Angeles County. Those within-state migrants from northern California tended to move the farthest; the largest streams were going to the Los Angeles and San Diego areas. Older intrastate migrants leaving Los Angeles also tended to move farther south within the state. Only the Bay Area migrants fought this southward drift and instead tended to settle in San Francisco's less populated surrounding counties, both to the north and south. Nonetheless, the predominant migration pattern within California is southward, just as it is nationally.

Finally, the Retirement Migration Project located several

major regional destinations of older migrants, using 1970 national microdata files similar to those used in the California study.[4] This project identified a chain of regional migration centers stretching from New England to the Pacific Northwest that attracted large proportions of older migrants from contiguous states, but not from distant states. Consistent with the findings of the two net migration studies, established tourist industries in coastal, lake or mountainous regions already existed in these states before retirement migration became prominent. Similar to the third study, both origins and destinations were used to determine migration patterns. But unlike the third study, the latter project was interested in migrants who entered the state from the outside, from contiguous or nearby states.

From east to west, the chain of regional migration destinations included coastal New England and New Jersey, certain zones in the mountainous Appalachian chain stretching from Pennsylvania to northern Alabama, and the mountainous Ozarks region of northern Arkansas and southern Missouri. The Great Plains states seem free of regional retirement centers, but the desert resort areas of southern and western Nevada receive migrants in large numbers from California.

Collectively, these research efforts reflect the range of demographic techniques available to the study of regional migration, but none of them can provide explicit information concerning the motives that drive migration. Because both the Midwest and New England studies relied on counties as their units of analysis, their view of the individual was obscure and implied. And although the California and national studies were able to track the movement of individuals from origin to destination, neither of these investigations addressed the migrants' motives for moving or the logic of their decision-making calculus.

Three Principles of Migration To Regional Destinations

The Cape Cod Retirement Migration Study was a five-year comparative investigation of migrants and non-migrants residing in three communities in Barnstable County, MA.[5] Data collection included surveys administered to two samples of residents, in-depth tape-recorded interviews with selected groups of older migrants, archival research of town census records and additional interviews and field observations in a number of Cape Cod communities. Cuba and Longino attempted to extract from these data the underlying principles of regional migration, from the standpoint of the migrant.[6] The principles that this study illustrated work in all regional centers.

Cape Cod attracts migrants from New England and surrounding states primarily for three reasons: It is a familiar place with which most migrants have some history; it is the setting for a variety of amenities desired by migrants of this age group; and it is relatively near these migrants' communities of origin, allowing them to maintain ties to their previous residences. These are the primary advantages of regional migration in all states where it exists.

Regional destinations are familiar. Almost every newcomer has had some experience linking them to the place:

family vacations, visits to friends or relatives, or conversations with others who have visited the retirement site.[7] Through their previous experience, migrants acquire a broad range of familiarities that are thought to be important. Migrants to regional destinations are not trying to escape their familiar climate; the seasons in the place of retirement mirror those of the migrant's origin. One retiree to Cape Cod put it this way: "It isn't any worse than back home, in fact it's very similar." The economic conditions, such as taxes and cost of housing, are familiar. More important, many migrants express a strong desire to remain in the accustomed social and cultural environment of their region. They do not wish to adjust to places that seem strange or foreign. For migrants who have traveled and moved around a great deal in their lives, a change of regions is not so daunting. But for migrants who are regionally rooted, a firmly established regional identity acts as a constraint on the choice of potential destinations. Although many retirement migrants are looking for a setting that will allow them a change of life in their later years, they are wary of shifting the cultural parameters that have bounded their experience and lifestyle. *This principle applies to the regionally rooted in all regions of the United States: They will only be in the market for a retirement move if a suitable location is nearby.*

The issue of lifestyle and available amenities is mentioned so frequently and so glibly in reports of retirement migration that this important issue, by repetition, is being drained of its meaning. It is important to put amenities in context.

In moving from metropolitan suburbs surrounding the larger cities, retirement-aged migrants are usually opting for a rural lifestyle. For most, the communities they are leaving were chosen primarily for occupational or family reasons; they wanted to live near their workplaces or in neighborhoods where they felt comfortable raising a family. But as retirement nears and children leave home, these suburbs may lose their appeal.

Yet while older migrants express a desire for a change of surroundings, they don't want to give up completely the comforts afforded by an urban lifestyle. Regional locations that are reasonably proximate to cities are especially attractive if the cultural and service amenities these migrants expect (e.g., museums, restaurants, theater, shopping, an international airport) can be found in a city, a couple of hours away. Sun City was built near Phoenix for a reason. The mountainous counties north of Atlanta and the coastal areas just south of Mobile are successfully attracting retirement development. Springfield, MO, just north of Branson, has a good airport, hospital and restaurants partly because of retirement market demand. It is no mystery that the highly concentrated retirement population in the North Carolina mountains is an easy drive from Asheville, the largest city in the western end of the state. And it is unthinkable that Cape Cod would have developed as it has without its proximity to Boston. One migrant described living on Cape Cod as "the best of both worlds," a place somewhere between the remoteness of rural living and the fast-paced life of the region's metropolitan centers. *This principle applies to retirees with more educated tastes and interests: The regional location must be accessible to metropolitan amen-*

ities but offer a relaxed small-town lifestyle.

A regional retirement center is also appealing for older migrants because it is close to the migrants' former communities. Moving within the region allows migrants to maintain ties with their previous residences, families and friends. Although relocating to another community means that everyday contact with people and places is no longer possible, the relatively short distance affords the opportunity for retaining meaningful place ties for those who desire them. One Cape Cod migrant phrased it this way, "We don't feel that we have left the community that we came from that completely."

Moving within the region also allows migrants to remain near parents, children or grandchildren who reside nearby. In some cases, retirement migrants to a regional center will be moving closer to some family members, a pattern first noted in a study of Sun City, AZ.[8] Having children in the vicinity seems like a security blanket, and proximity to the migrant's own parents grows in importance as they age. In a variety of ways, migrants feel that they have the opportunity to continue established patterns of family life and caregiving.[9]

Many migrants keep in mind that they are moving to a place that their family and friends will want to visit. Sometimes children put pressure on parents not to move too far away for fear that distance will reduce contact. Having visitors during the tourist season is a very common experience for migrants, and most will have some space set aside in their new homes for guests to use.

In the same way that retiring to an area relatively close to their previous residence allows migrants to maintain contact with friends and family, it also provides an opportunity to ease the transition out of work. Most migrants give up their jobs completely, but some retain occupational ties on a part-time basis (occasional consulting or technical advising). Others may travel between their new home and their residence of origin before moving full time, establishing a biweekly commuting pattern as a transitional phase. The proximity of regional destinations affords this flexibility of retirement transition from full-time work.

Moving is not the same as aging in place. The ties to previous communities are never totally transportable; new routines must be established, new friends made and new patterns of interaction created. Migrants, regardless of whether they move 100 or 1,000 miles, are faced with starting over. What may distinguish migrants who move to regional destinations from those who move farther away is that they are starting over on familiar turf, going toward something that is better, but not too far away. ***This principle applies to migrants to regional retirement centers: By moving a shorter distance from their community of origin, migrants can more easily maintain some degree of social continuity in their lives.***

• • • • • • • • • • • • • • • •

In Chapter 9, we will consider retirement migration as an economic development strategy.

CHAPTER NINE

RETIREMENT MIGRATION AS AN ECONOMIC DEVELOPMENT STRATEGY

Introduction

The strategy of recruiting manufacturing plants—smoke-stack chasing—to create jobs is familiar to small-town America. Chambers of commerce in counties approaching metropolitan area status (50,000 population) that have encouraged the development of industrial parks talk with anticipation about the benefits of bringing in plants. Unfortunately, enthusiasm for industrial recruitment tends to peak in times of economic recession, when lower numbers of manufacturing plants can afford to relocate. Many of these communities are not able to favorably compete with more urban areas for the plants that do relocate. They simply do not have the infrastructure. And many other factors of the relocation process are also out of the control of the local community. The result: Most industrial recruitment efforts amount to nothing more than a rain dance.[1] Because agriculture alone does not sustain economic growth in these communities, they experience economic decline.

Recent reports on employment growth in non-metropolitan counties substantiate the claim that manufacturing, agriculture and mining are declining in importance in rural counties as a source of jobs and earnings. After-inflation earnings in non-metropolitan manufacturing fell by 5 percent between 1979 and 1986. Mining lost employment during the same period and counties dependent on farming showed decline in income from 1979 to 1986.[2]

Further, 1990 Census counts by the Economic Research Service of the U.S. Department of Agriculture confirm a drop in non-metropolitan population growth between 1980 and 1990. Counties dependent on mining lost 5 percent of their population by 1990 and more than 75 percent of counties that depended on agriculture declined, with an overall drop of 1.4 percent. Areas dependent on manufacturing had a modest population increase of 1.7 percent, but nearly half of them declined.[3]

Stuart Rosenfeld and Ed Bergman reported for the Southern Growth Policies Board that "industrial recruitment should be used in moderation as an element of a comprehensive development strategy but not as the only or even the dominant strategy."[4] Although politically popular, relocating a manufacturing plant to a community does not always net job growth for that community. Used as an only strategy, it can even result in an overall loss of jobs in the long run due to the cyclical nature of certain manufacturing industries.

The tourism and retirement industries are not as visible and do not command as much political popularity, so many communities overlook their potential in developing a more service-based economy. Real hope, however, may lie beyond the smokestacks. The tourism and retirement industries more easily fit the infrastructures of these rural communities, especially if they are located within easy driving distance of a major city. In addition, these industries are

pump primers in that they bring money to a community that can then be used for further economic development. Rosenfeld and Bergman agree, showing that the fastest growth in non-metropolitan counties occurred because of tourism and retirement industries. They define growth as job creation and retention.

The USDA defines non-metropolitan retirement counties as those in which the population age 60 and over in 1980 was at least 15 percent higher than it would have been without the in-migration of older people from 1970 to 1980. The 15 percent net migration rate is based on the residual calculation method mentioned in Chapter 2. Start with the county's 60+ population in 1970, add the people who aged into the age 60+ category between 1970 and 1980 and subtract the people over 50 in the county who died during the decade. If the county's age 60+ population in 1980 was larger than expected after these maneuvers, it is assumed to have resulted from in-migration. This is a residual net migration rate; no migrants' noses are actually counted. Calvin Beale and Glenn Fuguitt, two eminent scholars of rural demography, declare that "retirement counties grew by 2 percent a year throughout the 1980s, twice the growth rate of the total U.S. population."[5]

Professor Nina Glasgow of Cornell University also reported in 1990 that population and employment growth in non-metropolitan retirement counties has outdistanced other non-metropolitan counties depending on manufacturing, mining and agriculture.[6] Retirement areas averaged 15.8 percent population growth in the 1980-1990 decade. Now one-fifth of all non-metropolitan counties are classed as retirement counties. Without the growth in these counties, there would have been no population increase at all in non-metropolitan America.[7]

This argument increasingly is being considered by leaders of metropolitan and non-metropolitan counties when determining economic development strategies. A strong case is presented for attracting tourists and retirees as effective strategies for economic development in rural areas. Generally, retirement areas evolve from areas with high tourism. It is also suggested that these strategies might provide a more efficient use of local resources than manufacturing recruitment in selected areas.

Asserting the Economic Impact of Retirees

A major advantage to recruiting older migrants is that most have steady incomes not vulnerable to normal down cycles in the national economy. Income derived from interest or stocks can fluctuate with business cycles, but Social Security and pension benefits are relatively stable. Spending this income locally leads to economic development and job creation in the community of relocation.

Another advantage to migration is the increase in the tax base. Retirees pay taxes to support institutions like public schools, but they do not attend or send their children there. Large investments in the infrastructure or tax abatements by governments are not required to attract retirees, though they are frequently part of the incentive package used to lure manufacturing plants. Migrants do not pollute or destroy the environment, and having a pool of young retirees available in the community benefits churches and increases the number of volunteers and contributors in local philanthropic and service organizations.

Retirement income can lead to job growth in the same way that industrial payrolls generate jobs. Retirees spend their income in the local economy, creating a demand for goods and services.[8] When the demand/supply ratio becomes more favorable for investment and employment, capital and labor often follow, stimulating economic growth. Jobs follow people with money. Many of the service jobs created will be low-paying as compared to manufacturing/mining. However, there will also be jobs created for higher-income professionals.

A 1986 study by the Federal Reserve Bank of Kansas City found that non-metropolitan counties whose incomes are based on retirees have outpaced all others in per capita income growth. Also, Glasgow reported that counties designated as retirement sites witnessed the largest increases in personal income and employment among all non-metropolitan counties.[9] She notes that per capita income in non-metropolitan retirement counties is still below the average for all non-metropolitan counties.[10]

Older migrants add to an existing mature market, increasing the importance of this segment. The consumption potential of older households is seen not just in their incomes but in their accumulated assets, a resource that can be drawn on for large purchases.[11] The balance in their savings accounts are larger than households in general and their homes are worth 20 percent more than the average home in the United States.[12] Consumption studies have shown that older consumers purchase not only houses and other durable goods, but non-durable goods and services as well, including food, travel, recreation, entertainment and medical care.

Eighty percent of the mature market own their home and 80 percent of those are mortgage-free. Most of these retirees come into the community and immediately purchase a home. They then invest the remainder of the proceeds from the sale of their last house into the host community financial institutions. Many of them also transfer significant assets into local investments.

Older amenity migrants will continue to be a good source of economic development[13] because such migrants tend more often to have multiple sources of income,[14] better health,[15] better education[16] and earlier retirements[17] than retirees who are aging in place.[18]

The consequences of retirement migration are quite different from those of younger migration. The elderly influence state economies primarily through their consumption demands rather than through participation in labor markets. The impacts of older migrants on state economies, annually, can be quite large. The migrant retiree "industry" impacts major segments of the economies where they settle, including real estate, financial institutions, recreation, health,

insurance and retail.[19] When rural counties float on a cushion of Social Security, pensions, annuities and asset income, local economic conditions improve, particularly in the service sector.

Retirement migration has a strong upside as a source of real economic development. It is no wonder, then, that towns, counties and entire states have begun to recruit older interstate migrants. Local and state governments are getting involved by financing the marketing of their communities and providing technical assistance to these communities during the organizing of their retiree attraction committees.

Empirical Evidence for the Economic Impact of Mobile Retirees

A Brandeis economist, William Crown, and the author examined the 1979 incomes of older interstate migrants, using 1980 Census microdata. The incomes were not imputed from national or regional averages or from all in- or out-migrants, but only from the individuals in the migration flows. The net income transfers for 1979 are shown in Table 1. These data do not include information on assets or on the multiplier effect of the income transfers into each state.[20]

The list of states gaining a net transfer of more than $100 million a year from older migrants reads like a Who's Who of the Sun Belt. Florida tops the list of states benefiting from retirement migration according to these estimates. It had a net gain of nearly $3.5 billion annually. Nine other states—Arizona, Texas, North Carolina, Arkansas, Oregon, South Carolina, Nevada, Georgia and Washington—posted net gains of $100 million or more annually from their elderly migrants. New Mexico and California just missed the elite top 10 in Table 1.

Regions that gain income as a result of elderly migrants do so at the expense of other regions. In a closed economy, the net value of these transfers must be zero. Thus, the migration of the elderly is primarily important because of its impact on the local, state and regional, rather than the national, economy.[21]

New York, at the bottom of the state list, stands alone as the only billion-dollar loser (it lost nearly $2 billion) in its exchange with all other states. The states of Illinois, Ohio, Michigan, Pennsylvania, New Jersey, Massachusetts, Indiana, Maryland and Connecticut round out the bottom 10 states in Table 1. Each lost more than $100 million a year in net income through retirement migration.

Table 2 contains the parallel estimates from the 1990 Census microdata covering the period 1985-1990. Constant dollars are not reported in Table 2. Even though inflation was relatively low in the 1980s, it is one factor accounting for the differences in the numbers between the two tables. In 1989 dollars, Florida's net income transfer from older migrants was more than $6.5 billion. In 1980, Florida was the only billionaire state due to migrant income. It was joined in 1990 by Arizona, which netted nearly $1.2 billion. North Carolina moved up from fourth to third place in net income from interstate migrants, with $742 million. Nevada jumped from eighth to fourth place, keeping $516 million. South Carolina, Georgia and Washington also moved up. Those in the top 10 that fell in the rankings over the decade were

Table 1 — Total Annual Income* Transferred to and from Each State, and the Net Amount, by Migrants Age 60+, 1975-1980

Rank	State	Income Transferred Into State	Income Transferred Out of State	Net Income Transferred
1	Florida	$4,103,914,000	$635,980,000	$3,467,934,000
2	Arizona	883,716,000	191,911,000	691,805,000
3	Texas	684,529,000	296,231,000	388,298,000
4	North Carolina	324,244,000	154,102,000	170,142,000
5	Arkansas	257,864,000	89,609,000	168,255,000
6	Oregon	260,814,000	133,189,000	127,625,000
7	South Carolina	186,096,000	68,775,000	117,321,000
8	Nevada	197,765,000	82,044,000	115,721,000
9	Georgia	272,284,000	157,634,000	114,650,000
10	Washington	302,173,000	189,479,000	112,694,000
11	New Mexico	158,908,000	65,447,000	93,461,000
12	California	1,227,512,000	1,137,358,000	90,154,000
13	Tennessee	196,395,000	151,862,000	44,533,000
14	Alabama	130,617,000	92,147,000	38,470,000
15	Mississippi	105,057,000	68,090,000	36,967,000
16	Hawaii	70,613,000	39,899,000	30,714,000
17	New Hampshire	92,748,000	66,905,000	25,843,000
18	Maine	77,938,000	55,800,000	22,138,000
19	Utah	66,435,000	47,147,000	19,288,000
20	Oklahoma	144,828,000	132,331,000	12,497,000
21	Colorado	229,307,000	218,378,000	10,929,000
22	Idaho	68,275,000	62,463,000	5,812,000
23	Delaware	49,264,000	45,574,000	3,690,000
24	Vermont	39,456,000	36,936,000	2,520,000
25	Virginia	332,850,000	335,487,000	-2,637,000
26	Kentucky	112,020,000	127,478,000	-15,458,000
27	South Dakota	29,309,000	46,977,000	-17,668,000
28	North Dakota	18,203,000	35,973,000	-17,770,000
29	Wyoming	18,711,000	37,814,000	-19,103,000
30	Nebraska	55,310,000	76,280,000	-20,970,000
31	Rhode Island	32,479,000	55,498,000	-23,019,000
32	Louisiana	92,054,000	116,069,000	-24,015,000
33	Alaska	19,589,000	47,834,000	-28,245,000
34	Montana	35,358,000	66,676,000	-31,318,000
35	West Virginia	56,996,000	96,458,000	-39,462,000
36	Kansas	99,726,000	158,681,000	-58,955,000
37	Missouri	212,738,000	272,734,000	-59,996,000
38	Minnesota	104,334,000	182,721,000	-78,387,000
39	Wisconsin	145,459,000	235,097,000	-89,638,000
40	Iowa	87,727,000	178,908,000	-91,181,000
41	D.C.	36,733,000	128,369,000	-91,636,000
42	Connecticut	178,969,000	328,573,000	-149,604,000
43	Maryland	212,441,000	372,075,000	-159,634,000
44	Indiana	162,435,000	323,028,000	-160,593,000
45	Massachusetts	177,229,000	404,774,000	-227,545,000
46	New Jersey	432,034,000	783,727,000	-351,693,000
47	Pennsylvania	296,202,000	683,618,000	-387,416,000
48	Michigan	157,891,000	629,123,000	-471,232,000
49	Ohio	206,984,000	707,090,000	-500,106,000
50	Illinois	251,039,000	1,089,509,000	-838,470,000
51	New York	257,403,000	2,213,114,000	-1,955,711,000

* Based on migrants' 1979 income, in 1979 dollars.

Table 2 — Total Annual Income* Transferred to and from Each State, and the Net Amount, by Migrants Age 60+, 1985-1990

Rank	State	Income Transferred Into State	Income Transferred Out of State	Net Income Transferred
1	Florida	$8,342,910,000	$1,818,332,000	$6,524,578,000
2	Arizona	1,710,692,000	538,890,000	1,171,802,000
3	North Carolina	1,150,396,000	408,826,000	741,570,000
4	Nevada	735,505,000	219,849,000	515,656,000
5	South Carolina	674,741,000	261,610,000	413,131,000
6	Oregon	638,641,000	314,019,000	324,622,000
7	Georgia	740,893,000	448,881,000	292,012,000
8	Washington	764,331,000	474,048,000	290,283,000
9	Arkansas	430,879,000	217,121,000	213,758,000
10	Texas	1,268,559,000	1,117,594,000	150,965,000
11	Tennessee	509,692,000	371,953,000	137,739,000
12	Alabama	357,643,000	257,282,000	100,361,000
13	New Mexico	312,226,000	214,832,000	97,394,000
14	Mississippi	242,324,000	171,859,000	70,465,000
15	Maine	208,046,000	152,367,000	55,679,000
16	New Hampshire	268,882,000	236,465,000	32,417,000
17	Utah	159,862,000	132,358,000	27,504,000
18	Kentucky	301,664,000	278,139,000	23,525,000
19	Colorado	505,026,000	490,154,000	14,872,000
20	Delaware	127,552,000	113,512,000	14,040,000
21	Hawaii	169,901,000	158,247,000	11,654,000
22	Oklahoma	326,043,000	314,760,000	11,283,000
23	Vermont	95,222,000	88,002,000	7,220,000
24	West Virginia	164,463,000	168,430,000	-3,967,000
25	Missouri	521,002,000	525,652,000	-4,650,000
26	Idaho	157,196,000	166,004,000	-8,808,000
27	North Dakota	40,135,000	54,808,000	-14,673,000
28	Montana	85,072,000	105,120,000	-20,048,000
29	South Dakota	52,882,000	75,230,000	-22,348,000
30	Nebraska	122,805,000	167,848,000	-45,043,000
31	Virginia	844,398,000	893,286,000	-48,888,000
32	Wyoming	53,135,000	103,098,000	-49,963,000
33	Alaska	43,382,000	103,379,000	-59,997,000
34	Rhode Island	98,880,000	163,500,000	-64,620,000
35	Kansas	239,985,000	330,750,000	-90,765,000
36	D.C.	119,621,000	221,273,000	-101,652,000
37	Louisiana	206,203,000	327,262,000	-121,059,000
38	Minnesota	271,092,000	392,675,000	-121,583,000
39	Wisconsin	366,607,000	543,345,000	-176,738,000
40	Indiana	421,973,000	602,752,000	-180,779,000
41	Iowa	149,046,000	332,637,000	-183,591,000
42	Maryland	610,670,000	841,704,000	-231,034,000
43	Pennsylvania	911,850,000	1,368,380,000	-456,530,000
44	Massachusetts	403,577,000	1,008,928,000	-605,351,000
45	Connecticut	346,312,000	955,668,000	-609,356,000
46	Ohio	605,979,000	1,255,894,000	-649,915,000
47	California	2,340,621,000	3,038,983,000	-698,362,000
48	Michigan	452,139,000	1,329,969,000	-877,830,000
49	New Jersey	799,547,000	1,959,365,000	-1,159,818,000
50	Illinois	549,803,000	1,884,766,000	-1,334,963,000
51	New York	675,423,000	3,975,621,000	-3,300,198,000

* Based on migrants' 1989 income, in 1989 dollars.

Figure 1 — State Distribution of the Annual Income Transferred by Migrants Age 60+, 1985-1990

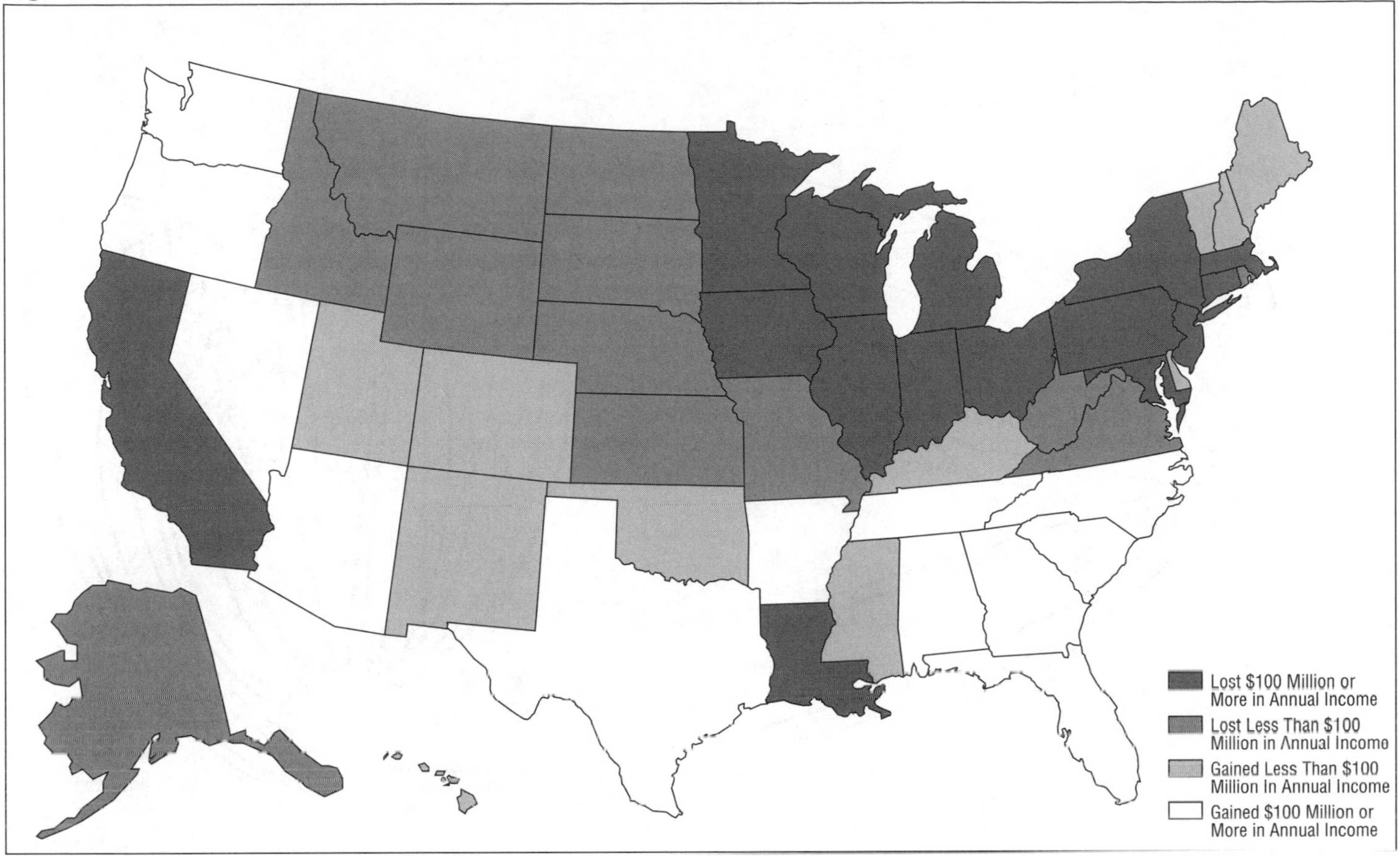

Legend:
- Lost $100 Million or More in Annual Income
- Lost Less Than $100 Million in Annual Income
- Gained Less Than $100 Million In Annual Income
- Gained $100 Million or More in Annual Income

Arkansas (from fifth to ninth) and Texas (from third to 10th). Oregon was sixth in net income transferred in both decades.

In 1990 there were 12 states that posted net gains of at least $100 million, the 10 already listed plus Tennessee and Alabama. Fifteen states and the District of Columbia lost at least $100 million, led by New York at $3.3 billion, Illinois at $1.3 billion and New Jersey at $1.2 billion. Michigan, California, Ohio, Connecticut, Massachusetts, Pennsylvania, Maryland, Iowa, Indiana, Wisconsin, Minnesota and Louisiana rounded out the list.

The relative stability of the net income transfer is remarkable. The same 10 states topped both tables, and nine of the bottom 10 states in 1980 were back in 1990. The only states to drop from positive to negative net income between 1980 and 1990 were Idaho and California, and the only state to move out of the negative numbers was Kentucky. Figure 1 illustrates the net income transfer picture for the entire United States in 1990.

If income transfers were thought of in the same way as stream migration, which states would be linked? Based on the 1980 Census, there were 18 specific state-to-state transfers of migrant income amounting to more than $100 million, from a total of 1,815 transfers in the entire matrix (see Table 3.) The largest single one-year transfer, by far, was $1.2 billion, from New York to Florida. Florida's bounty does not end there, however. Ten of the 18 largest transfers were to Florida — from New York, New Jersey, Ohio, Illinois, Pennsylvania, Michigan, Massachusetts, Maryland,

Table 3 — State-to-State Income Transfers Of More Than $100 Million* By In-migrants Age 60+, 1975-1980

Rank	Destination	Origin	Income Transferred	# of In-migrants
1	Florida	New York	$1,186,651,000	127,600
2	Florida	New Jersey	367,472,000	38,440
3	Florida	Ohio	322,304,000	37,720
4	Florida	Illinois	321,181,000	30,680
5	Florida	Pennsylvania	291,871,000	31,600
6	Florida	Michigan	269,896,000	28,320
7	New Jersey	New York	237,327,000	24,320
8	Florida	Massachusetts	180,645,000	19,840
9	California	New York	168,840,000	18,360
10	Arizona	California	142,358,000	16,440
11	Oregon	California	138,524,000	17,080
12	Florida	Maryland	135,134,000	11,480
13	California	Illinois	134,760,000	13,960
14	Florida	Connecticut	133,415,000	13,280
15	Florida	Indiana	126,610,000	14,320
16	Washington	California	115,346,000	12,360
17	Nevada	California	103,889,000	11,680
18	Arizona	Illinois	100,334,000	11,520

*Based on migrants' 1979 income, in 1979 dollars.

Figure 2 — State-to-State Income Transfers of More Than $100 Million* by In-migrants Age 60+, 1985-1990

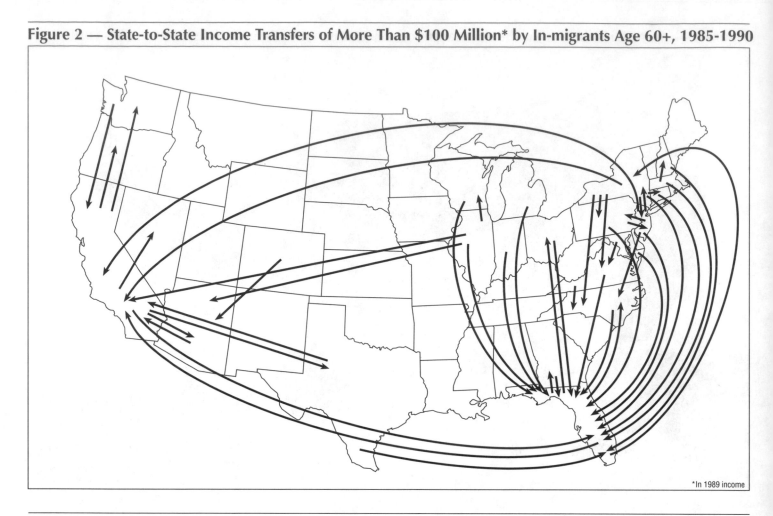

*In 1989 income

Table 4 — State-to-State Income Transfers of More Than $100 Million* by In-migrants Age 60+, 1985-1990

Rank	Destination	Origin	Income Transferred	# of In-migrants	Rank	Destination	Origin	Income Transferred	# of In-migrants
1	Florida	New York	$1,864,339,000	104,019	25	Georgia	Florida	166,925,000	11,533
2	Florida	New Jersey	729,275,000	41,315	26	Texas	California	164,353,000	10,134
3	Florida	Michigan	607,107,000	32,058	27	Arizona	Illinois	155,915,000	8,460
4	Florida	Pennsylvania	534,587,000	27,567	28	Florida	Georgia	151,993,000	9,210
5	Florida	Ohio	509,092,000	27,986	29	New Jersey	Pennsylvania	148,554,000	9,663
6	Florida	Illinois	481,950,000	25,893	30	North Carolina	Florida	145,133,000	8,841
7	Florida	Massachusetts	466,280,000	25,450	31	California	Arizona	141,690,000	9,134
8	New Jersey	New York	425,578,000	23,903	32	California	Florida	138,311,000	7,731
9	Florida	Connecticut	410,191,000	18,952	33	Wisconsin	Illinois	125,831,000	8,568
10	Arizona	California	384,917,000	23,331	34	Florida	North Carolina	123,418,000	6,385
11	Nevada	California	376,082,000	21,389	35	New York	New Jersey	122,773,000	7,716
12	Oregon	California	350,172,000	23,069	36	Florida	Texas	120,590,000	6,787
13	Washington	California	295,262,000	16,689	37	Virginia	New York	119,699,000	6,972
14	Florida	Virginia	263,315,000	11,582	38	Connecticut	New York	118,796,000	5,689
15	Pennsylvania	New Jersey	251,648,000	14,820	39	New Hampshire	Massachusetts	115,769,000	7,058
16	Florida	Maryland	242,999,000	11,432	40	New York	Florida	112,293,000	9,063
17	Florida	Indiana	226,915,000	13,327	41	North Carolina	New Jersey	110,772,000	5,871
18	California	New York	221,397,000	11,695	42	California	Washington	107,878,000	6,460
19	Florida	California	214,299,000	13,407	43	Virginia	Maryland	106,311,000	5,109
20	Florida	Wisconsin	207,023,000	9,763	44	North Carolina	Virginia	105,047,000	6,102
21	California	Illinois	184,795,000	9,136	45	California	New Jersey	103,553,000	4,611
22	Pennsylvania	New York	181,798,000	10,404	46	Florida	New Hampshire	102,105,000	5,504
23	North Carolina	New York	178,068,000	10,356	47	Arizona	Colorado	101,984,000	5,461
24	California	Texas	173,904,000	9,597	48	Ohio	Florida	100,463,000	8,707

*Based on migrants' 1989 income, in 1989 dollars.

Table 5 — Mean and Median Household Income* of Interstate In-migrants Age 60+, 1985-1990

State	# of In-migrants	Mean	Median	State	# of In-migrants	Mean	Median
Alabama	25,336	$27,623	$20,000	Montana	6,140	$22,408	$15,348
Alaska	2,395	44,788	38,883	Nebraska	9,852	21,389	15,816
Arizona	98,756	32,406	26,122	Nevada	43,131	33,491	25,617
Arkansas	29,848	25,889	19,002	New Hampshire	15,058	34,500	29,992
California	131,514	39,454	28,729	New Jersey	49,176	39,658	30,500
Colorado	30,672	31,988	23,672	New Mexico	19,872	30,844	22,972
Connecticut	17,351	41,265	31,476	New York	42,802	37,441	23,760
Delaware	8,026	31,206	23,000	North Carolina	64,530	33,254	27,576
D.C.	4,821	42,182	23,553	North Dakota	3,140	20,270	17,032
Florida	451,709	34,565	26,793	Ohio	44,459	27,135	19,395
Georgia	44,475	34,507	22,900	Oklahoma	23,572	25,228	16,424
Hawaii	8,053	43,378	35,200	Oregon	43,996	26,693	21,773
Idaho	10,832	27,522	19,180	Pennsylvania	57,538	31,294	22,378
Illinois	36,897	30,314	18,962	Rhode Island	5,842	34,025	24,000
Indiana	31,405	25,910	18,997	South Carolina	34,251	35,757	27,347
Iowa	11,669	21,329	16,657	South Dakota	4,141	22,497	17,838
Kansas	16,492	27,736	17,670	Tennessee	36,306	26,924	19,641
Kentucky	21,770	24,441	18,282	Texas	78,117	32,208	23,635
Louisiana	14,004	28,854	18,081	Utah	10,751	29,728	21,158
Maine	11,929	32,400	26,200	Vermont	5,916	27,989	25,853
Maryland	32,428	42,597	34,442	Virginia	46,554	38,585	27,566
Massachusetts	23,796	35,563	25,400	Washington	47,484	31,495	24,491
Michigan	31,885	30,413	20,124	West Virginia	12,919	24,960	16,304
Minnesota	19,370	24,533	19,630	Wisconsin	23,030	27,128	20,896
Mississippi	17,637	24,443	16,888	Wyoming	4,207	22,409	15,655
Missouri	35,251	29,076	19,164	**Overall U.S.**		**$32,769**	**$24,498**

*Based on migrants' 1989 income, in 1989 dollars.

Connecticut and Indiana. California received two long-distance transfers from New York and Illinois, and Arizona received transfers from California and Illinois. The other transfers were to New Jersey from New York, and to Oregon, Washington and Nevada from California.

By 1990, the number of streams containing more than $100 million in income had grown from 18 to 48. They are listed in Table 4 and illustrated in Figure 2. Seventeen were to Florida, actually a smaller share than in the earlier decade. The largest stream was the same in both decades: New York to Florida. New York sent nearly $1.9 billion of retirement income to Florida, a 57 percent increase from the prior decade.

After Florida there were seven streams to California, four to North Carolina, three to Arizona, two each to New Jersey, Pennsylvania, New York and Virginia, and one each to Nevada, Oregon, Washington, Georgia, Texas, Wisconsin, Connecticut, New Hampshire and Ohio.

New York originated the most streams, seven. California sent six and New Jersey and Florida each sent five. Illinois originated four streams and Pennsylvania, Massachusetts, Virginia, Maryland and Texas sent two streams apiece. Michigan, Ohio, Connecticut, Indiana, Wisconsin, Georgia, North Carolina, Washington, New Hampshire, Colorado and Arizona each originated one stream.

The economic impact of transferred income is not confined to the destination. State economies are interconnected.

If an older in-migrant to North Carolina buys a car, this will affect the production of automobiles in Michigan, which in turn will influence the production of tires in Ohio and car radios in Illinois. Moreover, if elderly migration influences the redistribution of wealth and regional labor markets, it may also influence patterns of regional investment and the efficiency with which goods and services get produced. Consequently, it is probable that retirement migration has an impact on national economic growth even though the net income transfer among regions of origin and destination is zero.

Household Income Distribution Among Migrants in 1990

Table 5 displays the mean and median household incomes of migrants into each state during the 1985-1990 migration period.

Mean migrant household incomes range from $44,788 for older migrants to Alaska (all 2,395 of them) to $20,270 for older migrants to North Dakota. Unfortunately, means can be skewed upward by only a few households with extremely high incomes. The median is sometimes preferred, because it cuts the distribution exactly in half and is not skewed in this way. Median household incomes range from $38,883 for Alaska in-migrants to $15,348 for migrants to Montana.

Migration boosters who imagine that older migrants are all well-to-do, with a great deal of discretionary income,

Table 6 — Distribution of Median Household Income* Among In-migrants Age 60+, 1985-1990

	0-$19,999	$20,000-29,999	$30,000-39,999	$40,000-49,999	$50,000+	Total
Percent	41.9	18.1	12.2	8.3	19.4	99.9†
Number	796,196	344,378	232,568	158,337	369,626	1,901,105

*Based on migrants' 1989 income, in 1989 dollars. †rounding error

may find the data in Table 5 disappointing. It is important to remember that all interstate migrants are not amenity migrants, the segment that appeals to economic developers. Many are dependency migrants, some of whom are widowed and living on one income. Their household incomes pull down the mean and median for the group as a whole. The most relevant issue to economic developers is the size and nature of the amenity migrant segment, but census data does not allow us to distinguish between the two types.

If there is a point of consensus today among research gerontologists, it is that the older population in America is more diverse than the general population on nearly every characteristic. Income means and medians do not demonstrate this diversity; they are measures of central tendency. In Table 6, however, household income of older migrants from 1985 to 1990 is broken into five categories. This spread should allow readers to examine whatever slices of the income range they find relevant.

Nationally, about one-fifth (19.4 percent) of interstate migrants have household incomes of $50,000 or more, 8.3 percent fall into the $40,000-$49,999 category, 12.2 percent earn $30,000-$39,999, 18.1 percent earn $20,000-$29,999 and 41.9 percent earn less than $20,000. More than a quarter (27.7 percent) have incomes of $40,000 or more, and these are the retirees who have the greatest positive impact on local economic development. Economic impact depends not only on the number of migrants, but upon their income as well.

Using the national averages for comparisons, it is possible to characterize the incomes of retirees who move into the various states. Table 7 shows the distribution of household income for each state. One might expect, for example, that Florida would receive large proportions of migrants with higher household incomes, because so many are from New York, a high income state. It was noted that a large amount of retirement income transfers to Florida from other states. Yet, a glance at the Florida line in Table 7 shows that it resembles the national averages shown in Table 6, with somewhat smaller proportions on the high and low ends, and somewhat more in the middle categories.

Arizona, Nevada, New Mexico and Washington have profiles similar to Florida's. Texas, Connecticut, Delaware, Massachusetts, New York, Rhode Island and the District of Columbia attract more migrants in both the highest and lowest categories.

Some states draw higher than average proportions of upper income interstate retirees and lower than average proportions of low income retirees. These states are illustrated in Figure 3, and include Alaska, California, Hawaii, Maryland, New Hampshire, New Jersey, North Carolina, South Carolina and Virginia.

The states that attract larger than average proportions of

migrants with lower household incomes, and smaller proportions of upper income retirees are Alabama, Arkansas, Colorado, Idaho, Indiana, Iowa, Kansas, Kentucky, Louisiana, Michigan, Minnesota, Mississippi, Missouri, Montana, Nebraska, North Dakota, Ohio, Oklahoma, Oregon, Pennsylvania, South Dakota, Tennessee, Utah, Vermont, West Virginia, Wisconsin and Wyoming. These states are also illustrated in Figure 3.

Illinois attracts a higher than average number of migrants in the lowest income category and matches the national average in the highest income category.

Income Breakdown For Top Receiving Counties

The 100 retirement counties or county groups that received the largest numbers of interstate migrants from 1985 to 1990 are arrayed in descending order by number of migrants in Table 8. The distribution of migrant household income is provided for each county.

Taken together, the distribution of household income in these counties is somewhat higher than that found in Table 6 for the United States as a whole. The proportion in the lowest income category is slightly smaller and those in the higher categories are slightly larger, but the differences are not impressive. About one-fifth (20.8 percent) of the migrants' households have incomes over $50,000, and 29.9 percent have incomes over $40,000.

Which counties receive the highest proportions of affluent retirees? The county group including Fairfax County and the independent cities of Fairfax and Falls Church, VA, has the highest proportion (51.1 percent) of migrants earning over $50,000. The data in Chapter 5 would suggest that many of these retirees moved from Washington, DC.

There are 14 counties or county groups where more than 30 percent of inbound migrants earn more than $50,000. Two other DC suburban counties, Montgomery (36.2 percent) and Prince Georges (35.8 percent) counties, in Maryland, join Fairfax, VA.

Four counties are in California, where the increasing value of housing may have discouraged retirees with more modest household incomes. San Diego (31.8 percent), Orange (39.3 percent) and Ventura (34.7 percent) counties in Southern California and Santa Clara County (49.0 percent) in the Bay Area made this elite list. The others are in the East. Palm Beach County (31.0 percent) and the county group consisting of Collier and Monroe counties (38.9 percent) are in Florida. Farther north, Middlesex County (45.1 percent) and Bergen County (47.6 percent), NJ, join Middlesex County (33.1 percent), MA, Fairfield County (40.9 percent), CT, and Bucks County (30.3 percent), PA.

In 1990, more than one-third (36.9 percent) of migrants into the leading 100 retirement counties or county groups

Table 7 — Distribution of Household Income Among In-migrants Age 60+, 1985-1990, by State

State	0-$19,999	$20,000-29,999	$30,000-39,999	$40,000-49,999	$50,000+	Totals
Alabama						
Percent	49.4	18.3	11.2	6.5	14.6	100.0
Number	12,528	4,633	2,841	1,643	3,691	25,336
Alaska						
Percent	27.1	7.3	17.8	13.8	33.9	99.9*
Number	650	175	427	330	813	2,395
Arizona						
Percent	36.1	22.8	14.3	9.2	17.6	100.0
Number	35,603	22,540	14,152	9,093	17,368	98,756
Arkansas						
Percent	48.1	19.2	13.3	8.6	10.7	99.9*
Number	14,364	5,741	3,967	2,570	3,206	29,848
California						
Percent	36.5	15.9	10.8	8.8	28.0	100.0
Number	47,946	20,865	14,269	11,591	36,843	131,514
Colorado						
Percent	43.5	18.4	11.5	7.6	19.0	100.0
Number	13,356	5,643	3,513	2,343	5,817	30,672
Connecticut						
Percent	43.6	9.8	7.7	7.7	31.1	99.9*
Number	7,558	1,708	1,343	1,339	5,403	17,351
Delaware						
Percent	43.6	17.4	10.4	8.2	20.4	100.0
Number	3,502	1,395	831	661	1,637	8,026
D.C.						
Percent	48.9	11.6	7.3	3.7	28.5	100.0
Number	2,359	558	350	178	1,376	4,821
Florida						
Percent	34.9	22.3	14.7	9.4	18.7	100.0
Number	157,756	100,653	66,361	42,449	84,490	451,709
Georgia						
Percent	43.3	15.6	12.0	7.2	21.8	99.9*
Number	19,261	6,945	5,347	3,205	9,717	44,475
Hawaii						
Percent	27.5	16.1	14.9	11.6	29.8	99.9*
Number	2,218	1,298	1,198	936	2,403	8,053
Idaho						
Percent	52.8	15.5	10.4	6.9	14.3	99.9*
Number	5,724	1,684	1,128	748	1,548	10,832
Illinois						
Percent	51.3	13.6	9.0	6.7	19.4	100.0
Number	18,930	5,004	3,318	2,484	7,161	36,897
Indiana						
Percent	51.4	17.5	10.8	6.5	13.7	99.9*
Number	16,140	5,498	3,405	2,047	4,315	31,405
Iowa						
Percent	59.1	18.0	7.4	4.7	10.8	100.0
Number	6,899	2,095	865	554	1,256	11,669
Kansas						
Percent	51.3	16.3	10.2	7.5	14.8	100.1*
Number	8,459	2,685	1,674	1,240	2,434	16,492

*rounding error

Table 7 — Distribution of Household Income Among In-migrants Age 60+, 1985-1990, by State

State	0-$19,999	$20,000-29,999	$30,000-39,999	$40,000-49,999	$50,000+	Totals
Kentucky						
Percent	55.7	17.5	10.0	4.9	12.0	100.1*
Number	12,117	3,800	2,169	1,072	2,612	21,770
Louisiana						
Percent	54.5	10.4	8.8	9.0	17.3	100.0
Number	7,635	1,458	1,227	1,257	2,427	14,004
Maine						
Percent	36.4	20.2	14.1	10.2	19.1	100.0
Number	4,343	2,410	1,685	1,211	2,280	11,929
Maryland						
Percent	35.4	11.4	13.8	9.3	30.2	100.1*
Number	11,464	3,693	4,464	3,010	9,797	32,428
Massachusetts						
Percent	47.7	10.7	10.3	5.7	25.6	100.0
Number	11,361	2,546	2,458	1,348	6,083	23,796
Michigan						
Percent	49.2	16.3	10.5	5.3	18.7	100.0
Number	15,698	5,189	3,361	1,684	5,953	31,885
Minnesota						
Percent	58.1	13.7	6.1	8.2	13.9	100.0
Number	11,262	2,656	1,172	1,586	2,694	19,370
Mississippi						
Percent	57.5	14.4	8.1	6.8	13.3	100.1*
Number	10,134	2,547	1,425	1,191	2,340	17,637
Missouri						
Percent	49.7	16.7	9.5	7.6	16.5	100.0
Number	17,524	5,892	3,336	2,689	5,810	35,251
Montana						
Percent	55.4	13.9	13.9	6.9	10.0	100.1*
Number	3,399	854	851	421	615	6,140
Nebraska						
Percent	57.9	15.5	13.3	5.4	7.8	99.9*
Number	5,708	1,529	1,312	530	773	9,852
Nevada						
Percent	36.8	21.6	14.2	10.0	17.4	100.0
Number	15,872	9,314	6,137	4,318	7,490	43,131
New Hampshire						
Percent	34.1	18.4	13.4	10.3	23.8	100.0
Number	5,132	2,776	2,021	1,545	3,584	15,058
New Jersey						
Percent	36.6	14.8	11.3	8.3	29.0	100.0
Number	17,999	7,301	5,562	4,063	14,251	49,176
New Mexico						
Percent	40.9	19.6	12.7	10.1	16.7	100.0
Number	8,121	3,885	2,526	2,013	3,327	19,872
New York						
Percent	44.5	13.1	10.3	7.4	24.7	100.0
Number	19,028	5,619	4,406	3,183	10,566	42,802
North Carolina						
Percent	37.2	18.6	13.7	10.5	20.0	100.0
Number	24,003	12,024	8,829	6,777	12,897	64,530

*rounding error

State	0-$19,999	$20,000-29,999	Range of Household Income $30,000-39,999	$40,000-49,999	$50,000+	Totals
North Dakota						
Percent	58.3	20.5	9.1	4.6	7.5	100.0
Number	1,830	645	285	145	235	3,140
Ohio						
Percent	51.0	17.6	9.9	7.2	14.3	100.0
Number	22,675	7,831	4,411	3,191	6,351	44,459
Oklahoma						
Percent	56.7	16.8	8.5	5.6	12.4	100.0
Number	13,358	3,966	2,007	1,325	2,916	23,572
Oregon						
Percent	46.7	21.2	11.9	8.5	11.6	99.9*
Number	20,554	9,312	5,255	3,758	5,117	43,996
Pennsylvania						
Percent	45.5	15.7	12.4	8.0	18.5	100.1*
Number	26,152	9,024	7,117	4,582	10,663	57,538
Rhode Island						
Percent	42.2	15.3	9.9	7.9	24.7	100.0
Number	2,464	896	579	462	1,441	5,842
South Carolina						
Percent	37.2	18.8	13.8	7.3	22.9	100.0
Number	12,753	6,435	4,713	2,517	7,833	34,251
South Dakota						
Percent	55.8	21.0	7.5	5.0	10.8	100.1*
Number	2,309	869	311	205	447	4,141
Tennessee						
Percent	50.8	17.2	9.8	6.7	15.6	100.1*
Number	18,444	6,240	3,543	2,424	5,655	36,306
Texas						
Percent	44.0	16.1	11.4	8.6	19.9	100.0
Number	34,366	12,570	8,925	6,687	15,569	78,117
Utah						
Percent	44.0	21.4	12.0	6.3	16.2	99.9*
Number	4,733	2,306	1,292	678	1,742	10,751
Vermont						
Percent	45.4	20.5	11.9	7.4	14.8	100.0
Number	2,685	1,214	706	438	873	5,916
Virginia						
Percent	39.1	13.6	10.9	8.4	28.1	100.1*
Number	18,192	6,345	5,055	3,891	13,071	46,554
Washington						
Percent	40.7	17.7	13.7	8.8	19.2	100.1*
Number	19,335	8,385	6,486	4,176	9,102	47,484
West Virginia						
Percent	59.4	12.5	8.0	6.5	13.6	100.0
Number	7,679	1,609	1,030	845	1,756	12,919
Wisconsin						
Percent	51.4	15.8	11.5	6.8	14.5	100.0
Number	11,846	3,632	2,646	1,571	3,335	23,030
Wyoming						
Percent	65.8	11.6	6.6	3.2	12.9	100.1*
Number	2,768	486	277	133	543	4,207

Table 8 — Distribution of Household Income Among In-migrants Age 60+, 1985-1990, for Top 100 Receiving Counties

County or County Group	0-$19,999	$20,000-29,999	$30,000-39,999	$40,000-49,999	$50,000+	Totals
1. MARICOPA COUNTY, ARIZONA						
Percent	32.7	23.1	14.6	9.6	20.0	100.0
Number	17,744	12,516	7,934	5,215	10,882	54,291
2. PALM BEACH COUNTY, FLORIDA						
Percent	27.3	17.9	13.8	9.9	31.0	99.9*
Number	12,958	8,500	6,570	4,695	14,721	47,444
3. BROWARD COUNTY, FLORIDA						
Percent	36.1	18.2	15.0	10.7	19.9	99.9*
Number	14,543	7,316	6,060	4,319	8,034	40,272
4. PINELLAS COUNTY, FLORIDA						
Percent	39.2	22.1	14.8	9.0	15.0	100.1*
Number	13,733	7,738	5,187	3,145	5,262	35,065
5. CLARK COUNTY, NEVADA						
Percent	35.6	21.7	15.0	10.5	17.2	100.0
Number	10,996	6,693	4,635	3,243	5,298	30,865
6. LEE COUNTY, FLORIDA						
Percent	29.3	23.0	16.9	9.5	21.4	100.1*
Number	7,391	5,798	4,263	2,399	5,404	25,255
7. LOS ANGELES COUNTY, CALIFORNIA						
Percent	41.0	12.0	9.7	9.4	27.8	99.9*
Number	9,845	2,888	2,323	2,268	6,681	24,005
8. SARASOTA COUNTY, FLORIDA						
Percent	22.5	23.6	15.5	10.9	27.5	100.0
Number	5,010	5,242	3,445	2,425	6,103	22,225
9. PASCO COUNTY, FLORIDA						
Percent	45.5	26.0	12.8	9.0	6.6	99.9*
Number	10,062	5,755	2,830	1,992	1,465	22,104
10. DADE COUNTY, FLORIDA						
Percent	46.2	18.0	8.8	8.0	19.0	100.0
Number	9,846	3,825	1,879	1,715	4,040	21,305
11. SAN DIEGO COUNTY, CALIFORNIA						
Percent	29.3	17.1	12.6	9.3	31.8	100.1*
Number	5,903	3,443	2,538	1,870	6,401	20,155
12. PIMA COUNTY, ARIZONA						
Percent	33.7	20.1	15.2	10.2	20.9	100.1*
Number	6,127	3,647	2,770	1,847	3,791	18,182
13. VOLUSIA COUNTY, FLORIDA						
Percent	38.8	24.8	15.3	8.9	12.1	99.9*
Number	6,753	4,313	2,671	1,557	2,113	17,407
14. POLK COUNTY , FLORIDA						
Percent	40.1	26.9	14.9	7.7	10.5	100.1*
Number	6,242	4,188	2,312	1,197	1,627	15,566
15. BREVARD COUNTY, FLORIDA						
Percent	34.5	23.6	16.6	10.3	15.0	100.0
Number	5,048	3,451	2,432	1,499	2,191	14,621
16. COLLIER AND MONROE COUNTIES, FLORIDA						
Percent	17.9	16.2	16.1	10.8	38.9	99.9*
Number	2,579	2,344	2,331	1,558	5,622	14,434
17. HILLSBOROUGH COUNTY, FLORIDA						
Percent	37.9	20.1	13.4	9.2	19.4	100.0
Number	5,326	2,817	1,884	1,291	2,718	14,036

* rounding error †independent city

| County or County Group | Range of Household Income | | | | | |
	0-$19,999	$20,000-29,999	$30,000-39,999	$40,000-49,999	$50,000+	Totals
18. RIVERSIDE COUNTY, CALIFORNIA						
Percent	34.4	21.3	12.6	8.9	22.8	100.0
Number	4,688	2,904	1,725	1,216	3,111	13,644
19. CHARLOTTE COUNTY, FLORIDA						
Percent	31.1	29.0	13.8	9.9	16.3	100.1*
Number	4,085	3,809	1,807	1,295	2,138	13,134
20. MANATEE COUNTY, FLORIDA						
Percent	29.1	24.4	18.3	11.3	16.9	100.0
Number	3,795	3,177	2,388	1,473	2,210	13,043
21. COOK COUNTY, ILLINOIS						
Percent	48.5	14.9	7.0	5.2	24.4	100.0
Number	6,213	1,905	894	666	3,123	12,801
22. LAKE COUNTY, FLORIDA						
Percent	36.2	30.1	15.6	8.5	9.5	99.9*
Number	4,539	3,778	1,956	1,071	1,192	12,536
23. MARION COUNTY, FLORIDA						
Percent	36.4	29.6	18.0	8.7	7.3	100.0
Number	4,404	3,576	2,170	1,055	882	12,087
24. HERNANDO COUNTY, FLORIDA						
Percent	34.6	29.6	16.5	6.4	12.9	100.0
Number	4,045	3,461	1,924	746	1,509	11,685
25. CITRUS, LEVY AND SUMTER COUNTIES, FLORIDA						
Percent	42.3	25.6	13.6	7.8	10.6	99.9*
Number	4,825	2,925	1,557	892	1,209	11,408
26. ORANGE COUNTY, CALIFORNIA						
Percent	28.7	11.5	10.6	9.9	39.3	100.0
Number	3,247	1,297	1,197	1,121	4,451	11,313
27. KING COUNTY, WASHINGTON						
Percent	32.5	15.4	15.5	12.5	24.2	100.1*
Number	3,645	1,731	1,734	1,398	2,709	11,217
28. HARRIS COUNTY, TEXAS						
Percent	42.5	13.3	12.3	6.3	25.6	100.0
Number	4,549	1,421	1,317	675	2,743	10,705
29. ORANGE COUNTY, FLORIDA						
Percent	41.1	22.3	12.7	7.7	16.2	100.0
Number	4,313	2,336	1,327	811	1,699	10,486
30. DOUGLAS, LYON, STOREY AND WASHOE COUNTIES AND CARSON CITY †, NEVADA						
Percent	39.1	20.4	12.5	8.2	19.7	99.9*
Number	4,030	2,106	1,293	848	2,032	10,309
31. FLAGLER, PUTNAM AND ST. JOHNS COUNTIES, FLORIDA						
Percent	30.1	21.3	14.0	11.5	23.1	100.0
Number	2,863	2,032	1,330	1,100	2,202	9,527
32. ST. LUCIE COUNTY, FLORIDA						
Percent	25.9	26.5	19.8	10.6	17.1	99.9*
Number	2,337	2,395	1,791	957	1,543	9,023
33. DE SOTO, GLADES, HARDEE, HENDRY AND HIGHLANDS COUNTIES, FLORIDA						
Percent	40.7	28.5	16.1	6.9	7.9	100.1*
Number	3,568	2,501	1,410	602	692	8,773
34. COOS, CURRY, DOUGLAS AND JOSEPHINE COUNTIES, OREGON						
Percent	48.3	24.3	9.9	8.9	8.6	100.0
Number	4,054	2,036	834	745	718	8,387

Table 8 — Distribution of Household Income Among In-migrants Age 60+, 1985-1990, for Top 100 Receiving Counties

County or County Group	0-$19,999	$20,000-29,999	$30,000-39,999	$40,000-49,999	$50,000+	Totals
35. OCEAN COUNTY, NEW JERSEY						
Percent	42.8	21.9	14.3	8.8	12.3	100.1*
Number	3,556	1,815	1,185	731	1,018	8,305
36. LA PAZ AND MOHAVE COUNTIES, ARIZONA						
Percent	41.2	25.1	14.2	8.3	11.2	100.0
Number	3,416	2,084	1,178	687	929	8,294
37. MONTGOMERY COUNTY, MARYLAND						
Percent	34.7	12.8	9.0	7.2	36.2	99.9*
Number	2,677	990	693	556	2,789	7,705
38. COCONINO AND YAVAPAI COUNTIES, ARIZONA						
Percent	44.1	24.9	13.0	8.2	9.7	99.9*
Number	3,285	1,858	973	615	725	7,456
39. INDIAN RIVER AND OKEECHOBEE COUNTIES, FLORIDA						
Percent	29.2	20.2	16.0	10.0	24.6	100.0
Number	2,173	1,502	1,189	744	1,831	7,439
40. MARTIN COUNTY, FLORIDA						
Percent	25.4	18.4	17.0	12.9	26.3	100.0
Number	1,810	1,309	1,209	920	1,876	7,124
41. SAN BERNARDINO COUNTY, CALIFORNIA						
Percent	45.2	17.3	8.8	8.2	20.5	100.0
Number	3,120	1,195	604	563	1,415	6,897
42. FAIRFAX COUNTY, FALLS CHURCH † AND FAIRFAX†, VIRGINIA						
Percent	21.6	10.1	7.2	10.0	51.1	100.0
Number	1,425	666	471	657	3,363	6,582
43. BERNALILLO COUNTY, NEW MEXICO						
Percent	32.2	17.2	9.4	14.8	26.4	100.0
Number	2,064	1,101	600	945	1,692	6,402
44. DALLAS COUNTY, TEXAS						
Percent	48.0	11.4	11.1	6.0	23.5	100.0
Number	2,907	691	671	361	1,423	6,053
45. BEXAR COUNTY, TEXAS						
Percent	32.2	17.2	13.0	10.9	26.7	100.0
Number	1,892	1,010	766	642	1,569	5,879
46. HORRY COUNTY, SOUTH CAROLINA						
Percent	32.4	25.4	19.0	6.9	16.3	100.0
Number	1,899	1,488	1,110	402	954	5,853
47. WAYNE COUNTY, MICHIGAN						
Percent	48.0	17.6	8.8	3.4	22.3	100.1*
Number	2,779	1,017	509	195	1,293	5,793
48. ST. LOUIS COUNTY AND ST. LOUIS †, MISSOURI						
Percent	46.3	9.3	9.0	7.9	27.5	100.0
Number	2,674	538	517	456	1,585	5,770
49. BALTIMORE COUNTY AND BALTIMORE†, MARYLAND						
Percent	46.2	9.6	14.3	8.6	21.3	100.0
Number	2,542	530	787	471	1,171	5,501
50. SEMINOLE COUNTY, FLORIDA						
Percent	37.8	17.2	13.4	9.4	22.1	99.9*
Number	2,075	944	736	515	1,213	5,483
51. MECKLENBURG COUNTY, NORTH CAROLINA						
Percent	35.6	19.2	13.7	6.5	25.0	100.0
Number	1,926	1,041	741	354	1,353	5,415

* rounding error †independent city

County or County Group	Range of Household Income					
	0-$19,999	$20,000-29,999	$30,000-39,999	$40,000-49,999	$50,000+	Totals
52. DUVAL COUNTY, FLORIDA						
Percent	47.0	16.4	12.8	8.2	15.5	99.9*
Number	2,513	878	684	438	830	5,343
53. CUYAHOGA COUNTY, OHIO						
Percent	51.3	15.1	10.9	10.1	12.6	100.0
Number	2,692	792	575	530	663	5,252
54. CARBON, MONROE, PIKE AND WAYNE COUNTIES, PENNSYLVANIA						
Percent	42.6	17.8	12.2	9.9	17.4	99.9*
Number	2,214	925	636	516	901	5,192
55. HENDERSON, MADISON AND TRANSYLVANIA COUNTIES, NORTH CAROLINA						
Percent	24.5	21.3	12.9	14.3	27.1	100.1
Number	1,269	1,101	669	738	1,401	5,178
56. SACRAMENTO COUNTY, CALIFORNIA						
Percent	36.8	18.8	13.9	8.5	22.0	100.0
Number	1,903	974	721	438	1,136	5,172
57. SHELBY COUNTY, TENNESSEE						
Percent	48.3	13.8	10.4	8.0	19.4	99.9*
Number	2,430	696	525	402	975	5,028
58. ESCAMBIA AND SANTA ROSA COUNTIES, FLORIDA						
Percent	43.2	18.3	8.5	12.7	17.3	100.0
Number	2,169	920	425	635	867	5,016
59. SANTA CLARA COUNTY, CALIFORNIA						
Percent	25.0	9.0	10.9	6.1	49.0	100.0
Number	1,244	449	545	302	2,443	4,983
60. TARRANT COUNTY, TEXAS						
Percent	37.9	18.8	13.9	5.7	23.7	100.0
Number	1,861	922	680	282	1,161	4,906
61. MONMOUTH COUNTY, NEW JERSEY						
Percent	35.6	18.0	11.3	6.6	28.5	100.0
Number	1,730	874	551	322	1,389	4,866
62. D.C.						
Percent	48.9	11.6	7.3	3.7	28.5	100.0
Number	2,359	558	350	178	1,376	4,821
63. PRINCE GEORGES COUNTY, MARYLAND						
Percent	26.6	9.4	14.3	13.8	35.8	99.9*
Number	1,283	454	689	664	1,726	4,816
64. FAIRFIELD COUNTY, CONNECTICUT						
Percent	38.8	6.1	8.2	6.0	40.9	100.0
Number	1,862	292	395	287	1,959	4,795
65. LANE COUNTY, OREGON						
Percent	46.9	22.6	13.8	5.2	11.5	100.0
Number	2,244	1,081	661	250	549	4,785
66. HONOLULU COUNTY, HAWAII						
Percent	29.6	16.3	15.3	9.5	29.3	100.0
Number	1,413	780	729	453	1,397	4,772
67. PHILADELPHIA COUNTY, PENNSYLVANIA						
Percent	49.3	13.2	13.0	6.0	18.5	100.0
Number	2,320	619	613	284	870	4,706
68. MIDDLESEX COUNTY, NEW JERSEY						
Percent	19.6	13.9	11.1	10.3	45.1	100.0
Number	919	651	522	482	2,113	4,687

Table 8 — Distribution of Household Income Among In-migrants Age 60+, 1985-1990, for Top 100 Receiving Counties

County or County Group	0-$19,999	$20,000-29,999	$30,000-39,999	$40,000-49,999	$50,000+	Totals
69. HENNEPIN COUNTY, MINNESOTA						
Percent	42.2	18.3	5.0	10.2	24.3	100.0
Number	1,933	837	229	465	1,113	4,577
70. BENTON AND MADISON COUNTIES, ARKANSAS						
Percent	37.4	15.2	20.9	12.1	14.4	100.0
Number	1,706	693	954	551	656	4,560
71. CLARK COUNTY, WASHINGTON						
Percent	43.2	16.6	16.8	7.5	16.0	100.1*
Number	1,962	753	762	339	726	4,542
72. BAXTER, BOONE, CARROLL, MARION, NEWTON AND SEARCY COUNTIES, ARKANSAS						
Percent	41.2	27.3	16.2	6.8	8.6	100.1*
Number	1,867	1,237	736	308	389	4,537
73. JACKSON COUNTY, OREGON						
Percent	46.3	22.2	14.5	6.6	10.4	100.0
Number	2,099	1,004	657	299	470	4,529
74. JACKSON COUNTY, MISSOURI						
Percent	42.2	9.4	11.2	11.8	25.5	100.1*
Number	1,894	422	504	528	1,143	4,491
75. CLALLAM, JEFFERSON AND MASON COUNTIES, WASHINGTON						
Percent	38.8	28.1	12.1	7.1	13.9	100.0
Number	1,740	1,263	543	318	624	4,488
76. FULTON COUNTY, GEORGIA						
Percent	49.1	14.0	10.6	4.4	22.0	100.1*
Number	2,181	624	470	195	976	4,446
77. PIERCE COUNTY, WASHINGTON						
Percent	48.4	12.1	18.3	4.0	17.2	100.0
Number	2,142	537	810	177	759	4,425
78. BARRY, CHRISTIAN, DADE, DALLAS, LAWRENCE, MCDONALD, POLK, STONE, TANEY AND WEBSTER COUNTIES, MISSOURI						
Percent	45.6	24.8	10.0	9.6	10.0	100.0
Number	1,990	1,081	437	421	435	4,364
79. MULTNOMAH COUNTY, OREGON						
Percent	55.4	19.7	3.4	10.2	11.4	100.1*
Number	2,373	845	144	437	488	4,287
80. HIDALGO COUNTY, TEXAS						
Percent	44.5	25.8	13.5	11.5	4.7	100.0
Number	1,868	1,084	566	482	198	4,198
81. EL PASO COUNTY, COLORADO						
Percent	41.9	13.9	17.6	8.1	18.4	99.9*
Number	1,749	582	735	339	768	4,173
82. SNOHOMISH COUNTY, WASHINGTON						
Percent	39.1	15.2	13.2	10.0	22.4	99.9
Number	1,614	627	546	414	924	4,125*
83. BUCKS COUNTY, PENNSYLVANIA						
Percent	31.1	9.1	18.0	11.6	30.3	100.1*
Number	1,276	373	741	475	1,244	4,109
84. ROCKINGHAM COUNTY, NEW HAMPSHIRE						
Percent	34.9	18.3	9.2	15.0	22.6	100.0
Number	1,407	739	373	605	912	4,036
85. OKLAHOMA COUNTY, OKLAHOMA						
Percent	46.9	15.6	11.8	8.7	17.0	100.0
Number	1,885	626	475	351	684	4,021

* rounding error

County or County Group	Range of Household Income					
	0-$19,999	$20,000-29,999	$30,000-39,999	$40,000-49,999	$50,000+	Totals
86. ALLEGHENY COUNTY, PENNSYLVANIA						
Percent	49.0	14.1	9.8	8.1	19.0	100.0
Number	1,968	566	395	326	762	4,017
87. BERGEN COUNTY, NEW JERSEY						
Percent	28.3	8.5	7.9	7.6	47.6	99.9*
Number	1,126	340	316	302	1,894	3,978
88. HARTFORD COUNTY, CONNECTICUT						
Percent	46.0	10.2	8.7	6.7	28.5	100.1*
Number	1,825	405	344	266	1,131	3,971
89. NEW HAVEN COUNTY, CONNECTICUT						
Percent	48.8	11.0	6.2	8.0	26.1	100.1*
Number	1,924	432	245	315	1,028	3,944
90. MIDDLESEX COUNTY, MASSACHUSETTS						
Percent	47.2	8.3	8.7	2.7	33.1	100.0
Number	1,845	325	339	105	1,295	3,909
91. RAMSEY COUNTY, MINNESOTA						
Percent	81.9	3.5	3.3	3.0	8.2	99.9*
Number	3,197	137	129	119	321	3,903
92. GILA AND PINAL COUNTIES, ARIZONA						
Percent	52.6	20.7	12.8	6.6	7.3	100.0
Number	2,032	800	494	254	282	3,862
93. MARION COUNTY, OREGON						
Percent	41.1	22.2	18.2	6.7	11.8	100.0
Number	1,586	855	702	258	456	3,857
94. DE KALB COUNTY, GEORGIA						
Percent	33.9	12.9	17.3	10.5	25.3	99.9^
Number	1,307	498	667	403	976	3,851
95. TULSA COUNTY, OKLAHOMA						
Percent	57.3	15.3	6.6	7.9	12.9	100.0
Number	2,199	587	254	303	496	3,839
96. FRANKLIN COUNTY, OHIO						
Percent	43.5	21.4	13.0	5.8	16.3	100.0
Number	1,669	821	498	222	624	3,834
97. VENTURA COUNTY, CALIFORNIA						
Percent	27.6	17.7	8.6	11.4	34.7	100.0
Number	1,052	675	329	433	1,325	3,814
98. OSCEOLA COUNTY, FLORIDA						
Percent	45.4	26.5	10.7	4.0	13.3	99.9*
Number	1,727	1,009	409	154	506	3,805
99. HAMILTON COUNTY, OHIO						
Percent	56.7	14.7	8.3	6.7	13.6	100.0
Number	2,153	560	316	255	515	3,799
100. WASHINGTON COUNTY, OREGON						
Percent	39.2	23.3	15.2	8.5	13.8	100.0
Number	1,485	883	577	320	522	3,787
Totals	**36.9**	**19.8**	**13.4**	**9.1**	**20.8**	**100.0**
	352,732	188,829	128,323	86,660	199,113	955,657

Figure 3 — Attraction of Migrants Age 60+ in Highest and Lowest Income Categories, 1985-1990

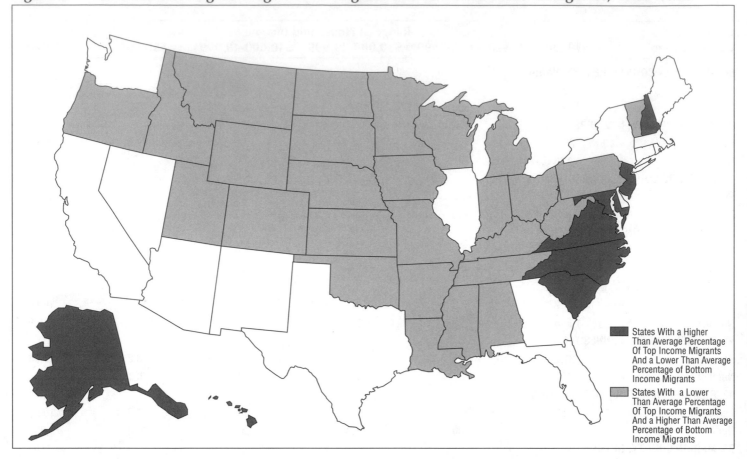

States With a Higher Than Average Percentage Of Top Income Migrants And a Lower Than Average Percentage of Bottom Income Migrants

States With a Lower Than Average Percentage Of Top Income Migrants And a Higher Than Average Percentage of Bottom Income Migrants

lived in households whose incomes were less than $20,000. Six of the leading 100 retirement counties received high proportions (more than 50 percent) of such lower income migrants. The county with the highest proportion (81.9 percent) of migrants earning less than $20,000 is Ramsey County, MN. Noted in Chapter 5, this is the county which received two large migration streams from rural Kansas.

There are five other areas where more than 50 percent of inbound migrants earn less that $20,000. They are Cuyahoga County (51.3 percent) and Hamilton County (56.7 percent), OH, Multnomah County (55.4 percent), OR, Tulsa County (57.3 percent), OK, and the county group consisting of Gila and Pinal counties (52.6 percent), AZ.

Income Distribution for Migrants From Abroad

The income ranges of migrants from abroad are displayed in Table 9. The two largest categories of migrants are those with the highest and lowest household incomes. There is certainly economic diversity among older migrants from abroad. Interpreting these differences, however, may be compounded by cultural factors.

No doubt there are some upper-middle-class and well-to-do retirees who move from abroad to the United States. Migrants from abroad include U.S. citizens who were living abroad and immigrants who are not yet citizens but who are residing in the United States legitimately. Many U.S. companies have employees living overseas and they usually earn

higher incomes than they would if working in this country. Furthermore, illegal aliens usually hide from government nose counters, so they are not well represented in these numbers.

When interpreting these data, one should note that the household income of a migrant is often elevated when he or she lives in a three-generation household where several incomes are involved. The same person living alone would have a much lower household income. Most research that examines the values, lifestyles and institutions of American Hispanics and Asians supports the position that the extended family remains one of the most important structural components of these cultures regardless of the country of origin, racial and ethnic ancestry, social class or religious preference. Older Hispanic and Asian migrants from abroad have tended to nurture traditional values stressing the importance of kin living together for economic and social support. The extended family has remained viable and is considered by some to be the single most important buffer against discriminatory practices and poverty suffered by most Hispanics in this country.[22]

For example, Donald Gelfand, a Wayne State University sociologist, reports in his study of older Salvadorans that immigration creates needs that are not intrinsically part of normal aging.[23] Older migrant Salvadorans are more dependent on adult children for assistance related to adjustment to a foreign society, such as translation, financial assistance, housekeeping, transportation, advice and English tutoring.

Table 9 — Distribution of Household Income Among In-migrants from Abroad Age 60+, 1985-1990

State	0-$19,999	$20,000-29,999	$30,000-39,999	$40,000-49,999	$50,000+	Totals
Alabama						
Percent	35.3	4.3	22.4	10.2	27.8	100.0
Number	131	16	83	38	103	371
Alaska						
Percent	-	17.5	13.2	38.5	30.7	99.9*
Number	-	45	34	99	79	257
Arizona						
Percent	43.4	14.0	11.2	8.8	22.6	100.0
Number	1,543	497	399	313	804	3,556
Arkansas						
Percent	22.2	25.5	22.7	5.0	24.6	100.0
Number	129	148	132	29	143	581
California						
Percent	32.7	14.0	12.2	10.2	31.0	100.1*
Number	25,361	10,889	9,449	7,900	24,039	77,638
Colorado						
Percent	45.6	11.4	4.5	15.1	23.5	100.1*
Number	699	174	69	231	360	1,533
Connecticut						
Percent	35.3	11.0	4.6	12.7	36.5	100.1*
Number	822	256	107	295	849	2,329
Delaware						
Percent	29.6	16.0	-	-	54.4	100.0
Number	37	20	-	-	68	125
D.C.						
Percent	38.9	6.9	14.6	13.1	26.5	100.0
Number	271	48	102	91	185	697
Florida						
Percent	44.6	17.4	11.7	9.4	16.9	100.0
Number	13,720	5,338	3,600	2,881	5,207	30,746
Georgia						
Percent	35.4	12.6	11.0	9.5	31.5	100.0
Number	660	236	206	177	588	1,867
Hawaii						
Percent	20.4	7.8	18.0	9.7	44.1	100.0
Number	705	268	623	335	1,522	3,453
Idaho						
Percent	54.0	36.5	-	-	9.5	100.0
Number	136	92	-	-	24	252
Illinois						
Percent	33.9	12.2	11.2	10.8	31.9	100.0
Number	3,492	1,257	1,152	1,113	3,279	10,293
Indiana						
Percent	37.2	18.2	12.2	12.9	19.5	100.0
Number	330	161	108	114	173	886
Iowa						
Percent	65.0	9.6	14.3	1.7	9.4	100.0
Number	345	51	76	9	50	531
Kansas						
Percent	43.6	1,3.0	8.9	5.6	28.9	100.0
Number	281	84	57	36	186	644

*rounding error

Table 9 — Distribution of Household Income Among In-migrants from Abroad Age 60+, 1985-1990

State	0-$19,999	$20,000-29,999	$30,000-39,999	$40,000-49,999	$50,000+	Totals
Kentucky						
Percent	38.6	27.6	16.9	13.4	3.5	100.0
Number	155	111	68	54	14	402
Louisiana						
Percent	36.1	7.4	10.6	10.2	35.6	99.9*
Number	234	48	69	66	231	648
Maine						
Percent	36.6	16.8	2.3	8.8	35.6	100.1*
Number	146	67	9	35	142	399
Maryland						
Percent	29.8	7.4	9.9	7.6	45.4	100.1*
Number	1,271	315	421	324	1,935	4,266
Massachusetts						
Percent	44.8	14.1	11.3	8.6	21.2	100.0
Number	3,064	961	772	591	1,447	6,835
Michigan						
Percent	37.7	6.8	9.8	11.1	34.7	100.1*
Number	1,127	204	293	331	1,037	2,992
Minnesota						
Percent	50.2	15.5	9.3	7.1	17.9	100.0
Number	747	231	138	105	267	1,488
Mississippi						
Percent	17.4	30.3	18.1	11.0	23.2	100.0
Number	81	141	84	51	108	465
Missouri						
Percent	31.6	6.2	24.2	16.0	21.9	99.9*
Number	333	65	255	169	231	1,053
Montana						
Percent	82.9	4.6	12.6	-	-	100.1*
Number	145	8	22	-	-	175
Nebraska						
Percent	61.1	4.2	-	-	34.7	100.0
Number	58	4	-	-	33	95
Nevada						
Percent	24.3	19.9	17.9	12.2	25.6	99.9*
Number	304	249	223	153	320	1,249
New Hampshire						
Percent	35.4	14.9	-	21.0	28.8	100.1*
Number	145	61	-	86	118	410
New Jersey						
Percent	19.3	14.2	11.0	12.2	43.3	100.0
Number	1,936	1,420	1,099	1,225	4,333	10,013
New Mexico						
Percent	38.6	18.2	3.2	13.2	26.8	100.0
Number	255	120	21	87	177	660
New York						
Percent	38.3	12.5	13.0	10.5	25.7	100.0
Number	12,516	4,091	4,249	3,437	8,399	32,692
North Carolina						
Percent	24.5	30.8	13.1	12.3	19.3	100.0
Number	381	480	204	192	300	1,557

*rounding error

State	Range of Household Income 0-$19,999	$20,000-29,999	$30,000-39,999	$40,000-49,999	$50,000+	Totals
North Dakota						
Percent	100.0	-	-	-	-	100.0
Number	65	-	-	-	-	65
Ohio						
Percent	41.9	13.8	12.4	9.4	22.4	99.9*
Number	820	270	243	184	438	1,955
Oklahoma						
Percent	31.4	28.8	13.0	19.9	7.0	100.1*
Number	322	295	133	204	72	1,026
Oregon						
Percent	45.8	7.6	14.8	4.8	27.0	100.0
Number	703	117	227	74	414	1,535
Pennsylvania						
Percent	42.2	14.3	11.2	7.3	25.0	100.0
Number	1,708	581	455	297	1,011	4,052
Rhode Island						
Percent	52.3	6.7	19.9	12.6	8.5	100.0
Number	450	58	171	108	73	860
South Carolina						
Porcent	12.8	1,7.5	22.0	11.3	35.8	100.0
Number	99	135	174	87	276	771
South Dakota						
Porccnt	89.6	-	-	-	10.4	100.0
Number	86	-	-	-	10	96
Tennessee						
Percent	35.1	8.7	19.5	3.9	32.7	99.9*
Number	351	87	195	39	327	999
Texas						
Percent	37.2	16.1	12.3	8.1	26.4	100.1*
Number	4,972	2,149	1,648	1,077	3,526	13,372
Utah						
Percent	13.0	23.0	24.4	12.7	26.8	99.9*
Number	48	85	90	47	99	369
Vermont						
Percent	70.3	-	29.7	-	-	100.0
Number	26	-	11	-	-	37
Virginia						
Percent	16.8	8.1	16.6	11.3	47.2	100.0
Number	717	348	711	483	2,016	4,275
Washington						
Percent	39.2	12.2	11.8	10.4	26.4	100.0
Number	1,479	462	444	393	999	3,777
West Virginia						
Percent	40.0	-	19.2	7.3	33.5	100.0
Number	98	-	47	18	82	245
Wisconsin						
Percent	42.0	15.8	9.5	6.2	26.5	100.0
Number	550	207	124	81	346	1,308
Wyoming						
Percent	14.1	28.2	-	5.1	52.6	100.0
Number	11	22	-	4	41	78
Totals	35.6	14.0	12.2	10.0	28.2	100.0
	84,065	32,972	28,797	23,663	66,481	235,978

Are family ties as strong among older Hispanic and Asian migrants who have lived in the United States for an extended period of time as they are among newcomers? Extended family values may not originate from tradition alone, but also from a defensive adaptive response by dependent and vulnerable migrants attempting to cope with a new culture and society.

Without knowing the living arrangements of older migrants from abroad, it is difficult to interpret the household income distribution in Table 9.

Regional Economic Impact Studies

The major observable economic impact of older migrants is on the local community. Some convincing evidence of such local consequences has been turned up by investigators using local surveys.

Guntersville, in the mountain lakes region of Alabama, for example, has a large river reservoir along with other recreational amenities appropriate for retirees. Mark Fagan, a regional planning scholar at Jacksonville State University in Alabama, administered a general economic survey to 185 older in-migrants to this community. The data suggest that these migrants had a positive influence on the local economy in Guntersville.[24] Other local surveys have come to very similar conclusions.[25]

The Appalachian Regional Commission funded a study of retirees who had moved into six western North Carolina counties. This 1989 telephone survey of 814 retirees represents one of the most thorough surveys of economic behavior conducted on older retirees. William Haas, a sociology professor at the University of North Carolina at Asheville and Professor William Serow found that their sample divided about equally into four parts: 22 percent had annual household incomes under $20,000, 25 percent had incomes between $20,000 and $29,999, 23 percent had incomes between $30,000 and $39,999 and 30 percent had incomes above $40,000.

More than three-quarters (79 percent) had settled in non-metropolitan counties, the average household bank deposit was $44,868, the average investment portfolio was $198,000, the average weekly household expenditure was $332 and reported mean home value was $108,884. The 630 households who kept spending records showed that they had collectively spent an annualized $22.6 million, not counting houses and cars, with a multiplier effect totaling $45.1 million a year. The researchers estimated that these retirees had the following measurable impacts on the economy: the creation of 943 jobs with an average annual salary of $14,900; local revenues of $384,300 in property tax and $331,800 in sales tax; state revenues of $708,120 in income tax, $289,000 in intangibles tax and $497,070 in sales tax. Further, 77 percent of the retirees volunteered an average of 7.4 hours a week of community service and 55 percent held positions of leadership in community churches and organizations. Almost one-half (41 percent) had an opportunity to vote on a school bond issue and 82 percent supported the increase. From the perspective of direct public sector receipts and expenditures, the retirees demonstrated that they had paid their own way—through the indirect economic

effects of their consumption expenditures. Migrant retirees represent an addition to the fiscal status of local governments.[26]

Bernal Green, an agricultural economist at the U.S. Department of Agriculture, and Mary Jo Schneider, a professor of anthropology at the University of Arkansas, sought to compare the direct economic effects of two growth options: factory jobs or retirement recruitment. They point out several advantages that retirement recruitment has for a local economy. For example, factory workers often commute from adjacent counties to their place of work, spending their money outside the local economy, while retirees tend to spend most of their money locally. Green and Schneider concluded that it takes 3.7 factory jobs to equal the same economic impact on a community as one new retiree household.[27] When counties receive retirees with higher incomes, the substitution rate would be even more favorable.

Local surveys do not necessarily provide a generalizable picture of all retired migrants in a state, or even a county. Samples often are drawn from residential areas where concentrations of retirees are known to live. These surveys, thus, may be tapping the high end of the income distribution among migrants. Those on the low end of the range are not likely to be living in concentrations, but scattered throughout the neighborhood to be near children and other relatives. This may be a moot point because it is the market segment with more discretionary income that is usually targeted by marketers, and this is the segment that these surveys usually study.

Graham Rowles, a cultural geographer, and his colleague John Watkins, a geographical statistician, both from the University of Kentucky, conducted a study of the older Appalachian population for the Appalachian Regional Commission. Their goal was to understand the ways in which retirement migration is altering the older population in the mountains. In the final report of this project, they emphasize the fact that in rural amenity areas, especially in the mountains, there is considerable overlap in older populations.[28]

"In each county the elderly population comprises a unique mixture of those who have spent their entire lives in the community, outsiders who migrated into the area and are now aging in place, return migrants who spent their working lives in metropolitan areas on the margin of the region, weekend vacationers who have decided to make the country their permanent residences, first-time amenity retirees, and several other subpopulations" (p.10).

This overlap in population groups is important to keep in mind when considering economic diversity among older migrants. Populations with different histories of involvement in the region generate different needs, expectations and aspirations. The result of this diversity is to increase local variation in the retired population, in its composition, resources and needs.

Rowles and Watkins argue that the business community that would address the needs of older migrants, no less than scholars, must come to understand the processes that contribute to the formation of local elderly populations and the melding of these groups within the fabric of the society. It is exactly this diversity of older migrants that affords one of the greatest challenges to those who would supply goods and services to them.

Attracting Retirees for Economic Development

Economic development agencies are mounting efforts to attract mature migrants. This is leading to sharpened competition among destinations for these migrants as new residents. Tom Graff and Robert Wiseman predicted in 1990 that within a short period, counties throughout the southeastern United States will proclaim themselves as retirement counties.[29] According to Leonard J. Hansen, a marketing consultant, mature adults can be reached, informed and motivated through newspapers and magazines that are designed to their specific information needs and interests. Advertising by local communities about their amenities can influence future migration patterns and therefore the economic development of these retirement destinations. Referred to in Chapter 3 as "selective recruitment," these efforts can stimulate and reinforce stream migration from one place to another, especially if supplemented by a healthy dose of network recruitment from family members and friends in the area.

A litany of the benefits of attracting retirees is beginning to replace the smokestack litany in rural chambers of commerce. The chant: In migrating retirees will increase the tax base, the number of positive taxpayers (residents who use fewer services than they pay for through taxes), the deposit base that can be used for commercial and industrial financing, retail sales, the level of expertise in the community, the number of unpaid community service volunteers, church contributions and employment.

The new litany has a second verse. In-migrating retirees will not strain social services, health-care services, school systems, the local criminal justice system or the natural environment.

The veracity of these claims is not contradicted in the research literature, but the impact of elderly migration, as a social phenomenon, has not yet generated enough research to provide definitive statements. The primary industries that expect to benefit from the retiree in-migrants are among the migration boosters: real estate, finance, insurance and utilities. All are housing-related.

The benefiting markets may go considerably beyond housing, however. The increasing amount of disposable income of 50- to 64-year-olds coupled with their fears of running out of money in old age presents a great opportunity for financial services marketers. There are recognizable trends in upscale empty nest lifestyles that are now emerging in the marketplace that include increases in mobility, spending on self and concern for long-term personal security. These put financial institutions in important positions to benefit from services to these retirees.

States with high numbers of older in-migrants have experienced substantial increases in the demand for food, housing, transportation and entertainment. This is a result of older migrants allocating more of their expenditures to these areas. They also spend relatively more on health insurance, medical services, prescription drugs and medical supplies than younger households.[30]

Pioneers in the Race to Recruit Retirees

A number of state-level efforts to attract retirees have been formed in the past few years. Since 1988, the state of Alabama has published *Alabama Advantage for Retirees*, an informational packet. The Governor's Program to Attract Retirees organized 90 local retiree attraction committees throughout the state and sponsors an annual conference to discuss strategy and recognize the most successful programs. The state provides technical support and co-ops brochure costs for local committees. In 1991, the state began national advertising to attract inquiries.

Since 1988, North Carolina has published the *Official Guide to Retiring in North Carolina*, a biannual magazine. The effort is coordinated by the State Department of Aging.

In 1989, South Carolina's office of State Parks and Tourism funded the publication of *South Carolina Mature Lifestyles*, an annual magazine aimed at turning visitors into residents. An association of South Carolina retirement communities was founded to promote in-migration to the state.

New Mexico publishes "Retirement in New Mexico," a paperback book, to attract out-of-state residents. Pennsylvania recently launched *Silver and Gold*, a magazine touting the virtues of retirement to the Keystone State. Arkansas publishes a tabloid for potential retiree migrants called *Share Arkansas*. The Louisiana Office of Tourism now advertises for retirees, and at least a half dozen other states are currently discussing the merits of starting their own campaign to attract retirees. Even Florida, long content to let retirees find their way to the Sunshine State unassisted, has launched its own magazine aimed at retiree migrants.

On a regional and local level, Hot Springs, AR, has been successfully promoting retiree in-migration for several years. The popular resort town advertises the benefits of retirement, mails a brochure to respondents that encourages a visit, greets prospects upon arrival and may even arrange for local retirees to show the visitors around town. A number of other city and regional efforts have been based on the Hot Springs model.

There are well over 100 local governments or chambers of commerce now actively involved in attracting retirees. They range from Alamogordo, NM, to Fayetteville, AR, and from Sierra Vista, AZ, to Pinehurst, NC.

Still, the lion's share of promotion to out-of-state retirees is done by more than 300 retirement community developers nationwide that depend on in-migrants for a large percentage of new home sales. Major developers like Del Webb Corporation and Cooper Communities build retirement communities so large they rival small towns in size, and recruit residents on a regional or national scale.

Conclusion

From the perspective of local government, economic development and job creation can be enhanced through attracting retirees. Retirement migration is increasingly seen as the clean, growth industry of the 1990s in small-town America because it increases economic consumption and broadens the tax base.[31] Glasgow concluded that retirees typically do not add increased demands for jobs, but help to create income opportunities for younger workers.[32] The retirement industry can help to diversify and stabilize a local economy. As active recruitment of retirees increases in scenic places with budding tourist industries, some retirees will be dipped from the large, powerful migration streams and redirected to these greener pastures. From a demographic perspective, the outcome of this process will be the continued dechannelization of retirement migration that was noted in Chapter 2. The huge gap between Florida and other destination states may continue to be chipped away in future decades, inch by inch. Older migrants are increasingly seen as economic saviors for some rural areas. This growth of rural retirement has helped to revitalize many small towns in the Sun Belt and Northwest.[33] Retirement counties are experiencing growth in business, services and retail activity.

Attracting retirees is a low-risk strategy because even if no retirees relocate to a community, the efforts should increase tourism. Retirees are visitors first and migrants later, and people visit an area several times before they decide to retire to that location. The greater the exposure to an area before people retire, the greater their chances of moving there after they retire. Once migration streams attach themselves to the recruitment location from specific other communities, they tend to be self-perpetuating.

Launching a strategy to attract retirees does not require extensive funds at the outset. Industrial recruitment strategies, on the other hand, require large outlays for developing industrial property, building access roads, installing utilities, providing industrial development bonds and issuing tax exemptions. Retirees can purchase vacant houses in existing neighborhoods. Most of the investment will be spent on promotional materials and advertising. However, certain amenities desired by retirees, such as health care and transportation, may require investments to develop and maintain.

As with any economic development activity, attracting retirees takes time. The seed must be planted and cultivated. Furthermore, attracting retirees is no panacea, and there are stresses associated with this strategy as with any other. Many rural communities with the potential for growing a tourism industry, however, can justify adding retiree attraction to their economic development arsenal. Smokestack chasing and retiree attraction may even be complementary, since promoting a community as a nice place to live puts forth quality of life features that industrialists considering a plant relocation find attractive. It is not suggested that retiree recruitment replace manufacturing recruitment altogether. A mixed strategy is usually best. However, in some cases, resources might be better used to attract retirees than gambling on capturing one of the few plants being chased by so many communities.

APPENDIX A
State-to-State Streams During Five-Year Periods Ending in 1970, 1980 And 1990

ALABAMA

TO ALABAMA FROM							FROM ALABAMA TO					
1970		1980		1990			1970		1980		1990	
#	%	#	%	#	%		#	%	#	%	#	%
0	–	0	–	7	–	ALASKA	0	–	0	–	8	–
0	–	40	0.2	187	0.7	ARIZONA	0	–	200	1.5	173	0.9
100	0.8	240	1.3	231	0.9	ARKANSAS	200	1.8	240	1.8	289	1.5
400	3.2	1,080	5.8	1,323	5.2	CALIFORNIA	600	5.3	440	3.3	580	3.0
100	0.8	80	0.4	66	0.3	COLORADO	100	0.9	240	1.8	183	0.9
0	–	240	1.3	129	0.5	CONNECTICUT	0	–	0	–	0	–
0	–	0	–	39	0.2	DELAWARE	0	–	40	0.3	0	–
0	–	120	0.6	51	0.2	D.C.	0	–	80	0.6	16	0.1
2,300	18.4	3,520	19.0	4,729	18.7	FLORIDA	1,900	16.7	2,880	21.8	5,217	26.7
1,800	14.4	1,280	6.9	2,958	11.7	GEORGIA	1,100	9.6	1,040	7.9	3,396	17.4
0	–	0	–	61	0.2	HAWAII	0	–	0	–	25	0.1
0	–	40	0.2	7	–	IDAHO	0	–	0	–	0	–
500	4.0	1,200	6.5	1,845	7.3	ILLINOIS	400	3.5	160	1.2	501	2.6
200	1.6	400	2.2	463	1.8	INDIANA	0	–	240	1.8	290	1.5
200	1.6	200	1.1	54	0.2	IOWA	200	1.8	40	0.3	106	0.5
100	0.8	120	0.6	90	0.4	KANSAS	100	0.9	160	1.2	0	–
0	–	160	0.9	304	1.2	KENTUCKY	200	1.8	120	0.9	358	1.8
300	2.4	640	3.5	926	3.7	LOUISIANA	300	2.6	680	5.1	642	3.3
0	–	80	0.4	51	0.2	MAINE	200	1.8	0	–	70	0.4
0	–	440	2.4	160	0.6	MARYLAND	100	0.9	200	1.5	119	0.6
0	–	160	0.9	42	0.2	MASSACHUSETTS	100	0.9	0	–	51	0.3
600	4.8	1,040	5.6	1,137	4.5	MICHIGAN	1,000	8.8	400	3.0	374	1.9
200	1.6	240	1.3	95	0.4	MINNESOTA	0	–	80	0.6	9	0.1
800	6.4	680	3.7	1,348	5.3	MISSISSIPPI	1,200	10.5	1,280	9.7	1,419	7.3
300	2.4	440	2.4	415	1.6	MISSOURI	100	0.9	240	1.8	101	0.5
0	–	40	0.2	0	–	MONTANA	0	–	0	–	0	–
0	–	40	0.2	19	0.1	NEBRASKA	0	–	0	–	0	–
0	–	40	0.2	137	0.5	NEVADA	0	–	0	–	94	0.5
100	0.8	40	0.2	115	0.5	NEW HAMPSHIRE	0	–	0	–	24	0.1
100	0.8	80	0.4	503	2.0	NEW JERSEY	100	0.9	40	0.3	145	0.7
0	–	40	0.2	22	0.1	NEW MEXICO	0	–	40	0.3	60	0.3
400	3.2	1,360	7.3	947	3.7	NEW YORK	200	1.8	360	2.7	243	1.2
200	1.6	280	1.5	355	1.4	NORTH CAROLINA	200	1.8	200	1.5	441	2.3
0	–	0	–	0	–	NORTH DAKOTA	0	–	0	–	0	–
800	6.4	840	4.5	872	3.4	OHIO	400	3.4	280	2.1	494	2.5
100	0.8	120	0.6	143	0.6	OKLAHOMA	200	1.8	280	2.1	92	0.5
200	1.6	80	0.4	20	0.1	OREGON	0	–	0	–	134	0.7
300	2.4	400	2.2	567	2.2	PENNSYLVANIA	200	1.8	240	1.8	87	0.4
0	–	40	0.2	87	0.3	RHODE ISLAND	100	0.9	0	–	0	–
100	0.8	120	0.6	416	1.6	SOUTH CAROLINA	0	–	240	1.8	381	2.0
0	–	0	–	80	0.3	SOUTH DAKOTA	0	–	0	–	0	–
700	5.6	960	5.2	1,667	6.6	TENNESSEE	1,200	10.5	1,120	8.5	1,764	9.0
800	6.4	760	4.1	1,676	6.6	TEXAS	900	7.9	720	5.4	1,006	5.1
100	0.8	40	0.2	16	0.1	UTAH	0	–	0	–	17	0.1
0	–	80	0.4	32	0.1	VERMONT	0	–	40	0.3	26	0.1
600	4.8	360	1.9	435	1.7	VIRGINIA	0	–	680	5.1	291	1.5
0	–	40	0.2	154	0.6	WASHINGTON	0	–	80	0.6	117	0.6
100	0.8	120	0.6	129	0.5	WEST VIRGINIA	0	–	80	0.6	114	0.6
0	–	80	0.4	226	0.9	WISCONSIN	100	0.9	80	0.6	96	0.5
0	–	120	0.6	0	–	WYOMING	0	–	0	–	18	0.1
12,500	100.0	18,520	99.5*	25,336	99.9*	TOTAL U.S.	11,400	100.4*	13,240	99.8*	19,571	100.2*

*rounding error

ALASKA

TO ALASKA FROM							FROM ALASKA TO					
1970		1980		1990			1970		1980		1990	
#	%	#	%	#	%		#	%	#	%	#	%
0	–	0	–	8	0.3	ALABAMA	0	–	0	–	7	0.1
0	–	0	–	92	3.8	ARIZONA	0	–	240	4.4	266	4.6
0	–	0	–	110	4.6	ARKANSAS	0	–	0	–	198	3.4
100	9.1	240	15.8	381	15.9	CALIFORNIA	300	14.3	920	16.9	1,082	18.5
0	–	120	7.9	65	2.7	COLORADO	0	–	120	2.2	144	2.5
0	–	0	–	12	0.5	CONNECTICUT	0	–	0	–	0	–
0	–	40	2.6	0	–	DELAWARE	0	–	0	–	0	–
100	9.1	40	2.6	0	–	D.C.	0	–	0	–	0	–
0	–	160	10.5	34	1.4	FLORIDA	0	–	240	4.4	211	3.6
0	–	0	–	0	–	GEORGIA	400	19.0	200	3.7	40	0.7
0	–	0	–	45	1.9	HAWAII	0	–	40	0.7	235	4.0
0	–	80	5.2	29	1.2	IDAHO	0	–	360	6.6	264	4.5
0	–	0	–	38	1.6	ILLINOIS	0	–	0	–	30	0.5
0	–	0	–	0	–	INDIANA	0	–	0	–	45	0.8
0	–	120	7.9	0	–	IOWA	0	–	0	–	71	1.2
0	–	0	–	15	0.6	KANSAS	0	–	40	0.7	57	1.0
0	–	40	2.6	0	–	KENTUCKY	0	–	40	0.7	32	0.6
0	–	0	–	38	1.6	LOUISIANA	0	–	40	0.7	0	–
0	–	0	–	7	0.3	MAINE	0	–	0	–	9	0.2
0	–	0	–	0	–	MARYLAND	0	–	0	–	0	–
0	–	0	–	0	–	MASSACHUSETTS	0	–	0	–	33	0.6
0	–	0	–	71	3.0	MICHIGAN	0	–	0	–	28	0.5
0	–	0	–	30	1.3	MINNESOTA	0	–	120	2.2	143	2.5
0	–	0	–	23	1.0	MISSISSIPPI	0	–	40	0.7	3	0.1
0	–	0	–	0	–	MISSOURI	300	14.3	80	1.5	10	0.2
0	–	40	2.6	80	3.3	MONTANA	0	–	80	1.5	77	1.3
0	–	0	–	11	0.5	NEBRASKA	0	–	0	–	0	–
100	9.1	40	2.6	0	–	NEVADA	0	–	120	2.2	65	1.1
0	–	0	–	0	–	NEW HAMPSHIRE	0	–	0	–	31	0.5
0	–	0	–	38	1.6	NEW JERSEY	0	–	0	–	18	0.3
0	–	0	–	83	3.5	NEW MEXICO	100	4.8	80	1.5	0	–
0	–	0	–	31	1.3	NEW YORK	0	–	0	–	19	0.3
0	–	0	–	8	0.3	NORTH CAROLINA	0	–	0	–	87	1.5
0	–	0	–	0	–	NORTH DAKOTA	0	–	0	–	0	–
0	–	0	–	37	1.5	OHIO	0	–	0	–	51	0.9
300	27.3	0	–	0	–	OKLAHOMA	0	–	0	–	35	0.6
100	9.1	80	5.2	219	9.1	OREGON	300	14.3	400	7.4	611	10.5
0	–	0	–	0	–	PENNSYLVANIA	0	–	0	–	39	0.7
0	–	0	–	0	–	RHODE ISLAND	0	–	0	–	0	–
0	–	0	–	19	0.8	SOUTH CAROLINA	0	–	0	–	0	–
0	–	0	–	0	–	SOUTH DAKOTA	0	–	0	–	19	0.3
0	–	0	–	0	–	TENNESSEE	0	–	0	–	0	–
100	9.1	200	13.2	114	4.8	TEXAS	100	4.8	400	7.4	189	3.2
0	–	0	–	111	4.6	UTAH	200	9.5	80	1.5	37	0.6
0	–	0	–	0	–	VERMONT	0	–	0	–	0	–
0	–	0	–	15	0.6	VIRGINIA	0	–	160	2.9	78	1.3
200	18.2	320	21.1	501	20.9	WASHINGTON	400	19.0	1,600	29.4	1,482	25.4
0	–	0	–	0	–	WEST VIRGINIA	0	–	0	–	0	–
100	–	0	–	77	3.2	WISCONSIN	0	–	40	0.7	83	1.4
0	–	0	–	53	2.2	WYOMING	0	–	0	–	8	0.1
1,100	100.1*	1,520	99.8*	2,395	99.9*	TOTAL U.S.	2,100	100.0	5,440	99.8*	5,837	100.1*

*rounding error

ARIZONA

							1970		1980		1990	
	TO ARIZONA FROM									**FROM ARIZONA TO**		
1970		**1980**		**1990**			**1970**		**1980**		**1990**	
#	%	#	%	#	%		#	%	#	%	#	%
0	–	200	0.2	173	0.2	ALABAMA	0	–	40	0.1	187	0.5
0	–	240	0.3	266	0.3	ALASKA	0	–	0	–	92	0.2
500	1.1	320	0.3	476	0.5	ARKANSAS	700	4.2	880	3.1	427	1.1
7,500	15.8	16,440	17.4	23,331	23.6	CALIFORNIA	5,800	34.9	8,600	30.1	9,134	23.9
1,800	3.8	3,640	3.8	5,461	5.5	COLORADO	800	4.8	1,000	3.5	2,031	5.3
500	1.1	1,320	1.4	774	0.8	CONNECTICUT	100	0.6	160	0.6	261	0.7
0	–	80	0.1	190	0.2	DELAWARE	0	–	0	–	22	0.1
0	–	40	0.1	21	–	D.C.	0	–	40	0.1	55	0.1
1,200	2.5	1,400	1.5	2,714	2.8	FLORIDA	600	3.6	1,320	4.6	2,021	5.3
0	–	200	0.2	423	0.4	GEORGIA	200	1.2	280	1.0	274	0.7
0	–	200	0.2	435	0.4	HAWAII	0	–	120	0.4	212	0.6
600	1.3	960	1.0	931	0.9	IDAHO	0	–	240	0.8	444	1.2
5,200	10.9	11,520	12.2	8,460	8.6	ILLINOIS	600	3.6	1,360	4.8	1,386	3.6
900	1.9	2,480	2.6	1,903	1.9	INDIANA	500	3.0	400	1.4	486	1.3
1,500	3.2	2,800	2.9	2,257	2.3	IOWA	100	0.6	440	1.5	558	1.5
300	0.6	1,160	1.2	1,599	1.6	KANSAS	200	1.2	560	2.0	821	2.1
100	0.2	480	0.5	105	0.1	KENTUCKY	0	–	80	0.3	307	0.8
100	0.2	200	0.2	289	0.3	LOUISIANA	200	1.2	360	1.3	90	0.2
0	–	160	0.2	247	0.3	MAINE	100	0.6	0	–	18	0.1
100	0.2	760	0.8	574	0.6	MARYLAND	0	–	80	0.3	250	0.7
500	1.1	1,600	1.7	868	0.9	MASSACHUSETTS	200	1.2	400	1.4	211	0.6
4,100	8.6	5,280	5.6	4,857	4.9	MICHIGAN	500	3.0	440	1.5	1,329	3.5
1,700	3.6	3,000	3.2	3,704	3.8	MINNESOTA	400	2.4	320	1.1	673	1.8
200	0.4	120	0.1	128	0.1	MISSISSIPPI	0	–	40	0.1	297	0.8
2,000	4.2	2,640	2.8	1,740	1.8	MISSOURI	300	1.8	800	2.8	941	2.5
1,000	2.1	840	0.9	802	0.8	MONTANA	0	–	120	0.4	188	0.5
800	1.7	1,600	1.7	851	0.9	NEBRASKA	100	0.6	440	1.5	343	0.9
200	0.4	520	0.5	1,718	1.7	NEVADA	200	1.2	560	2.0	2,076	5.4
0	–	200	0.2	101	0.1	NEW HAMPSHIRE	0	–	80	0.3	7	–
1,200	2.5	2,760	2.9	2,414	2.4	NEW JERSEY	500	3.0	320	1.1	311	0.8
500	1.1	1,560	1.6	2,009	2.0	NEW MEXICO	400	2.4	720	2.5	1,512	4.0
3,300	6.9	6,840	7.2	5,116	5.2	NEW YORK	0	–	560	2.0	821	2.1
0	–	40	0.1	266	0.3	NORTH CAROLINA	0	–	200	0.7	387	1.0
600	1.3	560	0.6	465	0.5	NORTH DAKOTA	0	–	40	0.1	65	0.2
2,400	5.0	5,080	5.4	3,375	3.4	OHIO	200	1.2	400	1.4	987	2.6
200	0.4	640	0.7	1,178	1.2	OKLAHOMA	800	4.8	520	1.8	822	2.2
500	1.1	1,800	1.9	1,971	2.0	OREGON	100	0.6	840	2.9	1,181	3.1
1,900	4.0	3,280	3.5	2,686	2.7	PENNSYLVANIA	300	1.8	480	1.7	697	1.8
100	0.2	0	–	146	0.2	RHODE ISLAND	0	–	0	–	36	0.1
0	–	120	0.1	232	0.2	SOUTH CAROLINA	0	–	0	–	123	0.3
300	0.6	520	0.5	859	0.9	SOUTH DAKOTA	0	–	80	0.3	206	0.5
0	–	440	0.4	347	0.4	TENNESSEE	0	–	120	0.4	471	1.2
1,200	2.5	1,920	2.0	3,244	3.3	TEXAS	1,900	11.4	2,520	8.8	2,025	5.3
400	0.8	1,080	1.1	1,058	1.1	UTAH	200	1.2	480	1.7	435	1.1
100	0.2	40	0.1	67	0.1	VERMONT	0	–	40	0.1	32	0.1
700	1.5	680	0.7	621	0.6	VIRGINIA	100	0.6	360	1.3	273	0.7
1,100	2.3	3,160	3.3	3,732	3.8	WASHINGTON	200	1.2	1,320	4.6	1,566	4.1
200	0.4	200	0.2	116	0.1	WEST VIRGINIA	0	–	80	0.3	257	0.7
1,600	3.4	3,200	3.4	2,763	2.8	WISCONSIN	300	1.8	320	1.1	751	2.0
500	1.1	280	0.3	693	0.7	WYOMING	0	–	40	0.1	181	0.5
47,600	**100.2***	**94,600**	**99.8***	**98,756**	**100.2***	**TOTAL U.S.**	**16,600**	**99.7***	**28,600**	**99.9***	**38,280**	**100.4***

*rounding error

ARKANSAS

TO ARKANSAS FROM							FROM ARKANSAS TO					
1970		1980		1990			1970		1980		1990	
#	%	#	%	#	%		#	%	#	%	#	%
200	1.1	240	0.7	289	1.0	ALABAMA	100	0.9	240	1.5	231	1.3
0	–	0	–	198	0.7	ALASKA	0	–	0	–	110	0.6
700	3.9	880	2.6	427	1.4	ARIZONA	500	4.7	320	1.9	476	2.6
1,500	8.4	4,560	13.5	3,879	13.0	CALIFORNIA	1,700	16.0	1,200	7.3	1,362	7.4
0	–	400	1.2	343	1.2	COLORADO	300	2.8	120	0.7	405	2.2
0	–	120	0.4	122	0.4	CONNECTICUT	0	–	80	0.5	14	0.1
100	0.6	0	–	14	0.1	DELAWARE	0	–	0	–	0	–
0	–	80	0.2	25	0.1	D.C.	100	0.9	0	–	0	–
0	–	960	2.8	1,108	3.7	FLORIDA	500	4.7	1,160	7.0	1,446	7.8
0	–	200	0.6	169	0.6	GEORGIA	100	0.9	200	1.2	346	1.9
0	–	0	–	0	–	HAWAII	0	–	0	–	34	0.2
0	–	80	0.2	25	0.1	IDAHO	0	–	0	–	8	–
3,500	19.6	6,680	19.8	3,380	11.3	ILLINOIS	400	3.8	1,400	8.5	1,410	7.7
500	2.8	880	2.6	415	1.4	INDIANA	0	–	360	2.2	446	2.4
100	0.6	1,680	5.0	1,106	3.7	IOWA	100	0.9	120	0.7	457	2.5
800	4.5	1,120	3.3	1,280	4.3	KANSAS	300	2.8	600	3.6	409	2.2
100	0.6	160	0.5	53	0.2	KENTUCKY	0	–	160	1.0	259	1.4
800	4.5	600	1.8	1,225	4.1	LOUISIANA	400	3.8	920	5.6	540	2.9
0	–	0	–	15	0.1	MAINE	0	–	0	–	0	–
100	0.6	200	0.6	120	0.4	MARYLAND	0	–	0	–	54	0.3
0	–	40	0.1	55	0.2	MASSACHUSETTS	0	–	80	0.5	62	0.3
500	2.8	1,520	4.5	795	2.7	MICHIGAN	300	2.8	440	2.7	450	2.4
300	1.7	560	1.7	526	1.8	MINNESOTA	0	–	80	0.5	221	1.2
100	0.6	600	1.8	655	2.2	MISSISSIPPI	400	3.8	600	3.6	498	2.7
1,400	7.8	2,360	7.0	2,164	7.3	MISSOURI	900	8.5	1,280	7.8	1,716	9.3
100	0.6	240	0.7	0	–	MONTANA	0	–	0	–	4	–
0	–	520	1.5	217	0.7	NEBRASKA	0	–	40	0.2	219	1.2
100	0.6	120	0.4	171	0.6	NEVADA	0	–	120	0.7	188	1.0
0	–	80	0.2	0	–	NEW HAMPSHIRE	0	–	0	–	7	–
0	–	120	0.4	234	0.8	NEW JERSEY	0	–	0	–	39	0.2
100	0.6	200	0.6	181	0.6	NEW MEXICO	100	0.9	400	2.4	180	1.0
700	3.9	720	2.1	256	0.9	NEW YORK	100	0.9	120	0.7	46	0.3
0	–	120	0.4	208	0.7	NORTH CAROLINA	100	0.9	40	0.2	270	1.5
0	–	0	–	115	0.4	NORTH DAKOTA	0	–	0	–	0	–
100	0.6	480	1.4	427	1.4	OHIO	200	1.9	120	0.7	278	1.5
1,500	8.4	1,920	5.9	1,721	5.8	OKLAHOMA	700	6.6	1,400	8.5	1,514	8.2
100	0.6	440	1.3	166	0.6	OREGON	100	0.9	160	1.0	125	0.7
0	–	280	0.8	237	0.8	PENNSYLVANIA	0	–	160	1.0	183	1.0
0	–	0	–	0	–	RHODE ISLAND	0	–	0	–	0	–
0	–	0	–	57	0.2	SOUTH CAROLINA	100	0.9	40	0.2	81	0.4
0	–	80	0.2	58	0.2	SOUTH DAKOTA	0	–	120	0.7	9	0.1
900	5.0	760	2.2	957	3.2	TENNESSEE	200	1.9	1,000	6.1	1,005	5.5
2,900	16.2	2,640	7.8	4,783	16.0	TEXAS	2,500	23.6	2,960	18.0	2,599	14.1
0	–	0	–	47	0.2	UTAH	0	–	0	–	17	0.1
0	–	0	–	0	–	VERMONT	0	–	0	–	0	–
0	–	80	0.2	119	0.4	VIRGINIA	100	0.9	0	–	177	1.0
100	0.6	120	0.4	259	0.9	WASHINGTON	0	–	200	1.2	258	1.4
0	–	40	0.1	143	0.5	WEST VIRGINIA	0	–	0	–	50	0.3
600	3.4	680	2.0	980	3.3	WISCONSIN	300	2.8	200	1.2	237	1.3
0	–	200	0.6	124	0.4	WYOMING	0	–	40	0.2	14	0.1
17,900	100.6*	33,760	100.1*	29,848	100.6*	TOTAL U.S.	10,600	99.5*	16,480	99.8*	18,454	100.3*

*rounding error

CALIFORNIA

TO CALIFORNIA FROM							FROM CALIFORNIA TO					
1970		1980		1990			1970		1980		1990	
#	%	#	%	#	%		#	%	#	%	#	%
600	0.6	440	0.3	580	0.4	ALABAMA	400	0.5	1,080	0.8	1,323	0.7
300	0.3	920	0.6	1,082	0.8	ALASKA	100	0.1	240	0.2	381	0.2
5,800	5.4	8,600	5.9	9,134	7.0	ARIZONA	7,500	10.1	16,440	11.6	23,331	12.5
1,700	1.6	1,200	0.8	1,362	1.0	ARKANSAS	1,500	2.0	4,560	3.2	3,879	2.1
2,800	2.6	4,640	3.2	3,555	2.7	COLORADO	1,800	2.4	4,480	3.2	4,524	2.4
1,200	1.1	2,240	1.5	1,827	1.4	CONNECTICUT	300	0.4	680	0.5	735	0.4
0	–	400	0.3	102	0.1	DELAWARE	0	–	0	–	121	0.1
700	0.7	520	0.4	369	0.3	D.C.	100	0.1	160	0.1	257	0.1
2,300	2.1	6,960	4.8	7,731	5.9	FLORIDA	4,700	6.3	7,160	5.1	13,407	7.2
700	0.7	1,000	0.7	1,059	0.8	GEORGIA	700	0.9	1,240	0.9	1,942	1.0
900	0.8	1,520	1.0	3,092	2.4	HAWAII	2,600	3.4	2,440	1.7	3,459	1.9
1,100	1.0	1,680	1.2	1,901	1.5	IDAHO	1,300	1.7	2,720	1.9	2,680	1.4
12,400	11.6	13,960	9.6	9,136	7.0	ILLINOIS	2,300	3.0	3,600	2.5	3,255	1.7
1,500	1.4	2,240	1.5	1,670	1.3	INDIANA	1,000	1.3	1,040	0.7	2,433	1.3
2,100	2.0	2,040	1.4	1,443	1.1	IOWA	800	1.1	1,480	1.0	1,295	0.7
1,700	1.6	1,640	1.1	1,533	1.2	KANSAS	1,200	1.6	1,960	1.4	1,566	0.8
100	0.1	840	0.6	512	0.4	KENTUCKY	200	0.2	520	0.4	998	0.5
800	0.7	1,120	0.8	1,438	1.1	LOUISIANA	900	1.2	1,320	0.9	1,482	0.8
400	0.4	360	0.2	368	0.3	MAINE	200	0.2	320	0.2	537	0.3
900	0.8	1,640	1.1	1,796	1.4	MARYLAND	300	0.4	400	0.3	1,355	0.7
2,100	2.0	2,800	1.9	2,490	1.9	MASSACHUSETTS	500	0.7	1,120	0.8	1,031	0.6
5,200	4.9	7,160	4.9	4,639	3.5	MICHIGAN	1,200	1.6	1,800	1.3	2,721	1.5
3,200	3.0	2,800	1.9	2,598	2.0	MINNESOTA	500	0.7	1,120	0.8	1,676	0.9
100	0.1	800	0.6	558	0.4	MISSISSIPPI	800	1.1	760	0.5	843	0.5
3,800	3.6	3,560	2.5	2,578	2.0	MISSOURI	2,400	3.2	5,320	3.8	4,675	2.5
1,400	1.3	1,480	1.0	504	0.4	MONTANA	1,000	1.3	1,400	1.0	1,044	0.6
900	0.8	1,400	1.0	1,209	0.9	NEBRASKA	700	0.9	1,480	1.0	1,322	0.7
1,800	1.7	4,240	2.9	5,199	4.0	NEVADA	3,400	4.6	11,680	8.3	21,389	11.4
100	0.1	440	0.3	345	0.3	NEW HAMPSHIRE	0	–	80	0.1	539	0.3
3,900	3.6	5,400	3.7	4,611	3.5	NEW JERSEY	1,100	1.5	1,000	0.7	1,335	0.7
1,400	1.3	1,280	0.9	1,583	1.2	NEW MEXICO	1,800	2.4	2,440	1.7	3,708	2.0
11,000	10.3	18,360	12.7	11,695	8.9	NEW YORK	2,200	3.0	2,160	1.5	3,280	1.8
400	0.4	840	0.6	626	0.5	NORTH CAROLINA	900	1.2	1,080	0.8	1,962	1.1
500	0.5	440	0.3	457	0.4	NORTH DAKOTA	700	0.9	200	0.1	375	0.2
6,000	5.6	6,760	4.7	4,039	3.1	OHIO	2,400	3.2	1,600	1.1	3,241	1.7
1,600	1.5	1,880	1.3	2,746	2.1	OKLAHOMA	3,300	4.4	4,880	3.5	4,451	2.4
4,400	4.1	5,960	4.1	6,151	4.7	OREGON	7,600	10.2	17,080	12.1	23,069	12.3
3,400	3.2	4,840	3.3	4,378	3.3	PENNSYLVANIA	1,300	1.7	1,600	1.1	2,998	1.6
200	0.2	760	0.5	598	0.5	RHODE ISLAND	300	0.4	120	0.1	323	0.2
500	0.5	200	0.1	237	0.2	SOUTH CAROLINA	200	0.3	640	0.5	1,020	0.5
500	0.5	600	0.4	411	0.3	SOUTH DAKOTA	0	–	520	0.4	485	0.3
400	0.4	1,040	0.7	1,019	0.8	TENNESSEE	500	0.7	1,400	1.0	1,527	0.8
5,200	4.9	6,960	4.8	9,597	7.3	TEXAS	4,600	6.2	11,240	7.9	10,134	5.4
1,200	1.1	960	0.7	1,678	1.3	UTAH	2,100	2.8	3,440	2.4	3,674	2.0
100	0.1	240	0.2	196	0.2	VERMONT	0	–	40	0.1	172	0.1
300	0.3	1,520	1.0	2,173	1.7	VIRGINIA	1,600	2.2	1,400	1.0	2,121	1.1
5,200	4.9	5,600	3.9	6,460	4.9	WASHINGTON	4,900	6.6	12,360	8.7	16,689	8.9
300	0.3	280	0.2	200	0.2	WEST VIRGINIA	100	0.1	200	0.1	332	0.2
2,800	2.6	2,120	1.5	2,330	1.8	WISCONSIN	400	0.5	1,080	0.7	1,398	0.8
1,100	1.0	200	0.1	519	0.4	WYOMING	0	–	360	0.2	746	0.4
107,000	100.3*	144,880	99.7*	131,514	100.8*	TOTAL U.S.	74,400	99.3*	141,440	99.9*	187,240	100.3*

*rounding error

COLORADO

	TO COLORADO FROM							FROM COLORADO TO					
1970		**1980**		**1990**			**1970**		**1980**		**1990**	
#	%	#	%	#	%		#	%	#	%	#	%
100	0.7	240	0.9	183	0.6	ALABAMA	100	0.7	80	0.3	66	0.2
0	–	120	0.4	144	0.5	ALASKA	0	–	120	0.5	65	0.2
800	5.6	1,000	3.7	2,031	6.6	ARIZONA	1,800	13.3	3,640	15.7	5,461	19.0
300	2.1	120	0.4	405	1.3	ARKANSAS	0	–	400	1.7	343	1.2
1,800	12.7	4,480	16.5	4,524	14.8	CALIFORNIA	2,800	20.7	4,640	20.0	3,555	12.3
400	2.8	120	0.4	291	1.0	CONNECTICUT	0	–	0	–	87	0.3
0	–	40	0.1	21	0.1	DELAWARE	0	–	200	0.9	0	–
0	–	40	0.1	0	–	D.C.	0	–	0	–	0	–
100	0.7	720	3.0	1,404	4.6	FLORIDA	700	5.2	960	4.1	1,702	5.9
0	–	160	0.6	114	0.4	GEORGIA	0	–	80	0.3	142	0.5
0	–	0	–	240	0.8	HAWAII	0	–	120	0.5	108	0.4
100	0.7	40	0.1	273	0.9	IDAHO	0	–	280	1.2	176	0.6
1,300	9.2	2,200	8.1	1,950	6.4	ILLINOIS	700	5.2	560	2.4	618	2.1
0	–	440	1.6	690	2.3	INDIANA	300	2.2	160	0.7	283	1.0
500	3.5	1,080	4.0	783	2.6	IOWA	200	1.5	280	1.2	404	1.4
400	2.8	1,000	3.7	987	3.2	KANSAS	500	3.7	1,000	4.3	865	3.0
0	–	80	0.3	57	0.2	KENTUCKY	300	2.2	80	0.3	161	0.6
0	–	160	0.6	354	1.2	LOUISIANA	0	–	0	–	66	0.2
0	–	40	0.1	27	0.1	MAINE	0	–	120	0.5	49	0.2
100	0.7	320	1.2	219	0.7	MARYLAND	0	–	120	0.5	188	0.7
0	–	160	0.6	120	0.4	MASSACHUSETTS	100	0.7	160	0.7	96	0.3
100	0.7	1,160	4.3	789	2.6	MICHIGAN	300	2.2	200	0.9	465	1.6
500	3.5	520	1.9	450	1.5	MINNESOTA	0	–	120	0.5	562	2.0
0	–	40	0.1	18	0.1	MISSISSIPPI	0	–	0	–	90	0.3
800	5.6	960	3.5	795	2.6	MISSOURI	600	4.4	640	2.8	880	3.1
100	0.7	320	1.2	225	0.7	MONTANA	0	–	280	1.2	360	1.3
1,300	9.2	1,240	4.6	1,176	3.8	NEBRASKA	1,100	8.1	760	3.3	1,150	4.0
0	–	160	0.6	276	0.9	NEVADA	100	0.7	400	1.7	522	1.8
100	0.7	120	0.4	69	0.2	NEW HAMPSHIRE	0	–	0	–	0	–
300	2.1	520	1.9	876	2.9	NEW JERSEY	100	0.7	320	1.4	99	0.3
1,400	9.9	600	2.2	1,326	4.3	NEW MEXICO	500	3.7	1,120	4.8	1,662	5.8
400	2.8	1,440	5.3	1,146	3.7	NEW YORK	100	0.7	160	0.7	221	0.8
100	0.7	80	0.3	177	0.6	NORTH CAROLINA	0	–	40	0.2	321	1.1
0	–	80	0.3	384	1.3	NORTH DAKOTA	0	–	80	0.3	150	0.5
400	2.8	800	3.0	678	2.2	OHIO	100	0.7	440	1.9	437	1.5
100	0.7	800	3.0	438	1.4	OKLAHOMA	0	–	880	3.8	985	3.4
0	–	240	0.9	429	1.4	OREGON	300	2.2	1,040	4.5	838	2.9
100	0.7	320	1.2	528	1.7	PENNSYLVANIA	0	–	0	–	235	0.8
100	0.7	0	–	12	–	RHODE ISLAND	0	–	0	–	21	0.1
0	–	0	–	87	0.3	SOUTH CAROLINA	0	–	0	–	207	0.7
300	2.1	560	2.1	279	0.9	SOUTH DAKOTA	400	3.0	80	0.3	224	0.8
0	–	240	0.9	132	0.4	TENNESSEE	200	1.5	120	0.5	156	0.5
600	4.2	1,560	5.7	2,448	8.0	TEXAS	1,300	9.6	1,920	8.3	2,240	7.8
400	2.8	480	1.8	516	1.7	UTAH	500	3.7	520	2.2	447	1.6
0	–	0	–	0	–	VERMONT	0	–	0	–	10	–
600	4.2	440	1.6	321	1.1	VIRGINIA	0	–	160	0.7	159	0.6
400	2.8	520	1.9	603	2.0	WASHINGTON	100	0.7	440	1.9	954	3.3
0	–	120	0.4	6	–	WEST VIRGINIA	0	–	0	–	18	0.1
100	0.7	560	2.1	561	1.8	WISCONSIN	300	2.2	120	0.5	307	1.1
100	0.7	720	2.7	1,110	3.6	WYOMING	0	–	400	1.7	660	2.3
14,200	**99.8***	**27,160**	**100.3***	**30,672**	**100.4***	**TOTAL U.S.**	**13,500**	**99.5***	**23,240**	**99.9***	**28,815**	**100.2***

*rounding error

CONNECTICUT

TO CONNECTICUT FROM							FROM CONNECTICUT TO					
1970		1980		1990			1970		1980		1990	
#	%	#	%	#	%		#	%	#	%	#	%
0	–	0	–	0	–	ALABAMA	0	–	240	0.7	129	0.3
0	–	0	–	0	–	ALASKA	0	–	0	–	12	–
100	0.7	160	0.9	261	1.5	ARIZONA	500	2.6	1,320	4.1	774	1.8
0	–	80	0.4	14	0.1	ARKANSAS	0	–	120	0.4	122	0.3
300	2.0	680	3.7	735	4.2	CALIFORNIA	1,200	6.3	2,240	6.9	1,827	4.3
0	–	0	–	87	0.5	COLORADO	400	2.1	120	0.4	291	0.7
0	–	40	0.2	50	0.3	DELAWARE	100	0.5	40	0.1	136	0.3
0	–	40	0.2	5	–	D.C.	0	–	40	0.1	34	0.1
700	4.7	1,720	9.4	1,810	10.4	FLORIDA	8,200	42.7	13,280	40.9	18,952	44.9
0	–	0	–	244	1.4	GEORGIA	200	1.0	480	1.5	660	1.6
0	–	0	–	25	0.1	HAWAII	0	–	0	–	0	–
0	–	0	–	0	–	IDAHO	0	–	40	0.1	36	0.1
0	–	160	0.9	411	2.4	ILLINOIS	200	1.0	240	0.7	303	0.7
100	0.7	160	0.9	100	0.6	INDIANA	100	0.5	160	0.5	32	0.1
0	–	120	0.7	0	–	IOWA	0	–	0	–	142	0.3
0	–	0	–	68	0.4	KANSAS	200	1.0	120	0.4	18	–
0	–	40	0.2	17	0.1	KENTUCKY	0	–	40	0.1	36	0.1
100	0.7	120	0.7	28	0.2	LOUISIANA	0	–	40	0.1	57	0.1
900	6.0	400	2.2	379	2.2	MAINE	700	3.6	960	3.0	1,315	3.1
300	2.0	240	1.3	217	1.3	MARYLAND	200	1.0	440	1.4	725	1.7
2,000	13.3	1,960	10.7	2,296	13.2	MASSACHUSETTS	1,600	8.3	2,480	7.6	2,447	5.8
200	1.3	200	1.1	135	0.8	MICHIGAN	100	0.5	200	0.6	84	0.2
0	–	0	–	25	0.1	MINNESOTA	0	–	160	0.5	218	0.5
0	–	0	–	17	0.1	MISSISSIPPI	0	–	80	0.2	66	0.2
100	0.7	160	0.9	196	1.1	MISSOURI	0	–	120	0.4	105	0.3
0	–	0	–	28	0.2	MONTANA	0	–	40	0.1	0	–
0	–	80	0.4	0	–	NEBRASKA	0	–	0	–	63	0.2
0	–	40	0.2	76	0.4	NEVADA	0	–	120	0.4	211	0.5
100	0.7	160	0.9	217	1.3	NEW HAMPSHIRE	300	1.6	720	2.2	761	1.8
500	3.3	1,400	7.6	1,409	8.1	NEW JERSEY	400	2.1	680	2.1	847	2.0
0	–	120	0.7	23	0.1	NEW MEXICO	0	–	80	0.2	261	0.6
8,000	53.3	7,480	40.8	5,689	32.8	NEW YORK	3,000	15.6	2,000	6.2	2,672	6.3
200	1.3	120	0.7	249	1.4	NORTH CAROLINA	300	1.6	880	2.7	1,428	3.4
0	–	40	0.2	0	–	NORTH DAKOTA	0	–	0	–	0	–
0	–	160	0.9	418	2.4	OHIO	400	2.1	80	0.2	532	1.3
0	–	0	–	31	0.2	OKLAHOMA	100	0.5	0	–	156	0.4
0	–	80	0.4	47	0.3	OREGON	0	–	40	0.1	118	0.3
100	0.7	840	4.6	496	2.9	PENNSYLVANIA	200	1.0	1,080	3.3	951	2.3
600	4.0	480	2.6	461	2.7	RHODE ISLAND	300	1.6	760	2.3	1,011	2.4
0	–	40	0.2	73	0.4	SOUTH CAROLINA	0	–	360	1.1	1,545	3.7
0	–	0	–	0	–	SOUTH DAKOTA	0	–	0	–	19	0.1
200	1.3	80	0.4	124	0.7	TENNESSEE	100	0.5	240	0.7	210	0.5
0	–	80	0.4	277	1.6	TEXAS	100	0.5	480	1.5	563	1.3
0	–	0	–	20	0.1	UTAH	0	–	40	0.1	72	0.2
400	2.7	520	2.8	293	1.7	VERMONT	0	–	840	2.6	769	1.8
0	–	240	1.3	216	1.2	VIRGINIA	300	1.6	680	2.1	963	2.3
100	0.7	0	–	25	0.1	WASHINGTON	0	–	0	–	357	0.9
0	–	40	0.2	22	0.1	WEST VIRGINIA	0	–	40	0.1	7	–
0	–	40	0.2	37	0.2	WISCONSIN	0	–	320	1.0	135	0.3
0	–	0	–	0	–	WYOMING	0	–	0	–	0	–
15,000	100.1*	18,320	99.9*	17,351	99.9*	TOTAL U.S.	19,200	99.8*	32,440	99.7*	42,172	100.1*

*rounding error

DELAWARE

TO DELAWARE FROM							FROM DELAWARE TO					
1970		1980		1990			1970		1980		1990	
#	%	#	%	#	%		#	%	#	%	#	%
0	–	40	0.6	0	–	ALABAMA	0	–	0	–	39	0.6
0	–	0	–	0	–	ALASKA	0	–	40	1.0	0	–
0	–	0	–	22	0.3	ARIZONA	0	–	80	1.9	190	3.0
0	–	0	–	0	–	ARKANSAS	100	2.9	0	–	14	0.2
0	–	0	–	121	1.5	CALIFORNIA	0	–	400	9.6	102	1.6
0	–	200	3.0	0	–	COLORADO	0	–	40	1.0	21	0.3
100	2.7	40	0.6	136	1.7	CONNECTICUT	0	–	40	1.0	50	0.8
100	2.7	40	0.6	23	0.3	D.C.	0	–	0	–	15	0.2
100	2.7	560	8.4	459	5.7	FLORIDA	700	20.6	1,080	26	1,762	27.8
0	–	0	–	32	0.4	GEORGIA	0	–	0	–	54	0.9
0	–	0	–	0	–	HAWAII	0	–	0	–	0	–
0	–	0	–	0	–	IDAHO	0	–	0	–	0	–
100	2.7	280	4.2	62	0.8	ILLINOIS	0	–	40	1.0	21	0.3
0	–	0	–	88	1.1	INDIANA	0	–	0	–	0	–
0	–	0	–	0	–	IOWA	0	–	0	–	0	–
100	2.7	0	–	0	–	KANSAS	0	–	0	–	0	–
0	–	0	–	0	–	KENTUCKY	0	–	40	1.0	25	0.4
0	–	0	–	102	1.3	LOUISIANA	0	–	0	–	0	–
0	–	0	–	0	–	MAINE	0	–	80	1.9	31	0.5
500	13.5	1,120	16.8	2,074	25.8	MARYLAND	500	14.7	800	19.2	964	15.2
0	–	80	1.2	234	2.9	MASSACHUSETTS	0	–	0	–	28	0.4
0	–	0	–	74	0.9	MICHIGAN	0	–	40	1.0	63	1.0
0	–	0	–	0	–	MINNESOTA	0	–	0	–	0	–
0	–	40	0.6	83	1.0	MISSISSIPPI	0	–	0	–	63	1.0
0	–	0	–	32	0.4	MISSOURI	200	5.9	0	–	0	–
0	–	0	–	0	–	MONTANA	0	–	0	–	0	–
0	–	0	–	0	–	NEBRASKA	0	–	0	–	0	–
0	–	0	–	7	0.1	NEVADA	0	–	0	–	93	1.5
0	–	0	–	0	–	NEW HAMPSHIRE	0	–	40	1.0	50	0.8
700	18.9	920	13.8	1,272	15.9	NEW JERSEY	500	14.7	280	6.7	229	3.6
0	–	0	–	0	–	NEW MEXICO	0	–	0	–	9	0.1
200	5.4	920	13.8	615	7.7	NEW YORK	200	5.9	80	1.9	189	3.0
100	2.7	80	1.2	114	1.4	NORTH CAROLINA	500	14.7	0	–	174	2.7
0	–	0	–	0	–	NORTH DAKOTA	0	–	0	–	0	–
0	–	80	1.2	79	1.0	OHIO	0	–	120	2.9	37	0.6
0	–	0	–	0	–	OKLAHOMA	0	–	0	–	23	0.4
0	–	0	–	20	0.3	OREGON	0	–	80	1.9	0	–
1,400	37.8	1,840	27.5	1,793	22.3	PENNSYLVANIA	500	14.7	560	13.5	1,399	22.1
0	–	0	–	0	–	RHODE ISLAND	0	–	0	–	0	–
0	–	0	–	0	–	SOUTH CAROLINA	0	–	40	1.0	138	2.2
0	–	0	–	0	–	SOUTH DAKOTA	0	–	0	–	0	–
200	5.4	0	–	38	0.5	TENNESSEE	0	–	0	–	48	0.8
0	–	0	–	27	0.3	TEXAS	100	2.9	120	2.9	121	1.9
0	–	0	–	0	–	UTAH	0	–	0	–	0	–
0	–	0	–	19	0.2	VERMONT	0	–	0	–	0	–
0	–	240	3.6	410	5.1	VIRGINIA	100	2.9	80	1.9	354	5.6
0	–	0	–	7	0.1	WASHINGTON	0	–	80	1.9	18	0.3
100	2.7	200	3.0	67	0.8	WEST VIRGINIA	0	–	0	–	0	–
0	–	0	–	16	0.2	WISCONSIN	0	–	0	–	0	–
0	–	0	–	0	–	WYOMING	0	–	0	–	21	0.3
3,700	99.9*	6,680	100.1*	8,026	100.0	TOTAL U.S.	3,400	99.9*	4,160	100.2*	6,345	100.1*

*rounding error

DISTRICT OF COLUMBIA

TO DISTRICT OF COLUMBIA FROM							FROM DISTRICT OF COLUMBIA TO					
1970		1980		1990			1970		1980		1990	
#	%	#	%	#	%		#	%	#	%	#	%
0	–	80	2.2	16	0.3	ALABAMA	0	–	120	1.0	51	0.5
0	–	0	–	0	–	ALASKA	100	0.6	40	0.3	0	–
0	–	40	1.1	55	1.1	ARIZONA	0	–	40	0.3	21	0.2
100	3.1	0	–	0	–	ARKANSAS	0	–	80	0.7	25	0.2
100	3.1	160	4.5	257	5.3	CALIFORNIA	700	4.2	520	4.5	369	3.6
0	–	0	–	0	–	COLORADO	0	–	40	0.3	0	–
0	–	40	1.1	34	0.7	CONNECTICUT	0	–	40	0.3	5	0.1
0	–	0	–	15	0.3	DELAWARE	100	0.6	40	0.3	23	0.2
100	3.1	80	2.2	142	3.0	FLORIDA	700	4.2	960	8.3	744	7.2
0	–	40	1.1	38	0.8	GEORGIA	0	–	200	1.7	122	1.2
0	–	0	–	87	1.8	HAWAII	0	–	0	–	17	0.2
0	–	0	–	0	–	IDAHO	0	–	0	–	24	0.2
100	3.1	160	4.5	19	0.4	ILLINOIS	100	0.6	120	1.0	69	0.7
0	–	0	–	45	0.9	INDIANA	0	–	80	0.7	38	0.4
0	–	0	–	0	–	IOWA	0	–	0	–	0	–
0	–	80	2.2	0	–	KANSAS	100	0.6	40	0.3	28	0.3
0	–	0	–	43	0.9	KENTUCKY	0	–	40	0.3	49	0.5
0	–	0	–	21	0.4	LOUISIANA	100	0.6	0	–	39	0.4
0	–	40	1.1	28	0.6	MAINE	0	–	40	0.3	49	0.5
900	28.1	880	24.7	1,405	29.1	MARYLAND	7,300	44.2	4,360	37.6	4,160	40.4
0	–	40	1.1	52	1.1	MASSACHUSETTS	100	0.6	320	2.8	65	0.6
0	–	80	2.2	80	1.7	MICHIGAN	300	1.8	160	1.4	37	0.4
0	–	0	–	0	–	MINNESOTA	0	–	0	–	28	0.3
0	–	0	–	56	1.7	MISSISSIPPI	0	–	40	0.3	0	–
0	–	0	–	34	0.7	MISSOURI	0	–	40	0.3	34	0.3
0	–	0	–	0	–	MONTANA	0	–	0	–	27	0.3
0	–	0	–	0	–	NEBRASKA	0	–	40	0.3	59	0.6
0	–	40	1.1	0	–	NEVADA	100	0.6	0	–	0	–
0	–	0	–	0	–	NEW HAMPSHIRE	0	–	40	0.3	0	–
0	–	80	2.2	76	1.6	NEW JERSEY	300	1.8	120	1.0	76	0.7
0	–	0	–	0	–	NEW MEXICO	0	–	80	0.7	60	0.6
400	12.5	200	5.6	424	8.8	NEW YORK	500	3.0	160	1.4	442	4.3
0	–	360	10.1	248	5.1	NORTH CAROLINA	900	5.5	400	3.4	573	5.6
100	3.1	0	–	0	–	NORTH DAKOTA	0	–	0	–	60	0.6
200	6.3	160	4.5	45	0.9	OHIO	100	0.6	80	0.7	143	1.4
0	–	0	–	27	0.6	OKLAHOMA	100	0.6	0	–	37	0.4
0	–	0	–	81	1.7	OREGON	0	–	40	0.3	0	–
500	15.6	240	6.7	257	5.3	PENNSYLVANIA	200	1.2	240	2.1	220	2.1
0	–	0	–	0	–	RHODE ISLAND	0	–	0	–	16	0.2
0	–	80	2.2	232	4.8	SOUTH CAROLINA	100	0.6	440	3.8	147	1.4
0	–	0	–	0	–	SOUTH DAKOTA	0	–	0	–	0	–
0	–	0	–	60	1.2	TENNESSEE	300	1.8	120	1.0	0	–
0	–	200	5.6	88	1.8	TEXAS	400	2.4	280	2.4	99	1.0
0	–	0	–	0	–	UTAH	0	–	0	–	0	–
0	–	0	–	0	–	VERMONT	100	0.6	0	–	114	1.1
700	21.9	360	10.1	603	12.5	VIRGINIA	3,700	22.4	2,160	18.6	1,815	17.6
0	–	40	1.1	186	3.9	WASHINGTON	0	–	40	0.3	105	1.0
0	–	80	2.2	36	0.8	WEST VIRGINIA	0	–	0	–	231	2.3
0	–	0	–	31	0.6	WISCONSIN	100	0.6	40	0.3	67	0.7
0	–	0	–	0	–	WYOMING	0	–	0	–	0	–
3,200	99.9*	3,560	99.4*	4,821	99.9*	TOTAL U.S.	16,500	99.7*	11,600	99.3*	10,288	100.3*

*rounding error

FLORIDA

TO FLORIDA FROM							FROM FLORIDA TO					
1970		1980		1990			1970		1980		1990	
#	%	#	%	#	%		#	%	#	%	#	%
1,900	0.7	2,880	0.7	5,217	1.2	ALABAMA	2,300	5.0	3,520	3.8	4,729	3.7
0	–	240	0.1	211	0.1	ALASKA	0	–	160	0.2	34	–
600	0.2	1,320	0.3	2,021	0.5	ARIZONA	1,200	2.6	1,400	1.5	2,714	2.1
500	0.2	1,160	0.3	1,446	0.3	ARKANSAS	0	–	960	1.0	1,108	0.9
4,700	1.8	7,160	1.6	13,407	3.0	CALIFORNIA	2,300	5.0	6,960	7.5	7,731	6.0
700	0.3	960	0.2	1,702	0.4	COLORADO	100	0.2	720	0.8	1,404	1.1
8,200	3.1	13,280	3.0	18,952	4.2	CONNECTICUT	700	1.5	1,720	1.9	1,810	1.4
700	0.3	1,080	0.2	1,762	0.4	DELAWARE	100	0.2	560	0.6	459	0.4
700	0.3	960	0.2	744	0.2	D.C.	100	0.2	80	0.1	142	0.1
5,100	1.9	6,960	1.6	9,210	2.0	GEORGIA	3,600	7.8	8,360	9.1	11,533	9.0
0	–	120	–	811	0.2	HAWAII	0	–	280	0.3	145	0.1
100	–	80	–	152	–	IDAHO	0	–	120	0.1	64	0.1
20,900	7.9	30,680	7.0	25,893	5.7	ILLINOIS	1,800	3.9	3,160	3.4	5,148	4.0
9,700	3.7	14,320	3.3	13,327	3.0	INDIANA	1,700	3.7	1,680	1.8	4,773	3.7
1,000	0.4	1,800	0.4	2,435	0.5	IOWA	300	0.7	560	0.6	398	0.3
400	0.2	600	0.1	871	0.2	KANSAS	0	–	280	0.3	413	0.3
3,000	1.1	3,840	0.9	4,704	1.0	KENTUCKY	1,500	3.3	1,640	1.8	2,253	1.8
600	0.2	800	0.2	2,089	0.5	LOUISIANA	200	0.4	1,120	1.2	834	0.7
2,200	0.8	2,720	0.6	4,726	1.1	MAINE	300	0.7	440	0.5	821	0.6
4,400	1.7	11,480	2.6	11,432	2.5	MARYLAND	800	1.7	1,880	2.0	3,470	2.7
11,000	4.2	19,840	4.5	25,450	5.6	MASSACHUSETTS	2,100	4.6	2,640	2.9	3,232	2.5
24,300	9.2	28,320	6.5	32,058	7.1	MICHIGAN	1,900	4.1	3,480	3.8	6,712	5.2
2,200	0.8	2,680	0.6	3,836	0.9	MINNESOTA	400	0.9	920	1.0	1,190	0.9
700	0.3	840	0.2	1,101	0.2	MISSISSIPPI	800	1.7	1,160	1.3	1,062	0.8
3,200	1.2	4,440	1.0	4,507	1.0	MISSOURI	300	0.7	1,240	1.3	1,911	1.5
0	–	200	–	268	0.1	MONTANA	0	–	0	–	230	0.2
400	0.2	400	0.1	803	0.2	NEBRASKA	0	–	160	0.2	179	0.1
200	0.1	440	0.1	1,045	0.2	NEVADA	100	0.2	920	1.0	1,336	1.0
1,800	0.7	2,840	0.6	5,504	1.2	NEW HAMPSHIRE	300	0.7	840	0.9	1,127	0.9
21,800	8.3	38,440	8.8	41,315	9.2	NEW JERSEY	2,200	4.0	4,040	5.0	4,173	3.3
400	0.2	360	0.1	647	0.1	NEW MEXICO	100	0.2	360	0.4	612	0.5
73,500	27.9	127,600	29.2	104,019	23.0	NEW YORK	3,700	8.0	9,000	9.8	9,063	7.1
2,600	1.0	4,800	1.1	6,385	1.4	NORTH CAROLINA	1,900	4.1	5,680	6.2	8,841	6.9
0	–	160	–	76	–	NORTH DAKOTA	0	–	0	–	45	–
19,300	7.3	37,720	8.6	27,986	6.2	OHIO	4,600	10.0	5,120	5.5	8,707	6.8
700	0.3	840	0.2	1,084	0.2	OKLAHOMA	200	0.4	680	0.7	662	0.5
0	–	160	–	457	0.1	OREGON	300	0.7	800	0.9	938	0.7
15,500	5.9	31,600	7.2	27,567	6.1	PENNSYLVANIA	2,500	5.4	4,480	4.9	6,831	5.3
1,900	0.7	2,040	0.5	4,278	1.0	RHODE ISLAND	500	1.1	360	0.4	377	0.3
600	0.2	2,080	0.5	3,090	0.7	SOUTH CAROLINA	1,200	2.6	1,800	2.0	2,910	2.3
400	0.2	200	–	141	–	SOUTH DAKOTA	0	–	120	0.1	109	0.1
2,500	0.9	3,840	0.9	4,257	0.9	TENNESSEE	1,400	3.0	2,720	2.9	4,572	3.6
1,500	0.6	2,920	0.7	6,787	1.5	TEXAS	1,900	4.1	3,760	4.1	5,070	3.9
0	–	360	0.1	169	–	UTAH	300	0.7	80	0.1	143	0.1
800	0.3	2,120	0.5	1,908	0.4	VERMONT	200	0.4	80	0.1	326	0.3
4,400	1.7	8,040	1.8	11,582	2.6	VIRGINIA	1,100	2.4	2,720	2.9	3,897	3.0
700	0.3	480	0.1	897	0.2	WASHINGTON	100	0.2	640	0.7	1,413	1.1
3,000	1.1	3,440	0.8	3,441	0.8	WEST VIRGINIA	300	0.7	760	0.8	1,137	0.9
4,400	1.7	7,200	1.6	9,763	2.2	WISCONSIN	600	1.3	1,440	1.6	1,737	1.4
0	–	200	–	176	–	WYOMING	0	–	80	0.1	36	–
263,200	100.1*	437,040	99.6*	451,709	100.1*	TOTAL U.S.	46,000	99.9*	92,280	100.1*	128,561	100.2*

*rounding error

GEORGIA

TO GEORGIA FROM							FROM GEORGIA TO					
1970		1980		1990			1970		1980		1990	
#	%	#	%	#	%		#	%	#	%	#	%
1,100	7.0	1,040	3.1	3,396	7.6	ALABAMA	1,800	13.4	1,280	6.4	2,958	10.4
400	2.5	200	0.6	40	0.1	ALASKA	0	–	0	–	0	–
200	1.3	280	0.8	274	0.6	ARIZONA	0	–	200	1.0	423	1.5
100	0.6	200	0.6	346	0.8	ARKANSAS	0	–	200	1.0	169	0.6
700	4.5	1,240	3.7	1,942	4.4	CALIFORNIA	700	5.2	1,000	5.0	1,059	3.7
0	–	80	0.2	142	0.3	COLORADO	0	–	160	0.8	114	0.4
200	1.3	480	1.4	660	1.5	CONNECTICUT	0	–	0	–	244	0.9
0	–	0	–	54	0.1	DELAWARE	0	–	0	–	32	0.1
0	–	200	0.6	122	0.3	D.C.	0	–	40	0.2	38	0.1
3,600	22.9	8,360	25.1	11,533	25.9	FLORIDA	5,100	38.1	6,960	34.7	9,210	32.3
0	–	0	–	0	–	HAWAII	0	–	160	0.8	17	0.1
0	–	80	0.2	30	0.1	IDAHO	0	–	0	–	8	–
200	1.3	2,080	6.2	2,014	4.5	ILLINOIS	100	0.7	200	1.0	252	0.9
0	–	480	1.4	582	1.3	INDIANA	0	–	320	1.6	392	1.4
0	–	120	0.4	64	0.1	IOWA	0	–	40	0.2	8	–
100	0.6	80	0.2	122	0.3	KANSAS	0	–	80	0.4	119	0.4
200	1.3	200	0.6	488	1.1	KENTUCKY	0	–	0	–	492	1.7
300	1.9	200	0.6	553	1.2	LOUISIANA	100	0.7	200	1.0	390	1.4
0	–	80	0.2	84	0.2	MAINE	0	–	0	–	31	0.1
100	0.6	600	1.8	622	1.4	MARYLAND	100	0.7	80	0.4	238	0.8
100	0.6	520	1.6	607	1.4	MASSACHUSETTS	300	2.2	120	0.6	314	1.1
800	5.1	1,320	4.0	1,376	3.1	MICHIGAN	0	–	480	2.4	670	2.4
300	1.9	160	0.5	164	0.4	MINNESOTA	0	–	40	0.2	65	0.2
200	1.3	400	1.2	343	0.8	MISSISSIPPI	600	4.5	760	3.8	318	1.1
600	3.8	320	1.0	627	1.4	MISSOURI	100	0.7	40	0.2	327	1.2
0	–	0	–	58	0.1	MONTANA	0	–	0	–	0	–
0	–	80	0.2	0	–	NEBRASKA	0	–	0	–	0	–
0	–	120	0.4	79	0.2	NEVADA	0	–	40	0.2	42	0.2
0	–	200	0.6	191	0.4	NEW HAMPSHIRE	0	–	0	–	0	–
100	0.6	1,400	4.2	1,838	4.1	NEW JERSEY	200	1.5	360	1.8	497	1.8
0	–	200	0.6	111	0.3	NEW MEXICO	0	–	120	0.6	126	0.4
300	1.9	2,240	6.7	3,396	7.6	NEW YORK	300	2.2	360	1.8	384	1.4
1,300	8.3	1,720	5.2	1,506	3.4	NORTH CAROLINA	400	3.0	1,040	5.2	2,172	7.6
0	–	0	–	0	–	NORTH DAKOTA	0	–	0	–	0	–
800	5.1	1,160	3.5	1,618	3.6	OHIO	600	4.5	400	2.0	519	1.8
100	0.6	120	0.4	87	0.2	OKLAHOMA	0	–	0	–	143	0.5
0	–	40	0.1	74	0.2	OREGON	0	–	40	0.2	29	0.1
400	2.5	1,080	3.2	1,223	2.8	PENNSYLVANIA	300	2.2	240	1.2	508	1.8
0	–	120	0.4	67	0.2	RHODE ISLAND	0	–	80	0.4	26	0.1
900	5.7	1,760	5.3	1,948	4.4	SOUTH CAROLINA	1,300	9.7	1,640	8.2	2,202	7.7
0	–	80	0.2	86	0.2	SOUTH DAKOTA	0	–	0	–	29	0.1
1,700	10.8	2,120	6.4	2,210	5.0	TENNESSEE	600	4.5	1,680	8.4	1,806	6.3
400	2.5	960	2.9	1,760	4.0	TEXAS	400	3.0	1,080	5.4	936	3.3
0	–	0	–	67	0.2	UTAH	0	–	0	–	47	0.2
0	–	40	0.1	22	0.1	VERMONT	0	–	0	–	0	–
300	1.9	880	2.6	1,103	2.5	VIRGINIA	400	3.0	600	3.0	690	2.4
0	–	40	0.1	208	0.5	WASHINGTON	0	–	0	–	177	0.6
0	–	120	0.4	260	0.6	WEST VIRGINIA	0	–	0	–	116	0.4
200	1.3	160	0.5	328	0.7	WISCONSIN	0	–	40	0.2	138	0.5
0	–	0	–	50	0.1	WYOMING	0	–	0	–	0	–
15,700	99.7*	33,360	100.0	44,475	100.3*	TOTAL U.S.	13,400	99.8*	20,080	100.3*	28,475	100.0

*rounding error

HAWAII

TO HAWAII FROM							FROM HAWAII TO					
1970		1980		1990			1970		1980		1990	
#	%	#	%	#	%		#	%	#	%	#	%
0	–	0	–	25	0.3	ALABAMA	0	–	0	–	61	0.7
0	–	40	0.7	235	2.9	ALASKA	0	–	0	–	45	0.5
0	–	120	2.1	212	2.6	ARIZONA	0	–	200	5.2	435	5.2
0	–	0	–	34	0.4	ARKANSAS	0	–	0	–	0	–
2,600	72.2	2,440	43.3	3,459	43.0	CALIFORNIA	900	42.9	1,520	39.2	3,092	37.1
0	–	120	2.1	108	1.3	COLORADO	0	–	0	–	240	2.9
0	–	0	–	0	–	CONNECTICUT	0	–	0	–	25	0.3
0	–	0	–	0	–	DELAWARE	0	–	0	–	0	–
0	–	0	–	17	0.2	D.C.	0	–	0	–	87	1.0
0	–	280	5.0	145	1.8	FLORIDA	0	–	120	3.1	811	9.7
0	–	160	2.8	17	0.2	GEORGIA	0	–	0	–	0	–
0	–	80	1.4	57	0.7	IDAHO	0	–	0	–	0	–
200	5.6	160	2.8	269	3.3	ILLINOIS	200	9.5	40	1.0	39	0.5
0	–	0	–	67	0.8	INDIANA	200	9.5	40	1.0	54	0.7
0	–	120	2.1	42	0.5	IOWA	0	–	80	2.1	0	–
0	–	0	–	16	0.2	KANSAS	0	–	0	–	0	–
0	–	0	–	36	0.5	KENTUCKY	0	–	0	–	0	–
100	2.8	80	1.4	34	0.4	LOUISIANA	0	–	40	1.0	54	0.7
0	–	0	–	0	–	MAINE	0	–	0	–	36	0.4
0	–	80	1.4	14	0.2	MARYLAND	0	–	80	2.1	76	0.9
0	–	200	3.5	96	1.2	MASSACHUSETTS	0	–	40	1.0	26	0.3
0	–	80	1.4	365	4.5	MICHIGAN	0	–	0	–	92	1.1
0	–	40	0.7	157	2.0	MINNESOTA	0	–	40	1.0	0	–
0	–	0	–	0	–	MISSISSIPPI	0	–	0	–	54	0.7
0	–	40	0.7	20	0.3	MISSOURI	0	–	40	1.0	82	1.0
0	–	80	1.4	110	1.4	MONTANA	0	–	0	–	0	–
0	–	0	–	0	–	NEBRASKA	0	–	0	–	0	–
0	–	40	0.7	45	0.6	NEVADA	0	–	120	3.1	307	3.7
0	–	0	–	109	1.4	NEW HAMPSHIRE	0	–	0	–	0	–
0	–	120	2.1	255	3.2	NEW JERSEY	0	–	0	–	125	1.5
100	2.8	0	–	0	–	NEW MEXICO	0	–	40	1.0	105	1.3
300	8.3	200	3.5	304	3.8	NEW YORK	0	–	40	1.0	151	1.8
200	5.6	0	–	23	0.3	NORTH CAROLINA	0	–	40	1.0	192	2.3
0	–	0	–	0	–	NORTH DAKOTA	0	–	0	–	0	–
0	–	80	1.4	56	0.7	OHIO	0	–	80	2.1	94	1.1
0	–	80	1.4	17	0.2	OKLAHOMA	0	–	0	–	100	1.2
0	–	0	–	261	3.2	OREGON	0	–	320	8.2	566	6.8
0	–	40	0.7	211	2.6	PENNSYLVANIA	100	4.8	80	2.1	140	1.7
100	2.8	80	1.4	16	0.2	RHODE ISLAND	0	–	0	–	0	–
0	–	0	–	0	–	SOUTH CAROLINA	100	4.8	40	1.0	18	0.2
0	–	0	–	0	–	SOUTH DAKOTA	0	–	0	–	38	0.5
0	–	0	–	17	0.2	TENNESSEE	0	–	40	1.0	48	0.6
0	–	80	1.4	233	2.9	TEXAS	100	4.8	280	7.2	233	2.8
0	–	80	1.4	320	4.0	UTAH	0	–	160	4.1	58	0.7
0	–	0	–	0	–	VERMONT	0	–	0	–	0	–
0	–	40	0.7	133	1.7	VIRGINIA	300	14.3	40	1.0	150	1.8
0	–	680	12.1	476	5.9	WASHINGTON	200	9.5	320	8.2	672	8.1
0	–	0	–	0	–	WEST VIRGINIA	0	–	0	–	22	0.3
0	–	0	–	20	0.3	WISCONSIN	0	–	0	–	0	–
0	–	0	–	22	0.3	WYOMING	0	–	40	1.0	7	0.1
3,600	100.1*	5,640	99.6*	8,053	100.2*	TOTAL U.S.	2,100	100.1*	3,880	99.7*	8,335	100.2*

*rounding error

IDAHO

							TO IDAHO FROM →←FROM IDAHO TO						
1970		1980		1990			1970		1980		1990	
#	%	#	%	#	%		#	%	#	%	#	%
0	–	0	–	0	–	ALABAMA	0	–	40	0.5	7	0.1
0	–	360	3.9	264	2.4	ALASKA	0	–	80	0.9	29	0.3
0	–	240	2.6	444	4.1	ARIZONA	600	11.3	960	10.8	931	9.1
0	–	0	–	8	0.1	ARKANSAS	0	–	80	0.9	25	0.2
1,300	31.0	2,720	29.8	2,680	24.7	CALIFORNIA	1,100	20.8	1,680	18.9	1,901	18.6
0	–	280	3.1	176	1.6	COLORADO	100	1.9	40	0.5	273	2.7
0	–	40	0.4	36	0.3	CONNECTICUT	0	–	0	–	0	–
0	–	0	–	0	–	DELAWARE	0	–	0	–	0	–
0	–	0	–	24	0.2	D.C.	0	–	0	–	0	–
0	–	120	1.3	64	0.6	FLORIDA	100	1.9	80	0.9	152	1.5
0	–	0	–	8	0.1	GEORGIA	0	–	80	0.9	30	0.3
0	–	0	–	0	–	HAWAII	0	–	80	0.9	57	0.6
100	2.4	120	1.3	12	0.1	ILLINOIS	0	–	120	1.4	0	–
0	–	40	0.4	60	0.6	INDIANA	0	–	0	–	10	0.1
0	–	0	–	80	0.7	IOWA	0	–	0	–	13	0.1
200	4.8	80	0.9	36	0.3	KANSAS	0	–	40	0.5	61	0.6
0	–	0	–	24	0.2	KENTUCKY	0	–	0	–	0	–
0	–	0	–	8	0.1	LOUISIANA	0	–	0	–	9	0.1
0	–	0	–	20	0.2	MAINE	0	–	0	–	0	–
0	–	80	0.9	56	0.5	MARYLAND	0	–	80	0.9	14	0.1
0	–	40	0.4	0	–	MASSACHUSETTS	0	–	0	–	0	–
0	–	80	0.9	184	1.7	MICHIGAN	0	–	0	–	61	0.6
100	2.4	160	1.8	112	1.0	MINNESOTA	100	1.9	120	1.4	47	0.5
0	–	0	–	28	0.3	MISSISSIPPI	0	–	0	–	15	0.2
0	–	120	1.3	128	1.2	MISSOURI	0	–	120	1.4	170	1.7
300	7.1	120	1.3	468	4.3	MONTANA	0	–	120	1.4	395	3.9
100	2.4	40	0.4	116	1.1	NEBRASKA	0	–	0	–	102	1.0
200	4.8	120	1.3	384	3.6	NEVADA	400	7.5	240	2.7	567	5.6
0	–	0	–	28	0.3	NEW HAMPSHIRE	0	–	0	–	31	0.3
0	–	40	0.4	84	0.8	NEW JERSEY	0	–	0	–	23	0.2
0	–	0	–	88	0.8	NEW MEXICO	100	1.9	0	–	186	1.8
0	–	80	0.9	216	2.0	NEW YORK	0	–	0	–	45	0.4
0	–	40	0.4	0	–	NORTH CAROLINA	0	–	40	0.5	21	0.2
0	–	240	2.6	124	1.1	NORTH DAKOTA	0	–	0	–	0	–
0	–	40	0.4	92	0.9	OHIO	0	–	120	1.4	71	0.7
0	–	40	0.4	60	0.6	OKLAHOMA	0	–	120	1.4	48	0.5
300	7.1	1,000	11.0	1,520	14.0	OREGON	600	11.3	1,000	11.3	1,245	12.2
0	–	0	–	28	0.3	PENNSYLVANIA	0	–	0	–	7	0.1
0	–	0	–	0	–	RHODE ISLAND	0	–	0	–	0	–
0	–	40	0.4	0	–	SOUTH CAROLINA	0	–	80	0.9	0	–
100	2.4	0	–	36	0.3	SOUTH DAKOTA	0	–	0	–	29	0.3
0	–	80	0.9	68	0.6	TENNESSEE	0	–	0	–	0	–
200	4.8	200	2.2	188	1.7	TEXAS	100	1.9	480	5.4	385	3.8
200	4.8	560	6.1	656	6.1	UTAH	100	1.9	680	7.7	972	9.5
0	–	0	–	8	0.1	VERMONT	0	–	0	–	0	–
0	–	0	–	24	0.2	VIRGINIA	0	–	80	0.9	51	0.5
1,000	23.8	1,840	20.2	1,692	15.6	WASHINGTON	1,900	35.8	2,120	23.9	1,959	19.2
0	–	0	–	0	–	WEST VIRGINIA	0	–	0	–	0	–
0	–	0	–	140	1.3	WISCONSIN	0	–	0	–	162	1.6
100	2.4	160	1.8	360	3.3	WYOMING	100	1.9	200	2.3	101	1.0
4,200	100.2*	9,120	99.7*	10,832	100.0	TOTAL U.S.	5,300	100.0	8,880	100.6*	10,205	100.2*

*rounding error

ILLINOIS

TO ILLINOIS FROM							FROM ILLINOIS TO					
1970		1980		1990			1970		1980		1990	
#	%	#	%	#	%		#	%	#	%	#	%
400	1.4	160	0.4	501	1.4	ALABAMA	500	0.6	1,200	1.0	1,845	1.7
0	–	0	–	30	0.1	ALASKA	0	–	0	–	38	–
600	2.1	1,360	3.8	1,386	3.8	ARIZONA	5,200	6.0	11,520	9.6	8,460	7.9
400	1.4	1,400	3.9	1,410	3.8	ARKANSAS	3,500	4.0	6,680	5.6	3,380	3.2
2,300	8.0	3,600	10.1	3,255	8.8	CALIFORNIA	12,400	14.3	13,960	11.6	9,136	8.5
700	2.4	560	1.6	618	1.7	COLORADO	1,300	1.5	2,200	1.8	1,950	1.8
200	0.7	240	0.7	303	0.8	CONNECTICUT	0	–	160	0.1	411	0.4
0	–	40	0.1	21	0.1	DELAWARE	100	0.1	280	0.2	62	0.1
100	0.3	120	0.3	69	0.2	D.C.	100	0.1	160	0.1	19	–
1,800	6.3	3,160	8.8	5,148	14.0	FLORIDA	20,900	24.1	30,680	25.5	25,893	24.2
100	0.3	200	0.6	252	0.7	GEORGIA	200	0.2	2,080	1.7	2,014	1.9
200	0.7	40	0.1	39	0.1	HAWAII	200	0.2	160	0.1	269	0.3
0	–	120	0.3	0	–	IDAHO	100	0.1	120	0.1	12	–
3,400	11.8	3,520	9.9	2,172	5.9	INDIANA	4,200	4.8	5,600	4.7	5,574	5.2
1,400	4.9	1,200	3.4	1,488	4.0	IOWA	2,800	3.2	1,800	1.5	1,775	1.7
600	2.1	320	0.9	363	1.0	KANSAS	600	0.7	840	0.7	679	0.6
900	3.1	800	2.2	525	1.4	KENTUCKY	1,900	2.2	1,920	1.6	1,889	1.8
200	0.7	520	1.5	255	0.7	LOUISIANA	600	0.7	320	0.3	630	0.6
0	–	40	0.1	39	0.1	MAINE	0	–	40	0.1	231	0.2
200	0.7	360	1.0	213	0.6	MARYLAND	800	0.9	440	0.4	393	0.4
400	1.4	440	1.2	204	0.6	MASSACHUSETTS	600	0.7	520	0.4	435	0.4
1,700	5.9	1,960	5.5	1,962	5.3	MICHIGAN	4,500	5.2	3,640	3.0	3,665	3.4
1,000	3.5	680	1.9	432	1.2	MINNESOTA	1,600	1.8	1,440	1.2	1,130	1.1
1,100	3.8	640	1.8	990	2.7	MISSISSIPPI	1,000	1.2	1,560	1.3	1,233	1.2
2,500	8.7	3,240	9.1	3,282	8.9	MISSOURI	4,900	5.7	5,200	4.3	4,943	4.6
100	0.3	80	0.2	207	0.6	MONTANA	0	–	80	0.1	145	0.1
100	0.3	160	0.4	186	0.5	NEBRASKA	600	0.7	280	0.2	423	0.4
0	–	200	0.6	252	0.7	NEVADA	100	0.1	1,120	0.9	2,465	2.3
0	–	40	0.1	60	0.2	NEW HAMPSHIRE	0	–	120	0.1	136	0.1
200	0.7	640	1.8	558	1.5	NEW JERSEY	800	0.9	440	0.4	588	0.6
200	0.7	160	0.4	156	0.4	NEW MEXICO	600	0.7	1,000	0.8	969	0.9
1,700	5.9	1,240	3.5	933	2.5	NEW YORK	1,000	1.2	800	0.7	899	0.8
400	1.4	200	0.6	321	0.9	NORTH CAROLINA	300	0.3	920	0.8	2,199	2.1
0	–	0	–	51	0.1	NORTH DAKOTA	100	0.1	120	0.1	80	0.1
1,500	5.2	1,600	4.5	1,272	3.5	OHIO	2,100	2.4	1,440	1.2	1,762	1.6
100	0.3	240	0.7	423	1.2	OKLAHOMA	300	0.3	800	0.7	504	0.5
0	–	40	0.1	150	0.4	OREGON	400	0.5	560	0.5	484	0.5
900	3.1	840	2.4	948	2.6	PENNSYLVANIA	600	0.7	640	0.5	1,053	1.0
0	–	40	0.1	45	0.1	RHODE ISLAND	0	–	80	0.1	86	0.1
100	0.3	80	0.2	162	0.4	SOUTH CAROLINA	400	0.5	440	0.4	1,140	1.1
0	–	80	0.2	36	0.1	SOUTH DAKOTA	500	0.6	200	0.2	160	0.2
1,000	3.5	800	2.2	648	1.8	TENNESSEE	1,200	1.4	2,040	1.7	2,337	2.2
200	0.7	480	1.3	1,812	4.9	TEXAS	2,300	2.7	5,600	4.7	4,341	4.1
0	–	40	0.1	90	0.2	UTAH	0	–	200	0.2	113	0.1
0	–	0	–	18	0.1	VERMONT	0	–	0	–	78	0.1
200	0.7	520	1.5	255	0.7	VIRGINIA	400	0.5	1,080	0.9	1,224	1.1
400	1.4	320	0.9	213	0.6	WASHINGTON	700	0.8	920	0.8	1,131	1.1
0	–	160	0.4	57	0.2	WEST VIRGINIA	0	–	440	0.4	178	0.2
1,400	4.9	3,040	8.5	3,066	8.3	WISCONSIN	6,100	7.0	8,160	6.8	8,568	8.0
100	0.3	0	–	21	0.1	WYOMING	100	0.1	160	0.1	7	–
28,800	99.9*	35,720	99.9*	36,897	100.5*	TOTAL U.S.	86,600	99.8*	120,160	100.2*	107,136	100.5*

*rounding error

INDIANA

TO INDIANA FROM							FROM INDIANA TO					
1970		1980		1990			1970		1980		1990	
#	%	#	%	#	%		#	%	#	%	#	%
0	–	240	1.0	290	0.9	ALABAMA	200	0.7	400	1.0	463	1.2
0	–	0	–	45	0.1	ALASKA	0	–	0	–	0	–
500	2.7	400	1.7	486	1.6	ARIZONA	900	3.1	2,480	6.3	1,903	5.0
0	–	360	1.6	446	1.4	ARKANSAS	500	1.7	880	2.2	415	1.1
1,000	5.4	1,040	4.5	2,433	7.8	CALIFORNIA	1,500	5.1	2,240	5.7	1,670	4.4
300	1.6	160	0.7	283	0.9	COLORADO	0	–	440	1.1	690	1.8
100	0.5	160	0.7	32	0.1	CONNECTICUT	100	0.3	160	0.4	100	0.3
0	–	0	–	0	–	DELAWARE	0	–	0	–	88	0.2
0	–	80	0.3	38	0.1	D.C.	0	–	0	–	45	0.1
1,700	9.1	1,680	7.3	4,773	15.2	FLORIDA	9,700	33.2	14,320	36.3	13,327	34.7
0	–	320	1.4	392	1.3	GEORGIA	0	–	480	1.2	582	1.5
200	1.1	40	0.2	54	0.2	HAWAII	0	–	0	–	67	0.2
0	–	0	–	10	–	IDAHO	0	–	40	0.1	60	0.2
4,200	22.6	5,600	24.2	5,574	17.8	ILLINOIS	3,400	11.6	3,520	8.9	2,172	5.7
100	0.5	160	0.7	254	0.8	IOWA	100	0.3	200	0.5	377	1.0
0	–	360	1.6	318	1.0	KANSAS	400	1.4	80	0.2	107	0.3
2,400	12.9	2,000	8.7	3,272	10.4	KENTUCKY	1,700	5.8	2,400	6.1	2,538	6.6
100	0.5	40	0.2	96	0.3	LOUISIANA	0	–	160	0.4	180	0.5
0	–	0	–	74	0.2	MAINE	0	–	40	0.1	9	–
500	2.7	280	1.2	202	0.6	MARYLAND	300	1.0	200	0.5	99	0.3
300	1.6	80	0.3	26	0.1	MASSACHUSETTS	100	0.3	160	0.4	160	0.4
1,400	7.5	2,640	11.4	2,066	6.6	MICHIGAN	1,800	6.2	1,960	5.0	2,303	6.0
200	0.9	40	0.2	148	0.5	MINNESOTA	300	1.0	480	1.2	125	0.3
100	0.5	200	0.9	221	0.7	MISSISSIPPI	0	–	280	0.7	324	0.8
500	2.7	640	2.8	662	2.1	MISSOURI	600	2.1	760	1.9	811	2.1
0	–	0	–	55	0.2	MONTANA	0	–	40	0.1	42	0.1
200	1.1	160	0.7	48	0.2	NEBRASKA	0	–	40	0.1	126	0.3
0	–	0	–	94	0.3	NEVADA	0	–	80	0.2	261	0.7
100	0.5	0	–	0	–	NEW HAMPSHIRE	0	–	0	–	0	–
400	2.2	160	0.7	137	0.4	NEW JERSEY	400	1.4	360	0.9	94	0.2
0	–	0	–	156	0.5	NEW MEXICO	200	0.7	320	0.8	276	0.7
500	2.7	280	1.2	961	3.1	NEW YORK	500	1.7	320	0.8	204	0.5
300	1.6	120	0.5	272	0.9	NORTH CAROLINA	100	0.3	320	0.8	711	1.9
0	–	40	0.2	16	0.1	NORTH DAKOTA	0	–	0	–	65	0.2
1,900	10.2	2,800	12.1	3,283	10.5	OHIO	1,700	5.8	1,520	3.9	2,341	6.1
0	–	80	0.3	201	0.6	OKLAHOMA	100	0.3	200	0.5	244	0.6
0	–	40	0.2	129	0.4	OREGON	200	0.7	360	0.9	187	0.5
200	1.1	560	2.4	488	1.6	PENNSYLVANIA	600	2.1	160	0.4	224	0.6
0	–	0	–	26	0.1	RHODE ISLAND	0	–	0	–	19	0.1
0	–	0	–	194	0.6	SOUTH CAROLINA	0	–	200	0.5	369	1.0
0	–	0	–	7	–	SOUTH DAKOTA	0	–	0	–	0	–
200	1.1	520	2.2	1,060	3.4	TENNESSEE	600	2.1	1,160	2.9	1,611	4.2
500	2.7	760	3.3	1,095	3.5	TEXAS	1,100	3.8	1,600	4.1	1,463	3.8
100	0.5	0	–	23	0.1	UTAH	0	–	40	0.1	75	0.2
0	–	0	–	0	–	VERMONT	0	–	0	–	16	–
0	–	200	0.9	310	1.0	VIRGINIA	400	1.4	280	0.7	684	1.8
100	0.5	200	0.9	131	0.4	WASHINGTON	300	1.0	160	0.4	381	1.0
200	1.1	120	0.5	118	0.4	WEST VIRGINIA	100	0.3	160	0.4	52	0.1
300	1.6	560	2.4	339	1.1	WISCONSIN	300	1.6	440	1.1	348	0.9
0	–	0	–	67	0.2	WYOMING	0	–	0	–	18	0.1
18,600	**99.7***	**23,120**	**100.1***	**31,405**	**100.3***	**TOTAL U.S.**	**29,200**	**99.9***	**39,440**	**99.8***	**38,426**	**100.3***

*rounding error

IOWA

	TO IOWA FROM							FROM IOWA TO				
1970		**1980**		**1990**			**1970**		**1980**		**1990**	
#	%	#	%	#	%		#	%	#	%	#	%
200	1.9	40	0.4	106	0.9	ALABAMA	200	1.3	200	1.0	54	0.3
0	–	0	–	71	0.6	ALASKA	0	–	120	0.6	0	–
100	1.0	440	3.9	558	4.8	ARIZONA	1,500	9.5	2,800	13.5	2,257	10.8
100	1.0	120	1.1	457	3.9	ARKANSAS	100	0.6	1,680	8.1	1,106	5.3
800	7.7	1,480	13.0	1,295	11.1	CALIFORNIA	2,100	13.3	2,040	9.8	1,443	6.9
200	1.9	280	2.5	404	3.5	COLORADO	500	3.2	1,080	5.2	783	3.7
0	–	0	–	142	1.2	CONNECTICUT	0	–	120	0.6	0	–
0	–	0	–	0	–	DELAWARE	0	–	0	–	0	–
0	–	0	–	0	–	D.C.	0	–	0	–	0	–
300	2.9	560	4.9	398	3.4	FLORIDA	1,000	6.3	1,800	8.7	2,435	11.6
0	–	40	0.4	8	0.1	GEORGIA	0	–	120	0.6	64	0.3
0	–	80	0.7	0	–	HAWAII	0	–	120	0.6	42	0.2
0	–	0	–	13	0.1	IDAHO	0	–	0	–	80	0.4
2,800	26.9	1,800	15.9	1,775	15.2	ILLINOIS	1,400	8.9	1,200	5.8	1,488	7.1
100	1.0	200	1.8	377	3.2	INDIANA	100	0.6	160	0.8	254	1.2
200	1.9	280	2.5	243	2.1	KANSAS	200	1.3	200	1.0	343	1.6
0	–	80	0.7	37	0.3	KENTUCKY	0	–	80	0.4	118	0.6
0	–	40	0.4	84	0.7	LOUISIANA	200	1.3	0	–	66	0.3
0	–	40	0.4	50	0.4	MAINE	0	–	0	–	0	–
0	–	40	0.4	118	1.0	MARYLAND	0	–	40	0.2	110	0.5
0	–	80	0.7	0	–	MASSACHUSETTS	0	–	0	–	83	0.4
200	1.9	200	1.8	264	2.3	MICHIGAN	200	1.3	240	1.2	273	1.3
900	8.7	1,240	11.0	1,101	9.4	MINNESOTA	1,800	11.4	1,200	5.8	1,368	6.5
0	–	40	0.4	38	0.3	MISSISSIPPI	0	–	80	0.4	96	0.5
600	5.8	800	7.1	777	6.7	MISSOURI	1,400	8.9	1,320	6.4	1,096	9.0
0	–	40	0.4	76	0.7	MONTANA	0	–	0	–	87	0.4
1000	9.6	840	7.4	682	5.8	NEBRASKA	1,100	7.0	1,200	5.8	1,365	6.5
0	–	40	0.4	118	1.0	NEVADA	0	–	160	0.8	195	0.9
0	–	0	–	0	–	NEW HAMPSHIRE	0	–	0	–	0	–
0	–	80	0.7	97	0.8	NEW JERSEY	0	–	0	–	135	0.6
0	–	40	0.4	33	0.3	NEW MEXICO	200	1.3	360	1.7	69	0.3
300	2.9	120	1.1	228	2.0	NEW YORK	0	–	80	0.4	175	0.8
100	1.0	80	0.7	0	–	NORTH CAROLINA	400	2.5	80	0.4	114	0.5
0	–	80	0.7	38	0.3	NORTH DAKOTA	300	1.9	40	0.2	20	0.1
200	1.9	200	1.8	146	1.3	OHIO	1,000	6.3	40	0.2	65	0.3
400	3.8	0	–	142	1.2	OKLAHOMA	0	–	120	0.6	278	1.3
100	1.0	160	1.4	192	1.7	OREGON	300	1.9	120	0.6	338	1.6
0	–	40	0.4	0	–	PENNSYLVANIA	300	1.9	80	0.4	0	–
0	–	0	–	0	–	RHODE ISLAND	0	–	0	–	0	–
0	–	0	–	30	0.3	SOUTH CAROLINA	0	–	40	0.2	159	0.8
300	2.9	560	4.9	236	2.0	SOUTH DAKOTA	300	1.9	520	2.5	490	2.3
0	–	0	–	150	1.3	TENNESSEE	0	–	200	1.0	369	1.8
700	6.7	320	2.8	391	3.4	TEXAS	400	2.5	1,520	7.3	1,681	8.0
100	1.0	0	–	0	–	UTAH	0	–	40	0.2	68	0.3
0	–	80	0.7	8	0.1	VERMONT	0	–	0	–	68	0.3
0	–	200	1.8	122	1.1	VIRGINIA	0	–	80	0.4	81	0.4
300	2.9	40	0.4	159	1.4	WASHINGTON	800	5.1	560	2.7	282	1.4
0	–	0	–	8	0.1	WEST VIRGINIA	0	–	0	–	0	–
400	3.8	480	4.2	412	3.5	WISCONSIN	0	–	880	4.2	503	2.4
0	–	40	0.4	85	0.7	WYOMING	0	–	40	0.2	61	0.3
10,400	**100.1***	**11,320**	**100.6***	**11,669**	**100.2***	**TOTAL U.S.**	**15,800**	**100.2***	**20,760**	**100.5***	**20,962**	**99.8***

*rounding error

KANSAS

TO KANSAS FROM							FROM KANSAS TO					
1970		1980		1990			1970		1980		1990	
#	%	#	%	#	%		#	%	#	%	#	%
100	0.9	160	1.1	0	–	ALABAMA	100	0.8	120	0.6	90	0.4
0	–	40	0.2	57	0.4	ALASKA	0	–	0	–	15	0.1
200	1.7	560	3.8	821	5.0	ARIZONA	300	2.5	1,160	6.2	1,599	6.8
300	2.6	600	4.0	409	2.5	ARKANSAS	800	6.6	1,120	6.0	1,280	5.4
1,200	10.3	1,960	13.2	1,566	9.5	CALIFORNIA	1,700	13.9	1,640	8.8	1,533	6.5
500	4.3	1,000	6.7	865	5.2	COLORADO	400	3.3	1,000	5.4	987	4.2
200	1.7	120	0.8	18	0.1	CONNECTICUT	0	–	0	–	68	0.3
0	–	0	–	0	–	DELAWARE	100	0.8	0	–	0	–
100	0.9	40	0.2	28	0.2	D.C.	0	–	80	0.4	0	–
0	–	280	1.9	413	2.5	FLORIDA	400	3.3	600	3.2	871	3.7
0	–	80	0.5	119	0.7	GEORGIA	100	0.8	80	0.4	122	0.5
0	–	0	–	0	–	HAWAII	0	–	0	–	16	0.1
0	–	40	0.2	61	0.4	IDAHO	200	1.6	80	0.4	36	0.2
600	5.1	840	5.6	679	4.1	ILLINOIS	600	4.9	320	1.7	363	1.5
400	3.4	80	0.5	107	0.7	INDIANA	0	–	360	1.9	318	1.3
200	1.7	200	1.3	343	2.1	IOWA	200	1.6	280	1.5	243	1.0
0	–	120	0.8	132	0.8	KENTUCKY	0	–	120	0.6	54	0.2
200	1.7	160	1.1	86	0.5	LOUISIANA	100	0.8	240	1.3	171	0.7
0	–	0	–	33	0.2	MAINE	0	–	0	–	0	–
100	0.9	120	0.8	43	0.3	MARYLAND	200	1.6	160	0.9	179	0.8
0	–	40	0.2	0	–	MASSACHUSETTS	0	–	0	–	91	0.4
0	–	80	0.5	289	1.8	MICHIGAN	0	–	80	0.4	111	0.5
100	0.9	0	–	88	0.5	MINNESOTA	0	–	80	0.4	3,154	13.3
0	–	120	0.8	72	0.4	MISSISSIPPI	0	–	40	0.2	54	0.2
3,000	25.6	3,480	23.4	3,711	22.5	MISSOURI	2,700	22.1	3,840	20.6	4,490	19.0
0	–	0	–	125	0.8	MONTANA	0	–	160	0.9	42	0.2
400	3.4	800	5.4	1,058	6.4	NEBRASKA	800	6.6	760	4.1	952	4.0
0	–	0	–	235	1.4	NEVADA	100	0.8	160	0.9	287	1.2
0	–	0	–	0	–	NEW HAMPSHIRE	0	–	0	–	0	–
0	–	40	0.2	303	1.8	NEW JERSEY	0	–	0	–	96	0.4
400	3.4	560	3.8	183	1.1	NEW MEXICO	100	0.8	120	0.6	330	1.4
0	–	240	1.6	486	3.0	NEW YORK	0	–	0	–	78	0.3
0	–	40	0.2	0	–	NORTH CAROLINA	0	–	120	0.6	264	1.1
0	–	0	–	47	0.3	NORTH DAKOTA	100	0.8	0	–	0	–
200	1.7	80	0.5	172	1.0	OHIO	100	0.8	120	0.6	258	1.1
1,700	14.5	1,120	7.5	1,280	7.8	OKLAHOMA	1,300	10.7	2,320	12.4	1,949	8.2
200	1.7	40	0.2	43	0.3	OREGON	0	–	280	1.5	262	1.1
0	–	160	1.1	149	0.9	PENNSYLVANIA	200	1.6	80	0.4	80	0.3
0	–	0	–	0	–	RHODE ISLAND	0	–	0	–	0	–
0	–	0	–	87	0.5	SOUTH CAROLINA	0	–	0	–	15	0.1
0	–	40	0.2	64	0.4	SOUTH DAKOTA	0	–	40	0.2	56	0.2
0	–	40	0.2	151	0.9	TENNESSEE	200	1.6	280	1.5	135	0.6
900	7.7	840	5.6	1,314	8.0	TEXAS	800	6.6	2,400	12.9	2,028	8.6
0	–	120	0.8	82	0.5	UTAH	200	1.6	40	0.2	117	0.5
0	–	0	–	0	–	VERMONT	0	–	0	–	0	–
100	0.9	240	1.6	130	0.8	VIRGINIA	0	–	120	0.6	222	0.9
200	1.7	280	1.9	434	2.6	WASHINGTON	400	3.3	160	0.9	465	2.0
0	–	0	–	50	0.3	WEST VIRGINIA	0	–	40	0.2	0	–
400	3.4	120	0.8	99	0.6	WISCONSIN	0	–	0	–	134	0.6
0	–	0	–	60	0.7	WYOMING	0	–	40	0.2	29	0.1
11,700	100.1*	14,880	99.2*	16,492	100.5*	TOTAL U.S.	12,200	99.8*	18,640	99.6*	23,644	100.0

*rounding error

KENTUCKY

TO KENTUCKY FROM							FROM KENTUCKY TO					
1970		1980		1990			1970		1980		1990	
#	%	#	%	#	%		#	%	#	%	#	%
200	1.8	120	0.7	358	1.6	ALABAMA	0	–	160	0.9	304	1.5
0	–	40	0.2	32	0.2	ALASKA	0	–	40	0.2	0	–
0	–	80	0.4	307	1.4	ARIZONA	100	0.8	480	2.7	105	0.5
0	–	160	0.9	259	1.2	ARKANSAS	100	0.8	160	0.9	53	0.3
200	1.8	520	2.9	998	4.6	CALIFORNIA	100	0.8	840	4.7	512	2.5
300	2.7	80	0.4	161	0.7	COLORADO	0	–	80	0.5	57	0.3
0	–	40	0.2	36	0.2	CONNECTICUT	0	–	40	0.2	17	0.1
0	–	40	0.2	25	0.1	DELAWARE	0	–	0	–	0	–
0	–	40	0.2	49	0.2	D.C.	0	–	0	–	43	0.2
1,500	13.4	1,640	9.2	2,253	10.4	FLORIDA	3,000	22.9	3,840	21.6	4,704	23.0
0	–	0	–	492	2.3	GEORGIA	200	1.5	200	1.1	488	2.4
0	–	0	–	0	–	HAWAII	0	–	0	–	36	0.2
0	–	0	–	0	–	IDAHO	0	–	0	–	24	0.1
1,900	17.0	1,920	10.7	1,889	8.7	ILLINOIS	900	6.9	800	4.5	525	2.6
1,700	15.2	2,400	13.4	2,538	11.7	INDIANA	2,400	18.3	2,000	11.3	3,272	16.0
0	–	80	0.4	118	0.5	IOWA	0	–	80	0.5	37	0.2
0	–	120	0.7	54	0.3	KANSAS	0	–	120	0.7	132	0.7
0	–	200	1.1	333	1.5	LOUISIANA	0	–	0	–	42	0.2
0	–	0	–	22	0.1	MAINE	0	–	0	–	39	0.2
100	0.9	160	0.9	250	1.2	MARYLAND	0	–	160	0.9	128	0.6
0	–	40	0.2	102	0.5	MASSACHUSETTS	0	–	120	0.7	36	0.2
600	5.4	1,480	8.3	1,412	6.5	MICHIGAN	300	2.3	960	5.4	594	2.9
0	–	120	0.7	134	0.6	MINNESOTA	100	0.8	80	0.5	55	0.3
0	–	120	0.7	303	1.4	MISSISSIPPI	300	2.3	120	0.7	240	1.2
200	1.8	320	1.8	352	1.6	MISSOURI	700	5.3	240	1.4	320	1.6
0	–	0	–	0	–	MONTANA	0	–	0	–	35	0.2
0	–	0	–	21	0.1	NEBRASKA	100	0.8	0	–	54	0.3
0	–	80	0.4	130	0.6	NEVADA	100	0.8	80	0.5	70	0.3
0	–	0	–	65	0.3	NEW HAMPSHIRE	0	–	0	–	0	–
200	1.8	240	1.3	481	2.2	NEW JERSEY	100	0.8	120	0.7	144	0.7
0	–	160	0.9	134	0.6	NEW MEXICO	0	–	0	–	24	0.1
500	4.5	440	2.5	434	2.0	NEW YORK	100	0.8	120	0.7	194	1.0
0	–	120	0.7	360	1.7	NORTH CAROLINA	100	0.8	240	1.4	897	4.4
0	–	40	0.2	0	–	NORTH DAKOTA	0	–	0	–	10	0.1
2,100	18.8	4,120	23.0	3,810	17.5	OHIO	1,900	14.5	2,840	16.0	2,944	14.4
300	2.7	80	0.4	190	0.9	OKLAHOMA	0	–	160	0.9	31	0.2
0	–	0	–	101	0.5	OREGON	0	–	40	0.2	95	0.5
200	1.8	440	2.5	381	1.8	PENNSYLVANIA	100	0.8	120	0.7	233	1.1
0	–	80	0.4	25	0.1	RHODE ISLAND	0	–	0	–	0	–
0	–	0	–	144	0.7	SOUTH CAROLINA	0	–	80	0.5	309	1.5
0	–	0	–	0	–	SOUTH DAKOTA	0	–	0	–	0	–
300	2.7	1,040	5.8	1,386	6.4	TENNESSEE	1,500	11.5	1,560	8.6	2,082	10.2
100	0.9	280	1.6	497	2.3	TEXAS	300	2.3	600	3.4	624	3.1
0	–	40	0.2	26	0.1	UTAH	0	–	0	–	48	0.2
0	–	0	–	7	–	VERMONT	0	–	0	–	0	–
300	2.7	480	2.7	430	2.0	VIRGINIA	0	–	640	3.6	336	1.6
0	–	0	–	8	–	WASHINGTON	0	–	200	1.1	120	0.6
400	3.6	520	2.9	483	2.2	WEST VIRGINIA	500	3.8	360	2.0	340	1.7
100	0.9	0	–	166	0.8	WISCONSIN	0	–	80	0.5	80	0.4
0	–	0	–	14	0.1	WYOMING	100	0.8	0	–	11	0.1
11,200	100.4*	17,880	99.7*	21,770	100.4*	TOTAL U.S.	13,100	100.4*	17,760	100.2*	20,444	100.5*

*rounding error

LOUISIANA

TO LOUISIANA FROM							FROM LOUISIANA TO					
1970		1980		1990			1970		1980		1990	
#	%	#	%	#	%		#	%	#	%	#	%
300	3.1	680	5.6	642	4.6	ALABAMA	300	3.6	640	4.5	926	4.3
0	–	40	0.3	0	–	ALASKA	0	–	0	–	38	0.2
200	2.1	360	3.0	90	0.6	ARIZONA	100	1.2	200	1.4	289	1.4
400	4.2	920	7.6	540	3.9	ARKANSAS	800	9.6	600	4.2	1,225	5.7
900	9.4	1,320	10.9	1,482	10.6	CALIFORNIA	800	9.6	1,120	7.9	1,438	6.7
0	–	0	–	66	0.5	COLORADO	0	–	160	1.1	354	1.7
0	–	40	0.3	57	0.4	CONNECTICUT	100	1.2	120	0.8	28	0.1
0	–	0	–	0	–	DELAWARE	0	–	0	–	102	0.5
100	1.0	0	–	39	0.3	D.C.	0	–	0	–	21	0.1
200	2.1	1,120	9.2	834	6.0	FLORIDA	600	7.2	800	5.6	2,089	9.7
100	1.0	200	1.7	390	2.8	GEORGIA	300	3.6	200	1.4	553	2.6
0	–	40	0.3	54	0.4	HAWAII	100	1.2	80	0.6	34	0.2
0	–	0	–	9	0.1	IDAHO	0	–	0	–	8	–
600	6.3	320	2.6	630	4.5	ILLINOIS	200	2.4	520	3.7	255	1.2
0	–	160	1.3	180	1.3	INDIANA	100	1.2	40	0.3	96	0.5
200	2.1	0	–	66	0.5	IOWA	0	–	40	0.3	84	0.4
100	1.0	240	2.0	171	1.2	KANSAS	200	2.4	160	1.1	86	0.4
0	–	0	–	42	0.3	KENTUCKY	0	–	200	1.4	333	1.6
0	–	0	–	18	0.1	MAINE	0	–	0	–	0	–
200	2.1	160	1.3	120	0.9	MARYLAND	0	–	0	–	319	1.5
100	1.0	160	1.3	24	0.2	MASSACHUSETTS	100	1.2	0	–	62	0.3
100	1.0	400	3.3	204	1.5	MICHIGAN	600	7.2	160	1.1	230	1.1
100	1.0	0	–	51	0.4	MINNESOTA	0	–	40	0.3	9	–
1,500	15.6	1,000	8.3	1,602	11.4	MISSISSIPPI	400	4.8	2,360	16.6	3,891	18.2
100	1.0	160	1.3	228	1.6	MISSOURI	100	1.2	80	0.6	333	1.6
0	–	0	–	66	0.5	MONTANA	0	–	40	0.3	0	–
0	–	120	1.0	18	0.1	NEBRASKA	0	–	0	–	37	0.2
100	1.0	40	0.3	45	0.3	NEVADA	0	–	240	1.7	182	0.9
0	–	0	–	39	0.3	NEW HAMPSHIRE	100	1.2	0	–	28	0.1
0	–	0	–	201	1.4	NEW JERSEY	100	1.2	0	–	138	0.6
0	–	120	1.0	126	0.9	NEW MEXICO	0	–	160	1.1	96	0.5
100	1.0	280	2.3	321	2.3	NEW YORK	0	–	120	0.8	148	0.7
0	–	120	1.0	336	2.4	NORTH CAROLINA	0	–	240	1.7	327	1.5
0	–	0	–	0	–	NORTH DAKOTA	0	–	0	–	10	0.1
100	1.0	0	–	384	2.7	OHIO	0	–	120	0.8	421	2.0
100	1.0	120	1.0	213	1.5	OKLAHOMA	200	2.4	160	1.1	568	2.7
100	1.0	40	0.3	0	–	OREGON	100	1.2	40	0.3	44	0.2
100	1.0	440	3.6	201	1.4	PENNSYLVANIA	200	2.4	0	–	141	0.7
0	–	0	–	15	0.1	RHODE ISLAND	0	–	0	–	57	0.3
100	1.0	360	3.0	57	0.4	SOUTH CAROLINA	0	–	80	0.6	201	0.9
0	–	0	–	0	–	SOUTH DAKOTA	0	–	0	–	15	0.1
500	5.2	440	3.6	273	2.0	TENNESSEE	400	4.8	240	1.7	507	2.4
2,700	28.1	2,480	20.5	3,525	25.2	TEXAS	2,200	26.5	4,800	33.8	4,874	22.7
0	–	40	0.3	0	–	UTAH	0	–	0	–	0	–
0	–	0	–	60	0.4	VERMONT	0	–	0	–	0	–
400	4.2	40	0.3	156	1.1	VIRGINIA	0	–	160	1.1	354	1.7
100	1.0	40	0.3	168	1.2	WASHINGTON	200	2.4	80	0.6	288	1.3
0	–	40	0.3	90	0.6	WEST VIRGINIA	0	–	0	–	51	0.3
0	–	80	0.7	150	1.1	WISCONSIN	0	–	80	0.6	82	0.4
0	–	0	–	21	0.2	WYOMING	0	–	120	0.8	65	0.3
9,600	99.5*	12,120	99.8*	14,004	100.2*	TOTAL U.S.	8,300	99.7*	14,200	99.9*	21,437	100.6*

*rounding error

MAINE

TO MAINE FROM							FROM MAINE TO					
1970		1980		1990			1970		1980		1990	
#	%	#	%	#	%		#	%	#	%	#	%
200	4.2	0	–	70	0.6	ALABAMA	0	–	80	1.1	51	0.5
0	–	0	–	9	0.1	ALASKA	0	–	0	–	7	0.1
100	2.1	0	–	18	0.2	ARIZONA	0	–	160	2.2	247	2.3
0	–	0	–	0	–	ARKANSAS	0	–	0	–	15	0.1
200	4.2	320	3.6	537	4.5	CALIFORNIA	400	7.0	360	5.1	368	3.5
0	–	120	1.4	49	0.4	COLORADO	0	–	40	0.6	27	0.3
700	14.6	960	10.8	1,315	11.0	CONNECTICUT	900	15.8	400	5.6	379	3.6
0	–	80	0.9	31	0.3	DELAWARE	0	–	0	–	0	–
0	–	40	0.5	49	0.4	D.C.	0	–	40	0.6	28	0.3
300	6.3	440	5.0	821	6.9	FLORIDA	2,200	38.6	2,720	38.2	4,726	44.9
0	–	0	–	31	0.3	GEORGIA	0	–	80	1.1	84	0.8
0	–	0	–	36	0.3	HAWAII	0	–	0	–	0	–
0	–	0	–	0	–	IDAHO	0	–	0	–	20	0.2
0	–	40	0.5	231	1.9	ILLINOIS	0	–	40	0.6	39	0.4
0	–	40	0.5	9	0.1	INDIANA	0	–	0	–	74	0.7
0	–	0	–	0	–	IOWA	0	–	40	0.6	50	0.5
0	–	0	–	0	–	KANSAS	0	–	0	–	33	0.3
0	–	0		39	0.3	KENTUCKY	0	–	0	–	22	0.2
0	–	0	–	0	–	LOUISIANA	0	–	0	–	18	0.2
0	–	200	2.3	111	0.9	MARYLAND	0	–	40	0.6	42	0.4
1,400	29.2	3,480	39.2	3,557	30.0	MASSACHUSETTS	600	10.5	960	13.5	1,759	16.7
0	–	80	0.9	97	0.8	MICHIGAN	0	–	0	–	61	0.6
0	–	0	–	26	0.2	MINNESOTA	0	–	0	–	107	1.0
0	–	0	–	0	–	MISSISSIPPI	200	3.5	0	–	24	0.2
0	–	0	–	0	–	MISSOURI	0	–	40	0.6	54	0.5
0	–	0	–	0	–	MONTANA	0	–	0	–	0	–
0	–	0	–	9	0.1	NEBRASKA	0	–	0	–	29	0.3
0	–	0	–	30	0.3	NEVADA	0	–	40	0.6	0	–
1,000	20.8	800	9.0	1,269	10.6	NEW HAMPSHIRE	300	5.3	760	10.7	714	6.8
200	4.2	560	6.3	734	6.2	NEW JERSEY	300	5.3	200	2.8	77	0.7
0	–	0	–	26	0.2	NEW MEXICO	100	1.8	40	0.6	6	0.1
300	6.3	680	7.7	1,148	9.6	NEW YORK	200	3.5	120	1.7	274	2.6
0	–	40	0.5	79	0.7	NORTH CAROLINA	0	–	360	5.1	174	1.7
0	–	0	–	5	–	NORTH DAKOTA	0	–	0	–	0	–
100	2.1	200	2.3	273	2.3	OHIO	0	–	0	–	155	1.5
0	–	40	0.5	0	–	OKLAHOMA	0	–	0	–	24	0.2
0	–	0	–	8	0.1	OREGON	0	–	80	1.1	7	0.1
100	2.1	280	3.2	298	2.5	PENNSYLVANIA	100	1.8	40	0.6	227	2.2
200	4.2	80	0.9	234	2.0	RHODE ISLAND	0	–	80	1.1	138	1.3
0	–	0	–	0	–	SOUTH CAROLINA	0	–	80	1.1	42	0.4
0	–	0	–	0	–	SOUTH DAKOTA	0	–	0	–	0	–
0	–	0	–	57	0.5	TENNESSEE	0	–	0	–	66	0.6
0	–	120	1.4	215	1.8	TEXAS	100	1.8	80	1.1	195	1.9
0	–	0	–	48	0.4	UTAH	0	–	0	–	0	–
0	–	80	0.9	76	0.6	VERMONT	100	1.8	40	0.6	63	0.6
0	–	200	2.3	309	2.6	VIRGINIA	200	3.5	0	–	84	0.8
0	–	0	–	75	0.6	WASHINGTON	0	–	120	1.7	0	–
0	–	0	–	0	–	WEST VIRGINIA	0	–	0	–	0	–
0	–	0	–	0	–	WISCONSIN	0	–	80	1.1	24	0.2
0	–	0	–	0	–	WYOMING	0	–	0	–	0	–
4,800	100.3*	8,880	100.6*	11,929	100.3*	TOTAL U.S.	5,700	100.2*	7,120	100.3*	10,534	100.3*

*rounding error

MARYLAND

TO MARYLAND FROM							FROM MARYLAND TO					
1970		1980		1990			1970		1980		1990	
#	%	#	%	#	%		#	%	#	%	#	%
100	0.5	200	0.8	119	0.4	ALABAMA	0	–	440	1.2	160	0.4
0	–	0	–	0	–	ALASKA	0	–	0	–	0	–
0	–	80	0.3	250	0.8	ARIZONA	100	0.6	760	2.1	574	1.4
0	–	0	–	54	0.2	ARKANSAS	100	0.6	200	0.6	120	0.3
300	1.4	400	1.6	1,355	4.2	CALIFORNIA	900	5.6	1,640	4.6	1,796	4.4
0	–	120	0.5	188	0.6	COLORADO	100	0.6	320	0.9	219	0.5
200	0.9	440	1.7	725	2.2	CONNECTICUT	300	1.9	240	0.7	217	0.5
500	2.3	800	3.2	964	3.0	DELAWARE	500	3.1	1,120	3.1	2,074	5.0
7,300	34.0	4,360	17.7	4,160	12.8	D.C.	900	5.6	880	2.5	1,405	3.4
800	3.7	1,880	7.6	3,470	10.7	FLORIDA	4,400	27.3	11,480	32.2	11,432	27.7
100	0.5	80	0.3	238	0.7	GEORGIA	100	0.6	600	1.7	622	1.5
0	–	80	0.3	76	0.2	HAWAII	0	–	80	0.2	14	–
0	–	80	0.3	14	–	IDAHO	0	–	80	0.2	56	0.1
800	3.7	440	1.8	393	1.2	ILLINOIS	200	1.2	360	1.0	213	0.5
300	1.4	200	0.8	99	0.3	INDIANA	500	3.1	280	0.8	202	0.5
0	–	40	0.2	110	0.3	IOWA	0	–	40	0.1	118	0.3
200	0.9	160	0.7	179	0.6	KANSAS	100	0.6	120	0.3	43	0.1
0	–	160	0.7	128	0.4	KENTUCKY	100	0.6	160	0.4	250	0.6
0	–	0	–	319	1.0	LOUISIANA	200	1.2	160	0.4	120	0.3
0	–	40	0.2	42	0.1	MAINE	0	–	200	0.6	111	0.3
400	1.9	560	2.3	505	1.6	MASSACHUSETTS	0	–	440	1.2	228	0.6
300	1.4	200	0.8	240	0.7	MICHIGAN	100	0.6	360	1.0	253	0.6
100	0.5	40	0.2	158	0.5	MINNESOTA	0	–	80	0.2	183	0.4
0	–	0	–	147	0.5	MISSISSIPPI	100	0.6	40	0.1	96	0.2
100	0.5	120	0.5	158	0.5	MISSOURI	100	0.7	200	0.6	213	0.5
100	0.5	0	–	0	–	MONTANA	0	–	200	0.6	95	0.2
0	–	0	–	28	0.1	NEBRASKA	0	–	40	0.1	54	0.1
0	–	0	–	53	0.2	NEVADA	0	–	80	0.2	164	0.4
0	–	160	0.7	72	0.2	NEW HAMPSHIRE	0	–	80	0.2	157	0.4
1,300	6.0	1,720	7.0	2,494	7.7	NEW JERSEY	1,100	6.8	480	1.3	1,198	2.9
0	–	0	–	16	0.1	NEW MEXICO	100	0.6	160	0.4	246	0.6
2,400	11.2	3,280	13.3	4,185	12.9	NEW YORK	500	3.1	640	1.8	858	2.1
400	1.9	560	2.3	739	2.3	NORTH CAROLINA	700	4.3	2,040	5.7	2,844	6.9
0	–	0	–	3	–	NORTH DAKOTA	0	–	0	–	25	0.1
200	0.9	600	2.4	657	2.0	OHIO	0	–	800	2.2	758	1.8
0	–	40	0.2	136	0.4	OKLAHOMA	0	–	80	0.2	95	0.2
0	–	40	0.2	0	–	OREGON	100	0.6	40	0.1	121	0.3
1,600	7.4	3,160	12.8	3,621	11.2	PENNSYLVANIA	1,800	11.2	2,520	7.1	3,945	9.5
0	–	80	0.3	96	0.3	RHODE ISLAND	0	–	80	0.2	36	0.1
100	0.5	40	0.2	357	1.1	SOUTH CAROLINA	200	1.2	680	1.9	1,161	2.8
0	–	0	–	0	–	SOUTH DAKOTA	0	–	0	–	67	0.2
100	0.5	280	1.1	128	0.4	TENNESSEE	200	1.2	880	2.5	468	1.1
500	2.3	240	1.0	621	1.9	TEXAS	0	–	680	1.9	628	1.5
0	–	40	0.2	101	0.3	UTAH	0	–	80	0.2	85	0.2
500	2.3	40	0.2	0	–	VERMONT	0	–	0	–	42	0.1
2,200	10.2	3,160	12.8	3,802	11.7	VIRGINIA	2,000	12.4	4,080	11.4	5,109	12.4
0	–	160	0.7	268	0.8	WASHINGTON	0	–	280	0.8	267	0.7
400	1.9	520	2.1	826	2.6	WEST VIRGINIA	600	3.7	1,360	3.8	1,950	4.7
200	0.9	0	–	111	0.3	WISCONSIN	0	–	80	0.2	172	0.4
0	–	0	–	23	0.1	WYOMING	0	–	0	–	69	0.2
21,500	100.1*	24,600	100.0	32,428	100.1*	TOTAL U.S.	16,100	99.6*	35,640	99.5*	41,333	100.0

*rounding error

MASSACHUSETTS

	TO MASSACHUSETTS FROM							FROM MASSACHUSETTS TO					
	1970		1980		1990			1970		1980		1990	
	#	%	#	%	#	%		#	%	#	%	#	%
	100	0.7	0	–	51	0.2	ALABAMA	0	–	160	0.3	42	0.1
	0	–	0	–	33	0.1	ALASKA	0	–	0	–	0	–
	200	1.4	400	1.8	211	0.9	ARIZONA	500	1.7	1,600	3.4	868	1.5
	0	–	80	0.4	62	0.3	ARKANSAS	0	–	40	0.1	55	0.1
	500	3.4	1,120	5.1	1,031	4.3	CALIFORNIA	2,100	7.3	2,800	6.0	2,490	4.4
	100	0.7	160	0.7	96	0.4	COLORADO	0	–	160	0.3	120	0.2
	1,600	10.8	2,480	11.3	2,447	10.3	CONNECTICUT	2,000	6.9	1,960	4.2	2,296	4.1
	0	–	0	–	28	0.1	DELAWARE	0	–	80	0.2	234	0.4
	100	0.7	320	1.5	65	0.3	D.C.	0	–	40	0.1	52	0.1
	2,100	14.2	2,640	12.0	3,232	13.6	FLORIDA	11,000	38.2	19,840	42.2	25,450	44.9
	300	2.0	120	0.5	314	1.3	GEORGIA	100	0.3	520	1.1	607	1.1
	0	–	40	0.2	26	0.1	HAWAII	0	–	200	0.4	96	0.2
	0	–	0	–	0	–	IDAHO	0	–	40	0.1	0	–
	600	4.1	520	2.4	435	1.8	ILLINOIS	400	1.4	440	0.9	204	0.4
	100	0.7	160	0.7	160	0.7	INDIANA	300	1.0	80	0.2	26	0.1
	0	–	0	–	83	0.4	IOWA	0	–	80	0.2	0	–
	0	–	0	–	91	0.4	KANSAS	0	–	40	0.1	0	–
	0	–	120	0.5	36	0.2	KENTUCKY	0	–	40	0.1	102	0.2
	100	0.7	0	–	62	0.3	LOUISIANA	100	0.3	160	0.3	24	–
	600	4.1	960	4.4	1,759	7.4	MAINE	1,400	4.9	3,480	7.4	3,557	6.3
	0	–	440	2.0	228	1.0	MARYLAND	400	1.4	560	1.2	505	0.9
	0	–	280	1.3	324	1.4	MICHIGAN	200	0.7	160	0.3	252	0.4
	0	–	40	0.2	114	0.5	MINNESOTA	0	–	120	0.3	9	–
	0	–	40	0.2	32	0.1	MISSISSIPPI	0	–	80	0.2	12	–
	0	–	120	0.5	189	0.8	MISSOURI	0	–	40	0.1	232	0.4
	0	–	0	–	26	0.1	MONTANA	0	–	0	–	0	–
	0	–	0	–	0	–	NEBRASKA	0	–	80	0.2	42	0.1
	0	–	0	–	78	0.3	NEVADA	100	0.3	200	0.4	292	0.5
	1,100	7.4	2,120	9.7	1,167	4.9	NEW HAMPSHIRE	3,300	11.5	6,400	13.6	7,058	12.4
	1,200	8.1	1,880	8.6	2,009	8.4	NEW JERSEY	900	3.1	880	1.9	1,182	2.1
	0	–	40	0.2	52	0.2	NEW MEXICO	0	–	120	0.3	129	0.2
	3,600	24.3	4,080	18.6	4,680	19.7	NEW YORK	1,900	6.6	1,040	2.2	1,957	3.5
	100	0.7	80	0.4	295	1.2	NORTH CAROLINA	200	0.7	840	1.8	1,329	2.3
	0	–	0	–	29	0.1	NORTH DAKOTA	0	–	0	–	50	0.1
	100	0.7	240	1.1	319	1.3	OHIO	300	1.0	280	0.6	415	0.7
	0	–	0	–	70	0.3	OKLAHOMA	0	–	0	–	64	0.1
	0	–	40	0.2	33	0.1	OREGON	0	–	200	0.4	229	0.4
	600	4.1	800	3.6	739	3.1	PENNSYLVANIA	800	2.8	440	0.9	1,010	1.8
	1,000	6.8	1,360	6.2	1,401	5.9	RHODE ISLAND	1,400	4.9	1,120	2.4	1,812	3.2
	0	–	40	0.2	191	0.8	SOUTH CAROLINA	100	0.3	160	0.3	756	1.3
	0	–	0	–	60	0.3	SOUTH DAKOTA	100	0.3	0	–	0	–
	0	–	120	0.5	21	0.1	TENNESSEE	100	0.3	160	0.3	186	0.3
	0	–	80	0.4	544	2.3	TEXAS	300	1.0	640	1.4	1,042	1.8
	0	–	0	–	50	0.2	UTAH	0	–	80	0.2	88	0.2
	200	1.4	480	2.2	334	1.4	VERMONT	0	–	800	1.7	640	1.1
	100	0.7	240	1.1	323	1.4	VIRGINIA	300	1.0	520	1.1	750	1.3
	200	1.4	120	0.5	47	0.2	WASHINGTON	100	0.3	160	0.3	330	0.6
	100	0.7	0	–	26	0.1	WEST VIRGINIA	0	–	40	0.1	47	0.1
	100	0.7	120	0.5	193	0.8	WISCONSIN	400	1.4	120	0.3	96	0.2
	0	–	40	0.2	0	–	WYOMING	0	–	0	–	0	–
	14,800	99.8*	21,920	99.9*	23,796	100.1*	TOTAL U.S.	28,800	99.6*	47,000	100.1*	56,737	100.1*

*rounding error

MICHIGAN

TO MICHIGAN FROM							FROM MICHIGAN TO					
1970		1980		1990			1970		1980		1990	
#	%	#	%	#	%		#	%	#	%	#	%
1,000	4.5	400	1.6	374	1.2	ALABAMA	600	1.1	1,040	1.4	1,137	1.5
0	–	0	–	28	0.1	ALASKA	0	–	0	–	71	0.1
500	2.3	440	1.8	1,329	4.2	ARIZONA	4,100	7.8	5,280	7.3	4,857	6.5
300	1.4	440	1.8	450	1.4	ARKANSAS	500	1.0	1,520	2.1	795	1.1
1,200	5.5	1,800	7.2	2,721	8.5	CALIFORNIA	5,200	9.9	7,160	9.9	4,639	6.2
300	1.4	200	0.8	465	1.5	COLORADO	100	0.2	1,160	1.6	789	1.1
100	0.5	200	0.8	84	0.3	CONNECTICUT	200	0.4	200	0.3	135	0.2
0	–	40	0.2	63	0.2	DELAWARE	0	–	0	–	74	0.1
300	1.4	160	0.6	37	0.1	D.C.	0	–	80	0.1	80	0.1
1,900	8.6	3,480	14.0	6,712	21.1	FLORIDA	24,300	46.4	28,320	39.3	32,058	42.9
0	–	480	1.9	670	2.1	GEORGIA	800	1.5	1,320	1.8	1,376	1.8
0	–	0	–	92	0.3	HAWAII	0	–	80	0.1	365	0.5
0	–	0	–	61	0.2	IDAHO	0	–	80	0.1	184	0.3
4,500	20.5	3,640	14.6	3,665	11.5	ILLINOIS	1,700	3.2	1,960	2.7	1,962	2.6
1,800	8.2	1,960	7.9	2,303	7.2	INDIANA	1,400	2.7	2,640	3.7	2,066	2.8
200	0.9	240	1.0	273	0.9	IOWA	200	0.4	200	0.3	264	0.4
0	–	80	0.3	111	0.4	KANSAS	0	–	80	0.1	289	0.4
300	1.4	960	3.9	594	1.9	KENTUCKY	600	1.1	1,480	2.1	1,412	1.9
600	2.7	160	0.6	230	0.7	LOUISIANA	100	0.2	400	0.6	204	0.3
0	–	0	–	61	0.2	MAINE	0	–	80	0.1	97	0.1
100	0.5	360	1.4	253	0.8	MARYLAND	300	0.6	200	0.3	240	0.3
200	0.9	160	0.6	252	0.8	MASSACHUSETTS	0	–	280	0.4	324	0.4
600	2.7	360	1.4	422	1.3	MINNESOTA	700	1.3	400	0.6	365	0.5
300	1.4	160	0.6	236	0.7	MISSISSIPPI	200	0.4	840	1.2	273	0.4
500	2.3	520	2.1	447	1.4	MISSOURI	600	1.1	1,040	1.4	868	1.2
0	–	0	–	72	0.2	MONTANA	100	0.2	120	0.2	87	0.1
0	–	40	0.2	136	0.4	NEBRASKA	200	0.4	80	0.1	75	0.1
0	–	200	0.8	285	0.9	NEVADA	200	0.4	560	0.8	885	1.2
0	–	80	0.3	64	0.2	NEW HAMPSHIRE	0	–	80	0.1	95	0.1
600	2.7	400	1.6	474	1.5	NEW JERSEY	600	1.1	120	0.2	176	0.2
0	–	80	0.3	357	1.1	NEW MEXICO	800	1.5	840	1.2	306	0.4
600	2.7	1,000	4.0	820	2.6	NEW YORK	800	1.5	720	1.0	770	1.0
100	0.5	320	1.3	268	0.8	NORTH CAROLINA	500	1.0	840	1.2	2,127	2.9
0	–	0	–	0	–	NORTH DAKOTA	0	–	80	0.1	10	–
3,100	14.1	2,800	11.2	2,394	7.5	OHIO	2,800	5.3	3,640	5.1	3,433	4.6
0	–	80	0.3	197	0.6	OKLAHOMA	0	–	280	0.4	179	0.2
0	–	80	0.3	150	0.5	OREGON	200	0.4	120	0.2	224	0.3
600	2.7	960	3.9	711	2.2	PENNSYLVANIA	1,000	1.9	1,480	2.1	1,247	1.7
0	–	120	0.5	23	0.1	RHODE ISLAND	0	–	0	–	16	–
0	–	40	0.2	342	1.1	SOUTH CAROLINA	0	–	760	1.1	1,293	1.7
0	–	0	–	79	0.3	SOUTH DAKOTA	0	–	80	0.1	15	–
400	1.8	400	1.6	939	2.9	TENNESSEE	800	1.5	1,880	2.6	2,817	3.8
400	1.8	360	1.4	925	2.9	TEXAS	1,000	1.9	2,000	2.8	2,343	3.1
0	–	40	0.2	61	0.2	UTAH	0	–	0	–	228	0.3
100	0.5	40	0.2	0	–	VERMONT	0	–	0	–	0	–
300	1.4	320	1.3	334	1.1	VIRGINIA	900	1.7	960	1.3	1,065	1.4
100	0.5	120	0.5	292	0.9	WASHINGTON	200	0.4	320	0.4	759	1.0
300	1.4	240	1.0	126	0.4	WEST VIRGINIA	0	–	360	0.5	459	0.6
700	3.2	920	3.7	846	2.7	WISCONSIN	700	1.3	880	1.2	1,121	1.5
0	–	40	0.2	57	0.2	WYOMING	0	–	0	–	7	–
22,000	100.4*	24,920	100.1*	31,885	100.3*	TOTAL U.S.	52,400	99.8*	72,040	100.2*	74,661	99.9*

*rounding error

MINNESOTA

TO MINNESOTA FROM							FROM MINNESOTA TO					
1970		1980		1990			1970		1980		1990	
#	%	#	%	#	%		#	%	#	%	#	%
0	–	80	0.6	9	0.1	ALABAMA	200	1.0	240	1.1	95	0.4
0	–	120	0.9	143	0.7	ALASKA	0	–	0	–	30	0.1
400	3.3	320	2.3	673	3.5	ARIZONA	1,700	8.6	3,000	13.7	3,704	15.5
0	–	80	0.6	221	1.1	ARKANSAS	300	1.5	560	2.6	526	2.2
500	4.1	1,120	8.1	1,676	8.7	CALIFORNIA	3,200	16.2	2,800	12.8	2,598	10.8
0	–	120	0.9	562	2.9	COLORADO	500	2.5	520	2.4	450	1.9
0	–	160	1.2	218	1.1	CONNECTICUT	0	–	0	–	25	0.1
0	–	0	–	0	–	DELAWARE	0	–	0	–	0	–
0	–	0	–	28	0.1	D.C.	0	–	0	–	0	–
400	3.3	920	6.7	1,190	6.1	FLORIDA	2,200	11.1	2,680	12.2	3,836	16.0
0	–	40	0.3	65	0.3	GEORGIA	300	1.5	160	0.7	164	0.7
0	–	40	0.3	0	–	HAWAII	0	–	40	0.2	157	0.7
100	0.8	120	0.9	47	0.2	IDAHO	100	0.5	160	0.7	112	0.5
1,600	13.2	1,440	10.4	1,130	5.8	ILLINOIS	1,000	5.1	680	3.1	432	1.8
300	2.5	480	3.5	125	0.7	INDIANA	200	1.0	40	0.2	148	0.6
1,800	14.9	1,200	8.7	1,368	7.1	IOWA	900	4.5	1,240	5.7	1,101	4.6
0	–	80	0.6	3,154	16.3	KANSAS	100	0.5	0	–	88	0.4
100	0.8	80	0.6	55	0.3	KENTUCKY	0	–	120	0.5	134	0.6
0	–	40	0.3	9	0.1	LOUISIANA	100	0.5	0	–	51	0.2
0	–	0	–	107	0.6	MAINE	0	–	0	–	26	0.1
0	–	80	0.6	183	0.9	MARYLAND	100	0.5	40	0.2	158	0.7
0	–	120	0.9	9	0.1	MASSACHUSETTS	0	–	40	0.2	114	0.5
700	5.8	400	2.9	365	1.9	MICHIGAN	600	3.0	360	1.6	422	1.8
0	–	40	0.3	55	0.3	MISSISSIPPI	0	–	0	–	27	0.1
100	0.8	240	1.7	190	1.0	MISSOURI	1,000	5.1	200	0.9	698	2.9
200	1.7	360	2.6	217	1.1	MONTANA	0	–	160	0.7	84	0.4
700	5.8	120	0.9	166	0.9	NEBRASKA	300	1.5	520	2.4	63	0.3
0	–	200	1.4	112	0.6	NEVADA	100	0.5	280	1.3	648	2.7
0	–	80	0.6	91	0.5	NEW HAMPSHIRE	0	–	0	–	0	–
0	–	200	1.4	87	0.5	NEW JERSEY	0	–	80	0.4	32	0.1
100	0.8	0	–	282	1.5	NEW MEXICO	200	1.0	600	2.7	102	0.4
300	2.5	200	1.4	509	2.6	NEW YORK	100	0.5	240	1.1	70	0.3
0	–	0	–	189	1.0	NORTH CAROLINA	0	–	160	0.7	240	1.0
1,100	9.1	1,800	13.0	1,014	5.2	NORTH DAKOTA	1,300	6.6	600	2.7	1,045	4.4
400	3.3	240	1.7	363	1.9	OHIO	400	2.0	200	0.9	168	0.7
200	1.7	0	–	28	0.1	OKLAHOMA	200	1.0	240	1.1	118	0.5
400	3.3	280	2.0	209	1.1	OREGON	300	1.5	240	1.1	290	1.2
0	–	80	0.6	345	1.8	PENNSYLVANIA	200	1.0	80	0.4	172	0.7
0	–	0	–	0	–	RHODE ISLAND	0	–	0	–	0	–
0	–	0	–	36	0.2	SOUTH CAROLINA	0	–	40	0.2	66	0.3
500	4.1	480	3.5	628	3.2	SOUTH DAKOTA	900	4.5	680	3.1	383	1.6
0	–	120	0.9	166	0.9	TENNESSEE	0	–	80	0.4	51	0.2
200	1.7	160	1.2	744	3.8	TEXAS	500	2.5	1,880	8.6	1,574	6.6
300	2.5	40	0.3	65	0.3	UTAH	100	0.5	80	0.4	98	0.4
0	–	0	–	0	–	VERMONT	0	–	0	–	0	–
200	1.7	40	0.3	219	1.1	VIRGINIA	0	–	200	0.9	129	0.5
400	3.3	520	3.8	342	1.8	WASHINGTON	1,000	5.1	520	2.4	543	2.3
0	–	0	–	0	–	WEST VIRGINIA	0	–	40	0.2	14	0.1
1,100	9.1	1,480	10.7	1,967	10.2	WISCONSIN	1,700	8.6	2,120	9.7	2,914	12.2
0	–	80	0.6	9	0.1	WYOMING	0	–	0	–	58	0.2
12,100	100.1*	13,800	100.2*	19,370	100.3*	TOTAL U.S.	19,800	99.9*	21,920	100.2*	23,958	100.3*

*rounding error

MISSISSIPPI

TO MISSISSIPPI FROM							FROM MISSISSIPPI TO					
1970		1980		1990			1970		1980		1990	
#	%	#	%	#	%		#	%	#	%	#	%
1,200	13.5	1,280	7.9	1,419	8.1	ALABAMA	800	8.4	680	6.8	1,348	10.3
0	–	40	0.2	3	–	ALASKA	0	–	0	–	23	0.2
0	–	40	0.2	297	1.7	ARIZONA	200	2.1	120	1.2	128	1.0
400	4.5	600	3.7	498	2.8	ARKANSAS	100	1.1	600	6.0	655	5.0
800	9.0	760	4.7	843	4.8	CALIFORNIA	100	1.1	800	8.0	558	4.2
0	–	0	–	90	0.5	COLORADO	0	–	40	0.4	18	0.1
0	–	80	0.5	66	0.4	CONNECTICUT	0	–	0	–	17	0.1
0	–	0	–	63	0.4	DELAWARE	0	–	40	0.4	83	0.6
0	–	40	0.2	0	–	D.C.	0	–	0	–	56	0.4
800	9.0	1,160	7.2	1,062	6.0	FLORIDA	700	7.4	840	8.4	1,101	8.4
600	6.7	760	4.7	318	1.8	GEORGIA	200	2.1	400	4.0	343	2.6
0	–	0	–	54	0.3	HAWAII	0	–	0	–	0	–
0	–	0	–	15	0.1	IDAHO	0	–	0	–	28	0.2
1,000	11.2	1,560	9.7	1,233	7.0	ILLINOIS	1,100	11.6	640	6.4	990	7.5
0	–	280	1.7	324	1.8	INDIANA	100	1.1	200	2.0	221	1.7
0	–	80	0.5	96	0.5	IOWA	0	–	40	0.4	38	0.3
0	–	40	0.2	54	0.3	KANSAS	0	–	120	1.2	72	0.6
300	3.4	120	0.7	240	1.4	KENTUCKY	0	–	120	1.2	303	2.3
400	4.5	2,360	14.6	3,891	22.1	LOUISIANA	1,500	15.8	1,000	10.0	1,602	12.2
200	2.2	0	–	24	0.1	MAINE	0	–	0	–	0	–
100	1.1	40	0.2	96	0.5	MARYLAND	0	–	0	–	147	1.1
0	–	80	0.5	12	0.1	MASSACHUSETTS	0	–	40	0.4	32	0.2
200	2.2	840	5.2	273	1.6	MICHIGAN	300	3.2	160	1.6	236	1.8
0	–	0	–	27	0.2	MINNESOTA	0	–	40	0.4	55	0.4
500	5.6	680	4.2	327	1.6	MISSOURI	1,100	11.6	240	2.4	282	2.1
0	–	0	–	0	–	MONTANA	0	–	0	–	27	0.2
200	2.2	0	–	54	0.3	NEBRASKA	0	–	40	0.4	38	0.3
0	–	40	0.2	30	0.2	NEVADA	0	–	0	–	90	0.7
0	–	0	–	39	0.2	NEW HAMPSHIRE	0	–	0	–	0	–
100	1.1	240	1.5	45	0.3	NEW JERSEY	0	–	80	0.8	0	–
0	–	40	0.2	51	0.3	NEW MEXICO	0	–	40	0.4	27	0.2
300	3.4	640	4.0	225	1.3	NEW YORK	0	–	80	0.8	165	1.3
0	–	120	0.7	195	1.1	NORTH CAROLINA	0	–	200	2.0	204	1.6
0	–	0	–	0	–	NORTH DAKOTA	0	–	40	0.4	0	–
500	5.6	400	2.5	435	2.5	OHIO	200	2.1	120	1.2	235	1.8
0	–	160	1.0	84	0.5	OKLAHOMA	0	–	160	1.6	210	1.6
100	1.1	0	–	15	0.1	OREGON	0	–	120	1.2	13	0.1
0	–	360	2.2	192	1.1	PENNSYLVANIA	100	1.1	120	1.2	122	0.9
0	–	40	0.2	30	0.2	RHODE ISLAND	0	–	0	–	0	–
0	–	40	0.2	57	0.3	SOUTH CAROLINA	100	1.1	280	2.8	120	0.9
0	–	0	–	0	–	SOUTH DAKOTA	0	–	0	–	10	0.1
700	7.9	2,160	13.4	2,715	15.4	TENNESSEE	1,800	18.9	1,480	14.8	1,746	13.3
500	5.6	600	3.7	1,689	9.6	TEXAS	900	9.5	800	8.0	1,210	9.2
0	–	0	–	0	–	UTAH	0	–	0	–	68	0.5
0	–	0	–	0	–	VERMONT	0	–	0	–	26	0.2
0	–	120	0.7	117	0.7	VIRGINIA	200	2.1	160	1.6	111	0.8
0	–	0	–	51	0.3	WASHINGTON	0	–	0	–	300	2.3
0	–	0	–	0	–	WEST VIRGINIA	0	–	0	–	18	0.1
0	–	320	2.0	228	1.3	WISCONSIN	0	–	160	1.6	77	0.6
0	–	0	–	60	0.3	WYOMING	0	–	0	–	0	–
8,900	99.8*	16,120	99.3*	17,637	100.1*	TOTAL U.S.	9,500	100.3*	10,000	100.0	13,153	100.0

*rounding error

MISSOURI

TO MISSOURI FROM							FROM MISSOURI TO					
1970		1980		1990			1970		1980		1990	
#	%	#	%	#	%		#	%	#	%	#	%
100	0.4	240	0.8	101	0.3	ALABAMA	300	1.1	440	1.3	415	1.2
300	1.2	80	0.3	10	–	ALASKA	0	–	0	–	0	–
300	1.2	800	2.6	941	2.7	ARIZONA	2,000	7.6	2,640	7.6	1,740	5.0
900	3.6	1,280	4.2	1,716	4.9	ARKANSAS	1,400	5.3	2,360	6.8	2,164	6.3
2,400	9.5	5,320	17.5	4,675	13.3	CALIFORNIA	3,800	14.5	3,560	10.2	2,578	7.5
600	2.4	640	2.1	880	2.5	COLORADO	800	3.1	960	2.8	795	2.3
0	–	120	0.4	105	0.3	CONNECTICUT	100	0.4	160	0.5	196	0.6
200	0.8	0	–	0	–	DELAWARE	0	–	0	–	32	0.1
0	–	40	0.1	34	0.1	D.C.	0	–	0	–	34	0.1
300	1.2	1,240	4.1	1,911	5.4	FLORIDA	3,200	12.2	4,440	12.8	4,507	13.1
100	0.4	40	0.1	327	0.9	GEORGIA	600	2.3	320	0.9	627	1.8
0	–	40	0.1	82	0.2	HAWAII	0	–	40	0.1	20	0.1
0	–	120	0.4	170	0.5	IDAHO	0	–	120	0.3	128	0.4
4,900	19.4	5,200	17.1	4,943	14.0	ILLINOIS	2,500	9.5	3,240	9.3	3,282	9.5
600	2.4	760	2.5	811	2.3	INDIANA	500	1.9	640	1.8	662	1.9
1,400	5.5	1,320	4.3	1,896	5.4	IOWA	600	2.3	800	2.3	777	2.3
2,700	10.7	3,840	12.6	4,490	12.7	KANSAS	3,000	11.5	3,480	10.0	3,711	10.8
700	2.8	240	0.8	320	0.9	KENTUCKY	200	0.8	320	0.9	352	1.0
100	0.4	80	0.3	333	0.9	LOUISIANA	100	0.4	160	0.5	228	0.7
0	–	40	0.1	54	0.2	MAINE	0	–	0	–	0	–
100	0.4	200	0.7	213	0.6	MARYLAND	100	0.4	120	0.3	158	0.5
0	–	40	0.1	232	0.7	MASSACHUSETTS	0	–	120	0.3	189	0.6
600	2.4	1,040	3.4	868	2.5	MICHIGAN	500	1.9	520	1.5	447	1.3
1,000	4.0	200	0.7	698	2.0	MINNESOTA	100	0.4	240	0.7	190	0.6
1,100	4.3	240	0.8	282	0.8	MISSISSIPPI	500	1.9	680	2.0	327	1.0
100	0.4	0	–	113	0.3	MONTANA	0	–	120	0.3	72	0.2
400	1.6	480	1.6	611	1.7	NEBRASKA	300	1.1	440	1.3	550	1.6
200	0.8	0	–	292	0.8	NEVADA	100	0.4	280	0.8	297	0.9
0	–	0	–	99	0.3	NEW HAMPSHIRE	0	–	40	0.1	57	0.2
1,000	4.0	240	0.8	321	0.9	NEW JERSEY	200	0.8	200	0.6	143	0.4
300	1.2	160	0.5	216	0.6	NEW MEXICO	0	–	520	1.5	456	1.3
600	2.4	560	1.8	654	1.9	NEW YORK	300	1.1	320	0.9	386	1.1
0	–	160	0.5	118	0.3	NORTH CAROLINA	0	–	240	0.7	297	0.9
0	–	40	0.1	0	–	NORTH DAKOTA	0	–	80	0.2	10	–
500	2.0	560	1.8	668	1.9	OHIO	400	1.5	360	1.0	616	1.8
600	2.4	1,160	3.8	1,039	3.0	OKLAHOMA	1,400	5.3	1,320	3.8	1,548	4.5
100	0.4	440	1.4	174	0.5	OREGON	500	1.9	280	0.8	478	1.4
700	2.8	720	2.4	318	0.9	PENNSYLVANIA	0	–	160	0.5	309	0.9
0	–	40	0.1	0	–	RHODE ISLAND	100	0.4	0	–	31	0.1
300	1.2	80	0.3	169	0.5	SOUTH CAROLINA	0	–	200	0.6	297	0.9
0	–	120	0.4	58	0.2	SOUTH DAKOTA	0	–	80	0.2	91	0.3
200	0.8	320	1.1	701	2.0	TENNESSEE	500	1.9	560	1.6	864	2.5
800	3.2	920	3.0	2,335	6.6	TEXAS	1,600	6.1	2,880	8.3	3,085	8.9
100	0.4	80	0.3	119	0.3	UTAH	0	–	40	0.1	229	0.7
0	–	0	–	14	–	VERMONT	0	–	40	0.1	31	0.1
300	1.2	120	0.4	168	0.5	VIRGINIA	100	0.4	200	0.6	309	0.9
400	1.6	440	1.4	322	0.9	WASHINGTON	100	0.4	520	1.5	342	1.0
0	–	40	0.1	151	0.4	WEST VIRGINIA	0	–	0	–	146	0.4
300	1.2	520	1.7	393	1.1	WISCONSIN	300	1.1	560	1.6	253	0.7
0	–	40	0.1	106	0.3	WYOMING	0	–	0	–	58	0.2
25,300	100.6*	30,400	99.7*	35,251	100.0	TOTAL U.S.	26,200	99.9*	34,800	100.0	34,514	100.6*

*rounding error

MONTANA

	TO MONTANA FROM							FROM MONTANA TO				
	1970		1980		1990			1970		1980		1990	
#	%	#	%	#	%		#	%	#	%	#	%
0	–	0	–	0	–	ALABAMA	0	–	40	0.5	0	–
0	–	80	1.5	77	1.3	ALASKA	0	–	40	0.5	80	1.1
0	–	120	2.2	188	3.1	ARIZONA	1,000	17.5	840	11.4	802	11.1
0	–	0	–	4	0.1	ARKANSAS	100	1.8	240	3.3	0	–
1,000	50.0	1,400	26.1	1,044	17.0	CALIFORNIA	1,400	24.6	1,480	20.1	504	7.0
0	–	280	5.2	360	5.9	COLORADO	100	1.8	320	4.3	225	3.1
0	–	40	0.7	0	–	CONNECTICUT	0	–	0	–	28	0.4
0	–	0	–	0	–	DELAWARE	0	–	0	–	0	–
0	–	0	–	27	0.4	D.C.	0	–	0	–	0	–
0	–	0	–	230	3.8	FLORIDA	0	–	200	2.7	268	3.7
0	–	0	–	0	–	GEORGIA	0	–	0	–	58	0.8
0	–	0	–	0	–	HAWAII	0	–	80	1.1	110	1.5
0	–	120	2.2	395	6.4	IDAHO	300	5.3	120	1.6	468	6.5
0	–	80	1.5	145	2.4	ILLINOIS	100	1.8	80	1.1	207	2.9
0	–	40	0.7	42	0.7	INDIANA	0	–	0	–	55	0.8
0	–	0	–	87	1.4	IOWA	0	–	40	0.5	76	1.1
0	–	160	3.0	42	0.7	KANSAS	0	–	0	–	125	1.7
0	–	0	–	35	0.6	KENTUCKY	0	–	0	–	0	–
0	–	40	0.7	0	–	LOUISIANA	0	–	0	–	66	0.9
0	–	0	–	0	–	MAINE	0	–	0	–	0	–
0	–	200	3.7	95	1.6	MARYLAND	100	1.8	0	–	0	–
0	–	0	–	0	–	MASSACHUSETTS	0	–	0	–	26	0.4
100	5.0	120	2.2	87	1.4	MICHIGAN	0	–	0	–	72	1.0
0	–	160	3.0	84	1.4	MINNESOTA	200	3.5	360	4.9	217	3.0
0	–	0	–	27	0.4	MISSISSIPPI	0	–	0	–	0	–
0	–	120	2.2	72	1.2	MISSOURI	100	1.8	0	–	113	1.6
100	5.0	40	0.7	210	3.4	NEBRASKA	0	–	40	0.5	54	0.8
0	–	40	0.7	118	1.9	NEVADA	0	–	200	2.7	302	4.2
0	–	0	–	34	0.6	NEW HAMPSHIRE	0	–	0	–	0	–
0	–	80	1.5	217	3.5	NEW JERSEY	0	–	0	–	0	–
0	–	40	0.7	22	0.4	NEW MEXICO	0	–	120	1.6	21	0.3
0	–	40	0.7	86	1.4	NEW YORK	100	1.8	0	–	14	0.2
0	–	0	–	18	0.3	NORTH CAROLINA	0	–	80	1.1	102	1.4
100	5.0	280	5.2	257	4.2	NORTH DAKOTA	0	–	360	4.9	225	3.1
0	–	40	0.7	164	2.7	OHIO	0	–	40	0.5	58	0.8
100	5.0	0	–	49	0.8	OKLAHOMA	100	1.8	0	–	92	1.3
100	5.0	440	8.2	208	3.4	OREGON	300	5.3	800	10.9	492	6.8
0	–	0	–	145	2.4	PENNSYLVANIA	0	–	0	–	0	–
0	–	0	–	0	–	RHODE ISLAND	0	–	0	–	0	–
0	–	0	–	0	–	SOUTH CAROLINA	0	–	80	1.1	78	1.1
0	–	80	1.5	48	0.8	SOUTH DAKOTA	0	–	200	2.7	29	0.4
0	–	80	1.5	0	–	TENNESSEE	0	–	120	1.6	0	–
100	5.0	120	2.2	80	1.3	TEXAS	0	–	80	1.1	220	3.0
100	5.0	280	5.2	110	1.8	UTAH	100	1.8	200	2.7	292	4.0
0	–	0	–	8	0.1	VERMONT	0	–	0	–	0	–
0	–	40	0.7	0	–	VIRGINIA	0	–	0	–	111	1.5
300	15.0	480	9.0	841	13.7	WASHINGTON	1,500	26.3	960	13.0	1,203	16.7
0	–	0	–	0	–	WEST VIRGINIA	0	–	0	–	21	0.3
0	–	200	3.7	158	2.6	WISCONSIN	100	1.8	80	1.1	82	1.1
0	–	120	2.2	326	5.3	WYOMING	100	1.8	160	2.2	330	4.6
2,000	100.0	5,360	99.3*	6,140	100.4*	TOTAL U.S.	5,700	100.5*	7,360	99.7*	7,226	100.2*

*rounding error

NEBRASKA

TO NEBRASKA FROM							FROM NEBRASKA TO					
1970		1980		1990			1970		1980		1990	
#	%	#	%	#	%		#	%	#	%	#	%
0	–	0	–	0	–	ALABAMA	0	–	40	0.4	19	0.2
0	–	0	–	0	–	ALASKA	0	–	0	–	11	0.1
100	1.4	440	5.5	343	3.5	ARIZONA	800	9.8	1,600	14.8	851	7.9
0	–	40	0.5	219	2.2	ARKANSAS	0	–	520	4.8	217	2.0
700	9.9	1,480	18.6	1,322	13.4	CALIFORNIA	900	11.0	1,400	13.0	1,209	11.2
1,100	15.5	760	9.5	1,150	11.7	COLORADO	1,300	15.9	1,240	11.5	1,176	10.9
0	–	0	–	63	0.6	CONNECTICUT	0	–	80	0.7	0	–
0	–	0	–	0	–	DELAWARE	0	–	0	–	0	–
0	–	40	0.5	59	0.6	D.C.	0	–	0	–	0	–
0	–	160	2.0	179	1.8	FLORIDA	400	4.9	400	3.7	803	7.4
0	–	0	–	0	–	GEORGIA	0	–	80	0.7	0	–
0	–	0	–	0	–	HAWAII	0	–	0	–	0	–
0	–	0	–	102	1.0	IDAHO	100	1.2	40	0.4	116	1.1
600	8.5	280	3.5	423	4.3	ILLINOIS	100	1.2	160	1.5	186	1.7
0	–	40	0.5	126	1.3	INDIANA	200	2.4	160	1.5	48	0.4
1,100	15.5	1,200	15.1	1,365	13.9	IOWA	1,000	12.2	840	7.8	682	6.3
800	11.3	760	9.5	952	9.7	KANSAS	400	4.9	800	7.4	1,058	9.8
100	1.4	0	–	54	0.6	KENTUCKY	0	–	0	–	21	0.2
0	–	0	–	37	0.4	LOUISIANA	0	–	120	1.1	18	0.2
0	–	0	–	29	0.3	MAINE	0	–	0	–	9	0.1
0	–	40	0.5	54	0.6	MARYLAND	0	–	0	–	28	0.3
0	–	80	1.0	42	0.4	MASSACHUSETTS	0	–	0	–	0	–
200	2.8	80	1.0	75	0.8	MICHIGAN	0	–	40	0.4	136	1.3
300	4.2	520	6.5	63	0.6	MINNESOTA	700	8.5	120	1.1	166	1.5
0	–	40	0.5	38	0.4	MISSISSIPPI	200	2.4	0	–	54	0.5
300	4.2	440	5.5	550	5.6	MISSOURI	400	4.9	480	4.4	611	5.7
0	–	40	0.5	54	0.6	MONTANA	100	1.2	40	0.4	210	2.0
0	–	40	0.5	21	0.2	NEVADA	0	–	120	1.1	165	1.5
100	1.4	0	–	0	–	NEW HAMPSHIRE	0	–	0	–	0	–
0	–	0	–	98	1.0	NEW JERSEY	0	–	0	–	11	0.1
100	1.4	0	–	269	2.7	NEW MEXICO	100	1.2	0	–	273	2.5
100	1.4	160	2.0	100	1.0	NEW YORK	100	1.2	120	1.1	37	0.3
0	–	0	–	30	0.3	NORTH CAROLINA	0	–	40	0.4	42	0.4
0	–	80	1.0	50	0.5	NORTH DAKOTA	0	–	0	–	75	0.7
0	–	80	1.0	76	0.8	OHIO	100	1.2	80	0.7	80	0.7
0	–	80	1.0	190	1.9	OKLAHOMA	100	1.2	200	1.9	118	1.1
100	1.4	200	2.5	224	2.3	OREGON	200	2.4	280	2.6	206	1.9
0	–	80	1.0	28	0.3	PENNSYLVANIA	0	–	0	–	84	0.8
0	–	0	–	0	–	RHODE ISLAND	0	–	0	–	0	–
0	–	0	–	8	0.1	SOUTH CAROLINA	0	–	40	0.4	87	0.8
400	5.6	200	2.5	310	3.2	SOUTH DAKOTA	400	4.9	240	2.2	582	5.4
0	–	0	–	67	0.7	TENNESSEE	0	–	0	–	126	1.2
0	–	160	2.0	445	4.5	TEXAS	100	1.2	840	7.8	537	5.0
100	1.4	0	–	8	0.1	UTAH	100	1.2	80	0.7	102	0.9
0	–	0	–	0	–	VERMONT	0	–	0	–	0	–
0	–	120	1.5	41	0.4	VIRGINIA	0	–	0	–	18	0.2
300	4.2	160	2.0	197	2.0	WASHINGTON	300	3.7	400	3.7	267	2.5
0	–	0	–	33	0.3	WEST VIRGINIA	0	–	0	–	0	–
200	2.8	0	–	154	1.6	WISCONSIN	100	1.2	120	1.1	63	0.6
400	5.6	160	2.0	204	2.1	WYOMING	0	–	80	0.7	292	2.7
7,100	99.9*	7,960	99.7*	9,852	100.3*	TOTAL U.S.	8,200	99.9*	10,800	100.0	10,794	100.1*

*rounding error

NEVADA

TO NEVADA FROM							FROM NEVADA TO					
1970		1980		1990			1970		1980		1990	
#	%	#	%	#	%		#	%	#	%	#	%
0	–	0	–	94	0.2	ALABAMA	0	–	40	0.4	137	0.9
0	–	120	0.5	65	0.2	ALASKA	100	2.3	40	0.4	0	–
200	2.9	560	2.3	2,076	4.8	ARIZONA	200	4.5	520	5.2	1,718	10.6
0	–	120	0.5	188	0.4	ARKANSAS	100	2.3	120	1.2	171	1.1
3,400	48.6	11,680	48.3	21,389	49.6	CALIFORNIA	1,800	40.9	4,240	42.2	5,199	32.1
100	1.4	400	1.7	522	1.2	COLORADO	0	–	160	1.6	276	1.7
0	–	120	0.5	211	0.5	CONNECTICUT	0	–	40	0.4	76	0.5
0	–	0	–	93	0.2	DELAWARE	0	–	0	–	7	–
100	1.4	0	–	0	–	D.C.	0	–	40	0.4	0	–
100	1.4	920	3.8	1,336	3.1	FLORIDA	200	4.5	440	4.4	1,045	6.5
0	–	40	0.2	42	0.1	GEORGIA	0	–	120	1.2	79	0.5
0	–	120	0.5	307	0.7	HAWAII	0	–	40	0.4	45	0.3
400	5.7	240	1.0	567	1.3	IDAHO	200	4.5	120	1.2	384	2.4
100	1.4	1,120	4.6	2,465	5.7	ILLINOIS	0	–	200	2.0	252	1.6
0	–	80	0.3	261	0.6	INDIANA	0	–	0	–	94	0.6
0	–	160	0.7	195	0.5	IOWA	0	–	40	0.4	118	0.7
100	1.4	160	0.7	287	0.7	KANSAS	0	–	0	–	235	1.5
100	1.4	80	0.3	70	0.2	KENTUCKY	0	–	80	0.8	130	0.8
0	–	240	1.0	182	0.4	LOUISIANA	100	2.3	40	0.4	45	0.3
0	–	40	0.2	0	–	MAINE	0	–	0	–	30	0.2
0	–	80	0.3	164	0.4	MARYLAND	0	–	0	–	53	0.3
100	1.4	200	0.8	292	0.7	MASSACHUSETTS	0	–	0	–	78	0.5
200	2.9	560	2.3	885	2.1	MICHIGAN	0	–	200	2.0	285	1.8
100	1.4	280	1.2	648	1.5	MINNESOTA	0	–	200	2.0	112	0.7
0	–	0	–	90	0.2	MISSISSIPPI	0	–	40	0.4	30	0.2
100	1.4	280	1.2	297	0.7	MISSOURI	200	4.5	0	–	292	1.8
0	–	200	0.8	302	0.7	MONTANA	0	–	40	0.4	118	0.7
0	–	120	0.5	165	0.4	NEBRASKA	0	–	40	0.4	21	0.1
0	–	80	0.3	24	0.1	NEW HAMPSHIRE	0	–	0	–	0	–
200	2.9	280	1.2	592	1.4	NEW JERSEY	0	–	0	–	160	1.0
100	1.4	400	1.7	320	0.7	NEW MEXICO	0	–	120	1.2	192	1.2
300	4.3	1,080	4.5	1,980	4.6	NEW YORK	200	4.5	80	0.8	407	2.5
0	–	80	0.3	230	0.5	NORTH CAROLINA	0	–	40	0.4	114	0.7
0	–	40	0.2	0	–	NORTH DAKOTA	0	–	0	–	35	0.2
100	1.4	760	3.1	802	1.9	OHIO	0	–	40	0.4	192	1.2
0	–	200	0.8	265	0.6	OKLAHOMA	0	–	240	2.4	124	0.8
500	7.1	560	2.3	558	1.3	OREGON	300	6.8	760	7.6	1,406	8.7
0	–	240	1.0	867	2.0	PENNSYLVANIA	0	–	0	–	136	0.8
0	–	40	0.2	124	0.3	RHODE ISLAND	0	–	0	–	0	–
0	–	0	–	61	0.1	SOUTH CAROLINA	0	–	0	–	54	0.3
300	4.3	160	0.7	26	0.1	SOUTH DAKOTA	0	–	40	0.4	101	0.6
0	–	40	0.2	170	0.4	TENNESSEE	0	–	40	0.4	51	0.3
100	1.4	600	2.5	1,063	2.5	TEXAS	100	2.3	560	5.6	492	3.0
200	2.9	360	1.5	766	1.8	UTAH	600	13.6	560	5.6	586	3.6
0	–	0	–	16	–	VERMONT	0	–	0	–	0	–
0	–	160	0.7	148	0.3	VIRGINIA	0	–	80	0.8	123	0.8
0	–	640	2.6	869	2.0	WASHINGTON	200	4.5	640	6.4	795	4.9
100	1.4	80	0.3	13	–	WEST VIRGINIA	0	–	0	–	18	0.1
0	–	240	1.0	682	1.6	WISCONSIN	100	2.3	0	–	170	1.1
0	–	200	0.8	362	0.8	WYOMING	0	–	40	0.4	7	–
7,000	99.8*	24,160	100.1*	43,131	100.1*	TOTAL U.S.	4,400	99.8*	10,040	100.2*	16,193	100.2*

*rounding error

NEW HAMPSHIRE

TO NEW HAMPSHIRE FROM							FROM NEW HAMPSHIRE TO					
1970		1980		1990			1970		1980		1990	
#	%	#	%	#	%		#	%	#	%	#	%
0	–	0	–	24	0.2	ALABAMA	100	1.9	40	0.4	115	0.9
0	–	0	–	31	0.2	ALASKA	0	–	0	–	0	–
0	–	80	0.6	7	0.1	ARIZONA	0	–	200	2.1	101	0.8
0	–	0	–	7	0.1	ARKANSAS	0	–	80	0.9	0	–
0	–	80	0.6	539	3.6	CALIFORNIA	100	1.9	440	4.7	345	2.7
0	–	0	–	0	–	COLORADO	100	1.9	120	1.3	69	0.5
300	5.0	720	5.8	761	5.1	CONNECTICUT	100	1.9	160	1.7	217	1.7
0	–	40	0.3	50	0.3	DELAWARE	0	–	0	–	0	–
0	–	40	0.3	0	–	D.C.	0	–	0	–	0	–
300	5.0	840	6.7	1,127	7.5	FLORIDA	1,800	34.0	2,840	30.2	5,504	43.1
0	–	0	–	0	–	GEORGIA	0	–	200	2.1	191	1.5
0	–	0	–	0	–	HAWAII	0	–	0	–	109	0.9
0	–	0	–	31	0.2	IDAHO	0	–	0	–	28	0.2
0	–	120	1.0	136	0.9	ILLINOIS	0	–	40	0.4	60	0.5
0	–	0	–	0	–	INDIANA	100	1.9	0	–	0	–
0	–	0	–	0	–	IOWA	0	–	0	–	0	–
0	–	0	–	0	–	KANSAS	0	–	0	–	0	–
0	–	0	–	0	–	KENTUCKY	0	–	0	–	65	0.5
100	1.7	0	–	28	0.2	LOUISIANA	0	–	0	–	39	0.3
300	5.0	760	6.1	714	4.7	MAINE	1,000	18.9	800	8.5	1,269	9.9
0	–	80	0.6	157	1.0	MARYLAND	0	–	160	1.7	72	0.6
3,300	55.0	6,400	51.3	7,058	46.9	MASSACHUSETTS	1,100	20.8	2,120	22.6	1,167	9.1
0	–	80	0.6	95	0.6	MICHIGAN	0	–	80	0.9	64	0.5
0	–	0	–	0	–	MINNESOTA	0	–	80	0.9	91	0.7
0	–	0	–	0	–	MISSISSIPPI	0	–	0	–	39	0.3
0	–	40	0.3	57	0.4	MISSOURI	0	–	0	–	99	0.8
0	–	0	–	0	–	MONTANA	0	–	0	–	34	0.3
0	–	0	–	0	–	NEBRASKA	100	1.9	0	–	0	–
0	–	0	–	0		NEVADA	0	–	80	0.9	24	0.2
0	–	680	5.4	747	5.0	NEW JERSEY	0	–	200	2.1	155	1.2
0	–	0	–	0	–	NEW MEXICO	0	–	0	–	90	0.7
800	13.3	1,240	9.9	1,329	8.8	NEW YORK	0	–	120	1.3	509	4.0
100	1.7	80	0.6	106	0.7	NORTH CAROLINA	0	–	120	1.3	174	1.4
0	–	0	–	0	–	NORTH DAKOTA	0	–	0	–	0	–
0	–	40	0.3	191	1.3	OHIO	0	–	160	1.7	26	0.2
0	–	40	0.3	17	0.1	OKLAHOMA	0	–	0	–	0	–
0	–	0	–	37	0.3	OREGON	0	–	40	0.4	39	0.3
100	1.7	240	1.9	304	2.0	PENNSYLVANIA	0	–	80	0.9	82	0.6
0	–	160	1.3	194	1.3	RHODE ISLAND	0	–	120	1.3	89	0.7
0	–	80	0.6	78	0.5	SOUTH CAROLINA	100	1.9	160	1.7	321	2.5
0	–	0	–	0	–	SOUTH DAKOTA	0	–	0	–	0	–
0	–	0	–	31	0.2	TENNESSEE	100	1.9	120	1.3	99	0.8
0	–	120	1.0	115	0.8	TEXAS	0	–	0	–	179	1.4
0	–	0	–	0	–	UTAH	0	–	0	–	0	–
500	8.3	400	3.2	944	6.3	VERMONT	600	11.3	480	5.1	771	6.0
0	–	120	1.0	126	0.8	VIRGINIA	0	–	120	1.3	387	3.0
0	–	0	–	0	–	WASHINGTON	0	–	120	1.3	141	1.1
200	3.3	0	–	0	–	WEST VIRGINIA	0	–	0	–	0	–
0	–	0	–	17	0.1	WISCONSIN	0	–	120	1.3	0	–
0	–	0	–	0	–	WYOMING	0	–	0	–	21	0.2
6,000	100.0	12,480	99.7*	15,058	100.2*	TOTAL U.S.	5,300	100.2*	9,400	100.3*	12,785	100.1*

*rounding error

NEW JERSEY

TO NEW JERSEY FROM							FROM NEW JERSEY TO					
1970		1980		1990			1970		1980		1990	
#	%	#	%	#	%		#	%	#	%	#	%
100	0.2	40	0.1	145	0.3	ALABAMA	100	0.2	80	0.1	503	0.5
0	–	0	–	18	–	ALASKA	0	–	0	–	38	–
500	1.1	320	0.6	311	0.6	ARIZONA	1,200	2.4	2,760	3.2	2,414	2.3
0	–	0	–	39	0.1	ARKANSAS	0	–	120	0.1	234	0.2
1,100	2.4	1,000	2.0	1,335	2.7	CALIFORNIA	3,900	7.8	5,400	6.2	4,611	4.3
100	0.2	320	0.6	99	0.2	COLORADO	300	0.6	520	0.6	876	0.8
400	0.9	680	1.4	847	1.7	CONNECTICUT	500	1.0	1,400	1.6	1,409	1.3
500	1.1	280	0.6	229	0.5	DELAWARE	700	1.4	920	1.1	1,272	1.2
300	0.7	120	0.2	76	0.2	D.C.	0	–	80	0.1	76	0.1
2,200	4.8	4,640	9.4	4,173	8.5	FLORIDA	21,800	43.5	38,440	44.2	41,315	38.8
200	0.4	360	0.7	497	1.0	GEORGIA	100	0.2	1,400	1.6	1,838	1.7
0	–	0	–	125	0.3	HAWAII	0	–	120	0.1	255	0.2
0	–	0	–	23	0.1	IDAHO	0	–	40	0.1	84	0.1
800	1.7	440	0.9	588	1.2	ILLINOIS	200	0.4	640	0.7	558	0.5
400	0.9	360	0.7	94	0.2	INDIANA	400	0.8	160	0.2	137	0.1
0	–	0	–	135	0.3	IOWA	0	–	80	0.1	97	0.1
0	–	0	–	96	0.2	KANSAS	0	–	40	0.1	303	0.3
100	0.2	120	0.2	144	0.3	KENTUCKY	200	0.4	240	0.3	481	0.5
100	0.2	0	–	138	0.3	LOUISIANA	0	–	0	–	201	0.2
300	0.7	200	0.4	77	0.2	MAINE	200	0.4	560	0.6	734	0.7
1,100	2.4	480	1.0	1,198	2.4	MARYLAND	1,300	2.6	1,720	2.0	2,494	2.3
900	2.0	880	1.8	1,182	2.4	MASSACHUSETTS	1,200	2.4	1,880	2.2	2,009	1.9
600	1.3	120	0.2	176	0.4	MICHIGAN	600	1.2	400	0.5	474	0.4
0	–	80	0.2	32	0.1	MINNESOTA	0	–	200	0.2	87	0.1
0	–	80	0.2	0	–	MISSISSIPPI	100	0.2	240	0.3	45	–
200	0.4	200	0.4	143	0.3	MISSOURI	1,000	2.0	240	0.3	321	0.3
0	–	0	–	0	–	MONTANA	0	–	80	0.1	217	0.2
0	–	0	–	11	–	NEBRASKA	0	–	0	–	98	0.1
0	–	0	–	160	0.3	NEVADA	200	0.4	280	0.3	592	0.6
0	–	200	0.4	155	0.3	NEW HAMPSHIRE	0	–	680	0.8	747	0.7
0	–	0	–	115	0.2	NEW MEXICO	600	1.2	320	0.4	261	0.2
23,000	50.0	24,320	49.2	23,903	48.6	NEW YORK	7,500	15.0	7,120	8.2	7,716	7.2
300	0.7	240	0.5	374	0.8	NORTH CAROLINA	300	0.6	3,160	3.6	5,871	5.5
0	–	0	–	0	–	NORTH DAKOTA	0	–	80	0.1	35	–
500	1.1	640	1.3	585	1.2	OHIO	500	1.0	720	0.8	897	0.8
100	0.2	0	–	86	0.2	OKLAHOMA	0	–	320	0.4	306	0.3
0	–	80	0.2	35	0.1	OREGON	100	0.2	80	0.1	242	0.2
10,500	22.8	11,480	23.2	9,663	19.7	PENNSYLVANIA	4,600	9.2	10,200	11.7	14,820	13.9
200	0.4	200	0.4	128	0.3	RHODE ISLAND	300	0.6	240	0.3	227	0.2
200	0.4	280	0.6	214	0.4	SOUTH CAROLINA	300	0.6	760	0.9	3,021	2.8
0	–	0	–	0	–	SOUTH DAKOTA	100	0.2	40	0.1	0	–
100	0.2	40	0.1	161	0.3	TENNESSEE	0	–	480	0.6	891	0.8
100	0.2	320	0.6	454	0.9	TEXAS	500	1.0	1,960	2.3	1,325	1.2
0	–	0	–	0	–	UTAH	0	–	120	0.1	28	–
0	–	240	0.5	64	0.1	VERMONT	100	0.2	480	0.6	588	0.6
700	1.5	400	0.8	783	1.6	VIRGINIA	1,000	2.0	1,400	1.6	4,116	3.9
0	–	0	–	146	0.3	WASHINGTON	0	–	240	0.3	774	0.7
300	0.7	120	0.2	21	–	WEST VIRGINIA	0	–	280	0.3	582	0.6
100	0.2	120	0.2	108	0.2	WISCONSIN	200	0.4	160	0.2	297	0.3
0	–	0	–	90	0.2	WYOMING	0	–	0	–	39	–
46,000	**100.0**	**49,400**	**99.8***	**49,176**	**100.2***	**TOTAL U.S.**	**50,100**	**100.1***	**86,880**	**100.3***	**106,556**	**99.7***

*rounding error

NEW MEXICO

TO NEW MEXICO FROM							FROM NEW MEXICO TO					
1970		1980		1990			1970		1980		1990	
#	%	#	%	#	%		#	%	#	%	#	%
0	–	40	0.2	60	0.3	ALABAMA	0	–	40	0.4	22	0.2
100	0.9	80	0.5	0	–	ALASKA	0	–	0	–	83	0.6
400	3.7	720	4.2	1,512	7.6	ARIZONA	500	6.0	1,560	15.4	2,009	13.7
100	0.9	400	2.3	180	0.9	ARKANSAS	100	1.2	200	2.0	181	1.2
1,800	16.8	2,440	14.2	3,708	18.7	CALIFORNIA	1,400	16.9	1,280	12.6	1,583	10.8
500	4.7	1,120	6.5	1,662	8.4	COLORADO	1,400	16.9	600	5.9	1,326	9.0
0	–	80	0.5	261	1.3	CONNECTICUT	0	–	120	1.2	23	0.2
0	–	0	–	9	0.1	DELAWARE	0	–	0	–	0	–
0	–	80	0.5	60	0.3	D.C.	0	–	0	–	0	–
100	0.9	360	2.1	612	3.1	FLORIDA	400	4.8	360	3.5	647	4.4
0	–	120	0.7	126	0.6	GEORGIA	0	–	200	2.0	111	0.8
0	–	40	0.2	105	0.5	HAWAII	100	1.2	0	–	0	–
100	0.9	0	–	186	0.9	IDAHO	0	–	0	–	88	0.6
600	5.6	1,000	5.8	969	4.9	ILLINOIS	200	2.4	160	1.6	156	1.1
200	1.9	320	1.9	276	1.4	INDIANA	0	–	0	–	156	1.1
200	1.9	360	2.1	69	0.4	IOWA	0	–	40	0.4	33	0.2
100	0.9	120	0.7	330	1.7	KANSAS	400	4.8	560	5.5	183	1.3
0	–	0	–	24	0.1	KENTUCKY	0	–	160	1.6	134	0.9
0	–	160	0.9	96	0.5	LOUISIANA	0	–	120	1.2	126	0.9
100	0.9	40	0.2	6	–	MAINE	0	–	0		26	0.2
100	0.9	160	0.9	246	1.2	MARYLAND	0	–	0	–	16	0.1
0	–	120	0.7	129	0.7	MASSACHUSETTS	0	–	40	0.4	52	0.4
800	7.5	840	4.9	306	1.5	MICHIGAN	0	–	80	0.8	357	2.4
200	1.9	600	3.5	102	0.5	MINNESOTA	100	1.2	0	–	282	1.9
0	–	40	0.2	27	0.1	MISSISSIPPI	0	–	40	0.4	51	0.4
0	–	520	3.0	456	2.3	MISSOURI	300	3.6	160	1.6	216	1.5
0	–	120	0.7	21	0.1	MONTANA	0	–	40	0.4	22	0.2
100	0.9	0	–	273	1.4	NEBRASKA	100	1.2	0	–	269	1.8
100	0.9	120	0.7	192	1.0	NEVADA	100	1.2	400	3.9	320	2.2
0	–	0	–	90	0.5	NEW HAMPSHIRE	0	–	0	–	0	–
600	5.6	320	1.9	261	1.3	NEW JERSEY	0	–	0	–	115	0.8
500	4.7	1,040	6.1	795	4.0	NEW YORK	100	1.2	80	0.8	145	1.0
0	–	80	0.5	18	0.1	NORTH CAROLINA	0	–	0	–	60	0.4
100	0.9	0	–	90	0.5	NORTH DAKOTA	0	–	0	–	35	0.2
300	2.8	560	3.3	414	2.1	OHIO	0	–	200	2.0	157	1.1
200	1.9	800	4.7	546	2.8	OKLAHOMA	200	2.4	680	6.7	416	2.8
300	2.8	280	1.6	123	0.6	OREGON	200	2.4	80	0.8	169	1.2
800	7.5	280	1.6	288	1.5	PENNSYLVANIA	100	1.2	80	0.8	180	1.2
0	–	0	–	27	0.1	RHODE ISLAND	0	–	0	–	62	0.4
0	–	0	–	6	–	SOUTH CAROLINA	0	–	0	–	45	0.3
0	–	80	0.5	72	0.4	SOUTH DAKOTA	0	–	0	–	0	–
0	–	40	0.2	126	0.6	TENNESSEE	0	–	40	0.4	87	0.6
2,000	18.7	2,440	14.2	3,768	19.0	TEXAS	2,300	27.7	2,400	23.6	3,537	24.1
0	–	240	1.4	45	0.2	UTAH	200	2.4	40	0.4	370	2.5
0	–	0	–	27	0.1	VERMONT	0	–	0	–	0	–
0	–	80	0.5	336	1.7	VIRGINIA	100	1.2	160	1.6	189	1.3
200	1.9	240	1.4	270	1.4	WASHINGTON	0	–	80	0.8	267	1.8
0	–	200	1.2	18	0.1	WEST VIRGINIA	0	–	0	–	53	0.4
0	–	360	2.1	303	1.5	WISCONSIN	0	–	40	0.4	339	2.3
100	0.9	120	0.7	246	1.2	WYOMING	0	–	120	1.2	0	–
10,700	99.8*	17,160	100.0	19,872	100.2*	TOTAL U.S.	8,300	99.9*	10,160	100.3*	14,698	100.5*

*rounding error

NEW YORK

TO NEW YORK FROM							FROM NEW YORK TO					
1970		**1980**		**1990**			**1970**		**1980**		**1990**	
#	%	#	%	#	%		#	%	#	%	#	%
200	0.6	360	1.0	243	0.6	ALABAMA	400	0.3	1,360	0.6	947	0.4
0	–	0	–	19	–	ALASKA	0	–	0	–	31	–
0	–	560	1.6	821	1.9	ARIZONA	3,300	2.1	6,840	2.8	5,116	2.3
100	0.3	120	0.3	46	0.1	ARKANSAS	700	0.5	720	0.3	256	0.1
2,200	6.7	2,160	6.2	3,280	7.7	CALIFORNIA	11,000	7.1	18,360	7.6	11,695	5.3
100	0.3	160	0.5	221	0.5	COLORADO	400	0.3	1,440	0.6	1,146	0.5
3,000	9.1	2,000	5.7	2,672	6.2	CONNECTICUT	8,000	5.2	7,480	3.1	5,689	2.6
200	0.6	80	0.2	189	0.4	DELAWARE	200	0.1	920	0.4	615	0.3
500	1.5	160	0.5	442	1.0	D.C.	400	0.3	200	0.1	424	0.2
3,700	11.3	9,000	25.8	9,063	21.1	FLORIDA	73,500	47.6	127,600	52.5	104,019	46.7
300	0.9	360	1.0	384	0.9	GEORGIA	300	0.2	2,240	0.9	3,396	1.5
0	–	40	0.1	151	0.4	HAWAII	300	0.2	200	0.1	304	0.1
0	–	0	–	45	0.1	IDAHO	0	–	80	–	216	0.1
1,000	3.0	800	2.3	899	2.1	ILLINOIS	1,700	1.1	1,240	0.5	933	0.4
500	1.5	320	0.9	204	0.5	INDIANA	500	0.3	280	0.1	961	0.4
0	–	80	0.2	175	0.4	IOWA	300	0.2	120	–	228	0.1
0	–	0	–	78	0.2	KANSAS	0	–	240	0.1	486	0.2
100	0.3	120	0.3	194	0.5	KENTUCKY	500	0.3	440	0.2	434	0.2
0	–	120	0.3	148	0.4	LOUISIANA	100	0.1	280	0.1	321	0.1
200	0.6	120	0.3	274	0.6	MAINE	300	0.2	680	0.3	1,148	0.5
500	1.5	640	1.8	858	2.0	MARYLAND	2,400	1.6	3,280	1.4	4,185	1.9
1,900	5.8	1,040	3.0	1,957	4.6	MASSACHUSETTS	3,600	2.3	4,080	1.7	4,680	2.1
800	2.4	720	2.1	770	1.8	MICHIGAN	600	0.4	1,000	0.4	820	0.4
100	0.3	240	0.7	70	0.2	MINNESOTA	300	0.2	200	0.1	509	0.2
0	–	80	0.2	165	0.4	MISSISSIPPI	300	0.2	640	0.3	225	0.1
300	0.9	320	0.9	386	0.9	MISSOURI	600	0.4	560	0.2	654	0.3
100	0.3	0	–	14	–	MONTANA	0	–	40	–	86	–
100	0.3	120	0.3	37	0.1	NEBRASKA	100	0.1	160	0.1	100	–
200	0.6	80	0.2	407	1.0	NEVADA	300	0.2	1,080	0.4	1,980	0.9
0	–	120	0.3	509	1.2	NEW HAMPSHIRE	800	0.5	1,240	0.5	1,329	0.6
7,500	22.9	7,120	20.4	7,716	18.0	NEW JERSEY	23,000	14.9	24,320	10.0	23,903	10.7
100	0.3	80	0.2	145	0.3	NEW MEXICO	500	0.3	1,040	0.4	795	0.4
700	2.1	440	1.3	1,083	2.5	NORTH CAROLINA	1,600	1.0	6,200	2.6	10,356	4.7
0	–	0	–	0	–	NORTH DAKOTA	0	–	0	–	50	–
1,600	4.9	1,040	3.0	942	2.2	OHIO	2,000	1.3	2,280	0.9	2,263	1.0
100	0.3	80	0.2	71	0.2	OKLAHOMA	300	0.2	360	0.1	337	0.2
0	–	0	–	107	0.3	OREGON	0	–	680	0.3	440	0.2
4,600	14.0	3,200	9.2	3,570	8.3	PENNSYLVANIA	7,100	4.6	8,440	3.5	10,404	4.7
300	0.9	240	0.7	257	0.6	RHODE ISLAND	800	0.5	760	0.3	1,019	0.5
300	0.9	600	1.7	636	1.5	SOUTH CAROLINA	1,700	1.1	2,760	1.1	4,794	2.2
0	–	80	0.2	0	–	SOUTH DAKOTA	100	0.1	80	–	38	–
100	0.3	360	1.0	132	0.3	TENNESSEE	300	0.2	1,280	0.5	1,119	0.5
400	1.2	280	0.8	1,259	2.9	TEXAS	1,100	0.7	3,400	1.4	3,642	1.6
0	–	120	0.3	55	0.1	UTAH	0	–	160	0.1	84	–
0	–	160	0.5	401	0.9	VERMONT	1,500	1.0	1,280	0.5	1,603	0.7
700	2.1	600	1.7	1,333	3.1	VIRGINIA	1,900	1.2	5,320	2.2	6,972	3.1
200	0.6	240	0.7	90	0.2	WASHINGTON	600	0.4	1,040	0.4	1,146	0.5
100	0.3	40	0.1	134	0.3	WEST VIRGINIA	400	0.3	320	0.1	525	0.2
0	–	320	0.9	109	0.3	WISCONSIN	500	0.3	200	0.1	318	0.1
0	–	0	–	41	0.1	WYOMING	0	–	40	–	40	–
32,800	99.6*	34,920	99.6*	42,802	100.0	**TOTAL U.S.**	154,300	100.1*	242,960	99.9*	222,781	99.8*

*rounding error

NORTH CAROLINA

TO NORTH CAROLINA FROM							FROM NORTH CAROLINA TO					
1970		1980		1990			1970		1980		1990	
#	%	#	%	#	%		#	%	#	%	#	%
200	1.2	200	0.5	441	0.7	ALABAMA	200	1.5	280	1.5	355	1.3
0	–	0	–	87	0.1	ALASKA	0	–	0	–	8	–
0	–	200	0.5	387	0.6	ARIZONA	0	–	40	0.2	266	1.0
100	0.6	40	0.1	270	0.4	ARKANSAS	0	–	120	0.6	208	0.8
900	5.2	1,080	2.7	1,962	3.0	CALIFORNIA	400	3.1	840	4.4	626	2.4
0	–	40	0.1	321	0.5	COLORADO	100	0.8	80	0.4	177	0.7
300	1.7	880	2.2	1,428	2.2	CONNECTICUT	200	1.5	120	0.6	249	0.9
500	2.9	0	–	174	0.3	DELAWARE	100	0.8	80	0.4	114	0.4
900	5.2	400	1.0	573	0.9	D.C.	0	–	360	1.9	248	0.9
1,900	11.0	5,680	14.4	8,841	13.7	FLORIDA	2,600	19.8	4,800	25.0	6,385	24.2
400	2.3	1,040	2.6	2,172	3.4	GEORGIA	1,300	9.9	1,720	9.0	1,506	5.7
0	–	40	0.1	192	0.3	HAWAII	200	1.5	0	–	23	0.1
0	–	40	0.1	21	–	IDAHO	0	–	40	0.2	0	–
300	1.7	920	2.3	2,199	3.4	ILLINOIS	400	3.1	200	1.0	321	1.2
100	0.6	320	0.8	711	1.1	INDIANA	300	2.3	120	0.6	272	1.0
400	2.3	80	0.2	114	0.2	IOWA	100	0.8	80	0.4	0	–
0	–	120	0.3	264	0.4	KANSAS	0	–	40	0.2	0	–
100	0.6	240	0.6	897	1.4	KENTUCKY	0	–	120	0.6	360	1.4
0	–	240	0.6	327	0.5	LOUISIANA	0	–	120	0.6	336	1.3
0	–	360	0.9	174	0.3	MAINE	0	–	40	0.2	79	0.3
700	4.1	2,040	5.2	2,844	4.4	MARYLAND	400	3.1	560	2.9	739	2.8
200	1.2	840	2.1	1,329	2.1	MASSACHUSETTS	100	0.8	80	0.4	295	1.1
500	2.9	840	2.1	2,127	3.3	MICHIGAN	100	0.8	320	1.7	268	1.0
0	–	160	0.4	240	0.4	MINNESOTA	0	–	0	–	189	0.7
0	–	200	0.5	204	0.3	MISSISSIPPI	0	–	120	0.6	195	0.7
0	–	240	0.6	297	0.5	MISSOURI	0	–	160	0.8	118	0.5
0	–	80	0.2	102	0.2	MONTANA	0	–	0	–	18	0.1
0	–	40	0.1	42	0.1	NEBRASKA	0	–	0	–	30	0.1
0	–	40	0.1	114	0.2	NEVADA	0	–	80	0.4	230	0.9
0	–	120	0.3	174	0.3	NEW HAMPSHIRE	100	0.8	80	0.4	106	0.4
300	1.7	3,160	8.0	5,871	9.1	NEW JERSEY	300	2.3	240	1.3	374	1.4
0	–	0	–	60	0.1	NEW MEXICO	0	–	80	0.4	18	0.1
1,600	9.3	6,200	15.7	10,356	16.1	NEW YORK	700	5.3	440	2.3	1,083	4.1
0	–	80	0.2	18	–	NORTH DAKOTA	0	–	0	–	80	0.3
700	4.1	1,640	4.2	2,505	3.9	OHIO	200	1.5	240	1.3	769	2.9
0	–	200	0.5	213	0.3	OKLAHOMA	0	–	160	0.8	261	1.0
0	–	0	–	48	0.1	OREGON	0	–	120	0.6	83	0.3
1,200	7.0	1,720	4.4	3,003	4.7	PENNSYLVANIA	0	–	560	2.9	925	3.5
0	–	40	0.1	141	0.2	RHODE ISLAND	0	–	0	–	0	–
1,700	9.9	2,200	5.6	3,204	5.0	SOUTH CAROLINA	2,200	16.8	3,000	15.6	3,747	14.2
0	–	40	0.1	111	0.2	SOUTH DAKOTA	0	–	0	–	0	–
400	2.3	600	1.5	873	1.4	TENNESSEE	500	3.8	720	3.8	1,338	5.1
300	1.7	480	1.2	1,299	2.0	TEXAS	500	3.8	440	2.3	392	1.5
0	–	160	0.4	102	0.7	UTAH	100	0.8	40	0.2	58	0.2
100	0.6	120	0.3	273	0.4	VERMONT	0	–	40	0.2	16	0.1
3,000	17.4	5,080	12.9	6,102	9.5	VIRGINIA	1,900	14.5	2,080	10.8	2,901	11.0
100	0.6	80	0.2	114	0.2	WASHINGTON	100	0.8	120	0.6	186	0.7
100	0.6	720	1.8	891	1.4	WEST VIRGINIA	0	–	240	1.3	330	1.3
200	1.2	240	0.6	318	0.5	WISCONSIN	0	–	40	0.2	154	0.6
0	–	120	0.3	0	–	WYOMING	0	–	40	0.2	0	–
17,200	99.9*	39,400	99.6*	64,530	101.0*	TOTAL U.S.	13,100	100.2*	19,200	99.8*	26,436	100.2*

*rounding error

NORTH DAKOTA

	TO NORTH DAKOTA FROM							FROM NORTH DAKOTA TO					
	1970		**1980**		**1990**			**1970**		**1980**		**1990**	
	#	%	#	%	#	%		#	%	#	%	#	%
	0	–	0	–	0	–	ALABAMA	0	–	0	–	0	–
	0	–	0	–	0	–	ALASKA	0	–	0	–	0	–
	0	–	40	1.6	65	2.1	ARIZONA	600	15.4	560	11.1	465	10.8
	0	–	0	–	0	–	ARKANSAS	0	–	0	–	115	2.7
	700	23.3	200	7.8	375	11.9	CALIFORNIA	500	12.8	440	8.7	457	10.6
	0	–	80	3.1	150	4.8	COLORADO	0	–	80	1.6	384	8.9
	0	–	0	–	0	–	CONNECTICUT	0	–	40	0.8	0	–
	0	–	0	–	0	–	DELAWARE	0	–	0	–	0	–
	0	–	0	–	60	1.9	D.C.	100	2.6	0	–	0	–
	0	–	0	–	45	1.4	FLORIDA	0	–	160	3.2	76	1.8
	0	–	0	–	0	–	GEORGIA	0	–	0	–	0	–
	0	–	0	–	0	–	HAWAII	0	–	0	–	0	–
	0	–	0	–	0	–	IDAHO	0	–	240	4.8	124	2.9
	100	3.3	120	4.7	80	2.6	ILLINOIS	0	–	0	–	51	1.2
	0	–	0	–	65	2.1	INDIANA	0	–	40	0.8	16	0.4
	300	10.0	40	1.6	20	0.6	IOWA	0	–	80	1.6	38	0.9
	100	3.3	0	–	0	–	KANSAS	0	–	0	–	47	1.1
	0	–	0	–	10	0.3	KENTUCKY	0	–	40	0.8	0	–
	0	–	0	–	10	0.3	LOUISIANA	0	–	0	–	0	–
	0	–	0	–	0	–	MAINE	0	–	0	–	5	0.1
	0	–	0	–	25	0.8	MARYLAND	0	–	0	–	3	0.1
	0	–	0	–	50	1.6	MASSACHUSETTS	0	–	0	–	29	0.7
	0	–	80	3.1	10	0.3	MICHIGAN	0	–	0	–	0	–
	1,300	43.3	600	23.4	1,045	33.3	MINNESOTA	1,100	28.2	1,800	35.7	1,014	23.5
	0	–	40	1.6	0	–	MISSISSIPPI	0	–	0	–	0	–
	0	–	80	3.1	10	0.3	MISSOURI	0	–	40	0.8	0	–
	0	–	360	14.1	225	7.2	MONTANA	100	2.6	280	5.6	257	6.0
	0	–	0	–	75	2.4	NEBRASKA	0	–	80	1.6	50	1.2
	0	–	0	–	35	1.1	NEVADA	0	–	40	0.8	0	–
	0	–	0	–	0	–	NEW HAMPSHIRE	0	–	0	–	0	–
	0	–	80	3.1	35	1.1	NEW JERSEY	0	–	0	–	0	–
	0	–	0	–	35	1.1	NEW MEXICO	100	2.6	0	–	90	2.1
	0	–	0	–	50	1.6	NEW YORK	0	–	0	–	0	–
	0	–	0	–	80	2.6	NORTH CAROLINA	0	–	80	1.6	18	0.4
	0	–	80	3.1	0	–	OHIO	100	2.6	0	–	42	1.0
	0	–	0	–	10	0.3	OKLAHOMA	0	–	80	1.6	14	0.3
	0	–	160	6.3	45	1.4	OREGON	700	17.9	80	1.6	186	4.3
	100	3.3	0	–	95	3.0	PENNSYLVANIA	0	–	0	–	18	0.4
	0	–	0	–	0	–	RHODE ISLAND	0	–	0	–	0	–
	0	–	0	–	0	–	SOUTH CAROLINA	0	–	0	–	0	–
	300	10.0	320	12.5	260	8.3	SOUTH DAKOTA	200	5.1	280	5.6	156	3.6
	0	–	0	–	0	–	TENNESSEE	0	–	0	–	48	1.1
	0	–	40	1.6	0	–	TEXAS	0	–	160	3.2	121	2.8
	0	–	0	–	0	–	UTAH	0	–	0	–	75	1.7
	100	3.3	0	–	0	–	VERMONT	0	–	0	–	0	–
	0	–	40	1.6	0	–	VIRGINIA	0	–	0	–	0	–
	0	–	120	4.7	40	1.3	WASHINGTON	300	7.7	200	4.0	198	4.6
	0	–	0	–	30	1.0	WEST VIRGINIA	0	–	0	–	0	–
	0	–	80	3.1	50	1.6	WISCONSIN	100	2.6	200	4.0	68	1.6
	0	–	0	–	55	1.8	WYOMING	0	–	40	0.8	155	3.6
	3,000	**99.8***	**2,560**	**100.1***	**3,140**	**100.1***	**TOTAL U.S.**	**3,900**	**100.1***	**5,040**	**100.3***	**4,320**	**100.4***

*rounding error

142 Retirement Migration in America

OHIO

TO OHIO FROM							FROM OHIO TO					
1970		1980		1990			1970		1980		1990	
#	%	#	%	#	%		#	%	#	%	#	%
400	1.2	280	0.9	494	1.1	ALABAMA	800	1.5	840	1.0	872	1.2
0	–	0	–	51	0.1	ALASKA	0	–	0	–	37	0.1
200	0.6	400	1.2	987	2.2	ARIZONA	2,400	4.5	5,080	5.9	3,375	4.5
200	0.6	120	0.4	278	0.6	ARKANSAS	100	0.2	480	0.6	427	0.6
2,400	7.4	1,600	4.9	3,241	7.3	CALIFORNIA	6,000	11.2	6,760	7.9	4,039	5.4
100	0.3	440	1.3	437	1.0	COLORADO	400	0.7	800	0.9	678	0.9
400	1.2	80	0.2	532	1.2	CONNECTICUT	0	–	160	0.2	418	0.6
0	–	120	0.4	37	0.1	DELAWARE	0	–	80	0.1	79	0.1
100	0.3	80	0.2	143	0.3	D.C.	200	0.4	160	0.2	45	0.1
4,600	14.2	5,120	15.7	8,707	19.6	FLORIDA	19,300	36.1	37,720	44.0	27,986	37.7
600	1.9	400	1.2	519	1.2	GEORGIA	800	1.5	1,160	1.4	1,618	2.2
0	–	80	0.2	94	0.2	HAWAII	0	–	80	0.1	56	0.1
0	–	120	0.4	71	0.2	IDAHO	0	–	40	0.1	92	0.1
2,100	6.5	1,440	4.4	1,762	4.0	ILLINOIS	1,500	2.8	1,600	1.9	1,272	1.7
1,700	5.3	1,520	4.7	2,341	5.3	INDIANA	1,900	3.6	2,800	3.3	3,283	4.4
1,000	3.1	40	0.1	65	0.2	IOWA	200	0.4	200	0.2	146	0.2
100	0.3	120	0.4	258	0.6	KANSAS	200	0.4	80	0.1	172	0.2
1,900	5.9	2,840	8.7	2,944	6.6	KENTUCKY	2,100	3.9	4,120	4.8	3,810	5.1
0	–	120	0.4	421	1.0	LOUISIANA	100	0.2	0	–	384	0.5
0	–	0	–	155	0.4	MAINE	100	0.2	200	0.2	273	0.4
0	–	800	2.4	758	1.7	MARYLAND	200	0.4	600	0.7	657	0.9
300	0.9	280	0.9	415	0.9	MASSACHUSETTS	100	0.2	240	0.3	319	0.4
2,800	8.7	3,640	11.1	3,433	7.7	MICHIGAN	3,100	5.8	2,800	3.3	2,394	3.2
400	1.2	200	0.6	168	0.4	MINNESOTA	400	0.7	240	0.3	363	0.5
200	0.6	120	0.4	235	0.5	MISSISSIPPI	500	0.9	400	0.5	435	0.6
400	1.2	360	1.1	616	1.4	MISSOURI	500	0.9	560	0.7	668	0.9
0	–	40	0.1	58	0.1	MONTANA	0	–	40	0.1	164	0.2
100	0.3	80	0.2	80	0.2	NEBRASKA	0	–	80	0.1	76	0.1
0	–	40	0.1	192	0.4	NEVADA	100	0.2	760	0.9	802	1.1
0	–	160	0.5	26	0.1	NEW HAMPSHIRE	0	–	40	0.1	191	0.3
500	1.5	720	2.2	897	2.0	NEW JERSEY	500	0.9	640	0.7	585	0.8
0	–	200	0.6	157	0.4	NEW MEXICO	300	0.6	560	0.7	414	0.6
2,000	6.2	2,280	7.0	2,263	5.1	NEW YORK	1,600	3.0	1,040	1.2	942	1.3
200	0.6	240	0.7	769	1.7	NORTH CAROLINA	700	1.3	1,640	1.9	2,505	3.4
100	0.3	0	–	42	0.1	NORTH DAKOTA	0	–	80	0.1	0	–
100	0.3	160	0.5	341	0.8	OKLAHOMA	500	0.9	320	0.4	190	0.3
0	–	120	0.4	181	0.4	OREGON	200	0.4	240	0.3	328	0.4
3,300	10.2	2,880	8.8	3,161	7.1	PENNSYLVANIA	2,400	4.5	2,120	2.5	2,607	3.5
0	–	0	–	70	0.2	RHODE ISLAND	0	–	80	0.1	47	0.1
100	0.3	40	0.1	703	1.6	SOUTH CAROLINA	100	0.2	1,520	1.8	1,860	2.5
0	–	40	0.1	61	0.1	SOUTH DAKOTA	0	–	40	0.1	15	–
700	2.2	1,240	3.8	794	1.8	TENNESSEE	1,200	2.2	2,960	3.5	2,058	2.8
500	1.5	320	1.0	1,441	3.2	TEXAS	900	1.7	2,240	2.6	2,145	2.9
100	0.3	0	–	92	0.2	UTAH	0	–	0	–	111	0.2
0	–	0	–	112	0.3	VERMONT	0	–	0	–	93	0.1
800	2.5	600	1.8	774	1.7	VIRGINIA	400	0.7	920	1.1	1,740	2.3
200	0.6	80	0.2	228	0.5	WASHINGTON	500	0.9	560	0.7	468	0.6
3,300	10.2	2,800	8.6	2390	5.4	WEST VIRGINIA	2,500	4.7	2,160	2.5	2,638	3.6
400	1.2	320	1.0	427	1.0	WISCONSIN	600	1.1	400	0.5	322	0.4
0	–	0	–	38	0.1	WYOMING	0	–	120	0.1	72	0.1
32,300	99.6*	32,680	99.9*	44,459	100.3*	TOTAL U.S.	53,400	99.8*	85,760	100.7*	74,271	100.2*

*rounding error

OKLAHOMA

		TO OKLAHOMA FROM						FROM OKLAHOMA TO					
1970		**1980**		**1990**			**1970**		**1980**		**1990**	
#	%	#	%	#	%		#	%	#	%	#	%
200	1.4	280	1.2	92	0.4	ALABAMA	100	0.7	120	0.7	143	0.7
0	–	0	–	35	0.2	ALASKA	300	2.2	0	–	0	–
800	5.4	520	2.3	822	3.5	ARIZONA	200	1.5	640	3.5	1,178	5.6
700	4.7	1,400	6.2	1,514	6.4	ARKANSAS	1,500	10.9	1,920	10.6	1,721	8.2
3,300	22.3	4,880	21.6	4,451	18.9	CALIFORNIA	1,600	11.7	1,880	10.4	2,746	13.0
0	–	880	3.9	985	4.2	COLORADO	100	0.7	800	4.4	438	2.1
100	0.7	0	–	156	0.7	CONNECTICUT	0	–	0	–	31	0.2
0	–	0	–	23	0.1	DELAWARE	0	–	0	–	0	–
100	0.7	0	–	37	0.2	D.C.	0	–	0	–	27	0.1
200	1.4	680	3.0	662	2.8	FLORIDA	700	5.1	840	4.6	1,084	5.1
0	–	0	–	143	0.6	GEORGIA	100	0.7	120	0.7	87	0.4
0	–	0	–	100	0.4	HAWAII	0	–	80	0.4	17	0.1
0	–	120	0.5	48	0.2	IDAHO	0	–	40	0.2	60	0.3
300	2.0	800	3.5	504	2.1	ILLINOIS	100	0.7	240	1.3	423	2.0
100	0.7	200	0.9	244	1.0	INDIANA	0	–	80	0.4	201	1.0
0	–	120	0.5	278	1.2	IOWA	400	2.9	0	–	142	0.7
1,300	8.8	2,320	10.3	1,949	8.3	KANSAS	1,700	12.4	1,120	6.2	1,280	6.1
0	–	160	0.7	31	0.1	KENTUCKY	300	2.2	80	0.4	190	0.9
200	1.4	160	0.7	568	2.4	LOUISIANA	100	0.7	120	0.7	213	1.0
0	–	0	–	24	0.1	MAINE	0	–	40	0.2	0	–
0	–	80	0.4	95	0.4	MARYLAND	0	–	40	0.2	136	0.7
0	–	0	–	64	0.3	MASSACHUSETTS	0	–	0	–	70	0.3
0	–	280	1.2	179	0.8	MICHIGAN	0	–	80	0.4	197	0.9
200	1.4	240	1.1	118	0.5	MINNESOTA	200	1.5	0	–	28	0.1
0	–	160	0.7	210	0.9	MISSISSIPPI	0	–	160	0.9	84	0.4
1,400	9.5	1,320	5.8	1,548	6.6	MISSOURI	600	4.4	1,160	6.4	1,039	4.9
100	0.7	0	–	92	0.4	MONTANA	100	0.7	0	–	49	0.2
100	0.7	200	0.9	118	0.5	NEBRASKA	0	–	80	0.4	190	0.9
0	–	240	1.1	124	0.5	NEVADA	0	–	200	1.1	265	1.3
0	–	0	–	0	–	NEW HAMPSHIRE	0	–	40	0.2	17	0.1
0	–	320	1.4	306	1.3	NEW JERSEY	100	0.7	0	–	86	0.4
200	1.4	680	3.0	416	1.8	NEW MEXICO	200	1.5	800	4.4	546	2.6
300	2.0	360	1.6	337	1.4	NEW YORK	100	0.7	80	0.4	71	0.3
0	–	160	0.7	261	1.1	NORTH CAROLINA	0	–	200	1.1	213	1.0
0	–	80	0.4	14	0.1	NORTH DAKOTA	0	–	0	–	10	0.1
500	3.4	320	1.4	190	0.8	OHIO	100	0.7	160	0.9	341	1.6
0	–	280	1.2	201	0.9	OREGON	0	–	400	2.2	524	2.5
200	1.4	0	–	202	0.9	PENNSYLVANIA	200	1.5	120	0.7	88	0.4
0	–	0	–	30	0.1	RHODE ISLAND	0	–	0	–	0	–
0	–	0	–	102	0.4	SOUTH CAROLINA	0	–	120	0.7	63	0.3
0	–	120	0.5	0	–	SOUTH DAKOTA	0	–	40	0.2	34	0.2
200	1.4	200	0.9	173	0.7	TENNESSEE	100	0.7	400	2.2	318	1.5
3,800	25.7	4,080	18.1	5,562	23.6	TEXAS	4,300	31.4	5,560	30.8	5,965	28.3
0	–	40	0.2	102	0.4	UTAH	0	–	40	0.2	116	0.6
0	–	0	–	0	–	VERMONT	0	–	0	–	21	0.1
100	0.7	160	0.7	78	0.3	VIRGINIA	200	1.5	160	0.9	129	0.6
300	2.0	520	2.3	188	0.8	WASHINGTON	300	2.2	80	0.4	267	1.3
0	–	0	–	7	–	WEST VIRGINIA	0	–	40	0.2	44	0.2
0	–	40	0.2	87	0.4	WISCONSIN	0	–	0	–	105	0.5
100	0.7	200	0.9	102	0.4	WYOMING	0	–	0	–	77	0.4
14,800	**100.5***	**22,600**	**100.0**	**23,572**	**100.1***	**TOTAL U.S.**	**13,700**	**99.9***	**18,080**	**99.6***	**21,074**	**100.2***

*rounding error

OREGON

| TO OREGON FROM | | | | | | | FROM OREGON TO | | | | | |
| 1970 | | 1980 | | 1990 | | | 1970 | | 1980 | | 1990 | |
#	%	#	%	#	%		#	%	#	%	#	%
0	–	0	–	134	0.3	ALABAMA	200	1.7	80	0.4	20	0.1
300	1.7	400	1.2	611	1.4	ALASKA	100	0.9	80	0.4	219	1.0
100	0.6	840	2.5	1,181	2.7	ARIZONA	500	4.3	1,800	9.4	1,971	8.7
100	0.6	160	0.5	125	0.3	ARKANSAS	100	0.9	440	2.3	166	0.7
7,600	44.2	17,080	50.8	23,069	52.4	CALIFORNIA	4,400	37.9	5,960	31.0	6,151	27.0
300	1.7	1,040	3.1	838	1.9	COLORADO	0	–	240	1.2	429	1.9
0	–	40	0.1	118	0.3	CONNECTICUT	0	–	80	0.4	47	0.2
0	–	80	0.2	0	–	DELAWARE	0	–	0	–	20	0.1
0	–	40	0.1	0	–	D.C.	0	–	0	–	81	0.4
300	1.7	800	2.4	938	2.1	FLORIDA	0	–	160	0.8	457	2.0
0	–	40	0.1	29	0.1	GEORGIA	0	–	40	0.2	74	0.3
0	–	320	1.0	566	1.3	HAWAII	0	–	0	–	261	1.2
600	3.5	1,000	3.0	1,245	2.8	IDAHO	300	2.6	1,000	5.2	1,520	6.7
400	2.3	560	1.7	484	1.1	ILLINOIS	0	–	40	0.2	150	0.7
200	1.2	360	1.1	187	0.4	INDIANA	0	–	40	0.2	129	0.6
300	1.7	120	0.4	338	0.8	IOWA	100	0.9	160	0.8	192	0.8
0	–	280	0.8	262	0.6	KANSAS	200	1.7	40	0.2	43	0.2
0	–	40	0.1	95	0.2	KENTUCKY	0	–	0	–	101	0.4
100	0.6	40	0.1	44	0.1	LOUISIANA	100	0.9	40	0.2	0	–
0	–	80	0.2	7	–	MAINE	0	–	0	–	8	–
100	0.6	40	0.1	121	0.3	MARYLAND	0	–	40	0.2	0	–
0	–	200	0.6	229	0.5	MASSACHUSETTS	0	–	40	0.2	33	0.1
200	1.2	120	0.4	224	0.5	MICHIGAN	0	–	80	0.4	150	0.7
300	1.7	240	0.7	290	0.7	MINNESOTA	400	3.4	280	1.5	209	0.9
0	–	120	0.4	13	–	MISSISSIPPI	100	0.9	0	–	15	0.1
500	2.9	280	0.8	478	1.1	MISSOURI	100	0.9	440	2.3	174	0.8
300	1.7	800	2.4	492	1.1	MONTANA	100	0.9	440	2.3	208	0.9
200	1.2	280	0.8	206	0.5	NEBRASKA	100	0.9	200	1.0	224	1.0
300	1.7	760	2.3	1,406	3.2	NEVADA	500	4.3	560	2.9	558	2.5
0	–	40	0.1	39	0.1	NEW HAMPSHIRE	0	–	0	–	37	0.2
100	0.6	80	0.2	242	0.6	NEW JERSEY	0	–	80	0.4	35	0.2
200	1.2	80	0.2	169	0.4	NEW MEXICO	300	2.6	280	1.5	123	0.5
0	–	680	2.0	440	1.0	NEW YORK	0	–	0	–	107	0.5
0	–	120	0.4	83	0.2	NORTH CAROLINA	0	–	0	–	48	0.2
700	4.1	80	0.2	186	0.4	NORTH DAKOTA	0	–	160	0.8	45	0.2
200	1.2	240	0.7	328	0.8	OHIO	0	–	120	0.6	181	0.8
0	–	400	1.2	524	1.2	OKLAHOMA	0	–	280	1.5	201	0.9
100	0.6	240	0.7	314	0.7	PENNSYLVANIA	0	–	80	0.4	76	0.3
0	–	120	0.4	0	–	RHODE ISLAND	0	–	0	–	0	–
0	–	0	–	32	0.1	SOUTH CAROLINA	0	–	0	–	51	0.2
200	1.2	240	0.7	157	0.4	SOUTH DAKOTA	0	–	120	0.6	116	0.5
100	0.6	0	–	87	0.2	TENNESSEE	0	–	0	–	0	–
200	1.2	240	0.7	1,024	2.3	TEXAS	500	4.3	480	2.5	490	2.2
100	0.6	160	0.5	194	0.4	UTAH	100	0.9	320	1.7	373	1.6
0	–	0	–	13	–	VERMONT	0	–	0	–	0	–
100	0.6	200	0.6	186	0.4	VIRGINIA	200	1.7	80	0.4	156	0.7
2,900	16.9	4,040	12.0	5,762	13.1	WASHINGTON	3,200	27.6	4,760	24.7	6,870	30.2
0	–	40	0.1	34	0.1	WEST VIRGINIA	0	–	0	–	26	0.1
100	0.6	320	1.0	346	0.8	WISCONSIN	0	–	80	0.4	116	0.5
0	–	120	0.4	106	0.2	WYOMING	0	–	120	0.6	116	0.5
17,200	100.2*	33,600	100.0	43,996	100.1*	TOTAL U.S.	11,600	100.2*	19,240	99.8*	22,777	100.3*

*rounding error

PENNSYLVANIA

TO PENNSYLVANIA FROM							FROM PENNSYLVANIA TO					
1970		1980		1990			1970		1980		1990	
#	%	#	%	#	%		#	%	#	%	#	%
200	0.7	240	0.6	87	0.2	ALABAMA	300	0.6	400	0.5	567	0.7
0	–	0	–	39	0.1	ALASKA	0	–	0	–	0	–
300	1.0	480	1.2	697	1.2	ARIZONA	1,900	3.6	3,280	4.0	2,686	3.4
0	–	160	0.4	183	0.3	ARKANSAS	0	–	280	0.3	237	0.3
1,300	4.5	1,600	4.0	2,998	5.2	CALIFORNIA	3,400	6.4	4,840	6.0	4,378	5.6
0	–	0	–	235	0.4	COLORADO	100	0.2	320	0.4	528	0.7
200	0.7	1,080	2.7	951	1.7	CONNECTICUT	100	0.2	840	1.0	496	0.6
500	1.7	560	1.4	1,399	2.4	DELAWARE	1,400	2.6	1,840	2.3	1,793	2.3
200	0.7	240	0.6	220	0.4	D.C.	500	0.9	240	0.3	257	0.3
2,500	8.7	4,480	11.3	6,831	11.9	FLORIDA	15,500	29.0	31,600	38.9	27,567	34.9
300	1.0	240	0.6	508	0.9	GEORGIA	400	0.7	1,080	1.3	1,223	1.6
100	0.3	80	0.2	140	0.2	HAWAII	0	–	40	–	211	0.3
0	–	0	–	7	–	IDAHO	0	–	0	–	28	–
600	2.1	640	1.6	1,053	1.8	ILLINOIS	900	1.7	840	1.0	948	1.2
600	2.1	160	0.4	224	0.4	INDIANA	200	0.4	560	0.7	488	0.6
300	1.0	80	0.2	0	–	IOWA	0	–	40	–	0	–
200	0.7	80	0.2	80	0.1	KANSAS	0	–	160	0.2	149	0.2
100	0.3	120	0.3	233	0.4	KENTUCKY	200	0.4	440	0.5	381	0.5
200	0.7	0	–	141	0.3	LOUISIANA	100	0.2	440	0.5	201	0.3
100	0.3	40	0.1	227	0.4	MAINE	100	0.2	280	0.3	298	0.4
1,800	6.3	2,520	6.4	3,945	6.9	MARYLAND	1,600	3.0	3,160	3.9	3,621	4.6
800	2.8	440	1.1	1,010	1.8	MASSACHUSETTS	600	1.1	800	1.0	739	0.9
1,000	3.5	1,480	3.7	1,247	2.2	MICHIGAN	600	1.1	960	1.2	711	0.9
200	0.7	80	0.2	172	0.3	MINNESOTA	0	–	80	0.1	345	0.4
100	0.3	120	0.3	122	0.2	MISSISSIPPI	0	–	360	0.4	192	0.2
0	–	160	0.4	309	0.5	MISSOURI	700	1.3	720	0.9	318	0.4
0	–	0	–	0	–	MONTANA	0	–	0	–	145	0.2
0	–	0	–	84	0.2	NEBRASKA	0	–	80	0.1	28	–
0	–	0	–	136	0.2	NEVADA	0	–	240	0.3	867	1.1
0	–	80	0.2	82	0.1	NEW HAMPSHIRE	100	0.2	240	0.3	304	0.4
4,600	16.1	10,200	25.8	14,820	25.8	NEW JERSEY	10,500	19.7	11,480	14.1	9,663	12.3
100	0.3	80	0.2	180	0.3	NEW MEXICO	800	1.5	280	0.3	288	0.4
7,100	24.8	8,440	21.4	10,404	18.1	NEW YORK	4,600	8.6	3,200	3.9	3,570	4.5
0	–	560	1.4	925	1.6	NORTH CAROLINA	1,200	2.2	1,720	2.1	3,003	3.8
0	–	0	–	18	–	NORTH DAKOTA	100	0.2	0	–	95	0.1
2,400	8.4	2,120	5.4	2,607	4.5	OHIO	3,300	6.2	2,880	3.5	3,161	4.0
200	0.7	120	0.3	88	0.2	OKLAHOMA	200	0.4	0	–	202	0.3
0	–	80	0.2	76	0.1	OREGON	100	0.2	240	0.3	314	0.4
400	1.4	40	0.1	202	0.4	RHODE ISLAND	100	0.2	240	0.3	115	0.2
100	0.3	120	0.3	636	1.1	SOUTH CAROLINA	500	0.9	1,080	1.3	1,833	2.3
0	–	80	0.2	0	–	SOUTH DAKOTA	0	–	0	–	10	–
100	0.3	40	0.1	415	0.7	TENNESSEE	300	0.6	880	1.1	750	1.0
300	1.0	400	1.0	757	1.3	TEXAS	1,200	2.2	2,080	2.6	1,534	1.9
100	0.3	0	–	69	0.1	UTAH	0	–	40	–	37	0.1
0	–	0	–	130	0.2	VERMONT	200	0.4	80	0.1	93	0.1
900	3.1	1,360	3.4	1,615	2.8	VIRGINIA	500	0.9	1,640	2.0	2,853	3.6
200	0.7	80	0.2	284	0.5	WASHINGTON	200	0.2	640	0.8	345	0.4
300	1.0	520	1.3	663	1.2	WEST VIRGINIA	900	1.7	440	0.5	979	1.2
200	0.7	80	0.2	278	0.5	WISCONSIN	0	–	160	0.2	323	0.4
0	–	40	0.1	11	–	WYOMING	0	–	40	–	29	–
28,600	**99.2***	**39,520**	**99.7***	**57,538**	**100.1***	**TOTAL U.S.**	**53,400**	**99.9***	**81,280**	**99.5***	**78,903**	**100.0**

*rounding error

RHODE ISLAND

TO RHODE ISLAND FROM							FROM RHODE ISLAND TO					
1970		1980		1990			1970		1980		1990	
#	%	#	%	#	%		#	%	#	%	#	%
100	2.4	0	–	0	–	ALABAMA	0	–	40	0.6	87	0.9
0	–	0	–	0	–	ALASKA	0	–	0	–	0	–
0	–	0	–	36	0.6	ARIZONA	100	1.9	0	–	146	1.6
0	–	0	–	0	–	ARKANSAS	0	–	0	–	0	–
300	7.1	120	2.8	323	5.5	CALIFORNIA	200	3.7	760	11.4	598	6.4
0	–	0	–	21	0.4	COLORADO	100	1.9	0	–	12	0.1
300	7.1	760	17.4	1,011	17.3	CONNECTICUT	600	11.1	480	7.2	461	5.0
0	–	0	–	0	–	DELAWARE	0	–	0	–	0	–
0	–	0	–	16	0.3	D.C.	0	–	0	–	0	–
500	11.9	360	8.3	377	6.5	FLORIDA	1,900	35.2	2,040	30.5	4,278	46.1
0	–	80	1.8	26	0.5	GEORGIA	0	–	120	1.8	67	0.7
0	–	0	–	0	–	HAWAII	100	1.9	80	1.2	16	0.2
0	–	0	–	0	–	IDAHO	0	–	0	–	0	–
0	–	80	1.8	86	1.5	ILLINOIS	0	–	40	0.6	45	0.5
0	–	0	–	19	0.3	INDIANA	0	–	0	–	26	0.3
0	–	0	–	0	–	IOWA	0	–	0	–	0	–
0	–	0	–	0	–	KANSAS	0	–	0	–	0	–
0	–	0	–	0	–	KENTUCKY	0	–	80	1.2	25	0.3
0	–	0	–	57	1.0	LOUISIANA	0	–	0	–	15	0.2
0	–	80	1.8	138	2.4	MAINE	200	3.7	80	1.2	234	2.5
0	–	80	1.8	36	0.6	MARYLAND	0	–	80	1.2	96	1.0
1,400	33.3	1,120	25.7	1,812	31.0	MASSACHUSETTS	1,000	18.5	1,360	20.4	1,401	15.1
0	–	0	–	16	0.3	MICHIGAN	0	–	120	1.8	23	0.3
0	–	0	–	0	–	MINNESOTA	0	–	0	–	0	–
0	–	0	–	0	–	MISSISSIPPI	0	–	40	0.6	30	0.3
100	2.4	0	–	31	0.5	MISSOURI	0	–	40	0.6	0	–
0	–	0	–	0	–	MONTANA	0	–	0	–	0	–
0	–	0	–	0	–	NEBRASKA	0	–	0	–	0	–
0	–	0	–	0	–	NEVADA	0	–	40	0.6	124	1.3
0	–	120	2.8	89	1.5	NEW HAMPSHIRE	0	–	160	2.4	194	2.1
300	7.1	240	5.5	227	3.9	NEW JERSEY	200	3.7	200	3.0	128	1.4
0	–	0	–	62	1.1	NEW MEXICO	0	–	0	–	27	0.3
800	19.0	760	17.4	1,019	17.4	NEW YORK	300	5.6	240	3.6	257	2.8
0	–	0	–	0	–	NORTH CAROLINA	0	–	40	0.6	141	1.5
0	–	0	–	0	–	NORTH DAKOTA	0	–	0	–	0	–
0	–	80	1.8	47	0.8	OHIO	0	–	0	–	70	0.8
0	–	0	–	0	–	OKLAHOMA	0	–	0	–	30	0.3
0	–	0	–	0	–	OREGON	0	–	120	1.8	0	–
100	2.4	240	5.5	115	2.0	PENNSYLVANIA	400	7.4	40	0.6	202	2.2
0	–	0	–	57	1.0	SOUTH CAROLINA	0	–	40	0.6	87	0.9
0	–	0	–	0	–	SOUTH DAKOTA	0	–	0	–	0	–
0	–	0	–	0	–	TENNESSEE	100	1.9	80	1.2	87	0.9
0	–	80	1.8	117	2.0	TEXAS	100	1.9	120	1.8	81	0.9
0	–	0	–	0	–	UTAH	0	–	0	–	41	0.4
0	–	80	1.8	44	0.8	VERMONT	0	–	80	1.2	73	0.8
200	4.8	80	1.8	60	1.0	VIRGINIA	100	1.9	40	0.6	123	1.3
0	–	0	–	0	–	WASHINGTON	0	–	120	1.8	39	0.4
0	–	0	–	0	–	WEST VIRGINIA	0	–	0	–	0	–
100	2.4	0	–	0	–	WISCONSIN	0	–	0	–	0	–
0	–	0	–	0	–	WYOMING	0	–	0	–	25	0.3
4,200	99.9*	4,360	99.8*	5,842	100.2*	TOTAL U.S.	5,400	100.3*	6,680	100.1*	9,289	100.1*

*rounding error

SOUTH CAROLINA

TO SOUTH CAROLINA FROM							FROM SOUTH CAROLINA TO					
1970		1980		1990			1970		1980		1990	
#	%	#	%	#	%		#	%	#	%	#	%
0	–	240	1.2	381	1.1	ALABAMA	100	1.9	120	1.2	416	2.6
0	–	0	–	0	–	ALASKA	0	–	0	–	19	0.1
0	–	0	–	123	0.4	ARIZONA	0	–	120	1.2	232	1.5
100	1.0	40	0.2	81	0.2	ARKANSAS	0	–	0	–	57	0.4
200	2.1	640	3.1	1,020	3.0	CALIFORNIA	500	9.3	200	2.0	237	1.5
0	–	0	–	207	0.6	COLORADO	0	–	0	–	87	0.5
0	–	360	1.8	1,545	4.5	CONNECTICUT	0	–	40	0.4	73	0.5
0	–	40	0.2	138	0.4	DELAWARE	0	–	0	–	0	–
100	1.0	440	2.1	147	0.4	D.C.	0	–	80	0.8	232	1.5
1,200	12.4	1,800	8.8	2,910	8.5	FLORIDA	600	11.1	2,080	21.1	3,090	19.3
1,300	13.4	1,640	8.0	2,202	6.4	GEORGIA	900	16.7	1,760	17.8	1,948	12.2
100	1.0	40	0.2	18	0.1	HAWAII	0	–	0	–	0	–
0	–	80	0.4	0	–	IDAHO	0	–	40	0.4	0	–
400	4.1	440	2.1	1,140	3.3	ILLINOIS	100	1.9	80	0.8	162	1.0
0	–	200	1.0	369	1.1	INDIANA	0	–	0	–	194	1.2
0	–	40	0.2	159	0.5	IOWA	0	–	0	–	30	0.2
0	–	0	–	15	–	KANSAS	0	–	0	–	87	0.5
0	–	80	0.4	309	0.9	KENTUCKY	0	–	0	–	144	0.9
0	–	80	0.4	201	0.6	LOUISIANA	100	1.9	360	3.6	57	0.4
0	–	80	0.4	42	0.1	MAINE	0	–	0	–	0	–
200	2.1	680	3.3	1,161	3.4	MARYLAND	100	1.9	40	0.4	357	1.2
100	1.0	160	0.8	756	2.2	MASSACHUSETTS	0	–	40	0.4	191	1.2
0	–	760	3.7	1,293	3.8	MICHIGAN	0	–	40	0.4	342	2.1
0	–	40	0.2	66	0.2	MINNESOTA	0	–	0	–	36	0.2
100	1.0	280	1.4	120	0.4	MISSISSIPPI	0	–	40	0.4	57	0.4
0	–	200	1.0	297	0.9	MISSOURI	300	5.6	80	0.8	169	1.1
0	–	80	0.4	78	0.2	MONTANA	0	–	0	–	0	–
0	–	40	0.2	87	0.3	NEBRASKA	0	–	0	–	8	0.1
0	–	0	–	54	0.2	NEVADA	0	–	0	–	61	0.4
100	1.0	160	0.8	321	0.9	NEW HAMPSHIRE	0	–	80	0.8	78	0.5
300	3.1	760	3.7	3,021	8.8	NEW JERSEY	200	3.7	280	2.8	214	1.3
0	–	0	–	45	0.1	NEW MEXICO	0	–	0	–	6	–
1,700	17.5	2,760	13.4	4,794	14.0	NEW YORK	300	5.6	600	6.1	636	4.0
2,200	22.7	3,000	14.6	3,747	10.9	NORTH CAROLINA	1,700	31.5	2,200	22.3	3,204	20.0
0	–	0	–	0	–	NORTH DAKOTA	0	–	0	–	0	–
100	1.0	1,520	7.4	1,860	5.4	OHIO	100	1.9	40	0.4	703	4.4
0	–	120	0.6	63	0.2	OKLAHOMA	0	–	0	–	102	0.6
0	–	0	–	51	0.2	OREGON	0	–	0	–	32	0.2
500	5.2	1,080	5.3	1,833	5.4	PENNSYLVANIA	100	1.9	120	1.2	636	4.0
0	–	40	0.2	87	0.3	RHODE ISLAND	0	–	0	–	57	0.4
100	1.0	0	–	18	0.1	SOUTH DAKOTA	0	–	0	–	10	0.1
300	3.1	480	2.3	609	1.8	TENNESSEE	0	–	360	3.6	627	3.9
0	–	240	1.2	525	1.5	TEXAS	100	1.9	320	3.2	335	2.1
0	–	0	–	0	–	UTAH	0	–	0	–	14	0.1
0	–	200	1.0	63	0.2	VERMONT	0	–	0	–	32	0.2
400	4.1	1,200	5.8	1,683	4.9	VIRGINIA	200	3.7	720	7.3	798	5.0
0	–	120	0.6	195	0.6	WASHINGTON	0	–	0	–	96	0.6
200	2.1	240	1.2	270	0.8	WEST VIRGINIA	0	–	40	0.4	115	0.7
0	–	160	0.8	147	0.4	WISCONSIN	0	–	0	–	34	0.2
0	–	0	–	0	–	WYOMING	0	–	0	–	0	–
9,700	99.9*	20,560	100.4*	34,251	100.2*	TOTAL U.S.	5,400	100.5*	9,880	99.8*	16,015	100.3*

*rounding error

SOUTH DAKOTA

TO SOUTH DAKOTA FROM							FROM SOUTH DAKOTA TO					
1970		1980		1990			1970		1980		1990	
#	%	#	%	#	%		#	%	#	%	#	%
0	–	0	–	0	–	ALABAMA	0	–	0	–	80	1.5
0	–	0	–	19	0.5	ALASKA	0	–	0	–	0	–
0	–	80	2.0	206	5.0	ARIZONA	300	6.7	520	8.8	859	16.4
0	–	120	3.0	9	0.2	ARKANSAS	0	–	80	1.4	58	1.1
0	–	520	13.0	485	11.7	CALIFORNIA	500	11.1	600	10.2	411	7.8
400	12.5	80	2.0	224	5.4	COLORADO	300	6.7	560	9.5	279	5.3
0	–	0	–	19	0.5	CONNECTICUT	0	–	0	–	0	–
0	–	0	–	0	–	DELAWARE	0	–	0	–	0	–
0	–	0	–	0	–	D.C.	0	–	0	–	0	–
0	–	120	3.0	109	2.6	FLORIDA	400	8.9	200	3.4	141	2.7
0	–	0	–	29	0.7	GEORGIA	0	–	80	1.4	86	1.6
0	–	0	–	38	0.9	HAWAII	0	–	0	–	0	–
0	–	0	–	29	0.7	IDAHO	100	2.2	0	–	36	0.7
500	15.6	200	5.0	160	3.9	ILLINOIS	0	–	80	1.4	36	0.7
0	–	0	–	0	–	INDIANA	0	–	0	–	7	0.1
300	9.4	520	13.0	490	11.8	IOWA	300	6.7	560	9.5	236	4.5
0	–	40	1.0	56	1.4	KANSAS	0	–	40	0.7	64	1.2
0	–	0	–	0	–	KENTUCKY	0	–	0	–	0	–
0	–	0	–	15	0.4	LOUISIANA	0	–	0	–	0	–
0	–	0	–	0	–	MAINE	0	–	0	–	0	–
0	–	0	–	67	1.6	MARYLAND	0	–	0	–	0	–
100	3.1	0	–	0	–	MASSACHUSETTS	0	–	0	–	60	1.1
0	–	80	2.0	15	0.4	MICHIGAN	0	–	0	–	79	1.5
900	28.1	680	17.0	383	9.3	MINNESOTA	500	11.1	480	8.2	628	12.0
0	–	0	–	10	0.2	MISSISSIPPI	0	–	0	–	0	–
0	–	80	2.0	91	2.2	MISSOURI	0	–	120	2.0	58	1.1
0	–	200	5.0	29	0.7	MONTANA	0	–	80	1.4	48	0.9
400	12.5	240	6.0	582	14.1	NEBRASKA	400	8.9	200	3.4	310	5.9
0	–	40	1.0	101	2.4	NEVADA	300	6.7	160	2.7	26	0.5
0	–	0	–	0	–	NEW HAMPSHIRE	0	–	0	–	0	–
100	3.1	40	1.0	0	–	NEW JERSEY	0	–	0	–	0	–
0	–	0	–	0	–	NEW MEXICO	0	–	80	1.4	72	1.4
100	3.1	80	2.0	38	0.9	NEW YORK	0	–	80	1.4	0	–
0	–	0	–	0	–	NORTH CAROLINA	0	–	40	0.7	111	2.1
200	6.3	280	7.0	156	4.0	NORTH DAKOTA	300	6.7	320	5.4	260	5.0
0	–	40	1.0	15	0.4	OHIO	0	–	40	0.7	61	1.2
0	–	40	1.0	34	0.8	OKLAHOMA	0	–	120	2.0	0	–
0	–	120	3.0	116	2.8	OREGON	200	4.4	240	4.1	157	3.0
0	–	0	–	10	0.2	PENNSYLVANIA	0	–	80	1.4	0	–
0	–	0	–	0	–	RHODE ISLAND	0	–	0	–	0	–
0	–	0	–	10	0.2	SOUTH CAROLINA	100	2.2	0	–	18	0.3
100	3.1	0	–	29	0.7	TENNESSEE	200	4.4	40	0.7	63	1.2
0	–	0	–	109	2.6	TEXAS	0	–	680	11.6	361	6.9
0	–	80	2.0	72	1.7	UTAH	0	–	0	–	92	1.8
0	–	0	–	0	–	VERMONT	0	–	0	–	0	–
0	–	0	–	71	1.7	VIRGINIA	0	–	0	–	0	–
0	–	80	2.0	105	2.5	WASHINGTON	400	8.9	280	4.8	219	4.2
0	–	0	–	0	–	WEST VIRGINIA	0	–	0	–	25	0.5
0	–	80	2.0	47	1.1	WISCONSIN	0	–	40	0.7	154	2.9
100	3.1	160	4.0	163	3.9	WYOMING	200	4.4	80	1.4	149	2.8
3,200	99.9*	4,000	100.0	4,141	100.1*	TOTAL U.S.	4,500	100.0	5,880	100.3*	5,244	99.9*

*rounding error

TENNESSEE

TO TENNESSEE FROM							FROM TENNESSEE TO					
1970		1980		1990			1970		1980		1990	
#	%	#	%	#	%		#	%	#	%	#	%
1,200	7.5	1,120	3.9	1,764	4.9	ALABAMA	700	5.3	960	4.5	1,667	6.4
0	–	0	–	0	–	ALASKA	0	–	0	–	0	–
0	–	120	0.4	471	1.3	ARIZONA	0	–	440	2.1	347	1.3
200	1.2	1,000	3.4	1,005	2.8	ARKANSAS	900	6.9	760	3.6	957	3.7
500	3.1	1,400	4.8	1,527	4.2	CALIFORNIA	400	3.1	1,040	4.9	1,019	3.9
200	1.2	120	0.4	156	0.4	COLORADO	0	–	240	1.1	132	0.5
100	0.6	240	0.8	210	0.6	CONNECTICUT	200	1.5	80	0.4	124	0.5
0	–	0	–	48	0.1	DELAWARE	200	1.5	0	–	38	0.2
300	1.9	120	0.4	0	–	D.C.	0	–	0	–	60	0.2
1,400	8.7	2,720	9.4	4,572	12.6	FLORIDA	2,500	19.1	3,840	18.1	4,257	16.3
600	3.7	1,680	5.8	1,806	5.0	GEORGIA	1,700	13.0	2,120	10.0	2,210	8.5
0	–	40	0.1	48	0.1	HAWAII	0	–	0	–	17	0.1
0	–	0	–	0	–	IDAHO	0	–	80	0.4	68	0.3
1,200	7.5	2,040	7.0	2,337	6.4	ILLINOIS	1,000	7.6	800	3.8	648	2.5
600	3.7	1,160	4.0	1,611	4.4	INDIANA	200	1.5	520	2.5	1,060	4.1
0	–	200	0.7	369	1.0	IOWA	0	–	0	–	150	0.6
200	1.2	280	1.0	135	0.4	KANSAS	0	–	40	0.2	151	0.6
1,500	9.3	1,560	5.4	2,082	5.7	KENTUCKY	300	2.3	1,040	4.9	1,386	5.3
400	2.5	240	0.8	507	1.4	LOUISIANA	500	3.8	440	2.1	273	1.0
0	–	0	–	66	0.2	MAINE	0	–	0	–	57	0.2
200	1.2	880	3.0	468	1.3	MARYLAND	100	0.8	280	1.3	128	0.5
100	0.6	160	0.6	186	0.5	MASSACHUSETTS	0	–	120	0.6	21	0.1
800	5.0	1,880	6.5	2,817	7.8	MICHIGAN	400	3.1	400	1.9	939	3.6
0	–	80	0.3	51	0.1	MINNESOTA	0	–	120	0.6	166	0.6
1,800	11.1	1,480	5.1	1,746	4.8	MISSISSIPPI	700	5.3	2,160	10.2	2,715	10.4
500	3.1	560	1.9	864	2.4	MISSOURI	200	1.5	320	1.5	701	2.7
0	–	120	0.4	0	–	MONTANA	0	–	80	0.4	0	–
0	–	0	–	126	0.4	NEBRASKA	0	–	0	–	67	0.3
0	–	40	0.1	51	0.1	NEVADA	0	–	40	0.2	170	0.7
100	0.6	120	0.4	99	0.3	NEW HAMPSHIRE	0	–	0	–	31	0.1
0	–	480	1.7	891	2.5	NEW JERSEY	100	0.8	40	0.2	161	0.6
0	–	40	0.1	87	0.2	NEW MEXICO	0	–	40	0.2	126	0.5
300	1.9	1,280	4.4	1,119	3.1	NEW YORK	100	0.8	360	1.7	132	0.5
500	3.1	720	2.5	1,338	3.7	NORTH CAROLINA	400	3.1	600	2.8	873	3.3
0	–	0	–	48	0.1	NORTH DAKOTA	0	–	0	–	0	–
1,200	7.5	2,960	10.2	2,058	5.7	OHIO	700	5.3	1,240	5.8	794	3.0
100	0.6	400	1.4	318	0.9	OKLAHOMA	200	1.5	200	0.9	173	0.7
0	–	0	–	0	–	OREGON	100	0.8	0	–	87	0.3
300	1.9	880	3.0	750	2.1	PENNSYLVANIA	100	0.8	40	0.2	415	1.6
100	0.6	80	0.3	87	0.2	RHODE ISLAND	0	–	0	–	0	–
0	–	360	1.2	627	1.7	SOUTH CAROLINA	300	2.3	480	2.3	609	2.3
200	1.2	40	0.1	63	0.2	SOUTH DAKOTA	100	0.8	0	–	29	0.1
700	4.3	720	2.5	1,605	4.4	TEXAS	200	1.5	1,400	6.6	1,311	5.0
0	–	0	–	72	0.2	UTAH	0	–	0	–	17	0.1
0	–	0	–	33	0.1	VERMONT	0	–	0	–	0	–
400	2.5	1,320	4.5	1,326	3.7	VIRGINIA	600	4.6	640	3.0	1,524	5.8
0	–	120	0.4	108	0.3	WASHINGTON	100	0.8	80	0.4	141	0.5
100	0.6	120	0.4	249	0.7	WEST VIRGINIA	0	–	120	0.6	86	0.3
300	1.9	160	0.6	336	0.9	WISCONSIN	100	0.8	40	0.2	96	0.4
0	–	0	–	69	0.2	WYOMING	0	–	0	–	0	–
16,100	99.8*	29,040	99.9*	36,306	100.1*	TOTAL U.S.	13,100	100.2*	21,200	100.2*	26,133	100.2*

*rounding error

TEXAS

TO TEXAS FROM							FROM TEXAS TO					
1970		1980		1990			1970		1980		1990	
#	%	#	%	#	%		#	%	#	%	#	%
900	2.3	720	0.9	1,006	1.3	ALABAMA	800	2.6	760	1.9	1,676	2.4
100	0.3	400	0.5	189	0.2	ALASKA	100	0.3	200	0.5	114	0.2
1,900	4.8	2,520	3.2	2,025	2.6	ARIZONA	1,200	4.0	1,920	4.9	3,244	4.6
2,500	6.3	2,960	3.8	2,599	3.3	ARKANSAS	2,900	9.6	2,640	6.8	4,783	6.9
4,600	11.6	11,240	14.3	10,134	13.0	CALIFORNIA	5,200	17.2	6,960	17.8	9,597	13.7
1,300	3.3	1,920	2.4	2,240	2.9	COLORADO	600	2.0	1,560	4.0	2,448	3.5
100	0.3	480	0.6	563	0.7	CONNECTICUT	0	–	80	0.2	277	0.4
100	0.3	120	0.2	121	0.2	DELAWARE	0	–	0	–	27	–
400	1.0	280	0.4	99	0.1	D.C.	0	–	200	0.5	88	0.1
1,900	4.8	3,760	4.8	5,070	6.5	FLORIDA	1,500	5.0	2,920	7.5	6,787	9.7
400	1.0	1,080	1.4	936	1.2	GEORGIA	400	1.3	960	2.5	1,760	2.5
100	0.3	280	0.4	233	0.3	HAWAII	0	–	80	0.2	233	0.3
100	0.3	480	0.6	385	0.5	IDAHO	200	0.7	200	0.5	188	0.3
2,300	5.8	5,600	7.1	4,341	5.6	ILLINOIS	200	0.7	480	1.2	1,812	2.6
1,100	2.8	1,600	2.0	1,463	1.9	INDIANA	500	1.7	760	1.9	1,095	1.6
400	1.0	1,520	1.9	1,681	2.2	IOWA	700	2.3	320	0.8	391	0.6
800	2.0	2,400	3.1	2,028	2.6	KANSAS	900	3.0	840	2.2	1,314	1.9
300	0.8	600	0.8	624	0.8	KENTUCKY	100	0.3	280	0.7	497	0.7
2,200	5.5	4,800	6.1	4,874	6.2	LOUISIANA	2,700	8.9	2,480	6.4	3,525	5.1
100	0.3	80	0.1	195	0.3	MAINE	0	–	120	0.3	215	0.3
0	–	680	0.9	628	0.8	MARYLAND	500	1.7	240	0.6	621	0.9
300	0.8	640	0.8	1,042	1.3	MASSACHUSETTS	0	–	80	0.2	544	0.8
1,000	2.5	2,000	2.5	2,343	3.0	MICHIGAN	400	1.3	360	0.9	925	1.3
500	1.3	1,880	2.4	1,574	2.0	MINNESOTA	200	0.7	160	0.4	744	1.1
900	2.3	800	1.0	1,210	1.6	MISSISSIPPI	500	1.7	600	1.5	1,689	2.4
1,600	4.0	2,880	3.7	3,085	4.0	MISSOURI	800	2.6	920	2.4	2,335	3.3
0	–	80	0.1	220	0.3	MONTANA	100	0.3	120	0.3	80	0.1
100	0.3	840	1.1	537	0.7	NEBRASKA	0	–	160	0.4	445	0.6
100	0.3	560	0.7	492	0.6	NEVADA	100	0.3	600	1.5	1,063	1.5
0	–	0	–	179	0.2	NEW HAMPSHIRE	0	–	120	0.3	115	0.2
500	1.3	1,960	2.5	1,325	1.7	NEW JERSEY	100	0.3	320	0.8	454	0.7
2,300	5.8	2,400	3.1	3,537	4.5	NEW MEXICO	2,000	6.6	2,440	6.3	3,768	5.4
1,100	2.8	3,400	4.3	3,642	4.7	NEW YORK	400	1.3	280	0.7	1,259	1.8
500	1.3	440	0.6	392	0.5	NORTH CAROLINA	300	1.0	480	1.2	1,299	1.9
0	–	160	0.2	121	0.2	NORTH DAKOTA	0	–	40	0.1	0	–
900	2.3	2,240	2.9	2,145	2.8	OHIO	500	1.7	320	0.8	1,441	2.1
4,300	10.8	5,560	7.1	5,965	7.6	OKLAHOMA	3,800	12.5	4,080	10.5	5,562	8.0
500	1.3	480	0.6	490	0.6	OREGON	200	0.7	240	0.6	1,024	1.5
1,200	3.0	2,080	2.7	1,534	2.0	PENNSYLVANIA	300	1.0	400	1.0	757	1.1
100	0.3	120	0.2	81	0.1	RHODE ISLAND	0	–	80	0.2	117	0.2
100	0.3	320	0.4	335	0.4	SOUTH CAROLINA	0	–	240	0.6	525	0.8
0	–	680	0.9	361	0.5	SOUTH DAKOTA	0	–	0	–	109	0.2
200	0.5	1,400	1.8	1,311	1.7	TENNESSEE	700	2.3	720	1.8	1,605	2.3
200	0.5	360	0.5	410	0.5	UTAH	100	0.3	200	0.5	285	0.4
0	–	0	–	57	0.1	VERMONT	0	–	80	0.2	0	–
600	1.5	960	1.2	1,040	1.3	VIRGINIA	400	1.3	840	2.2	801	1.2
100	0.3	1,000	1.3	1,033	1.3	WASHINGTON	600	2.0	640	1.6	1,575	2.3
100	0.3	200	0.3	247	0.3	WEST VIRGINIA	200	0.7	120	0.3	141	0.2
1,000	2.5	1,000	1.3	1,687	2.2	WISCONSIN	100	0.3	360	0.9	449	0.6
0	–	520	0.7	288	0.4	WYOMING	0	–	40	0.1	53	0.1
39,800	101.1*	78,480	100.4*	78,117	100.3*	TOTAL U.S.	30,300	100.2*	39,040	99.7*	69,856	100.4*

*rounding error

UTAH

TO UTAH FROM							FROM UTAH TO					
1970		1980		1990			1970		1980		1990	
#	%	#	%	#	%		#	%	#	%	#	%
0	–	0	–	17	0.2	ALABAMA	100	2.3	40	0.6	16	0.2
200	3.8	80	0.9	37	0.3	ALASKA	0	–	0	–	111	1.4
200	3.8	480	5.6	435	4.1	ARIZONA	400	9.1	1,080	17.0	1,058	13.0
0	–	0	–	17	0.2	ARKANSAS	0	–	0	–	47	0.6
2,100	40.4	3,440	40.4	3,674	34.2	CALIFORNIA	1,200	27.3	960	15.1	1,678	20.6
500	9.6	520	6.1	447	4.2	COLORADO	400	9.1	480	7.5	516	6.3
0	–	40	0.5	72	0.7	CONNECTICUT	0	–	0	–	20	0.3
0	–	0	–	0	–	DELAWARE	0	–	0	–	0	–
0	–	0	–	0	–	D.C.	0	–	0	–	0	–
300	5.8	80	0.9	143	1.3	FLORIDA	0	–	360	5.7	169	2.1
0	–	0	–	47	0.4	GEORGIA	0	–	0	–	67	0.8
0	–	160	1.9	58	0.5	HAWAII	0	–	80	1.3	320	3.9
100	1.9	680	8.0	972	9.0	IDAHO	200	4.5	560	8.8	656	8.1
0	–	200	2.3	113	1.1	ILLINOIS	0	–	40	0.6	90	1.1
0	–	40	0.5	75	0.7	INDIANA	100	2.3	0	–	23	0.3
0	–	40	0.5	68	0.6	IOWA	100	2.3	0	–	0	–
200	3.8	40	0.5	117	1.1	KANSAS	0	–	120	1.9	82	1.0
0	–	0	–	48	0.5	KENTUCKY	0	–	40	0.6	26	0.3
0	–	0	–	0	–	LOUISIANA	0	–	40	0.6	0	–
0	–	0	–	0	–	MAINE	0	–	0	–	48	0.6
0	–	80	0.9	85	0.8	MARYLAND	0	–	40	0.6	101	1.2
0	–	80	0.9	88	0.8	MASSACHUSETTS	0	–	0	–	50	0.6
0	–	0	–	228	2.1	MICHIGAN	0	–	40	0.6	61	0.8
100	1.9	80	0.9	98	0.9	MINNESOTA	300	6.8	40	0.6	65	0.8
0	–	0	–	68	0.6	MISSISSIPPI	0	–	0	–	0	–
0	–	40	0.5	229	2.1	MISSOURI	100	2.3	80	1.3	119	1.5
100	1.9	200	2.3	292	2.7	MONTANA	100	2.3	280	4.4	110	1.4
100	1.9	80	0.9	102	1.0	NEBRASKA	100	2.3	0	–	8	0.1
600	11.5	560	6.6	586	5.5	NEVADA	200	4.5	360	5.7	766	9.4
0	–	0	–	0	–	NEW HAMPSHIRE	0	–	0	–	0	–
0	–	120	1.4	28	0.3	NEW JERSEY	0	–	0	–	0	–
200	3.8	40	0.5	370	3.4	NEW MEXICO	0	–	240	3.8	45	0.6
0	–	160	1.9	84	0.8	NEW YORK	0	–	120	1.9	55	0.7
100	1.9	40	0.5	58	0.5	NORTH CAROLINA	0	–	160	2.5	102	1.3
0	–	0	–	75	0.7	NORTH DAKOTA	0	–	0	–	0	–
0	–	0	–	111	1.0	OHIO	100	2.3	0	–	92	1.1
0	–	40	0.5	116	1.1	OKLAHOMA	0	–	40	0.6	102	1.3
100	1.9	320	3.8	373	3.5	OREGON	100	2.3	160	2.5	194	2.4
0	–	40	0.5	37	0.3	PENNSYLVANIA	100	2.3	0	–	69	0.9
0	–	0	–	41	0.4	RHODE ISLAND	0	–	0	–	0	–
0	–	0	–	14	0.1	SOUTH CAROLINA	0	–	0	–	0	–
0	–	0	–	92	0.9	SOUTH DAKOTA	0	–	80	1.3	72	0.9
0	–	0	–	17	0.2	TENNESSEE	0	–	0	–	72	0.9
100	1.9	200	2.3	285	2.7	TEXAS	200	4.5	360	5.7	410	5.0
0	–	0	–	0	–	VERMONT	0	–	0	–	0	–
0	–	120	1.4	101	0.9	VIRGINIA	200	4.5	0	–	117	1.4
100	1.9	160	1.9	368	3.4	WASHINGTON	200	4.5	520	8.2	336	4.1
100	1.9	0	–	17	0.2	WEST VIRGINIA	0	–	0	–	18	0.2
0	–	0	–	48	0.5	WISCONSIN	100	2.3	0	–	0	–
0	–	360	4.2	400	3.7	WYOMING	100	2.3	40	0.6	257	3.2
5,200	99.6*	8,520	100.0	10,751	100.2*	TOTAL U.S.	4,400	100.1*	6,360	100.0	8,148	100.4*

*rounding error

VERMONT

TO VERMONT FROM							FROM VERMONT TO					
1970		1980		1990			1970		1980		1990	
#	%	#	%	#	%		#	%	#	%	#	%
0	–	40	0.9	26	0.4	ALABAMA	0	–	80	1.6	32	0.6
0	–	0	–	0	–	ALASKA	0	–	0	–	0	–
0	–	40	0.9	32	0.5	ARIZONA	100	3.2	40	0.8	67	1.2
0	–	0	–	0	–	ARKANSAS	0	–	0	–	0	–
0	–	40	0.9	172	2.9	CALIFORNIA	100	3.2	240	4.7	196	3.6
0	–	0	–	10	0.2	COLORADO	0	–	0	–	0	–
0	–	840	18.3	769	13.0	CONNECTICUT	400	12.9	520	10.2	293	5.4
0	–	0	–	0	–	DELAWARE	0	–	0	–	19	0.4
100	3.3	0	–	114	1.9	D.C.	0	–	0	–	0	–
200	6.7	80	1.7	326	5.5	FLORIDA	800	25.8	2,120	41.7	1,908	35.0
0	–	0	–	0	–	GEORGIA	0	–	40	0.8	22	0.4
0	–	0	–	0	–	HAWAII	0	–	0	–	0	–
0	–	0	–	0	–	IDAHO	0	–	0	–	8	0.2
0	–	0	–	78	1.3	ILLINOIS	0	–	0	–	18	0.3
0	–	0	–	16	0.3	INDIANA	0	–	0	–	0	–
0	–	0	–	68	1.2	IOWA	0	–	80	1.6	8	0.2
0	–	0	–	0	–	KANSAS	0	–	0	–	0	–
0	–	0	–	0	–	KENTUCKY	0	–	0	–	7	0.1
0	–	0	–	0	–	LOUISIANA	0	–	0	–	60	1.1
100	3.3	40	0.9	63	1.1	MAINE	0	–	80	1.6	76	1.4
0	–	0	–	42	0.7	MARYLAND	500	16.1	40	0.8	0	–
0	–	800	17.4	640	10.8	MASSACHUSETTS	200	6.5	480	9.4	334	6.1
0	–	0	–	0	–	MICHIGAN	100	3.2	40	0.8	0	–
0	–	0	–	0	–	MINNESOTA	0	–	0	–	0	–
0	–	0	–	26	0.4	MISSISSIPPI	0	–	0	–	0	–
0	–	40	0.9	31	0.5	MISSOURI	0	–	0	–	14	0.3
0	–	0	–	0	–	MONTANA	0	–	0	–	8	0.2
0	–	0	–	0	–	NEBRASKA	0	–	0	–	0	–
0	–	0	–	0	–	NEVADA	0	–	0	–	16	0.3
600	20.0	480	10.4	771	13.0	NEW HAMPSHIRE	500	16.1	400	7.9	944	17.3
100	3.3	480	10.4	588	9.9	NEW JERSEY	0	–	240	4.7	64	1.2
0	–	0	–	0	–	NEW MEXICO	0	–	0	–	27	0.5
1,500	50.0	1,280	27.8	1,603	27.1	NEW YORK	0	–	160	3.1	401	7.4
0	–	40	0.9	16	0.3	NORTH CAROLINA	100	3.2	12	2.4	273	5.0
0	–	0	–	0	–	NORTH DAKOTA	100	3.2	0	–	0	–
0	–	0	–	93	1.6	OHIO	0	–	0	–	112	2.1
0	–	0	–	21	0.4	OKLAHOMA	0	–	0	–	0	–
0	–	0	–	0	–	OREGON	0	–	0	–	13	0.2
200	6.7	80	1.7	93	1.6	PENNSYLVANIA	0	–	0	–	130	2.4
0	–	80	1.7	73	1.2	RHODE ISLAND	0	–	80	1.6	44	0.8
0	–	0	–	32	0.5	SOUTH CAROLINA	0	–	200	3.9	63	1.2
0	–	0	–	0	–	SOUTH DAKOTA	0	–	0	–	0	–
0	–	0	–	0	–	TENNESSEE	0	–	0	–	33	0.6
0	–	80	1.7	0	–	TEXAS	0	–	0	–	57	1.1
0	–	0	–	0	–	UTAH	0	–	0	–	0	–
0	–	80	1.7	124	2.1	VIRGINIA	200	6.5	80	1.6	123	2.3
200	6.7	0	–	68	1.2	WASHINGTON	0	–	40	0.8	63	1.2
0	–	0	–	0	–	WEST VIRGINIA	0	–	0	–	0	–
0	–	80	1.7	0	–	WISCONSIN	0	–	0	–	14	0.3
0	–	0	–	21	0.4	WYOMING	0	–	0	–	0	–
2,900	100.0*	4,600	99.9*	5,916	100.0	TOTAL U.S.	3,100	99.9*	5,080	100.0	5,447	100.4*

*rounding error

VIRGINIA

<table>
<tr><th colspan="6">TO VIRGINIA FROM</th><th></th><th colspan="6">FROM VIRGINIA TO</th></tr>
<tr><th colspan="2">1970</th><th colspan="2">1980</th><th colspan="2">1990</th><th></th><th colspan="2">1970</th><th colspan="2">1980</th><th colspan="2">1990</th></tr>
<tr><th>#</th><th>%</th><th>#</th><th>%</th><th>#</th><th>%</th><th></th><th>#</th><th>%</th><th>#</th><th>%</th><th>#</th><th>%</th></tr>
<tr><td>0</td><td>–</td><td>680</td><td>2.0</td><td>291</td><td>0.6</td><td>ALABAMA</td><td>600</td><td>2.8</td><td>360</td><td>1.1</td><td>435</td><td>1.0</td></tr>
<tr><td>0</td><td>–</td><td>160</td><td>0.5</td><td>78</td><td>0.2</td><td>ALASKA</td><td>0</td><td>–</td><td>0</td><td>–</td><td>15</td><td>–</td></tr>
<tr><td>100</td><td>0.5</td><td>360</td><td>1.1</td><td>273</td><td>0.6</td><td>ARIZONA</td><td>700</td><td>3.3</td><td>680</td><td>2.1</td><td>621</td><td>1.5</td></tr>
<tr><td>100</td><td>0.5</td><td>0</td><td>–</td><td>177</td><td>0.4</td><td>ARKANSAS</td><td>0</td><td>–</td><td>80</td><td>0.2</td><td>119</td><td>0.3</td></tr>
<tr><td>1,600</td><td>7.5</td><td>1,400</td><td>4.1</td><td>2,121</td><td>4.6</td><td>CALIFORNIA</td><td>300</td><td>1.4</td><td>1,520</td><td>4.6</td><td>2,173</td><td>5.1</td></tr>
<tr><td>0</td><td>–</td><td>160</td><td>0.5</td><td>159</td><td>0.3</td><td>COLORADO</td><td>600</td><td>2.8</td><td>440</td><td>1.3</td><td>321</td><td>0.8</td></tr>
<tr><td>300</td><td>1.4</td><td>680</td><td>2.0</td><td>963</td><td>2.1</td><td>CONNECTICUT</td><td>0</td><td>–</td><td>240</td><td>0.7</td><td>216</td><td>0.5</td></tr>
<tr><td>100</td><td>0.5</td><td>80</td><td>0.2</td><td>354</td><td>0.8</td><td>DELAWARE</td><td>0</td><td>–</td><td>240</td><td>0.7</td><td>410</td><td>1.0</td></tr>
<tr><td>3,700</td><td>17.4</td><td>2,160</td><td>6.3</td><td>1,815</td><td>3.9</td><td>D.C.</td><td>700</td><td>3.3</td><td>360</td><td>1.1</td><td>603</td><td>1.4</td></tr>
<tr><td>1,100</td><td>5.2</td><td>2,720</td><td>8.0</td><td>3,897</td><td>8.4</td><td>FLORIDA</td><td>4,400</td><td>20.7</td><td>8,040</td><td>24.5</td><td>11,582</td><td>27.1</td></tr>
<tr><td>400</td><td>1.9</td><td>600</td><td>1.8</td><td>690</td><td>1.5</td><td>GEORGIA</td><td>300</td><td>1.4</td><td>880</td><td>2.7</td><td>1,103</td><td>2.6</td></tr>
<tr><td>300</td><td>1.4</td><td>40</td><td>0.1</td><td>150</td><td>0.3</td><td>HAWAII</td><td>0</td><td>–</td><td>40</td><td>0.1</td><td>133</td><td>0.3</td></tr>
<tr><td>0</td><td>–</td><td>80</td><td>0.2</td><td>51</td><td>0.1</td><td>IDAHO</td><td>0</td><td>–</td><td>0</td><td>–</td><td>24</td><td>0.1</td></tr>
<tr><td>400</td><td>1.9</td><td>1,080</td><td>3.2</td><td>1,224</td><td>2.6</td><td>ILLINOIS</td><td>200</td><td>0.9</td><td>520</td><td>1.6</td><td>255</td><td>0.6</td></tr>
<tr><td>400</td><td>1.9</td><td>280</td><td>0.8</td><td>684</td><td>1.5</td><td>INDIANA</td><td>0</td><td>–</td><td>200</td><td>0.6</td><td>310</td><td>0.7</td></tr>
<tr><td>0</td><td>–</td><td>80</td><td>0.2</td><td>81</td><td>0.2</td><td>IOWA</td><td>0</td><td>–</td><td>200</td><td>0.6</td><td>122</td><td>0.3</td></tr>
<tr><td>0</td><td>–</td><td>120</td><td>0.4</td><td>222</td><td>0.5</td><td>KANSAS</td><td>100</td><td>0.5</td><td>240</td><td>0.7</td><td>130</td><td>0.3</td></tr>
<tr><td>0</td><td>–</td><td>640</td><td>1.9</td><td>336</td><td>0.7</td><td>KENTUCKY</td><td>300</td><td>1.4</td><td>480</td><td>1.5</td><td>430</td><td>1.0</td></tr>
<tr><td>0</td><td>–</td><td>160</td><td>0.5</td><td>354</td><td>0.8</td><td>LOUISIANA</td><td>400</td><td>1.9</td><td>40</td><td>0.1</td><td>156</td><td>0.4</td></tr>
<tr><td>200</td><td>0.9</td><td>0</td><td>–</td><td>84</td><td>0.2</td><td>MAINE</td><td>0</td><td>–</td><td>200</td><td>0.6</td><td>309</td><td>0.7</td></tr>
<tr><td>2,000</td><td>9.4</td><td>4,080</td><td>11.9</td><td>5,109</td><td>11.0</td><td>MARYLAND</td><td>2,200</td><td>10.3</td><td>3,160</td><td>9.6</td><td>3,802</td><td>8.9</td></tr>
<tr><td>300</td><td>1.4</td><td>520</td><td>1.5</td><td>750</td><td>1.6</td><td>MASSACHUSETTS</td><td>100</td><td>0.5</td><td>240</td><td>0.7</td><td>323</td><td>0.8</td></tr>
<tr><td>900</td><td>4.2</td><td>960</td><td>2.8</td><td>1,065</td><td>2.3</td><td>MICHIGAN</td><td>300</td><td>1.4</td><td>320</td><td>1.0</td><td>334</td><td>0.8</td></tr>
<tr><td>0</td><td>–</td><td>200</td><td>0.6</td><td>129</td><td>0.3</td><td>MINNESOTA</td><td>200</td><td>0.9</td><td>40</td><td>0.1</td><td>219</td><td>0.5</td></tr>
<tr><td>200</td><td>0.9</td><td>160</td><td>0.5</td><td>111</td><td>0.2</td><td>MISSISSIPPI</td><td>0</td><td>–</td><td>120</td><td>0.4</td><td>117</td><td>0.3</td></tr>
<tr><td>100</td><td>0.5</td><td>200</td><td>0.6</td><td>309</td><td>0.7</td><td>MISSOURI</td><td>300</td><td>1.4</td><td>120</td><td>0.4</td><td>168</td><td>0.4</td></tr>
<tr><td>0</td><td>–</td><td>0</td><td>–</td><td>111</td><td>0.2</td><td>MONTANA</td><td>0</td><td>–</td><td>40</td><td>0.1</td><td>0</td><td>–</td></tr>
<tr><td>0</td><td>–</td><td>0</td><td>–</td><td>18</td><td>–</td><td>NEBRASKA</td><td>0</td><td>–</td><td>120</td><td>0.4</td><td>41</td><td>0.1</td></tr>
<tr><td>0</td><td>–</td><td>80</td><td>0.2</td><td>123</td><td>0.3</td><td>NEVADA</td><td>0</td><td>–</td><td>160</td><td>0.5</td><td>148</td><td>0.4</td></tr>
<tr><td>0</td><td>–</td><td>120</td><td>0.4</td><td>387</td><td>0.8</td><td>NEW HAMPSHIRE</td><td>0</td><td>–</td><td>120</td><td>0.4</td><td>126</td><td>0.3</td></tr>
<tr><td>1,000</td><td>4.7</td><td>1,400</td><td>4.1</td><td>4,116</td><td>8.8</td><td>NEW JERSEY</td><td>700</td><td>3.3</td><td>400</td><td>1.2</td><td>783</td><td>1.8</td></tr>
<tr><td>100</td><td>0.5</td><td>160</td><td>0.5</td><td>189</td><td>0.4</td><td>NEW MEXICO</td><td>0</td><td>–</td><td>80</td><td>0.2</td><td>336</td><td>0.8</td></tr>
<tr><td>1,900</td><td>8.9</td><td>5,320</td><td>15.6</td><td>6,972</td><td>15.0</td><td>NEW YORK</td><td>700</td><td>3.3</td><td>600</td><td>1.8</td><td>1,333</td><td>3.1</td></tr>
<tr><td>1,900</td><td>8.9</td><td>2,080</td><td>6.1</td><td>2,901</td><td>6.2</td><td>NORTH CAROLINA</td><td>3,000</td><td>14.1</td><td>5,080</td><td>15.5</td><td>6,102</td><td>14.3</td></tr>
<tr><td>0</td><td>–</td><td>0</td><td>–</td><td>0</td><td>–</td><td>NORTH DAKOTA</td><td>0</td><td>–</td><td>40</td><td>0.1</td><td>0</td><td>–</td></tr>
<tr><td>400</td><td>1.9</td><td>920</td><td>2.7</td><td>1,740</td><td>3.7</td><td>OHIO</td><td>800</td><td>3.8</td><td>600</td><td>1.8</td><td>774</td><td>1.8</td></tr>
<tr><td>200</td><td>0.9</td><td>160</td><td>0.5</td><td>129</td><td>0.3</td><td>OKLAHOMA</td><td>100</td><td>0.5</td><td>160</td><td>0.5</td><td>78</td><td>0.2</td></tr>
<tr><td>200</td><td>0.9</td><td>80</td><td>0.2</td><td>156</td><td>0.3</td><td>OREGON</td><td>100</td><td>0.5</td><td>200</td><td>0.6</td><td>186</td><td>0.4</td></tr>
<tr><td>500</td><td>2.3</td><td>1,640</td><td>4.8</td><td>2,853</td><td>6.1</td><td>PENNSYLVANIA</td><td>900</td><td>4.2</td><td>1,360</td><td>4.1</td><td>1,615</td><td>3.8</td></tr>
<tr><td>100</td><td>0.5</td><td>40</td><td>0.1</td><td>123</td><td>0.3</td><td>RHODE ISLAND</td><td>200</td><td>0.9</td><td>80</td><td>0.2</td><td>60</td><td>0.1</td></tr>
<tr><td>200</td><td>0.9</td><td>720</td><td>2.1</td><td>798</td><td>1.7</td><td>SOUTH CAROLINA</td><td>400</td><td>1.9</td><td>1,200</td><td>3.7</td><td>1,683</td><td>3.9</td></tr>
<tr><td>0</td><td>–</td><td>0</td><td>–</td><td>0</td><td>–</td><td>SOUTH DAKOTA</td><td>0</td><td>–</td><td>0</td><td>–</td><td>71</td><td>0.2</td></tr>
<tr><td>600</td><td>2.8</td><td>640</td><td>1.9</td><td>1,524</td><td>3.3</td><td>TENNESSEE</td><td>400</td><td>1.9</td><td>1,320</td><td>4.0</td><td>1,326</td><td>3.1</td></tr>
<tr><td>400</td><td>1.9</td><td>840</td><td>2.5</td><td>801</td><td>1.7</td><td>TEXAS</td><td>600</td><td>2.8</td><td>960</td><td>2.9</td><td>1,040</td><td>2.4</td></tr>
<tr><td>200</td><td>0.9</td><td>0</td><td>–</td><td>117</td><td>0.3</td><td>UTAH</td><td>0</td><td>–</td><td>120</td><td>0.4</td><td>101</td><td>0.2</td></tr>
<tr><td>200</td><td>0.9</td><td>80</td><td>0.2</td><td>123</td><td>0.3</td><td>VERMONT</td><td>0</td><td>–</td><td>80</td><td>0.2</td><td>124</td><td>0.3</td></tr>
<tr><td>0</td><td>–</td><td>200</td><td>0.6</td><td>216</td><td>0.5</td><td>WASHINGTON</td><td>0</td><td>–</td><td>320</td><td>1.0</td><td>480</td><td>1.1</td></tr>
<tr><td>1,200</td><td>5.6</td><td>1,840</td><td>5.4</td><td>1,497</td><td>3.2</td><td>WEST VIRGINIA</td><td>1,600</td><td>7.5</td><td>840</td><td>2.6</td><td>1,694</td><td>4.0</td></tr>
<tr><td>0</td><td>–</td><td>240</td><td>0.7</td><td>183</td><td>0.4</td><td>WISCONSIN</td><td>100</td><td>0.5</td><td>160</td><td>0.5</td><td>150</td><td>0.4</td></tr>
<tr><td>0</td><td>–</td><td>0</td><td>–</td><td>0</td><td>–</td><td>WYOMING</td><td>0</td><td>–</td><td>40</td><td>0.1</td><td>14</td><td>–</td></tr>
<tr><td>21,300</td><td>99.9*</td><td>34,160</td><td>100.3*</td><td>46,554</td><td>100.2*</td><td>TOTAL U.S.</td><td>21,300</td><td>100.1*</td><td>32,840</td><td>99.8*</td><td>42,695</td><td>100.1*</td></tr>
</table>

*rounding error

WASHINGTON

	TO WASHINGTON FROM							FROM WASHINGTON TO					
	1970		1980		1990			1970		1980		1990	
	#	%	#	%	#	%		#	%	#	%	#	%
ALABAMA	0	–	80	0.2	117	0.3	ALABAMA	0	–	40	0.2	154	0.5
ALASKA	400	1.9	1,600	4.5	1,482	3.1	ALASKA	200	1.2	320	1.3	501	1.7
ARIZONA	200	1.0	1,320	3.7	1,566	3.3	ARIZONA	1,100	6.7	3,160	13.3	3,732	12.7
ARKANSAS	0	–	200	0.6	258	0.5	ARKANSAS	100	0.6	120	0.5	259	0.9
CALIFORNIA	4,900	23.8	12,360	34.6	16,689	35.2	CALIFORNIA	5,200	31.9	5,600	23.6	6,460	22.0
COLORADO	100	0.5	440	1.2	954	2.0	COLORADO	400	2.5	520	2.2	603	2.1
CONNECTICUT	0	–	0	–	357	0.8	CONNECTICUT	100	0.6	0	–	25	0.1
DELAWARE	0	–	80	0.2	18	–	DELAWARE	0	–	0	–	7	–
D.C.	0	–	40	0.1	105	0.2	D.C.	0	–	40	0.2	186	0.6
FLORIDA	100	0.5	640	1.8	1,413	3.0	FLORIDA	700	4.3	480	2.0	897	3.1
GEORGIA	0	–	0	–	177	0.4	GEORGIA	0	–	40	0.2	208	0.1
HAWAII	200	1.0	320	0.9	672	1.4	HAWAII	0	–	680	2.9	476	1.6
IDAHO	1,900	9.2	2,120	5.9	1,959	4.1	IDAHO	1,000	6.1	1,840	7.8	1,692	5.8
ILLINOIS	700	3.4	920	2.6	1,131	2.4	ILLINOIS	400	2.5	320	1.3	213	0.7
INDIANA	300	1.5	160	0.4	381	0.8	INDIANA	100	0.6	200	0.8	131	0.5
IOWA	800	3.9	560	1.6	282	0.6	IOWA	300	1.8	40	0.2	159	0.5
KANSAS	400	1.9	160	0.4	465	1.0	KANSAS	200	1.2	280	1.2	434	1.5
KENTUCKY	0	–	200	0.6	120	0.3	KENTUCKY	0	–	0	–	8	–
LOUISIANA	200	1.0	80	0.2	288	0.6	LOUISIANA	100	0.6	40	0.2	168	0.6
MAINE	0	–	120	0.3	0	–	MAINE	0		0	–	75	0.3
MARYLAND	0	–	280	0.8	267	0.6	MARYLAND	0	–	160	0.7	268	0.9
MASSACHUSETTS	100	0.5	160	0.4	330	0.7	MASSACHUSETTS	200	1.2	120	0.5	47	0.2
MICHIGAN	200	1.0	320	0.9	759	1.6	MICHIGAN	100	0.6	120	0.5	292	1.0
MINNESOTA	1,000	4.9	520	1.5	543	1.1	MINNESOTA	400	2.5	520	2.2	342	1.2
MISSISSIPPI	0	–	0	–	300	0.6	MISSISSIPPI	0	–	0	–	51	0.2
MISSOURI	100	0.5	520	1.5	342	0.7	MISSOURI	400	2.5	440	1.9	322	1.1
MONTANA	1,500	7.3	960	2.7	1,203	2.5	MONTANA	300	1.8	480	2.0	841	2.9
NEBRASKA	300	1.5	400	1.1	267	0.6	NEBRASKA	300	1.8	160	0.7	197	0.7
NEVADA	200	1.0	640	1.8	795	1.7	NEVADA	0	–	640	2.7	869	3.0
NEW HAMPSHIRE	0	–	120	0.3	141	0.3	NEW HAMPSHIRE	0	–	0	–	0	–
NEW JERSEY	0	–	240	0.7	774	1.6	NEW JERSEY	0	–	0	–	146	0.5
NEW MEXICO	0	–	80	0.2	267	0.6	NEW MEXICO	200	1.2	240	1.0	270	0.9
NEW YORK	600	2.9	1,040	2.9	1,146	2.4	NEW YORK	200	1.2	240	1.0	90	0.3
NORTH CAROLINA	100	0.5	120	0.3	186	0.4	NORTH CAROLINA	100	0.6	80	0.3	114	0.4
NORTH DAKOTA	300	1.5	200	0.6	198	0.4	NORTH DAKOTA	0	–	120	0.5	40	0.1
OHIO	500	2.4	560	1.6	468	1.0	OHIO	200	1.2	80	0.3	228	0.8
OKLAHOMA	300	1.5	80	0.2	267	0.6	OKLAHOMA	300	1.8	520	2.2	188	0.6
OREGON	3,200	15.5	4,760	13.3	6,870	14.5	OREGON	2,900	17.8	4,040	17.0	5,762	19.6
PENNSYLVANIA	200	1.0	640	1.8	345	0.7	PENNSYLVANIA	200	1.2	80	0.3	284	1.0
RHODE ISLAND	0	–	120	0.3	39	0.1	RHODE ISLAND	0	–	0	–	0	–
SOUTH CAROLINA	0	–	0	–	96	0.2	SOUTH CAROLINA	0	–	120	0.5	195	0.7
SOUTH DAKOTA	400	1.9	280	0.8	219	0.5	SOUTH DAKOTA	0	–	80	0.3	105	0.4
TENNESSEE	100	0.5	80	0.2	141	0.3	TENNESSEE	0	–	120	0.5	108	0.4
TEXAS	600	2.9	640	1.8	1,575	3.3	TEXAS	100	0.6	1,000	4.2	1,033	3.5
UTAH	200	1.0	520	1.5	336	0.7	UTAH	100	0.6	160	0.7	368	1.3
VERMONT	0	–	40	0.1	63	0.1	VERMONT	200	1.2	0	–	68	0.2
VIRGINIA	0	–	320	0.9	480	1.0	VIRGINIA	0	–	200	0.8	216	0.7
WEST VIRGINIA	0	–	120	0.3	33	0.1	WEST VIRGINIA	0	–	40	0.2	53	0.2
WISCONSIN	400	1.9	360	1.0	366	0.8	WISCONSIN	200	1.2	120	0.5	154	0.5
WYOMING	100	0.5	240	0.7	234	0.5	WYOMING	0	–	120	0.5	306	1.0
TOTAL U.S.	20,600	100.3*	35,760	100.0	47,484	100.2*	TOTAL U.S.	16,300	99.6*	23,720	99.9*	29,345	100.2*

*rounding error

WEST VIRGINIA

TO WEST VIRGINIA FROM							FROM WEST VIRGINIA TO					
1970		1980		1990			1970		1980		1990	
#	%	#	%	#	%		#	%	#	%	#	%
0	–	80	0.9	114	0.9	ALABAMA	100	0.9	120	0.9	129	1.0
0	–	0	–	0	–	ALASKA	0	–	0	–	0	–
0	–	80	0.9	257	2.0	ARIZONA	200	1.0	200	1.5	116	0.9
0	–	0	–	50	0.4	ARKANSAS	0	–	40	0.3	143	1.1
100	1.4	200	2.3	332	2.6	CALIFORNIA	300	2.7	280	2.1	200	1.6
0	–	0	–	18	0.1	COLORADO	0	–	120	0.9	6	0.1
0	–	40	0.5	7	0.1	CONNECTICUT	0	–	40	0.3	22	0.2
0	–	0	–	0	–	DELAWARE	100	0.9	200	1.5	67	0.5
0	–	0	–	231	1.8	D.C.	0	–	80	0.6	36	0.3
300	4.2	760	8.8	1,137	8.8	FLORIDA	3,000	26.8	3,440	25.7	3,441	26.6
0	–	0	–	116	0.9	GEORGIA	0	–	120	0.9	260	2.0
0	–	0	–	22	0.2	HAWAII	0	–	0	–	0	–
0	–	0	–	0	–	IDAHO	0	–	0	–	0	–
0	–	440	5.1	178	1.4	ILLINOIS	0	–	160	1.2	57	0.4
100	1.4	160	1.9	52	0.4	INDIANA	200	1.8	120	0.9	118	0.9
0	–	0	–	0	–	IOWA	0	–	0	–	8	0.1
0	–	40	0.5	0	–	KANSAS	0	–	0	–	50	0.4
500	6.9	360	4.2	340	2.6	KENTUCKY	400	3.6	520	3.9	483	3.7
0	–	0	–	51	0.4	LOUISIANA	0	–	40	0.3	90	0.7
0	–	0	–	0	–	MAINE	0	–	0	–	0	–
600	8.3	1,360	15.8	1,950	15.1	MARYLAND	400	3.6	520	3.9	826	6.4
0	–	40	0.5	47	0.4	MASSACHUSETTS	100	0.9	0	–	26	0.2
0	–	360	4.2	459	3.6	MICHIGAN	300	2.7	240	1.8	126	1.0
0	–	40	0.5	14	0.1	MINNESOTA	0	–	0	–	0	–
0	–	0	–	18	0.1	MISSISSIPPI	0	–	0	–	0	–
0	–	0	–	146	1.1	MISSOURI	0	–	40	0.3	151	1.2
0	–	0	–	21	0.2	MONTANA	0	–	0	–	0	–
0	–	0	–	0	–	NEBRASKA	0	–	0	–	33	0.3
0	–	0	–	18	0.1	NEVADA	100	0.9	80	0.6	13	0.1
0	–	0	–	0	–	NEW HAMPSHIRE	200	1.8	0	–	0	–
0	–	280	3.3	582	4.5	NEW JERSEY	300	2.7	120	0.9	21	0.2
0	–	0	–	53	0.4	NEW MEXICO	0	–	200	1.5	18	0.1
400	5.6	320	3.7	525	4.1	NEW YORK	100	0.9	40	0.3	134	1.0
0	–	240	2.8	330	2.6	NORTH CAROLINA	100	0.9	720	5.4	891	6.9
0	–	0	–	0	–	NORTH DAKOTA	0	–	0	–	30	0.2
2,500	34.7	2,160	25.1	2,638	20.4	OHIO	3,300	29.5	2,800	21.0	2,390	18.5
0	–	40	0.5	44	0.3	OKLAHOMA	0	–	0	–	7	0.1
0	–	0	–	26	0.2	OREGON	0	–	40	0.3	34	0.3
900	12.5	440	5.1	979	7.6	PENNSYLVANIA	300	2.7	520	3.9	663	5.1
0	–	0	–	0	–	RHODE ISLAND	0	–	0	–	0	–
0	–	40	0.5	115	0.9	SOUTH CAROLINA	200	1.8	240	1.8	270	2.1
0	–	0	–	25	0.2	SOUTH DAKOTA	0	–	0	–	0	–
0	–	120	1.4	86	0.7	TENNESSEE	100	0.9	120	0.9	249	1.9
200	2.8	120	1.4	141	1.1	TEXAS	100	0.9	200	1.5	247	1.9
0	–	0	–	18	0.1	UTAH	100	0.9	0	–	17	0.1
0	–	0	–	0	–	VERMONT	0	–	0	–	0	–
1,600	22.2	840	9.8	1,694	13.1	VIRGINIA	1,200	10.7	1,840	13.8	1,497	11.6
0	–	40	0.5	53	0.4	WASHINGTON	0	–	120	0.9	33	0.3
0	–	0	–	32	0.3	WISCONSIN	0	–	0	–	34	0.3
0	–	0	–	0	–	WYOMING	0	–	40	0.3	0	–
7,200	100.0	8,600	100.2*	12,919	100.2*	TOTAL U.S.	11,200	100.3*	13,360	99.8*	12,936	100.3*

*rounding error

WISCONSIN

TO WISCONSIN FROM							FROM WISCONSIN TO					
1970		1980		1990			1970		1980		1990	
#	%	#	%	#	%		#	%	#	%	#	%
100	0.7	80	0.4	96	0.4	ALABAMA	0	–	80	0.3	226	0.7
0	–	40	0.2	83	0.4	ALASKA	100	0.6	0	–	77	0.3
300	2.0	320	1.6	751	3.3	ARIZONA	1,600	9.0	3,200	12.2	2,763	8.9
300	2.0	200	1.0	237	1.0	ARKANSAS	600	3.4	680	2.6	980	3.1
400	2.7	1,080	5.5	1,398	6.1	CALIFORNIA	2,800	15.7	2,120	8.1	2,330	7.5
300	2.0	120	0.6	307	1.3	COLORADO	100	0.6	560	2.1	561	1.8
0	–	320	1.6	135	0.6	CONNECTICUT	0	–	40	0.2	37	0.1
0	–	0	–	0	–	DELAWARE	0	–	0	–	16	0.1
100	0.7	40	0.2	67	0.3	D.C.	0	–	0	–	31	0.1
600	4.0	1,440	7.3	1,737	7.5	FLORIDA	4,400	24.7	7,200	27.5	9,763	31.3
0	–	40	0.2	138	0.6	GEORGIA	200	1.1	160	0.6	328	1.1
0	–	0	–	0	–	HAWAII	0	–	0	–	20	0.1
0	–	0	–	162	0.7	IDAHO	0	–	0	–	140	0.5
6,100	40.7	8,160	41.5	8,568	37.2	ILLINOIS	1,400	7.9	3,040	11.6	3,066	9.8
1,300	8.7	440	2.2	348	1.5	INDIANA	300	1.7	560	2.1	339	1.1
0	–	880	4.5	503	2.2	IOWA	400	2.2	480	1.8	412	1.3
0	–	0	–	134	0.6	KANSAS	400	2.2	120	0.5	99	0.3
0	–	80	0.4	80	0.4	KENTUCKY	100	0.6	0	–	166	0.5
0	–	80	0.4	82	0.4	LOUISIANA	0	–	80	0.3	150	0.5
0	–	80	0.4	24	0.1	MAINE	0	–	0	–	0	–
0	–	80	0.4	172	0.8	MARYLAND	200	1.1	0	–	111	0.4
400	2.7	120	0.6	96	0.4	MASSACHUSETTS	100	0.6	120	0.5	193	0.6
700	4.7	880	4.5	1,121	4.9	MICHIGAN	700	3.9	920	3.5	846	2.7
1,700	11.3	2,120	10.8	2,914	12.7	MINNESOTA	1,100	6.2	1,480	5.7	1,967	6.3
0	–	160	0.8	77	0.3	MISSISSIPPI	0	–	320	1.2	228	0.7
300	2.0	560	2.9	253	1.1	MISSOURI	300	1.7	520	2.0	393	1.3
100	0.7	80	0.4	82	0.4	MONTANA	0	–	200	0.8	158	0.5
100	0.7	120	0.6	63	0.3	NEBRASKA	200	1.1	0	–	154	0.5
100	0.7	0	–	170	0.7	NEVADA	0	–	240	0.9	682	2.2
0	–	120	0.6	0	–	NEW HAMPSHIRE	0	–	0	–	17	0.1
200	1.3	160	0.8	297	1.3	NEW JERSEY	100	0.6	120	0.5	108	0.4
0	–	40	0.2	339	1.5	NEW MEXICO	0	–	360	1.4	303	1.0
500	3.3	200	1.0	318	1.4	NEW YORK	0	–	320	1.2	109	0.4
0	–	40	0.2	154	0.7	NORTH CAROLINA	200	1.1	240	0.9	318	1.0
100	0.7	200	1.0	68	0.3	NORTH DAKOTA	0	–	80	0.3	50	0.2
600	4.0	400	2.0	322	1.4	OHIO	400	2.2	320	1.2	427	1.4
0	–	0	–	105	0.5	OKLAHOMA	0	–	40	0.2	87	0.3
0	–	80	0.4	116	0.5	OREGON	100	0.6	320	1.2	346	1.1
0	–	160	0.8	323	1.4	PENNSYLVANIA	200	1.1	80	0.3	278	0.9
0	–	0	–	0	–	RHODE ISLAND	100	0.6	0	–	0	–
0	–	0	–	34	0.2	SOUTH CAROLINA	0	–	160	0.6	147	0.5
0	–	40	0.2	154	0.7	SOUTH DAKOTA	0	–	80	0.3	47	0.2
100	0.7	40	0.2	96	0.4	TENNESSEE	300	1.7	160	0.6	336	1.1
100	0.7	360	1.8	449	2.0	TEXAS	1,000	5.6	1,000	3.8	1,687	5.4
100	0.7	0	–	0	–	UTAH	0	–	0	–	48	0.2
0	–	0	–	14	0.1	VERMONT	0	–	80	0.3	0	–
100	0.7	160	0.8	150	0.7	VIRGINIA	0	–	240	0.9	183	0.6
200	1.3	120	0.6	154	0.7	WASHINGTON	400	2.2	360	1.4	366	1.2
0	–	0	–	34	0.2	WEST VIRGINIA	0	–	0	–	32	0.1
100	0.7	0	–	105	0.5	WYOMING	0	–	80	0.3	50	0.2
15,000	100.4*	19,640	99.6*	23,030	100.7*	TOTAL U.S.	17,800	100.0	26,160	99.9*	31,175	100.6*

*rounding error

WYOMING

	TO WYOMING FROM							FROM WYOMING TO					
	1970		1980		1990			1970		1980		1990	
#	%	#	%	#	%		#	%	#	%	#	%	
0	–	0	–	18	0.4	ALABAMA	0	–	120	2.7	0	–
0	–	0	–	8	0.2	ALASKA	0	–	0	–	53	0.8
0	–	40	1.4	181	4.3	ARIZONA	500	17.9	280	6.3	693	10.7
0	–	40	1.4	14	0.3	ARKANSAS	0	–	200	4.5	124	1.9
0	–	360	12.3	746	17.7	CALIFORNIA	1,100	39.3	200	4.5	519	8.0
0	–	400	13.7	660	15.7	COLORADO	100	3.6	720	16.1	1,110	17.1
0	–	0	–	0	–	CONNECTICUT	0	–	0	–	0	–
0	–	0	–	21	0.5	DELAWARE	0	–	0	–	0	–
0	–	0	–	0	–	D.C.	0	–	0	–	0	–
0	–	80	2.7	36	0.9	FLORIDA	0	–	200	4.5	176	2.7
0	–	0	–	0	–	GEORGIA	0	–	0	–	50	0.8
0	–	40	1.4	7	0.2	HAWAII	0	–	0	–	22	0.3
100	14.3	200	6.8	101	2.4	IDAHO	100	3.6	160	3.6	360	5.6
100	14.3	160	5.5	7	0.2	ILLINOIS	100	3.6	0	–	21	0.3
0	–	0	–	18	0.4	INDIANA	0	–	0	–	67	1.0
0	–	40	1.4	61	1.4	IOWA	0	–	40	0.9	85	1.3
0	–	40	1.4	29	0.7	KANSAS	0	–	0	–	60	0.9
100	14.3	0	–	11	0.3	KENTUCKY	0	–	0	–	14	0.2
0	–	120	4.3	65	1.5	LOUISIANA	0	–	0	–	21	0.3
0	–	0	–	0	–	MAINE	0	–	0	–	0	–
0	–	0	–	69	1.6	MARYLAND	0	–	0	–	23	0.4
0	–	0	–	0	–	MASSACHUSETTS	0	–	40	0.9	0	–
0	–	0	–	7	0.2	MICHIGAN	0	–	40	0.9	57	0.9
0	–	0	–	58	1.4	MINNESOTA	0	–	80	1.8	9	0.1
0	–	0	–	0	–	MISSISSIPPI	0	–	0	–	60	0.9
0	–	0	–	58	1.4	MISSOURI	0	–	40	0.9	106	1.6
100	14.3	160	5.8	330	7.8	MONTANA	0	–	120	2.7	326	5.0
0	–	80	2.9	292	6.9	NEBRASKA	400	14.3	160	3.6	204	3.1
0	–	40	1.4	7	0.2	NEVADA	0	–	200	4.5	362	5.6
0	–	0	–	21	0.5	NEW HAMPSHIRE	0	–	0	–	0	–
0	–	0	–	39	0.9	NEW JERSEY	0	–	0	–	90	1.4
0	–	120	4.3	0	–	NEW MEXICO	100	3.6	120	2.7	246	3.8
0	–	40	1.4	40	1.0	NEW YORK	0	–	0	–	41	0.6
0	–	40	1.4	0	–	NORTH CAROLINA	0	–	120	2.7	0	–
0	–	40	1.4	155	3.7	NORTH DAKOTA	0	–	0	–	55	0.8
0	–	120	4.3	72	1.7	OHIO	0	–	0	–	38	0.6
0	–	0	–	77	1.8	OKLAHOMA	100	3.6	200	4.5	102	1.6
0	–	120	4.3	116	2.8	OREGON	0	–	120	2.7	106	1.6
0	–	40	1.4	29	0.7	PENNSYLVANIA	0	–	40	0.9	11	0.2
0	–	0	–	25	0.7	RHODE ISLAND	0	–	0	–	0	–
0	–	0	–	0	–	SOUTH CAROLINA	0	–	0	–	0	–
200	28.6	80	2.9	149	3.5	SOUTH DAKOTA	100	3.6	160	3.6	163	2.5
0	–	0	–	0	–	TENNESSEE	0	–	0	–	69	1.1
0	–	40	1.4	53	1.3	TEXAS	0	–	520	11.6	288	4.4
100	14.3	40	1.4	257	6.1	UTAH	0	–	360	8.0	400	6.2
0	–	0	–	0	–	VERMONT	0	–	0	–	21	0.3
0	–	40	1.4	14	0.3	VIRGINIA	0	–	0	–	0	–
0	–	120	4.3	306	7.3	WASHINGTON	100	3.6	240	5.4	234	3.6
0	–	40	1.4	0	–	WEST VIRGINIA	0	–	0	–	0	–
0	–	80	2.9	50	1.2	WISCONSIN	100	3.6	0	–	105	1.6
700	100.1*	2,760	99.0*	4,207	100.1*	TOTAL U.S.	2,800	100.3*	4,480	100.5*	6,491	99.8*

*rounding error

APPENDIX B
In-migration, Out-migration And Net Migration by County, 1985-1990

Migration by County or County Group

County or county group	Number of In-migrants	Number of Out-migrants	Net Number of Migrants
Alabama			
Baldwin and Escambia	2,213	1,025	1,188
Madison and Limestone	2,288	1,460	828
Bibb, Fayette, Greene, Hale, Lamar, Marion and Pickens	1,051	604	447
Chambers, Coosa, Randolph and Tallapoosa	920	488	432
Tuscaloosa	855	426	429
Dale, Houston, Barbour and Henry	1,497	1,107	390
Calhoun	608	280	328
St. Clair and Shelby	860	536	324
Colbert and Lauderdale	791	490	301
Coffee, Covington and Geneva	1,269	1,019	250
Lawrence and Morgan	754	540	214
Autauga, Elmore and Chilton	492	308	184
De Kalb, Jackson and Marshall	1,223	1,041	182
Mobile	2,232	2,117	115
Montgomery	1,067	954	113
Choctaw, Clarke, Conecuh, Monroe, Washington and Wilcox	564	456	108
Bullock, Butler, Crenshaw, Lowndes, Macon and Pike	438	336	102
Walker, Franklin and Winston	555	469	86
Blount and Cullman	409	351	58
Etowah and Cherokee	743	750	-7
Jefferson	2,843	2,861	-18
Russell and Lee	828	847	-19
Clay, Cleburne and Talladega	430	517	-87
Dallas, Marengo, Perry and Sumter	406	589	-183
Alaska*			
Aleutians East, Aleutians West, Bethel, Bristol Bay, Dillingham, Haines, Kodiak Island, Lake and Peninsula, Nome, North Slope, Northwest Arctic, Prince of Wales-Outer Ketchikan, Skagway-Yakutat-Angoon, Southeast Fairbanks, Valdez-Cordova, Wade Hampton, Wrangell-Petersburg and Yukon-Koyukuk	355	671	-316
Fairbanks North Star, Juneau, Kenai Peninsula, Ketchikan Gateway, Matanuska-Susitna and Sitka	874	2,233	-1,359
Anchorage	1,166	2,933	-1,767
Arizona			
Maricopa	54,291	19,213	35,078
Pima	18,182	7,053	11,129
La Paz and Mohave	8,294	2,846	5,448
Coconino and Yavapai	7,456	2,877	4,579
Yuma	3,742	1,696	2,046
Gila and Pinal	3,862	1,901	1,961
Cochise, Graham, Greenlee and Santa Cruz	2,334	2,059	275
Apache and Navajo	595	635	-40
Arkansas			
Benton and Madison	4,560	1,938	2,622
Baxter, Boone, Carroll, Marion, Newton and Searcy	4,537	2,360	2,177
Cleburne, Fulton, Independence, Izard, Jackson, Sharp, Stone, Van Buren, White and Woodruff	3,607	1,808	1,799
Clark, Garland, Hot Spring, Montgomery and Pike	3,229	1,630	1,599
Pulaski and Saline	2,660	1,864	796
Washington	1,518	874	644
Crawford, Sebastian, Franklin, Logan, Polk and Scott	2,333	1,732	601
Conway, Johnson, Perry, Pope and Yell	1,027	574	453
Faulkner, Lonoke, Monroe and Prairie	782	398	384

* The Census Microdata program only identifies boroughs and census areas for Alaska, not counties.

County or county group	Number of In-migrants	Number of Out-migrants	Net Number of Migrants
Clay, Craighead, Greene, Lawrence and Randolph	1,291	949	342
Miller, Hempstead, Howard, Lafayette, Little River, Nevada and Sevier	1,199	1,084	115
Cross, Lee, Phillips, Poinsett and St. Francis	607	501	106
Arkansas, Ashley, Bradley, Chicot, Desha, Drew and Lincoln	606	508	98
Calhoun, Columbia, Dallas, Ouachita and Union	865	774	91
Jefferson, Cleveland and Grant	518	569	-51
Crittenden and Mississippi	509	891	-382

California

County or county group	Number of In-migrants	Number of Out-migrants	Net Number of Migrants
Riverside	13,644	8,304	5,340
Sonoma	2,825	1,890	935
San Diego	20,155	19,354	801
Sacramento	5,172	4,745	427
Marin	1,391	1,110	281
Colusa, Glenn, Tehama and Trinity	679	420	259
San Joaquin	1,804	1,546	258
Tulare	1,201	946	255
Yolo	719	498	221
Fresno	1,825	1,643	182
Butte	1,238	1,058	180
Shasta	826	742	84
Napa	707	649	58
Placer	936	966	30
Madera and San Benito	354	384	-30
Nevada, Plumas and Sierra	937	1,022	-85
Stanislaus	1,505	1,591	-86
Kings	153	240	-87
Del Norte, Lassen, Modoc and Siskiyou	778	924	-146
Solano	1,349	1,534	-185
Merced	317	552	-235
Lake and Mendocino	730	972	-242
Humboldt	541	799	-250
Imperial	327	590	-263
San Luis Obispo	1,572	1,923	-351
Kern	1,877	2,284	-407
Sutter and Yuba	409	895	-486
Alpine, Amador, Calaveras, Inyo, Mariposa, Mono and Tuolumne	1,087	1,584	-497
Monterey	1,711	2,208	-497
El Dorado	659	1,310	-651
Ventura	3,814	4,639	-825
Santa Cruz	760	1,738	-978
Santa Barbara	2,183	3,321	-1,138
San Bernardino	6,897	8,322	-1,425
Contra Costa	2,973	4,677	-1,704
San Mateo	2,054	4,166	-2,112
San Francisco	1,652	3,879	-2,227
Alameda	3,452	6,612	-3,160
Santa Clara	4,983	8,283	-3,300
Orange	11,313	19,404	-8,091
Los Angeles	24,005	59,516	-35,511

Colorado

County or county group	Number of In-migrants	Number of Out-migrants	Net Number of Migrants
Delta and Mesa	2,448	1,334	1,114
Boulder	2,553	1,574	979
Larimer	2,427	1,500	927
Archuleta, Dolores, Gunnison, Hinsdale, La Plata, Mineral, Montezuma, Montrose, Ouray, San Juan and San Miguel	1,794	1,056	738

Migration by County or County Group

County or county group	Number of In-migrants	Number of Out-migrants	Net Number of Migrants
El Paso	4,173	3,647	526
Alamosa, Chaffee, Conejos, Costilla, Custer, Fremont, Huerfano, Lake, Las Animas, Rio Grande and Saguache	1,434	1,086	348
Douglas, Clear Creek, Elbert, Gilpin, Park and Teller	1,263	1,062	201
Eagle, Garfield, Grand, Jackson, Moffat, Pitkin, Rio Blanco, Routt and Summit	1,152	1,052	100
Pueblo	861	858	3
Weld	870	898	-28
Arapahoe	3,717	3,749	-32
Jefferson	3,321	3,561	-240
Adams	1,092	1,422	-330
Baca, Bent, Cheyenne, Crowley, Kiowa, Kit Carson, Lincoln, Logan Morgan, Otero, Phillips, Prowers, Sedgwick, Washington and Yuma	591	1,326	-735
Denver	2,976	4,690	-1,714

Connecticut

Windham	666	882	-216
Tolland	402	1,176	-774
New London	1,540	2,398	-858
Middlesex	805	1,986	-1,181
Litchfield	1,228	2,423	-1,195
Hartford	3,971	8,836	-4,865
New Haven	3,944	8,920	-4,976
Fairfield	4,795	15,551	-10,756

Delaware

Sussex	3,011	1,075	1,936
Kent	1,386	693	693
New Castle	3,629	4,577	-948

District of Columbia

Washington	4,821	10,288	-5,467

Florida

Palm Beach	47,444	8,855	38,589
Broward	40,272	13,458	26,814
Pinellas	35,065	14,322	20,743
Lee	25,255	4,807	20,448
Sarasota	22,225	5,588	16,637
Pasco	22,104	6,215	15,889
Volusia	17,407	5,192	12,215
Polk	15,566	3,717	11,849
Collier and Monroe	14,434	3,160	11,274
Charlotte	13,134	1,886	11,248
Brevard	14,621	3,785	10,836
Marion	12,087	2,070	10,017
Dade	21,305	11,322	9,983
Citrus, Levy and Sumter	11,408	1,663	9,745
Hernando	11,685	1,981	9,704
Manatee	13,043	3,670	9,373
Lake	12,536	3,287	9,249
Hillsborough	14,036	5,249	8,787
St. Johns, Flagler and Putnam	9,527	1,537	7,990
St. Lucie	9,023	1,342	7,681
De Soto, Glades, Hardee, Hendry and Highlands	8,773	1,590	7,183
Martin	7,124	1,444	5,680
Indian River and Okeechobee	7,439	1,875	5,564

County or county group	Number of In-migrants	Number of Out-migrants	Net Number of Migrants
Orange	10,486	5,012	5,474
Seminole	5,483	1,874	3,609
Osceola	3,805	931	2,874
Escambia and Santa Rosa	5,016	2,280	2,736
Bay, Holmes and Washington	3,033	1,030	2,003
Okaloosa and Walton	3,473	1,638	1,835
Bradford, Columbia, Dixie, Gilchrist, Hamilton, Lafayette, Madison, Suwannee, Taylor and Union	2,662	879	1,783
Duval	5,343	3,712	1,631
Clay, Nassau and Baker	2,210	1,004	1,206
Gadsden, Calhoun, Franklin, Gulf, Jackson and Liberty	1,342	312	1,030
Alachua	1,666	803	863
Leon, Jefferson and Wakulla	1,677	1,071	606

Georgia

County or county group	Number of In-migrants	Number of Out-migrants	Net Number of Migrants
Forsyth, Banks, Dawson, Franklin, Habersham, Hall, Hart, Lumpkin, Rabun, Stephens, Towns, Union and White	3,522	871	2,651
Cobb	3,486	2,131	1,355
Gwinnett	2,394	1,064	1,330
Chatham	2,720	1,439	1,281
Baker, Calhoun, Colquitt, Decatur, Early, Grady, Miller, Mitchell, Seminole, Terrell, Thomas and Worth	1,684	956	728
Effingham, Bryan, Camden, Glynn, Liberty, Long and McIntosh	1,636	948	688
De Kalb	3,851	3,228	623
Catoosa, Dade and Walker	1,301	684	617
Columbia, McDuffie and Richmond	1,836	1,231	605
Clayton	949	415	534
Ben Hill, Berrien, Brooks, Cook, Echols, Irwin, Lanier, Lowndes, Tift and Turner	1,214	706	508
Clarke, Jackson, Madison, Oconee and Oglethorpe	873	375	498
Appling, Bulloch, Candler, Evans, Jeff Davis, Tattnall, Toombs and Wayne	824	338	486
Paulding, Bartow, Gordon and Haralson	723	280	443
Cherokee and Pickens	793	380	413
Douglas and Fayette	1,236	846	390
Fannin, Gilmer, Murray and Whitfield	833	501	332
Houston, Jones, Peach, Crawford, Monroe and Twiggs	1,012	698	314
Chattooga, Floyd and Polk	747	470	277
Barrow, Walton, Elbert, Greene and Morgan	565	312	253
Bleckley, Dodge, Laurens, Montgomery, Pulaski, Telfair, Treutlen, Wheeler and Wilcox	665	426	239
Atkinson, Bacon, Brantley, Charlton, Clinch, Coffee, Pierce and Ware	771	541	230
Dougherty, Lee, Crisp, Dooly, Macon, Marion, Schley, Sumter, Taylor and Webster	1,041	830	211
Burke, Emanuel, Glascock, Jefferson, Jenkins, Lincoln, Screven, Taliaferro, Warren and Wilkes	495	293	202
Baldwin, Hancock, Jasper, Johnson, Putnam, Washington and Wilkinson	531	338	193
Butts, Newton, Spalding, Lamar, Pike and Upson	680	519	161
Henry and Rockdale	633	474	159
Bibb	682	541	141
Coweta, Carroll, Heard, Meriwether and Troup	927	831	96
Fulton	4,446	4,411	35
Chattahoochee, Muscogee, Clay, Harris, Quitman, Randolph, Stewart and Talbot	1,405	1,398	7

Hawaii

County or county group	Number of In-migrants	Number of Out-migrants	Net Number of Migrants
Kalawao, Kauai and Maui	1,660	970	690
Hawaii	1,621	1,082	539
Honolulu	4,772	6,283	-1,511

Migration by County or County Group

County or county group	Number of In-migrants	Number of Out-migrants	Net Number of Migrants
Idaho			
Ada	2,616	1,816	800
Adams, Boise, Canyon, Elmore, Gem, Owyhee, Payette, Valley and Washington	2,072	1,345	727
Benewah, Bonner, Boundary, Clearwater, Idaho, Kootenai, Latah, Lewis, Nez Perce and Shoshone	3,584	3,540	44
Bonneville, Butte, Clark, Custer, Fremont, Jefferson, Lemhi, Madison and Teton	716	859	-143
Blaine, Camas, Cassia, Gooding, Jerome, Lincoln, Minidoka and Twin Falls	1,204	1,513	-309
Bannock, Bear Lake, Bingham, Caribou, Franklin, Oneida and Power	640	1,132	-492
Illinois			
Clinton, Monroe, Bond, Randolph and Washington	792	644	148
Alexander, Edwards, Gallatin, Hamilton, Hardin, Johnson, Massac, Pope, Pulaski, Saline, Union, Wabash, Wayne and White	1,245	1,275	-30
Woodford, Fulton, Marshall, Mason and Stark	369	402	-33
La Salle	384	449	-65
Hancock, Henderson, Knox, McDonough and Warren	822	911	-89
Clark, Coles, Cumberland, Douglas, Edgar and Moultrie	612	713	-101
Franklin, Jackson, Jefferson, Perry and Williamson	1,008	1,127	-119
Adams, Brown, Pike, Schuyler and Scott	462	606	-144
Henry, Bureau, Mercer and Putnam	471	634	-163
Jersey, Calhoun, Greene, Macoupin, Montgomery, Morgan and Shelby	540	706	-166
McLean	504	716	-212
Jo Daviess, Ogle and Stephenson	453	776	-323
Tazewell	453	778	-325
Menard, Cass, Christian, De Witt and Logan	342	681	-339
Carroll, Lee and Whiteside	453	862	-409
Macon	384	806	-422
Sangamon	720	1,252	-532
Kendall and De Kalb	360	939	-579
Kankakee and Livingston	570	1,187	-617
Ford, Iroquois, Piatt and Vermilion	612	1,257	-645
Clay, Crawford, Effingham, Fayette, Jasper, Lawrence, Marion and Richland	645	1,305	-660
St. Clair	945	1,769	-824
Champaign	693	1,524	-831
McHenry	924	1,778	-854
Madison	996	1,914	-918
Rock Island	567	1,515	-948
Peoria	633	1,649	-1,016
Winnebago and Boone	1,248	2,689	-1,441
Will and Grundy	873	3,049	-2,176
Kane	681	3,051	-2,370
Lake	1,449	6,157	-4,708
Du Page	2,886	10,070	-7,184
Cook	12,801	53,945	-41,144
Indiana			
Vanderburgh, Warrick and Spencer	1,492	1,123	369
Harrison, Crawford, Orange, Scott and Washington	738	374	364
Daviess, Greene, Knox, Martin and Owen	751	488	263
Benton, Fulton, Jasper, Newton, Pulaski and Starke	660	473	187
Whitley, Adams, Huntington and Wells	804	676	128
Delaware	577	456	121
Dearborn, Jefferson, Ohio, Ripley and Switzerland	890	786	104
Clark and Floyd	1,334	1,238	96
Posey, Dubois, Gibson, Perry and Pike	295	267	28

County or county group	Number of In-migrants	Number of Out-migrants	Net Number of Migrants
Jackson, Jennings and Lawrence	487	493	-6
Madison	500	520	-20
Blackford, Grant, Henry, Jay and Randolph	1,014	1,066	-52
Boone and Hendricks	519	589	-70
Hamilton, Hancock and Shelby	1,095	1,187	-92
Fayette, Franklin, Rush, Union and Wayne	854	954	-100
Vigo	859	988	-129
Kosciusko and Marshall	713	857	-144
Howard, Tipton, Cass, Miami and Wabash	1,315	1,479	-164
Johnson and Morgan	552	727	-175
Elkhart	1,319	1,504	-185
Clay, Parke, Putnam, Sullivan and Vermillion	481	692	-211
Monroe	452	705	-253
Carroll, Clinton, Fountain, Montgomery, Warren and White	988	1,266	-278
Tippecanoe	254	557	-303
Bartholomew, Brown and Decatur	393	704	-311
De Kalb, Lagrange, Noble and Steuben	798	1,117	-319
La Porte	546	955	-409
Porter	602	1,022	-420
St. Joseph	1,637	2,285	-648
Lake	3,342	4,004	-662
Allen	1,483	2,332	-849
Marion	3,661	6,542	-2,881

Iowa

County or county group	Number of In-migrants	Number of Out-migrants	Net Number of Migrants
Bremer, Allamakee, Buchanan, Butler, Chickasaw, Clayton, Fayette, Grundy, Howard and Winneshiek	797	741	56
Warren, Jasper, Madison and Marion	344	519	-175
Cerro Gordo, Floyd, Franklin, Hancock, Kossuth, Mitchell, Winnebago and Worth	666	906	-240
Calhoun, Hamilton, Humboldt, Pocahontas, Webster and Wright	227	491	-264
Dallas, Boone and Story	703	978	-275
Des Moines, Henry, Lee, Louisa and Muscatine	832	1,144	-312
Buena Vista, Clay, Dickinson, Emmet, Lyon, O'Brien, Osceola, Palo Alto and Sioux	624	987	-363
Adair, Adams, Appanoose, Clarke, Davis, Decatur, Jefferson, Keokuk, Lucas, Mahaska, Monroe, Ringgold, Taylor, Union, Van Buren, Wapello and Wayne	993	1,393	-400
Linn	756	1,196	-440
Black Hawk	642	1,088	-446
Johnson, Benton, Hardin, Iowa, Jones, Marshall, Poweshiek, Tama and Washington	1,031	1,627	-596
Dubuque, Cedar, Clinton, Delaware and Jackson	534	1,227	-693
Scott	737	1,521	-784
Pottawattamie, Cass, Fremont, Harrison, Mills, Montgomery, Page and Shelby	768	1,717	-949
Woodbury, Audubon, Carroll, Cherokee, Crawford, Greene, Guthrie, Ida, Monona, Plymouth and Sac	851	1,815	-964
Polk	1,164	3,612	-2,448

Kansas

County or county group	Number of In-migrants	Number of Out-migrants	Net Number of Migrants
Clay, Geary, Marshall, Pottawatomie and Riley	721	555	166
Butler, Chase, Coffey, Dickinson, Greenwood, Lyon, Marion, Morris and Wabaunsee	901	765	136
Shawnee, Jefferson and Osage	1,487	1,424	63
Miami, Douglas and Franklin	820	796	24
Leavenworth, Atchison, Brown, Doniphan, Jackson and Nemaha	738	777	-39

Migration by County or County Group

County or county group	Number of In-migrants	Number of Out-migrants	Net Number of Migrants
Harvey, McPherson, Reno and Rice	806	994	-188
Barber, Barton, Comanche, Edwards, Harper, Kingman, Kiowa, Pawnee, Pratt, Rush, Stafford and Sumner	336	735	-399
Cheyenne, Decatur, Ellis, Gove, Graham, Logan, Norton, Osborne, Phillips, Rawlins, Rooks, Russell, Sheridan, Sherman, Smith, Thomas, Trego and Wallace	627	1,043	-416
Cherokee, Crawford, Labette, Montgomery and Neosho	993	1,461	-468
Wyandotte	1,316	1,831	-515
Allen, Anderson, Bourbon, Chautauqua, Cowley, Elk, Linn, Wilson and Woodson	654	1,354	-700
Johnson	3,476	4,232	-756
Cloud, Ellsworth, Jewell, Lincoln, Mitchell, Ottawa, Republic, Saline and Washington	587	1,592	-1,005
Sedgwick	2,543	3,608	-1,065
Clark, Finney, Ford, Grant, Gray, Greeley, Hamilton, Haskell, Hodgeman, Kearny, Lane, Meade, Morton, Ness, Scott, Seward, Stanton, Stevens and Wichita	487	2,477	-1,990

Kentucky

County or county group	Number of In-migrants	Number of Out-migrants	Net Number of Migrants
Adair, Casey, Clinton, Cumberland, Green, McCreary, Pulaski, Russell, Taylor and Wayne	1,782	900	882
Breckinridge, Grayson, Larue, Marion, Nelson and Washington	868	188	680
Allen, Barren, Butler, Edmonson, Hart, Metcalfe and Monroe	774	286	488
Clay, Jackson, Knox, Laurel and Rockcastle	688	217	471
Fayette	1,580	1,131	449
Christian, Caldwell, Crittenden, Hopkins, Livingston, Lyon, Muhlenberg, Todd and Trigg	1,304	866	438
Ballard, Calloway, Carlisle, Fulton, Graves, Hickman, McCracken and Marshall	2,057	1,801	256
Boyle, Estill, Garrard, Lincoln and Madison	779	529	250
Boone, Campbell, Carroll, Gallatin, Grant, Owen and Pendleton	1,266	1,023	243
Bourbon, Clark, Scott, Harrison, Nicholas and Powell	680	453	227
Bullitt, Oldham, Shelby, Henry, Spencer and Trimble	664	496	168
Bath, Bracken, Fleming, Lewis, Mason, Menifee, Montgomery, Morgan, Robertson and Rowan	492	396	96
Henderson, Daviess, Hancock, McLean, Ohio, Union and Webster	1,070	995	75
Jessamine, Woodford, Anderson, Franklin and Mercer	560	592	-32
Hardin and Meade	247	289	-42
Breathitt, Knott, Lee, Leslie, Letcher, Owsley, Perry and Wolfe	527	642	-115
Boyd, Carter, Greenup, Elliott and Lawrence	963	1,117	-154
Bell, Harlan and Whitley	550	796	-246
Kenton	766	1,046	-280
Floyd, Johnson, Magoffin, Martin and Pike	435	759	-324
Logan, Simpson and Warren	267	778	-511
Jefferson	3,451	5,144	-1,693

Louisiana

County or county group	Number of In-migrants	Number of Out-migrants	Net Number of Migrants
Rapides	753	586	167
St. Charles, St. John the Baptist, Assumption and St. James	276	170	106
Ouachita	717	697	20
Ascension and Livingston	312	308	4
Caldwell, East Carroll, Franklin, Jackson, Madison, Morehouse, Richland, Tensas, Union and West Carroll	657	732	-75
West Baton Rouge, East Feliciana, Iberville, Pointe Coupee, St. Helena and West Feliciana	216	295	-79
Evangeline and St. Landry	150	278	-128
Acadia and Vermilion	87	216	-129
Calcasieu, Allen, Beauregard, Cameron and Jefferson Davis	861	1,032	-171
Bienville, Claiborne, De Soto, Lincoln, Natchitoches, Red River, Sabine and Webster	1,149	1,349	-200

County or county group	Number of In-migrants	Number of Out-migrants	Net Number of Migrants
Lafourche and Terrebonne	174	386	-212
Tangipahoa and Washington	576	828	-252
Lafayette	501	784	-283
Bossier and Caddo	2,112	2,449	-337
Avoyelles, Catahoula, Concordia, Grant, La Salle, Vernon and Winn	600	948	-348
St. Martin, Iberia and St. Mary	141	579	-438
St. Bernard, St. Tammany and Plaquemines	876	1,588	-712
East Baton Rouge	1,197	1,976	-779
Jefferson	1,455	2,642	-1,187
Orleans	1,194	3,594	-2,400

Maine

Knox, Lincoln, Sagadahoc and Waldo	1,936	917	1,019
York	2,110	1,520	590
Androscoggin, Kennebec, Somerset, Franklin and Oxford	2,948	2,717	231
Cumberland	2,567	2,432	135
Aroostook and Washington	679	652	27
Penobscot, Piscataquis and Hancock	1,689	2,296	-607

Maryland

Queen Annes, Cecil, Caroline, Kent and Talbot	3,029	1,868	1,161
Dorchester, Somerset, Wicomico and Worcester	1,909	1,540	369
Frederick	938	745	193
Howard	1,259	1,116	143
Allegany and Garrett	843	802	41
Charles	687	691	-4
Calvert and St. Marys	863	1,024	-161
Washington	571	746	-175
Harford	812	1,018	-206
Carroll	519	850	-331
Anne Arundel	2,976	3,564	-588
Prince Georges	4,816	6,751	-1,935
Montgomery	7,705	10,089	-2,384
Baltimore and Baltimore*	5,501	10,529	-5,028

Massachusetts

Berkshire	1,514	1,963	-449
Barnstable, Dukes and Nantucket	3,740	4,257	-517
Hampshire and Franklin	921	1,705	-784
Plymouth	1,205	3,481	-2,276
Worcester	2,414	4,732	-2,318
Hampden	1,740	4,226	-2,486
Suffolk	2,481	4,979	-2,498
Bristol	1,867	4,577	-2,710
Norfolk	1,620	6,134	-4,514
Essex	2,385	8,006	-5,621
Middlesex	3,909	12,677	-8,768

Michigan

Cass and Van Buren	1,268	951	317
Ottawa	735	703	32
Dickinson, Gogebic, Houghton, Iron, Keweenaw and Ontonagon	697	742	-45
Barry, Branch and St. Joseph	948	1,023	-75
Lapeer and Shiawassee	519	669	-150
Baraga, Marquette and Menominee	573	737	-164
Allegan, Ionia and Montcalm	915	1,140	-225

*independent city

Migration by County or County Group

County or county group	Number of In-migrants	Number of Out-migrants	Net Number of Migrants
Alcona, Alpena, Cheboygan, Crawford, Montmorency, Oscoda, Otsego and Presque Isle	665	897	-232
Berrien	1,576	1,809	-233
Muskegon and Oceana	548	791	-243
Benzie, Grand Traverse, Leelanau and Manistee	757	1,000	-243
Monroe	501	750	-249
Huron, Sanilac and Tuscola	295	644	-349
Antrim, Charlevoix, Emmet, Kalkaska, Missaukee and Wexford	682	1,185	-503
Alger, Chippewa, Delta, Luce, Mackinac and Schoolcraft	229	793	-564
Bay	129	712	-583
Saginaw	444	1,054	-610
Jackson	393	1,004	-611
Calhoun	674	1,288	-614
Hillsdale and Lenawee	888	1,507	-619
Clinton and Eaton	330	973	-643
Livingston	512	1,165	-653
Clare, Gratiot and Isabella	324	980	-656
St. Clair	185	949	-764
Midland, Lake, Mason, Mecosta, Newaygo and Osceola	892	1,717	-825
Kalamazoo	502	1,333	-831
Arenac, Gladwin, Iosco, Ogemaw and Roscommon	540	1,627	-1,087
Ingham	777	2,063	-1,286
Washtenaw	934	2,221	-1,287
Kent	1,062	2,621	-1,559
Genesee	1,446	3,110	-1,664
Macomb	1,737	5,656	-3,919
Oakland	3,415	12,316	-8,901
Wayne	5,793	18,531	-12,738

Minnesota

County or county group	Number of In-migrants	Number of Out-migrants	Net Number of Migrants
Ramsey	3,903	3,222	681
Dodge, Goodhue, Le Sueur, Rice, Steele and Waseca	732	287	445
Fillmore, Houston, Wabasha and Winona	575	440	135
Olmsted	460	394	66
Stearns	362	314	48
Washington	1,074	1,033	41
Beltrami, Cass, Crow Wing and Hubbard	869	875	-6
Blue Earth, Brown, Nicollet, Sibley and Watonwan	315	347	-32
Clearwater, Kittson, Mahnomen, Marshall, Norman, Pennington, Polk, Red Lake and Roseau	446	480	-34
Carver and Scott	170	283	-113
Becker, Douglas, Grant, Otter Tail, Pope and Stevens	625	747	-122
Kandiyohi, McLeod, Meeker and Renville	273	431	-158
Chisago, Isanti, Wright, Benton and Sherburne	524	696	-172
Clay, Big Stone, Chippewa, Lac qui Parle, Swift, Traverse, Wilkin and Yellow Medicine	596	782	-186
Anoka	309	559	-250
Cottonwood, Jackson, Lincoln, Lyon, Murray, Nobles, Pipestone, Redwood and Rock	401	702	-301
Kanabec, Mille Lacs, Morrison, Pine, Todd and Wadena	306	659	-353
Faribault, Freeborn, Martin and Mower	616	987	-371
St. Louis	791	1,261	-470
Dakota	865	1,370	-505
Aitkin, Carlton, Cook, Itasca, Koochiching, Lake and Lake of the Woods	581	1,106	-525
Hennepin	4,577	6,983	-2,406

Mississippi

County or county group	Number of In-migrants	Number of Out-migrants	Net Number of Migrants
Hancock and Harrison	3,024	1,599	1,425

County or county group	Number of In-migrants	Number of Out-migrants	Net Number of Migrants
De Soto, Coahoma, Panola, Quitman, Tallahatchie, Tate and Tunica	2,004	1,222	782
Forrest, Lamar and Perry	1,176	402	774
Covington, Jefferson Davis, Marion, Pearl River and Stone	1,059	512	547
Alcorn, Benton, Marshall, Prentiss, Tippah and Tishomingo	1,167	750	417
Adams, Amite, Claiborne, Franklin, Jefferson, Lawrence, Lincoln, Pike, Walthall and Wilkinson	1,263	944	319
Calhoun, Chickasaw, Lafayette, Monroe and Union	951	674	277
Rankin, Copiah and Simpson	789	523	266
Kemper, Lauderdale and Newton	681	438	243
Itawamba, Lee and Pontotoc	705	549	156
Madison, Warren and Yazoo	573	452	121
Clarke, Jasper, Leake, Neshoba, Scott and Smith	354	274	80
Hinds	1,218	1,192	26
Choctaw, Clay, Lowndes, Noxubee, Oktibbeha, Webster and Winston	639	682	-43
George, Greene, Jones and Wayne	426	493	-67
Jackson	594	696	-102
Attala, Carroll, Grenada, Holmes, Leflore, Montgomery and Yalobusha	657	843	-186
Bolivar, Humphreys, Issaquena, Sharkey, Sunflower and Washington	357	908	-551

Missouri

County or county group	Number of In-migrants	Number of Out-migrants	Net Number of Migrants
Christian, Barry, Dade, Dallas, Lawrence, McDonald, Polk, Stone, Taney and Webster	4,364	2,234	2,130
Greene	2,344	1,046	1,298
Camden, Laclede, Miller, Morgan and Pulaski	1,615	895	720
Douglas, Howell, Oregon, Ozark, Shannon, Texas and Wright	1,523	942	581
Crawford, Dent, Gasconade, Maries, Phelps and Washington	816	395	421
Barton, Bates, Benton, Cedar, Henry, Hickory, St. Clair and Vernon	1,596	1,223	373
Carroll, Chariton, Johnson, Pettis and Saline	748	521	227
Atchison, Caldwell, Clinton, Daviess, Gentry, Grundy, Harrison, Holt, Mercer, Nodaway and Worth	925	730	195
Audrain, Callaway, Cole, Cooper, Howard, Moniteau and Osage	795	651	144
Lincoln, Marion, Monroe, Montgomery, Pike, Ralls, Randolph and Warren	1,048	917	131
Buchanan, Andrew and De Kalb	642	558	84
Cass, Lafayette and Ray	638	565	73
Adair, Clark, Knox, Lewis, Linn, Livingston, Macon, Putnam, Schuyler, Scotland, Shelby and Sullivan	827	755	72
Butler, Carter, Reynolds, Ripley, Stoddard and Wayne	845	837	8
Dunklin, Mississippi, New Madrid, Pemiscot and Scott	983	992	-9
St. Charles	907	957	-50
Boone	568	645	-77
Bollinger, Cape Girardeau, Iron, Madison, Perry, Ste. Genevieve and St. Francois	976	1,064	-88
Clay and Platte	1,130	1,272	-142
Jasper and Newton	1,095	1,377	-282
Franklin and Jefferson	605	1,024	-419
Jackson	4,491	5,420	-929
St. Louis and St. Louis*	5,770	9,494	-3,724

Montana

County or county group	Number of In-migrants	Number of Out-migrants	Net Number of Migrants
Mineral, Missoula and Ravalli	995	917	78
Yellowstone	956	923	33
Beaverhead, Broadwater, Deer Lodge, Gallatin, Granite, Jefferson, Lewis and Clark, Madison, Meagher, Park, Powell, Silver Bow and Yellowstone National Park	1,795	1,898	-103
Cascade, Chouteau, Glacier, Pondera, Teton and Toole	561	673	-112
Big Horn, Blaine, Carbon, Carter, Custer, Daniels, Dawson, Fallon, Fergus, Garfield, Golden Valley, Hill, Judith Basin, Liberty, McCone, Musselshell, (cont.)	793	1,282	-489

*independent city

Migration by County or County Group

County or county group	Number of In-migrants	Number of Out-migrants	Net Number of Migrants
(cont.) Petroleum, Phillips, Powder River, Prairie, Richland, Roosevelt, Rosebud, Sheridan, Stillwater, Sweet Grass, Treasure, Valley, Wheatland and Wibaux			
Flathead, Lake, Lincoln and Sanders	1,040	1,533	-493

Nebraska

Butler, Cass, Fillmore, Gage, Jefferson, Johnson, Nemaha, Otoe, Pawnee, Polk, Richardson, Saline, Saunders, Seward, Thayer and York	1,237	1,033	204
Lancaster	1,515	1,325	190
Sarpy and Washington	646	466	180
Dakota, Antelope, Cedar, Dixon, Knox, Madison, Pierce, Stanton and Wayne	698	641	57
Adams, Buffalo, Clay, Franklin, Harlan, Kearney, Nuckolls, Phelps and Webster	563	509	54
Blaine, Custer, Garfield, Greeley, Hall, Hamilton, Howard, Loup, Merrick, Sherman, Valley and Wheeler	552	547	5
Boone, Burt, Colfax, Cuming, Dodge, Nance, Platte and Thurston	364	447	-83
Arthur, Chase, Dawson, Dundy, Frontier, Furnas, Gosper, Grant, Hayes, Hitchcock, Hooker, Keith, Lincoln, Logan, McPherson, Perkins, Red Willow and Thomas	631	797	-166
Douglas	2,976	3,650	-674
Banner, Box Butte, Boyd, Brown, Cherry, Cheyenne, Dawes, Deuel, Garden, Holt, Keya Paha, Kimball, Morrill, Rock, Scotts Bluff, Sheridan and Sioux	670	1,379	-709

Nevada

Clark	30,865	9,060	21,805
Douglas, Lyon, Storey and Washoe and Carson City*	10,309	5,525	4,784
Churchill, Elko, Esmeralda, Eureka, Humboldt, Lander, Lincoln, Mineral, Nye, Pershing and White Pine	1,957	1,608	349

New Hampshire

Rockingham	4,036	2,860	1,176
Belknap, Carroll, Coos and Grafton	3,268	2,655	613
Strafford	1,478	1,103	375
Merrimack	1,233	1,029	204
Cheshire and Sullivan	1,631	1,477	154
Hillsborough	3,412	3,661	-249

New Jersey

Ocean	8,305	7,408	897
Cape May and Salem	2,999	2,838	161
Burlington	3,697	4,121	-424
Cumberland	530	1,011	-481
Gloucester	1,344	1,850	-506
Atlantic	2,023	2,783	-760
Hunterdon	654	1,871	-1,217
Camden	3,066	4,371	-1,305
Mercer	1,620	3,490	-1,870
Somerset	1,391	3,721	-2,330
Warren and Sussex	950	3,558	-2,608
Monmouth	4,866	7,699	-2,833
Middlesex	4,687	8,468	-3,781
Passaic	1,450	5,565	-4,115
Hudson	2,107	6,275	-4,168
Morris	1,703	7,168	-5,465
Union	1,754	8,488	-6,734

*independent city

County or county group	Number of In-migrants	Number of Out-migrants	Net Number of Migrants
Essex	2,052	9,645	-7,593
Bergen	3,978	16,226	-12,248
New Mexico			
Bernalillo	6,402	4,712	1,690
Sandoval, Torrance and Valencia	2,001	983	1,018
Dona Ana	2,196	1,239	957
Los Alamos and Santa Fe	1,878	1,018	860
Catron, Grant, Hidalgo, Lincoln, Luna, Otero, Sierra and Socorro	3,351	2,523	828
Cibola, McKinley and San Juan	1,071	885	186
Chaves and Eddy	1,347	1,198	149
Colfax, Mora, Rio Arriba, San Miguel and Taos	639	495	144
Curry, DeBaca, Guadalupe, Harding, Lea, Quay, Roosevelt and Union	987	1,645	-658
New York			
Saratoga	854	1,155	-301
Jefferson	280	592	-312
Warren, Washington and Hamilton	898	1,210	-312
Greene and Columbia	589	918	-329
Cayuga and Seneca	399	766	-367
Herkimer and Fulton	310	772	-462
Montgomery, Otsego and Schoharie	747	1,209	-462
Orleans, Genesee and Wyoming	347	809	-462
Oneida	1,044	1,520	-476
Madison and Chenango	359	842	-483
Rensselaer	487	1,005	-518
Lewis and St. Lawrence	275	831	-556
Clinton, Essex and Franklin	502	1,104	-602
Oswego	183	788	-605
Allegany and Cattaraugus	539	1,144	-605
Steuben and Yates	582	1,216	-634
Livingston, Ontario and Wayne	720	1,437	-717
Chemung and Schuyler	336	1,114	-778
Broome	823	1,773	-950
Chautauqua	440	1,402	-962
Tioga, Cortland and Tompkins	827	1,874	-1,047
Delaware and Sullivan	730	1,881	-1,151
Albany	892	2,177	-1,285
Niagara	578	1,994	-1,416
Schenectady	284	1,819	-1,535
Ulster	713	2,612	-1,899
Orange	1,568	3,482	-1,914
Onondaga	1,304	3,628	-2,324
Monroe	2,463	5,562	-3,099
Putnam and Dutchess	1,069	4,468	-3,399
Rockland	859	4,329	-3,470
Richmond	779	5,083	-4,304
Erie	2,841	8,505	-5,664
Bronx	1,124	11,230	-10,106
New York	3,022	14,155	-11,133
Westchester	2,009	15,197	-13,188
Suffolk	3,081	20,111	-17,030
Kings	2,716	28,606	-25,890
Nassau	2,492	30,902	-28,410
Queens	2,737	33,559	-30,822
North Carolina			
Henderson, Madison and Transylvania	5,178	1,608	3,570

Migration by County or County Group

County or county group	Number of In-migrants	Number of Out-migrants	Net Number of Migrants
Carteret, Craven, Jones and Pamlico	3,435	771	2,664
Anson, Montgomery, Moore and Richmond	3,495	891	2,604
Buncombe	3,684	1,249	2,435
Mecklenburg	5,415	3,294	2,121
Wake	3,450	1,388	2,062
Brunswick, Columbus and Pender	2,787	766	2,021
New Hanover	2,199	551	1,648
Cherokee, Clay, Graham, Haywood, Jackson, Macon and Swain	3,378	1,820	1,558
Camden, Chowan, Currituck, Dare, Gates, Hyde, Pasquotank, Perquimans, Tyrrell and Washington	2,487	969	1,518
Orange and Chatham	1,824	422	1,402
Cabarrus and Rowan	1,644	573	1,071
Alleghany, Ashe, Avery, Mitchell, Watauga, Wilkes and Yancey	1,485	466	1,019
Guilford	2,448	1,506	942
Franklin, Granville, Person, Vance and Warren	1,227	341	886
Johnston and Lee	1,068	218	850
Cumberland	1,482	700	782
Cleveland, McDowell, Polk and Rutherford	1,575	842	733
Durham	1,446	721	725
Forsyth	1,629	959	670
Davie, Stokes, Yadkin and Surry	951	292	659
Lincoln and Iredell	1,098	460	638
Pitt	723	97	626
Union and Stanly	672	179	493
Beaufort, Bertie, Hertford and Martin	1,077	596	481
Harnett and Sampson	591	140	451
Alexander, Burke and Caldwell	666	239	427
Bladen, Hoke, Robeson and Scotland	924	570	354
Gaston	879	530	349
Nash and Wilson	543	219	324
Alamance	702	398	304
Catawba	624	334	290
Edgecombe, Halifax and Northampton	744	468	276
Davidson	552	292	260
Wayne	390	157	233
Randolph	321	121	200
Duplin, Greene and Lenoir	549	349	200
Onslow	807	678	129
Caswell and Rockingham	381	262	119

North Dakota

County or county group	Number of In-migrants	Number of Out-migrants	Net Number of Migrants
Grand Forks, Pembina, Traill and Walsh	730	530	200
Barnes, Benson, Cavalier, Dickey, Eddy, Foster, Griggs, La Moure, Nelson, Ramsey, Ransom, Sargent, Steele, Stutsman, Towner and Wells	585	660	-75
Cass and Richland	810	1,134	-324
Morton, Adams, Billings, Bowman, Divide, Dunn, Golden Valley, Grant, Hettinger, McKenzie, Mercer, Oliver, Sioux, Slope, Stark and Williams	355	763	-408
Burleigh, Bottineau, Burke, Emmons, Kidder, Logan, McHenry, McIntosh, McLean, Mountrail, Pierce, Renville, Rolette, Sheridan and Ward	660	1,233	-573

Ohio

County or county group	Number of In-migrants	Number of Out-migrants	Net Number of Migrants
Washington, Monroe, Morgan and Noble	525	299	226
Fairfield	373	222	151
Butler	1,852	1,710	142
Lawrence, Gallia and Jackson	808	685	123
Auglaize, Hardin and Mercer	319	223	96
Ashland and Huron	450	379	71
Wood	430	380	50

County or county group	Number of In-migrants	Number of Out-migrants	Net Number of Migrants
Medina	664	672	-8
Adams, Pike and Scioto	748	758	-10
Licking	463	475	-12
Fulton, Henry and Williams	456	514	-58
Holmes and Tuscarawas	283	345	-62
Coshocton, Knox and Morrow	502	627	-125
Brown, Clinton, Fayette and Highland	553	688	-135
Defiance, Paulding, Putnam and Van Wert	425	605	-180
Richland	461	650	-189
Erie, Ottawa and Sandusky	988	1,178	-190
Pickaway and Ross	394	597	-203
Belmont and Guernsey	596	820	-224
Wayne	462	724	-262
Champaign, Logan and Shelby	168	433	-265
Clark	820	1,127	-307
Athens, Hocking, Meigs and Vinton	254	589	-335
Warren	568	907	-339
Hancock and Seneca	431	773	-342
Crawford, Marion and Wyandot	483	838	-355
Delaware, Madison and Union	438	819	-381
Lorain	952	1,354	-402
Allen	362	779	-417
Clermont	466	887	-421
Carroll, Jefferson and Harrison	513	939	-426
Columbiana	590	1,029	-439
Geauga and Ashtabula	959	1,427	-468
Portage	423	914	-491
Stark	1,784	2,280	-496
Miami, Darke and Preble	463	973	-510
Muskingum and Perry	250	806	-556
Greene	447	1,041	-594
Montgomery	2,935	3,598	-663
Trumbull	1,000	1,825	-825
Lake	759	1,830	-1,071
Mahoning	912	2,164	-1,252
Summit	2,107	4,548	-2,441
Franklin	3,834	6,372	-2,538
Lucas	1,738	4,457	-2,719
Hamilton	3,799	7,028	-3,229
Cuyahoga	5,252	11,983	-6,731

Oklahoma

County or county group	Number of In-migrants	Number of Out-migrants	Net Number of Migrants
Rogers, Craig, Delaware, Mayes, Nowata, Ottawa and Washington	2,376	1,824	552
Comanche, McClain, Caddo, Grady, Jefferson, Stephens and Tillman	1,779	1,303	476
Cleveland	1,055	603	452
Atoka, Bryan, Carter, Coal, Garvin, Johnston, Love, Marshall, Murray and Pontotoc	1,884	1,457	427
Canadian and Logan	676	363	313
Choctaw, Haskell, Latimer, Le Flore, McCurtain, Pittsburg and Pushmataha	1,486	1,263	223
Beaver, Beckham, Cimarron, Cotton, Custer, Dewey, Ellis, Greer, Harmon, Harper, Jackson, Kiowa, Roger Mills, Texas, Washita, Woods and Woodward	1,581	1,400	181
Oklahoma	4,021	3,902	119
Pottawatomie, Hughes, Lincoln, Okfuskee, Pawnee, Payne and Seminole	1,406	1,302	104
Creek and Osage	487	456	31
Garfield, Alfalfa, Blaine, Grant, Kay, Kingfisher, Major and Noble	1,083	1,135	-52
Sequoyah, Wagoner, Adair, Cherokee, McIntosh, Muskogee and Okmulgee	1,899	1,956	-57
Tulsa	3,839	4,110	-271

Migration by County or County Group

County or county group	Number of In-migrants	Number of Out-migrants	Net Number of Migrants
Oregon			
Coos, Curry, Douglas and Josephine	8,387	2,904	5,483
Jackson	4,529	1,624	2,905
Lane	4,785	1,992	2,793
Marion	3,857	1,644	2,213
Washington	3,787	1,873	1,914
Clatsop, Columbia, Lincoln and Tillamook	2,850	1,162	1,688
Benton and Linn	2,094	750	1,344
Clackamas	2,987	1,697	1,290
Crook, Deschutes, Hood River, Jefferson, Sherman and Wasco	2,547	1,343	1,204
Yamhill and Polk	1,339	730	609
Baker, Gilliam, Morrow, Umatilla, Union, Wallowa and Wheeler	1,134	1,164	-30
Grant, Harney, Klamath, Lake, Malheur	1,413	1,501	-88
Multnomah	4,287	4,393	-106
Pennsylvania			
Carbon, Monroe, Pike and Wayne	5,192	2,482	2,710
Lancaster	3,067	1,496	1,571
Adams and Franklin	1,714	973	741
York	1,906	1,314	592
Wyoming, Bradford, Sullivan, Susquehanna and Tioga	1,970	1,561	409
Lycoming	707	397	310
Bedford, Fulton and Huntingdon	700	404	296
Luzerne	1,988	1,723	265
Columbia, Montour and Northumberland	873	668	205
Centre	700	593	107
Cumberland and Perry	980	893	87
Northampton	1,713	1,644	69
Lehigh	1,439	1,410	29
Lebanon	533	538	-5
Clinton, Juniata, Mifflin, Snyder and Union	611	623	-12
Crawford and Warren	631	663	-32
Clarion, Forest and Venango	402	485	-83
Blair	522	634	-112
Clearfield and Jefferson	356	519	-163
Washington	892	1,056	-164
Fayette and Greene	836	1,043	-207
Lackawanna	892	1,138	-246
Butler	457	822	-365
Schuylkill	335	712	-377
Cameron, Elk, McKean and Potter	489	884	-395
Bucks	4,109	4,528	-419
Armstrong and Indiana	525	965	-440
Mercer	409	938	-529
Dauphin	687	1,244	-557
Westmoreland	1,328	2,044	-716
Beaver and Lawrence	1,059	1,781	-722
Cambria and Somerset	729	1,468	-739
Berks	1,071	1,910	-839
Chester	2,277	3,308	-1,031
Erie	1,103	2,434	-1,331
Delaware	2,783	5,086	-2,303
Montgomery	2,830	6,188	-3,358
Allegheny	4,017	10,498	-6,481
Philadelphia	4,706	11,836	-7,130
Rhode Island			
Washington	1,539	1,271	268

County or county group	Number of In-migrants	Number of Out-migrants	Net Number of Migrants
Newport and Bristol	828	1,332	-504
Kent	675	1,968	-1,293
Providence	2,800	4,718	-1,918

South Carolina

County or county group	Number of In-migrants	Number of Out-migrants	Net Number of Migrants
Horry	5,853	1,328	4,525
Beaufort, Colleton and Jasper	3,447	1,093	2,354
Pickens and Oconee	2,037	600	1,437
Charleston	3,168	1,782	1,386
Allendale, Bamberg, Barnwell, Calhoun, Hampton and Orangeburg	1,524	471	1,053
Richland	1,815	862	953
Clarendon, Georgetown and Williamsburg	1,350	455	895
York	1,503	666	837
Greenville	2,391	1,615	776
Berkeley and Dorchester	1,596	884	712
Anderson	1,053	381	672
Lexington	1,179	615	564
Spartanburg	1,245	789	456
Chesterfield, Darlington, Dillon, Marion and Marlboro	1,089	690	399
Fairfield, Laurens and Newberry	804	418	386
Sumter	537	226	311
Florence	678	439	239
Kershaw, Lancaster and Lee	741	576	165
Abbeville, Edgefield, Greenwood, McCormick and Saluda	744	627	117
Cherokee, Chester and Union	456	437	19
Aiken	1,041	1,061	-20

South Dakota

County or county group	Number of In-migrants	Number of Out-migrants	Net Number of Migrants
Pennington, Butte, Custer, Fall River, Harding, Lawrence and Meade	1,415	1,466	-51
Brookings, Clark, Codington, Deuel, Grant, Hamlin, Kingsbury, Lake, McCook, Miner and Moody	526	598	-72
Bennett, Brule, Buffalo, Campbell, Corson, Dewey, Gregory, Haakon, Hughes, Hyde, Jackson, Jones, Lyman, Mellette, Perkins, Potter, Shannon, Stanley, Sully, Todd, Tripp, Walworth and Zlebach	623	702	-79
Minnehaha and Lincoln	546	690	-144
Beadle, Brown, Day, Edmunds, Faulk, Hand, Jerauld, McPherson, Marshall, Roberts and Spink	515	831	-316
Aurora, Bon Homme, Charles Mix, Clay, Davison, Douglas, Hanson, Hutchinson, Sanborn, Turner, Union and Yankton	516	957	-441

Tennessee

County or county group	Number of In-migrants	Number of Out-migrants	Net Number of Migrants
Cumberland, Putnam and White	2,085	865	1,220
Campbell, Claiborne, Cocke, Hamblen, Loudon, Monroe, Morgan, Roane and Scott	2,361	1,279	1,082
Blount and Sevier	1,557	674	883
Marion, Sequatchie, Bledsoe, Grundy, Meigs, Polk and Rhea	1,248	434	814
Benton, Decatur, Hardin, Henry, Houston, Humphreys, Perry, Stewart and Wayne	1,689	930	759
Hamilton	2,469	1,736	733
Davidson	3,549	2,834	715
Anderson, Grainger, Jefferson and Union	972	381	591
Hawkins, Unicoi, Greene, Hancock and Johnson	969	383	586
Franklin, Giles, Lawrence, Lincoln and Moore	1,236	724	512
Madison, Chester, Hardeman, Henderson and McNairy	1,221	731	490
Cannon, Clay, De Kalb, Fentress, Jackson, Macon, Overton, Pickett, Smith, Trousdale, Van Buren and Warren	1,065	597	468
Knox	1,929	1,466	463

Migration by County or County Group

County or county group	Number of In-migrants	Number of Out-migrants	Net Number of Migrants
Rutherford	702	264	438
Sumner	705	307	398
Cheatham, Dickson, Robertson, Williamson and Wilson	1,377	990	387
Bradley and McMinn	654	271	383
Bedford, Coffee, Hickman, Lewis, Marshall and Maury	1,011	731	280
Tipton, Fayette, Haywood and Lauderdale	630	408	222
Sullivan	1,368	1,161	207
Carter and Washington	1,071	901	170
Carroll, Crockett, Dyer, Gibson, Lake, Obion and Weakley	1,122	965	157
Montgomery	288	253	35
Shelby	5,028	6,848	-1,820

Texas

County or county group	Number of In-migrants	Number of Out-migrants	Net Number of Migrants
Hidalgo	4,198	1,482	2,716
Bexar	5,879	3,885	1,994
Cameron	2,672	1,012	1,660
Comal, Guadalupe, Karnes and Wilson	1,301	290	1,011
Hays, Bastrop, Caldwell, Fayette, Lee and Milam	1,279	292	987
Travis	2,634	1,797	837
Collin	1,580	766	814
Atascosa, Bandera, Frio, Gillespie, Kendall, Kerr and Medina	1,335	709	626
Smith	1,166	598	568
Williamson	854	363	491
Fort Bend	863	387	476
Coryell, Blanco, Brown, Burnet, Coleman, Hamilton, Lampasas, Llano, Mills, Runnels and San Saba	1,291	821	470
Tarrant	4,906	4,480	426
Nueces	1,382	972	410
Camp, Rains, Upshur, Van Zandt and Wood	649	254	395
Brazos	529	189	340
Bell	1,097	773	324
Bowie and Cass	992	702	290
San Patricio, Aransas, Bee, Live Oak, McMullen and Refugio	544	255	289
Callahan, Comanche, Eastland, Erath, Palo Pinto, Shackelford, Stephens and Throckmorton	695	410	285
Hardin and Orange	619	347	272
Ellis, Kaufman and Rockwall	621	358	263
Denton	1,330	1,087	243
Delta, Franklin, Hopkins, Lamar, Marion, Morris, Red River and Titus	886	677	209
Jasper, Newton, Polk, Sabine, San Augustine, Shelby and Tyler	825	650	175
Grayson, Fannin and Hunt	1,213	1,045	168
Wichita	730	586	144
Taylor	505	368	137
Cherokee, Panola and Rusk	483	357	126
Dimmit, Edwards, Kinney, La Salle, Maverick, Real, Uvalde, Val Verde and Zavala	574	465	109
Potter and Randall	998	890	108
Anderson and Henderson	483	375	108
Midland	621	542	79
Tom Green, Coke, Concho, Crockett, Glasscock, Irion, Kimble, McCulloch, Mason, Menard, Reagan, Schleicher, Sterling and Sutton	621	545	76
Brazoria	637	573	64
Brooks, Duval, Jim Wells, Kenedy, Kleberg and Willacy	177	118	59
Bosque, Falls, Freestone, Hill, Limestone, Navarro and Somervell	546	504	42
Waller, Burleson, Grimes, Leon, Madison, Robertson and Washington	419	377	42
Victoria, Calhoun, De Witt, Goliad, Gonzales, Jackson and Lavaca	448	425	23
Webb, Jim Hogg, Starr and Zapata	480	459	21
Liberty, Chambers, Houston, San Jacinto, Trinity and Walker	484	504	-20

County or county group	Number of In-migrants	Number of Out-migrants	Net Number of Migrants
Jefferson	902	961	-59
Galveston	1,039	1,100	-61
Gregg and Harrison	790	857	-67
Angelina and Nacogdoches	334	425	-91
Montgomery	950	1,046	-96
McLennan	607	704	-97
Austin, Colorado, Matagorda and Wharton	296	420	-124
Johnson, Parker, Hood and Wise	930	1,064	-134
Bailey, Cochran, Crosby, Dickens, Floyd, Garza, Hale, Hockley, King, Lamb, Lynn, Motley, Terry and Yoakum	432	604	-172
Ector	494	795	-301
Borden, Dawson, Fisher, Haskell, Howard, Jones, Kent, Martin, Mitchell, Nolan, Scurry and Stonewall	395	706	-311
Andrews, Brewster, Crane, Culberson, Gaines, Hudspeth, Jeff Davis, Loving, Pecos, Presidio, Reeves, Terrell, Upton, Ward and Winkler	264	590	-326
Lubbock	686	1,061	-375
El Paso	2,569	2,948	-379
Archer, Baylor, Childress, Clay, Cooke, Cottle, Foard, Hardeman, Jack, Knox, Montague, Wilbarger and Young	529	1,088	-559
Armstrong, Briscoe, Carson, Castro, Collingsworth, Dallam, Deaf Smith, Donley, Gray, Hall, Hansford, Hartley, Hemphill, Hutchinson, Lipscomb, Moore, Ochiltree, Oldham, Parmer, Roberts, Sherman, Swisher and Wheeler	596	1,203	-607
Harris	10,705	12,791	-2,086
Dallas	6,053	9,804	-3,751

Utah

County or county group	Number of In-migrants	Number of Out-migrants	Net Number of Migrants
Beaver, Garfield, Iron, Juab, Kane, Millard, Piute, Sanpete, Sevier, Washington and Wayne	2,436	1,110	1,326
Utah	1,321	862	459
Salt Lake	3,661	3,272	389
Davis and Tooele	933	720	213
Weber and Morgan	1,272	1,180	92
Box Elder, Cache and Rich	436	365	71
Carbon, Daggett, Duchesne, Emery, Grand, San Juan, Summit, Uintah and Wasatch	692	639	53

Vermont

County or county group	Number of In-migrants	Number of Out-migrants	Net Number of Migrants
Franklin, Grand Isle, Orange and Washington	976	538	438
Addison, Bennington and Rutland	1,345	1,156	189
Caledonia, Essex, Lamoille and Orleans	1,232	1,105	127
Windham and Windsor	1,471	1,499	-28
Chittenden	892	1,149	-257

Virginia

County or county group	Number of In-migrants	Number of Out-migrants	Net Number of Migrants
James City, York, Accomack, Northampton, Poquoson* and Williamsburg*	2,805	1,022	1,783
Virginia Beach*	3,330	2,084	1,246
Gloucester, Essex, King and Queen, King William, Lancaster, Mathews, Middlesex, Northumberland, Richmond and Westmoreland	1,761	709	1,052
Amelia, Brunswick, Buckingham, Charlotte, Cumberland, Halifax, Lunenburg, Mecklenburg, Nottoway, Prince Edward and South Boston*	1,911	960	951
Albemarle, Fluvanna, Greene, Louisa, Nelson and Charlottesville*	1,713	810	903
Chesterfield	1,518	661	857
Amherst, Campbell, Appomattox, Bedford, Lynchburg* and Bedford*	1,713	982	731
Clarke, Frederick, Page, Shenandoah, Warren and Winchester*	1,911	1,189	722
Culpeper, Fauquier, Madison, Orange and Rappahannock	1,263	701	562
Roanoke* and Salem*	771	300	471
Newport News*	1,209	784	425

*independent city

Migration by County or County Group

County or county group	Number of In-migrants	Number of Out-migrants	Net Number of Migrants
Washington, Bland, Carroll, Grayson, Smyth, Wythe, Bristol* and Galax*	1,743	1,374	369
Stafford, Caroline, King George, Spotsylvania and Fredericksburg*	1,365	1,048	317
Augusta, Bath, Highland, Rockbridge, Rockingham, Buena Vista*, Harrisonburg*, Lexington*, Staunton* and Waynesboro*	1,344	1,028	316
Isle of Wight, Southampton, Suffolk* and Franklin*	666	402	264
Franklin, Henry, Patrick and Martinsville*	627	407	220
Richmond*	1,203	1,044	159
Pittsylvania and Danville*	666	531	135
Floyd, Giles, Montgomery, Pulaski and Radford*	738	619	119
Loudoun, Prince William, Manassas* and Manassas Park*	2,154	2,048	106
Charles City, Goochland, Hanover, New Kent and Powhatan	351	271	80
Henrico	1,248	1,190	58
Chesapeake*	804	829	-25
Botetourt, Roanoke, Alleghany, Craig, Clifton Forge* and Covington*	1,002	1,065	-63
Portsmouth*	474	631	-157
Dinwiddie, Prince George, Greensville, Surry, Sussex, Colonial Heights*, Hopewell*, Petersburg* and Emporia*	495	731	-236
Buchanan, Russell and Tazewell	354	631	-277
Hampton*	726	1,075	-349
Scott, Dickenson, Lee, Wise and Norton*	618	993	-375
Norfolk*	987	1,382	-395
Alexandria*	939	1,877	-938
Arlington	1,563	3,035	-1,472
Fairfax, Fairfax* and Falls Church*	6,582	10,282	-3,700

Washington

County or county group	Number of In-migrants	Number of Out-migrants	Net Number of Migrants
Clallam, Jefferson and Mason	4,488	1,179	3,309
Clark	4,542	1,319	3,223
King	11,217	8,422	2,795
Snohomish	4,125	2,052	2,073
Pierce	4,425	2,471	1,954
Island, San Juan and Skagit	2,748	1,281	1,467
Grays Harbor, Lewis and Pacific	1,980	940	1,040
Kitsap	1,764	849	915
Whatcom	1,440	551	889
Benton and Franklin	1,404	648	756
Thurston	1,875	1,323	552
Chelan, Douglas, Kittitas and Okanogan	819	756	63
Asotin, Columbia, Garfield, Walla Walla and Whitman	1,056	1,062	-6
Cowlitz, Klickitat, Skamania and Wahkiakum	1,209	1,242	-33
Adams, Ferry, Grant, Lincoln, Pend Oreille and Stevens	753	922	-169
Yakima	696	983	-287
Spokane	2,943	3,345	-402

West Virginia

County or county group	Number of In-migrants	Number of Out-migrants	Net Number of Migrants
Mineral, Berkeley, Grant, Hampshire, Hardy, Jefferson, Morgan and Pendleton	3,071	1,512	1,559
Doddridge, Harrison, Marion, Monongalia, Preston and Taylor	1,693	1,271	422
Fayette, Greenbrier, Nicholas, Pocahontas and Webster	977	620	357
Barbour, Braxton, Gilmer, Lewis, Randolph, Tucker and Upshur	1,037	826	211
Wood, Calhoun, Jackson, Pleasants, Ritchie, Roane, Tyler and Wirt	1,025	1,317	-292
Cabell, Wayne, Lincoln, Logan, Mason and Mingo	1,579	2,021	-442
McDowell, Mercer, Monroe, Raleigh, Summers and Wyoming	1,334	1,830	-496
Brooke, Hancock, Marshall, Ohio and Wetzel	950	1,520	-570
Kanawha, Putnam, Boone and Clay	1,253	2,019	-766

Wisconsin

County or county group	Number of In-migrants	Number of Out-migrants	Net Number of Migrants
La Crosse, Crawford and Vernon	996	492	504

*independent city

County or county group	Number of In-migrants	Number of Out-migrants	Net Number of Migrants
Grant, Green, Iowa, Lafayette and Richland	841	373	468
Douglas, Ashland, Bayfield, Burnett, Iron, Price, Rusk, Sawyer, Taylor and Washburn	1,938	1,582	356
Buffalo, Jackson, Monroe, Pepin, Pierce and Trempealeau	808	651	157
St. Croix, Barron, Clark, Dunn and Polk	1,236	1,124	112
Columbia, Dodge and Sauk	902	798	104
Chippewa and Eau Claire	520	561	-41
Rock	842	888	-46
Fond du Lac and Green Lake	510	559	-49
Forest, Langlade, Lincoln, Oneida and Vilas	1,218	1,281	-63
Marathon	303	386	-83
Adams, Juneau, Portage and Wood	839	929	-90
Kenosha	1,197	1,290	-93
Marquette, Menominee, Shawano, Waupaca and Waushara	715	886	-171
Racine	532	814	-282
Calumet and Outagamie	355	725	-370
Jefferson and Walworth	1,193	1,627	-434
Winnebago	398	1,026	-628
Ozaukee and Washington	423	1,075	-652
Dane	1,408	2,061	-653
Brown, Sheboygan, Door, Florence, Kewaunee, Manitowoc, Marinette and Oconto	1,809	2,475	-666
Waukesha	1,081	2,587	-1,506
Milwaukee	2,966	6,985	-4,019

Wyoming

County or county group	Number of In-migrants	Number of Out-migrants	Net Number of Migrants
Big Horn, Campbell, Crook, Hot Springs, Johnson, Park, Sheridan, Washakie and Weston	1,539	1,628	-89
Natrona, Converse, Fremont and Niobrara	956	1,478	-522
Carbon, Lincoln, Sublette, Sweetwater, Teton and Uinta	656	1,453	-797
Laramie, Albany, Goshen and Platte	1,056	1,932	-876

REFERENCES

Introduction

[1] S. L. Barsby and D. R. Cox, *Interstate Migration of the Elderly*, (Lexington, MA: D.C. Heath, 1975).

[2] Michael Greenwood and G. L. Hunt, "Jobs Versus Amenities in the Analysis of Metropolitan Migration," *Journal of Urban Economics* 25 (1989): pp. 1-16.

[3] William J. Serow, "Why the Elderly Move," *Research on Aging* 9 (1987): pp. 582-597.

[4] William J. Serow, Douglas A. Charity, Gary M. Fournier and David W. Rasmussen, "Cost of Living Differentials and Elderly Interstate Migration," *Research on Aging* 8 (1986): pp. 317-327.

[5] Cynthia B. Flynn, "General vs. Aged Interstate Migration," *Research on Aging* 2 (1980): pp. 165-176.

[6] Jeanne C. Biggar, *The Sunning of America: Migration to the Sunbelt*, Population Bulletin No. 34 (Washington, DC: Population Reference Bureau, 1979).

[7] Charles F. Longino Jr., "Going Home: Aged Return Migration in the United States, 1965-1970," *Journal of Gerontology* 34 (1979).

[8] Robert F. Wiseman, "Why Older People Move: Theoretical Issues," *Research on Aging* 2 (1979): pp. 141-154.

[9] Jeanne C. Biggar, Diane C. Cowper and Dale E. Yeatts, "National Elderly Migration Patterns and Selectivity, 1955-1960, 1965-1970 and Decade Trends," *Research on Aging* 6 (1984): pp. 163-188.

[10] Charles F. Longino Jr., "Returning from the Sunbelt," *Returning from the Sunbelt: Myths and Realities of Migratory Patterns Among the Elderly*, ed. Abraham Monk (Proceedings of an Invitational Symposium, Columbia University in the City of New York: The Brookdale Institute on Aging and Adult Human Development, 1985).

[11] Eugene Litwak and Charles F. Longino Jr., "Migration Patterns Among the Elderly: A Developmental Perspective," *The Gerontologist* 27(1987): pp. 266-272.

[12] Frank Biafora and Charles F. Longino Jr., "Elderly Hispanic Migration in the United States," *Journal of Gerontology: Social Sciences* 45 (1990): pp. S212-S219.

[13] Charles F. Longino Jr. and Kenneth J. Smith, "Black Retirement Migration in the United States," *Journal of Gerontology: Social Sciences* 46 (1991): pp. S125-S132.

[14] Charles F. Longino Jr. and William H. Crown, "Retirement Migration and Interstate Income Transfers," *The Gerontologist* 30 (1990): pp. 784-789.

[15] Frank D. Bean, George C. Myers, Jacqueline L. Angel and Omer R. Galle, "Geographic Concentration, Migration and Population Redistribution Among the Elderly," *Demography of Aging*, ed. Linda G. Martin and Samuel H. Preston (Washington, DC: National Academy Press, 1994).

Chapter 1

[1] Richard Boyer and David Savageau, *Retirement Places Rated* (New York: Rand McNally and Company, 1987) p. vii.

[2] Charles F. Longino Jr., "Personal Determinants and Consequences of Independent Housing Choices," *Housing in an Aging Society,* ed. Robert J. Newcomer and M. Powell Lawton (New York: Van Nostrand Reinhold, 1986) pp. 83-93.

[3] Raymond K. Oldakowski and Curtis C. Roseman, "The Development of Migration Expectations: Changes Throughout the Lifecourse," *Journal of Gerontology* 41 (1986): pp. 290-295.

[4] Charles F. Longino Jr., "Geographic Distribution and Migration," *Handbook of Aging and the Social Sciences, 3d ed.*, ed. Robert H. Binstock and Linda K. George (San Diego: Academic Press, 1990), pp. 45-63.

[5] Charles F. Longino Jr., "Where Retirees Prefer to Live: The Geographical Distribution and Migratory Patterns of Retirees," *Columbia Handbook on Retirement*, ed. Abraham Monk (New York: Columbia University Press, 1994), pp. 405-416.

[6] Patricia Gober and Leo E. Zonn, "Kin and Elderly Amenity Migration," *The Gerontologist* 23 (1983): pp. 288-294.

[7] Clifford H. Patrick, "Health and Migration of the Elderly," *Research on Aging* 2 (1980): pp. 290-295.

[8] Charles F. Longino Jr., David J. Jackson, Rick S. Zimmerman and Julia E. Bradsher, "The Second Move: Health and Geographic Mobility," *Journal of Gerontology: Social Sciences* 46 (1991): pp. S218-S224.

[9] Julia E. Bradsher, Charles F. Longino Jr., David J. Jackson, and Rick S. Zimmerman, "Health and Geographic Mobility Among the Recently Widowed," *Journal of Gerontology: Social Sciences* 47 (1993): pp. S261-S268.

[10] Lee Cuba, "Reorientations of Self: Residential Identification in Anchorage, Alaska," *Studies in Symbolic Interaction* 5 (1984): pp. 219-237.

[11] Lee Cuba, "From Visitor to Resident: Retiring to Vacationland," *Generations* 13 (1989): pp. 63-67.

[12] Robert F. Wiseman and Curtis C. Roseman, "A Typology of Elderly Migration Based on the Decision-Making Process," *Economic Geography* 55 (1979): pp. 324-337.

[13] Lee Cuba, "Models of Migration Decision Making Reexamined: The Destination Search of Older Migrants to Cape Cod," *The Gerontologist* 31 (1989): pp. 204-209.

[14] Tom Graff and Robert F. Wiseman, "Changing Patterns of Retirement Counties Since 1965," *Geographical Review* 80 (1990): pp. 239-251.

Chapter 2

[1] Jeanne C. Biggar, *The Sunning of America: Migration to the Sunbelt* (Washington, DC: Population Reference Bureau, 1979).

[2] Hiram J. Friedsam, "Inter-regional Migration of the Aged

in the United States," *The Journal of Gerontology* 6 (1951): pp. 237-242.

[3] Jeanne C. Biggar, "Reassessing Elderly Sunbelt Migration," *Research on Aging* 2 (1980): pp. 177-190.

[4] Cynthia B. Flynn, "General Versus Aged Interstate Migration, 1965-1970," *Research on Aging* 2 (1980): pp. 165-176.

[5] Cynthia B. Flynn, Charles F. Longino Jr., Robert F. Wiseman and Jeanne C. Biggar, "The Redistribution of America's Older Population: Major National Migration Patterns for Three Census Decades, 1960-1980," *The Gerontologist* 25 (1985): pp. 292-296.

[6] Cheryl Russell, *The Master Trend: How the Baby Boom Generation is Remaking America* (New York: Plenum Press, 1993).

[7] Susan L. Cutter, *Rating Places: A Geographer's View on Quality of Life* (Washington, DC: Resource Publications in Geography, 1985); Charles F. Longino Jr., "Rating Places: A Demographer Thinks Aloud About Retirement Guides," *Generations* 13 (1989): pp. 61-62.

[8] Frank A. Biafora and Charles F. Longino Jr., "Elderly Hispanic Migration in the United States," *Journal of Gerontology: Social Sciences* 45 (1990): pp. S212-S219.

Chapter 3

[1] E.G. Ravenstein, "The Laws of Migration," Paper 1, *Journal of the Royal Statistical Society* 48 (1885); reprinted in *Demography, ed. Kingsley Davis* (New York: Arno Press, 1976), pp. 168-235.

[2] S. Barsby and D.R. Cox, *Interstate Migration of the Elderly* (Lexington, MA: D.C. Heath, 1975).

[3] Charles F. Longino Jr., "Retirement Communities," *The Dynamics of Aging: Original Essays on the Experiences and Processes of Growing Old,* ed. Forrest Berghorn and Donna Schafer (Boulder, CO: Westview, 1980), pp. 391-417.

[4] Lee Cuba, "From Visitor to Resident: Retiring to Vacationland," *Generations* 13 (1989): pp. 63-67.

[5] Charles F. Longino Jr., "American Retirement Communities and Residential Relocation," *Geographical Perspectives on the Elderly*, ed. Anthony M. Warnes (London: John Wiley & Sons, Ltd., 1982), pp. 239-262.

[6] E.G. Ravenstein, "The Laws of Migration," Paper 2, *Journal of the Royal Statistical Society* 52 (1889): pp. 241-301.

[7] Charles F. Longino Jr., "Returning From the Sunbelt," *Returning from the Sunbelt: Myths and Realities of Migratory Patterns Among the Elderly*, ed. Abraham Monk (Proceedings of an Invitational Symposium, Columbia University in the City of New York: The Brookdale Institute on Aging and Adult Human Development, 1985), pp. 7-21.

[8] William J. McAuley and C. Nutty, "Residential Preferences and Moving Behavior: A Family Life-Cycle Analysis," *Journal of Marriage and the Family* 44 (1982): pp. 301-309.

[9] Eugene Litwak and Charles F. Longino Jr., "Migration Patterns Among the Elderly: A Developmental Perspective," *The Gerontologist* 27 (1987): pp. 266-272; William J. Serow, "Why the Elderly Move," *Research on Aging* 9 (1987): pp. 582-597.

[10] Alden Speare Jr. and Judith W. Meyer, "Types of Elderly Residential Mobility and Their Determinants," *Journal of Gerontology: Social Sciences* 43 (1988): pp. S74-S81.

[11] Cuba, "From Visitor to Resident," pp. 64-65.

[12] Julia E. Bradsher, Charles F. Longino Jr., David J. Jackson and Rick S. Zimmerman, "Health and Geographic Mobility Among the Recently Widowed," *Journal of Gerontology: Social Sciences* 47 (1992): pp. S261-S268.

[13] Charles F. Longino Jr., "Migration Winners and Losers," *American Demographics* 6 (1984): pp. 27-29; Longino Jr., *Returning from the Sunbelt.*

[14] Alden Speare Jr., Roger Avery and Leora Lawton, "Disability, Residential Mobility and Changes in Living Arrangements," *Journal of Gerontology: Social Sciences* 46 (1991): pp. S133-S142.

Chapter 4

[1] Charles F. Longino Jr., "Geographical Mobility and Family Caregiving in Nonmetropolitan America: Three-Decade Evidence from the U.S. Census," *Family Relations* 39 (1990): pp. 38-43.

[2] Cheryl Russell, *The Master Trend: How the Baby Boom Generation is Remaking America* (New York: Plenum Press, 1993).

Chapter 5

[1] David L. Chandler, *Henry Flagler: The Astonishing Life and Times of the Visionary Robber Baron Who Founded Florida* (New York: Macmillan, 1986).

[2] Mark S. Foster, *From Streetcar to Superhighway: American City Planners and Urban Transportation, 1900-1940* (Philadelphia: Temple University Press, 1981).

[3] Peter O. Muller, *Contemporary Suburban America* (Englewood Cliffs, New Jersey: Prentice-Hall, Inc., 1981).

[4] Spencer Miller Jr., "History of the Modern Highway in the United States," *Highways in our National Life*, ed. Jean Labatut and Wheaton J. Lane (New York: Arno Press, 1972).

[5] H. Jerome Cranmer, *New Jersey in the Automobile Age: A History of Transportation* (Princeton, NJ: D. Van Nostrand, 1964).

[6] John Anson Ford, *Thirty Explosive Years in Los Angeles County* (San Marino, CA: The Huntington Library, 1961).

[7] Barry Norman, *The Story of Hollywood* (New York: NAL

REFERENCES

Penguin, Inc., 1987).

[8] H. Wayne Morgan and Anne Hodges Morgan, *Oklahoma: A Bicentennial History* (New York: W.W. Norton, 1977).

[9] Margaret S. Gordon, *Employment Expansion and Population Growth: The California Experience 1900-1950* (Berkeley, CA: University of California Press, 1954).

[10] John B. Rae, *The Road and the Car in American Life* (Cambridge, MA: M.I.T. Press, 1971).

[11] James J. Flink, *The Car Culture* (Cambridge, MA: M.I.T. Press, 1975).

[12] Bessie Louise Pierce, *A History of Chicago* (New York: A.A. Knopf, 1937).

[13] Charles F. Longino Jr. and Ralph B. McNeal, "The Elderly Population in South Florida," *South Florida: The Winds of Change*, ed. T.D. Boswell (Miami, FL: Association of American Geographers, 1991), pp. 181-194.

[14] Charles F. Longino Jr. and Philip J. Perricone, "The Elderly Population of South Florida, 1950-1990," *The Florida Geographer* 25 (1991): pp 2-19.

[15] Charles F. Longino Jr. and William H. Haas III, "Migration and the Rural Elderly," *Aging in Rural America* ed. C. Neil Bull (Newbury Park, California: Sage Publications, 1993): pp. 17-29.

[16] Everett S. Lee, "A Theory of Migration," *Demography* 3 (1966): pp. 47-57.

[17] Charles F. Longino Jr., "The Forest and the Trees: Microlevel Considerations in the Study of Geographical Mobility in Old Age," *Elderly Migration and Population Redistribution: A Comparative Perspective,* ed. Andrei Rogers (London: Belhaven Press, 1992), pp. 23-34.

Chapter 6

[1] William J. Serow, "Return Migration of the Elderly in the U.S.A.: 1955-1960 and 1965-1970," *Journal of Gerontology* 33 (1978): pp. 288-295.

[2] Charles F. Longino Jr., "Going Home: Aged Return Migration in the United States, 1965-1970," *Journal of Gerontology* 34 (1979): pp. 736-745.

[3] Andrei Rogers, "Return Migration to Region of Birth Among Retirement-Age Persons in the United States," *Journal of Gerontology: Social Sciences* 45 (1990): pp. S128-S134.

[4] Thomas L. Smith, *The Sociology of Rural Life* (New York: Harper and Brothers, 1947).

[5] Daniel M. Johnson, *Black Migration in America: A Social Demographic History* (Durham, NC: Duke University Press, 1981).

[6] James H. Johnson Jr. and Curtis C. Roseman, "Increasing Black Out-migration From Los Angeles: The Role of Household Dynamics and Kinship Systems," *Annals of the Association of American Geographers* 80 (1990): pp. 205-222.

[7] Isaac Robinson, "Back to the South," *American Demographics* 8 (1986): pp. 40-43.

[8] William O'Hare, Jane-yu Li, Roy Chatterjee and Margaret Shukur, *Blacks on the Move: A Decade of Demographic Change* (Washington, DC: Joint Center for Political Studies, 1982).

[9] Mark Abrahamson and Valerie Carter, "Tolerance, Urbanism and Region," *American Sociological Review* 51 (1986): pp. 287-293.

[10] Charles F. Longino Jr. and Kenneth J. Smith, "Black Retirement Migration in the United States," *Journal of Gerontology: Social Sciences* 46 (1991): pp. S125-S132.

[11] Pastora S.J. Cafferty and William C. McCready, *Hispanics in the United States: A New Social Agenda* (New Brunswick, NJ: Transaction Books, 1985).

[12] Chairman of the House Select Committee on Aging, *Demographic Characteristics of the Older Hispanic Population, Committee Publication No. 100-696* (Washington, DC: U.S. Government Printing Office, 1988).

[13] Frank D. Bean and Marta Tienda, *The Hispanic Population of the United States* (New York: Sage, 1988).

[14] Frank A. Biafora and Charles F. Longino Jr., "Elderly Hispanic Migration in the United States," *Journal of Gerontology: Social Sciences* 45 (1990): pp. S212-S219.

[15] Longino Jr., "Going Home: Aged Return Migration in the United States 1965-1970," pp. 736-745.

[16] William J. Serow and Douglas A. Charity, "Return Migration of the Elderly in the United States: Recent Trends," *Research on Aging* 10 (1988): pp. 155-168.

[17] Francoise Cribier, "A European Assessment of Aged Migration," *Research on Aging* 2 (1980): pp. 225-270.

[18] Dexter Burley, "Occupations as a Motivating Factor in Retirement Migration: An Extreme Case Study," *The Gerontologist* 22 (1982): pp. 435-437.

[19] Charles F. Longino Jr., Jeanne C. Biggar, Cynthia B. Flynn and Robert F. Wiseman, *The Retirement Migration Project: A Final Report to the National Institute on Aging* (Coral Gables, FL: University of Miami Center for Social Research in Aging, 1984).

[20] Andrei Rogers and John Watkins, "General Versus Elderly Interstate Migration and Population Redistribution in the United States," *Research on Aging* 9 (1987): pp. 483-529.

[21] Graham Rowles, "Between Worlds: A Relocation Dilemma for the Appalachian Elderly," *International Journal of Aging and Human Development* 19 (1983): pp. 301-314.

[22] William J. Serow, "Why the Elderly Move," *Research on Aging* 9 (1987): pp. 582-597.

[23] Serow, "Return Migration of the Elderly in the U.S.A.: 1955-1960 and 1965-1970," pp. 288-295; Charles F. Longino Jr., "Going Home: Aged Return Migration in the United States 1965-1970," pp. 736-745.

[24] Charles F. Longino Jr., "Migration Winners and Losers," *American Demographics* 6 (1984): pp. 22-25, 37.

[25] Charles F. Longino Jr. and William J. Serow, "Regional Differences in the Characteristics of Elderly Return Mi-

grants," *Journal of Gerontology: Social Sciences* 47 (1992): pp. 538-543.

[26] Rogers and Watkins, "General Versus Elderly Interstate Migration and Population Redistribution in the United States," pp. 301-314.

Chapter 7

[1] Charles F. Longino Jr., "Geographic Distribution and Migration," *Handbook of Aging and the Social Sciences 3d ed.*, ed. Robert H. Binstock and Linda K. George (San Diego, CA: Academic Press, 1990), pp. 45-63.

[2] U.S. Bureau of the Census, "Nonpermanent Residents by States and Selected Counties and Incorporated Places: 1980," *1980 Census of Population Supplementary Report PC80-S1-6.* (Washington, DC: Government Printing Office, 1982).

[3] Patricia Gober and Robert C. Mings, "A Geography of Non-permanent Residence in the United States," *Professional Geographer* 36 (1984): pp. 292-296.

[4] *Woodall's Campground Directory: North American Edition* (Bannockburn, Illinois: Woodall Publishing, 1988).

[5] Kevin E. McHugh and Robert C. Mings, "On the Road Again: Seasonal Migration to a Sunbelt Metropolis," *Urban Geography* 12 (1991): pp. 1-18.

[6] Wolfgang Weissleder, "Retiring in Two Places," *Aging in Place: Housing Adaptations and Options for Remaining in the Community*, ed. Gloria Gutman and N. Blackie (Burnaby, BC: Gerontology Research Centre, Simon Fraser University, 1986).

[7] McHugh and Mings, "On the Road Again: Seasonal Migration to a Sunbelt Metropolis," pp. 1-18.

[8] Harry W. Martin, Sue K. Hoppe, Victor W. Marshall and Joanne F. Daciuk, "Sociodemographic and Health Characteristics of Anglophone Canadian and U.S. Snowbirds," *Journal of Aging and Health* 4 (1992): pp. 500-513.

[9] Timothy D. Hogan, "Determinants of the Seasonal Migration of the Elderly to Sunbelt States." *Research on Aging* 8 (1987): pp. 23-37.

[10] Weissleder, "Retiring in Two Places."

[11] Herbert C. Northcott, *Changing Residence: The Geographic Mobility of Elderly Canadians* (Toronto: Butterworths, 1988).

[12] *Canadian Travel to the United States* (Ottawa: International Travel Section, Statistics Canada, 1984).

[13] Richard D. Tucker, Victor W. Marshall, Charles F. Longino Jr. and Larry C. Mullins, "Canadian Snowbirds in Florida: A Descriptive Profile," *Canadian Journal on Aging* 7 (1988): pp. 218-232.

[14] Richard D. Tucker, Larry C. Mullins, Francoise Beland, Charles F. Longino Jr. and Victor W. Marshall, "Older Canadians in Florida: A Comparison of Anglophone and Francophone Seasonal Migrants." *Canadian Journal on Aging* 11 (1992): pp. 281-297.

[15] L. Dupont, *La Presence Quebecoise en Floride et ses Implications Pour le Quebec* (Quebec City: Secretariat Permanent des Peuples Francophones, 1984).

[16] Lee Cuba, "From Visitor to Resident: Retiring to Vacationland," *Generations* 13 (1989): pp. 63-67.

[17] John A. Krout, "Seasonal Migration of the Elderly," *The Gerontologist* 23 (1983): pp. 295-299.

[18] G.C. Hoyt, "The Life of the Retired in a Trailer Park," *American Journal of Sociology* 19 (1954): pp. 361-370.

[19] C.H. Rush, "Winter Texans in the Lower Rio Grande Valley," *Texas Business Review* (May-June 1980): pp. 171-175.

[20] Larry C. Mullins and Richard D. Tucker, ed., *Snowbirds in the Sun Belt: Older Canadians in Florida* (Tampa, FL: University of South Florida, International Exchange Center on Gerontology, 1988).

[21] Tucker, Marshall, Longino Jr. and Mullins, "Canadian Snowbirds in Florida," pp. 218-232.

[22] Kevin E. McHugh, "Seasonal Migration and a Substitute for, or Precursor to, Permanent Migration," *Research on Aging* 12 (1990): pp. 229-245.

[23] McHugh, "Seasonal Migration," pp. 229-245.

[24] Victor W. Marshall, Charles F. Longino Jr., Richard D. Tucker and Larry C. Mullins, "Health Care Utilization of Canadian Snowbirds," *Journal of Aging and Health* 1 (1989): pp. 150-168.

[25] Victor W. Marshall and Charles F. Longino Jr., "Older Canadians in Florida: The Social Networks of International Seasonal Migrants," *Comprehensive Gerontology* (B) 2 (1988): pp. 53-68.

[26] Larry C. Mullins, Charles F. Longino Jr., Victor G. Marshall and Richard D. Tucker, "An Examination of Loneliness and Social Isolation Among Elderly Canadian Seasonal Migrants in Florida," *Journal of Gerontology: Social Sciences* 44 (1989): pp. 580-586.

[27] Charles F. Longino Jr., Victor W. Marshall, Larry C. Mullins and Richard D. Tucker, "On the Nesting of Snowbirds," *Journal of Applied Gerontology* 10 (1991): pp. 157-168.

Chapter 8

[1] John Fraser Hart, "Facets of the Geography of Populations in the Midwest," *Journal of Geography* 85 (1986): pp. 201-211.

[2] Judith W. Meyer, "A Regional Scale Temporal Analysis of the Migration Patterns of Elderly Persons Over Time," *Journal of Gerontology* 42 (1987): pp. 366-375.

[3] Richard K. Ormrod, "Evidence that California's Elderly are Migrating Southward," *Social Science Research* 70 (1986): pp. 149-151.

[4] Charles F. Longino Jr., Jeanne C. Biggar, Cynthia B. Flynn

REFERENCES

and Robert F. Wiseman, *The Retirement Migration Project: A Final Report to the National Institute on Aging* (Coral Gables, FL: University of Miami, 1984).

[5] Lee Cuba, *The Cape Cod Retirement Migration Study: A Final Report to the National Institute on Aging* (Wellesley, MA: Wellesley College, 1992).

[6] Lee Cuba and Charles F. Longino Jr., "Regional Retirement Migration: The Case of Cape Cod," *Journal of Gerontology: Social Sciences* 46 (1991): pp. S33-S42.

[7] Nina Glasgow, "The Older Metropolitan Origin Migrant as a Factor in Rural Population Growth," *Rebirth of Rural America: Rural Migration in the Midwest,* ed. Andrew J. Sofranko and James D. Williams (Ames, IA: Iowa State University, 1980); Valerie A. Karn, *Retiring to the Seaside* (Boston: Routledge and Kegan Paul, 1977).

[8] Patricia Gober and Leo Zonn, "Kin and Elderly Amenity Migration," *The Gerontologist* 23 (1983): pp. 292-296.

[9] Lee Cuba, "Family and Retirement in the Context of Elderly Migration," *Families and Retirement,* ed. Maximiliane Szinovacz, David Ekerdt and Barbara Vinich (Newbury Park: Sage, 1992).

Chapter 9

[1] Thomas M. Power, "Broader Vision, Narrower Focus in Local Economic Development," *Forum for Applied Research and Public Policy* (Fall 1989): pp.40-49.

[2] T. Hady and P. Ross, "Nonmetro Counties Less Dependent on Farming, Manufacturing, and Mining," *Rural Development Perspectives* 6 (1990): pp. 43-45.

[3] United States Department of Agriculture, Economic Research Service, *Rural Conditions and Trends* 1 (1991): p. 10.

[4] Stuart Rosenfeld and Ed Bergman, "Charting Growth in the South," report submitted to the Southern Growth Policies Board, Research Triangle Park, North Carolina (1988).

[5] Calvin Beale and Glenn Fuguitt, "Decade of Pessimistic Nonmetropolitan Population Trends Ends on Optimistic Note," *Rural Development Perspectives* 6 (1990): pp. 14-18.

[6] Nina Glasgow, "Attracting Retirees as a Community Development Option," *Journal of the Community Development Society* 21 (1990): pp. 102-114.

[7] Mark Fagan and Charles F. Longino Jr. "Migrating Retirees: A Source for Economic Development," *Economic Development Quarterly* 7 (1993): pp. 98-106.

[8] Tom Exter, "Incomes of the Mature Market," *American Demographics* 9 (1987): p. 62.

[9] Nina Glasgow and Richard J. Reeder, "Economic and Fiscal Implications of Non-metropolitan Retirement Migration," *Journal of Applied Gerontology* 9 (1990): pp. 433-451.

[10] Richard J. Reeder and Nina Glasgow, "Nonmetro Retirement Counties' Strengths and Weaknesses," *Rural Development Perspectives* 6 (1990): pp. 12-18.

[11] William H. Crown, Charles F. Longino Jr. and Neal E. Cutler, "Net Worth and the Economic Diversity of the Elderly," *Journal of Aging and Social Policy* 5 (1993): pp. 99-118.

[12] Robert S. Menchin, *The Mature Market* (Chicago: Probus Publishing, 1989).

[13] William Crown and Charles F. Longino Jr. "State and Regional Policy Implications of Elderly Migration," *Journal of Aging and Social Policy* 3 (1991): pp. 185-207.

[14] Charles F. Longino Jr. "Retirement Migration Streams: Trends and Implications for North Carolina Communities," *Journal of Applied Gerontology* 9 (1990): pp. 393-404.

[15] William Haas and Lee Crandall, "Physicians' Views of Retirement Migrants' Impact on Rural Medical Practice," *The Gerontologist* 28 (1988): pp. 663-666.

[16] Jeanne C. Biggar, "Who Moved Among the Elderly, 1965-1970: A Comparison of Types of Older Movers," *Research on Aging* 2 (1980): pp. 73-91.

[17] Jeanne C. Biggar, Diane Cowper and Dale Yeatts, "National Elderly Migration Patterns and Selectivity: 1955-1960, 1965-1970 and Decade Trends," *Research on Aging* 6 (1984): pp. 163-188.

[18] Charles F. Longino Jr., Jeanne C. Biggar, Cynthia B. Flynn and Robert F. Wiseman, *The Retirement Migration Project: A Final Report to the National Institute on Aging* (Miami, FL: University of Miami Center for Social Research in Aging, 1984).

[19] Mark Fagan. *Attracting Retirees for Economic Development* (Jacksonville, AL: Jacksonville State University Center for Economic Development, 1988).

[20] Charles F. Longino Jr. and William H. Crown, "Retirement Migration and Interstate Income Transfers," *The Gerontologist* 30 (1990): pp. 784-789.

[21] William H. Crown and Charles F. Longino Jr., "State and Regional Policy Implications of Elderly Migration," *Journal of Aging and Social Policy* 3 (1991): pp. 185-207.

[22] Fernando Torres-Gil, "An Examination of Factors Affecting Future Cohorts of Elderly Hispanics," *The Gerontologist* 26 (1986): pp. 140-146.

[23] Donald E. Gelfand, "Immigration, Aging and Intergenerational Relationships," *The Gerontologist* 25 (1989): pp. 292-296.

[24] Mark Fagan, "Economic Impact of Retirees on a Community," *Social Science Perspectives* (September 1990): pp.72-81.

[25] Gordon Bennett, "Retirement Migration and Economic Development in High-Amenity, Nonmetropolitan Areas," *Journal of Applied Gerontology* 12 (1993): pp. 466-481.

[26] William Haas and William Serow, "The Influence of Retirement In-Migration on Local Economic Development," report submitted to the Appalachian Regional Commission, (September 29, 1990).

27 Bernal Green and Mary Jo Schneider, "Manufacturing or Retirement: A Comparison of the Direct Economic Effects of Two Growth Options," unpublished paper, University of Arkansas, (1989).

28 Graham D. Rowles and John F. Watkins, "Change in the Mountains: Elderly Migration and Population Dynamics in Appalachia," Occasional Publication Number 2, Sanders-Brown Center on Aging, Lexington, KY, (1991).

29 Tom Graff and Robert F. Wiseman, "Changing Patterns of Retirement Counties," *The Geographical Review* 80 (1990): pp. 239-251.

30 William H. Crown, "State Economic Implications of Elderly Interstate Migration," *The Gerontologist* 28 (1988): pp. 533-539.

31 William H. Crown and Charles F. Longino Jr., "State and Regional Policy Implications of Elderly Migration," *Journal of Aging and Social Policy* 3 (1991): pp. 185-207.

32 Nina Glasgow, "A Place in the Country," *American Demographics* 14 (1991): pp.24-30.

33 Calvin Beale and Glenn Fuguitt, "Decade of Pessimistic Nonmetro Population Trends End on Optimistic Note," *Rural Development Perspectives* 6 (1990): pp. 14-18.